THE FABRIC OF THE CITY

STUDIES IN EUROPEAN URBAN HISTORY (1100-1800)

VOLUME 59

Series Editors
Marc Boone
Anne-Laure Van Bruaene
Ghent University

The Fabric of the City

A Social History of Cloth Manufacture in Medieval Ypres

PETER STABEL

BREPOLS

Cover illustration: **Front:** Anonymous coloured woodcut by Johannes or Lucas van Doetechum (Yprae, 1562) published in Lodovico Guicciardini, *Descrittione di M. Lodovico Guicciardini di tutti i Paesi Bassi, altrimenti detti Germania inferiore. Con piu carte di geographia del paese & col ritratto naturale di piu terre principali.* (Antwerp: Willem Silvius, 1567). The cloth hall of gigantic proportions stands proudly in the centre of the city, even at the time when Ypres had almost lost its industrial output completely (© Yper Museum, SM 000700). **Back:** A horizontal loom in medieval Ypres. Fragment of a miniature in the register of privileges of the Ypres cloth industry, 1363 (the register was destroyed during World War I but the miniatures had been copied by François Böhm and are preserved as a chromolithography. The illustration was used for a Diploma of the "Société Historique, Archéologique et Littéraire de la ville d'Ypres et de l'ancienne West-Flandre" in 1861 (© Yper Museum, 000396).

© 2022, Brepols Publishers n.v., Turnhout, Belgium.

All rights reserved. No part of this publication may be reproduced, stored in a retrieval system, or transmitted, in any form or by any means, electronic, mechanical, photocopying, recording, or otherwise without the prior permission of the publisher.

D/2022/0095/200
ISBN 978-2-503-60051-2
eISBN 978-2-503-60052-9
DOI 10.1484/M.SEUH-EB.5.129628
ISSN 1780-3241
eISSN 2294-8368

Printed in the EU on acid-free paper.

Contents

List of Illustrations	9
Acknowledgements	11
Money Matters	15
Introduction. Growth and Decline of a Textile City	17
Chapter 1. Flemish Resilience? Cloth and its Markets	25
Ypres Cloth in Medieval Europe	26
Heavy and Light Cloth: A Broken Balance	32
An Industry in Continuous Transition	35
Conclusions: Rise and Decline of an Industry	40
Chapter 2. Of Weaving Looms, Spinning Wheels and Fuller's Troughs. Cloth and Technology	43
Labour and Textile Technology	43
A Mercantile Prelude	47
Wool preparation	51
Weaving	53
Fulling	58
Cloth finishing	61
Dyeing	64
Conclusions: technological innovation and the emergence of the 'grande draperie'	69
Chapter 3. The Rise and Fall of Industrial Suburbia. Cloth and the Urban Fabric	71
Urban Change in Medieval Ypres	71
Revolt and Taxation	72
Textiles in the Urban Fabric	80
City Walls and Social Segregation	83
The 'Marshy Meadow'	87
Towards a Post-Industrial City?	90
Conclusions	95

Chapter 4. The Boinebrokes of Ypres. Cloth and Mercantile Capital — 97
- The Shadow of Boinebroke — 98
- The Boinebrokes of Ypres — 102
- A Hostile Take-Over? — 108
- How did Woollens Find their Way to International Customers? Merchants and Brokers — 114
- Conclusions — 118

Chapter 5. The Clothiers' Century. Cloth and Entrepreneurship — 121
- From merchant entrepreneurs to clothiers: a social revolution in 1280? — 124
- Access to Entrepreneurship — 130
- Monitoring Cloth Manufacture — 134
- Access to Capital — 138
- Conclusions: A Dance of Capital and Labour — 145

Chapter 6. The Rules of the Game. Cloth, Labour and Guilds — 151
- Craftsmen and Guilds — 151
- Clothiers and their Workers — 155
- Running a Textile Workshop — 156
- Starting a Guild Career: Apprenticeship — 159
- The Rewards of Skill: Journeymen and Unskilled Workers — 163
- Hiring a Labour Force — 166
- The Bells of Labour — 168
- Conclusions — 170

Chapter 7. All in a Wage… Cloth and its Rewards — 173
- Labour and Cloth — 176
- A Textile Wage: What is in a Name? — 178
- Wages in Ypres — 183
  - The preparation of wool — 183
  - Weaving — 185
  - Fulling — 186
  - Shearing and cloth finishing — 187
  - Dyeing — 189
- Textile Wages and Builders' Wages in the Fourteenth Century: a Comparison — 189

Chapter 8. 'Whether He or She'. Cloth and Gender — 193
- Women, Guilds and Entrepreneurship — 194
- Gender Inclusivity in the Ypres Cloth Industry — 199
- It is (Becoming) a Man's World — 203

Chapter 9. A Time to Protest. Cloth and Revolt — 207
- Medieval Revolts in Flanders — 207
- Cokerulle: A True Social Conflict? — 214
- Revolt and Restoration 1302-1328 — 217

Social Friction and Political Dissent 1328-1377   219
The Last Revolts (Late Fourteenth-Fifteenth Centuries)   225
Labour Conflict, Political Conflict   228

Chapter 10. Roads of Capitalism   231
A Rural Epilogue to an Urban Industry?   234
Ypres and Florence: Two Sides of the Same Coin?   245
Rise and Fall of a Textile City   252

Bibliography   257

Glossary of textile terms (in the Ypres sources)   275

List of Illustrations

Figures

Figure 1.1   Leaden cloth seal from before 1383. This is one of the hundreds of leaden cloth seals that were found in Ypres, most notably from the excavations in the *Verdronken Weide*, south of the inner city. It has a representation of an Ypres cross and was never used as a quality mark (© Yper Museum, obj. nr. 5411).   38

Figure 2.1   Transport and sale at the cloth hall of wool sacks (miniature from the *Keurboek*, register of statutes of the Ypres cloth industry, destroyed in WWI). Chromolithography of the "Société Historique, Archéologique et Littéraire de la ville d'Ypres et de l'ancienne West-Flandre" in 1861 (© Yper Museum, obj. nr. 000396). See also cover image.   49

Figure 2.2   The Ypres cloth hall (miniature from the *Keurboek*, register of statutes of the Ypres cloth industry, destroyed in WWI). Chromolithography of the "Société Historique, Archéologique et Littéraire de la ville d'Ypres et de l'ancienne West-Flandre" in 1861 (© Yper Museum, obj. nr. 000396). See also cover image.   50

Figure 2.3   Women spinning (with distaff), carding and combing. These three labour-intensive stages of cloth manufacture were mostly done by women, in Ypres all of them inhabitants of the city. Fragment of miniature representing Gaia Caecilia, wife of Tarquinius Priscus, first King of Rome, from Giovanni Boccaccio, *De claris mulieribus* (anonymous French translation: *Le livre de femmes nobles et renomées*), Rouen, c. 1440 (anonymous artist).   52

Figure 2.4   Warping spun yarn (measuring and preparing warp yarn for the weaver's warp beam) was a task often executed by female assistants in the weaver's workshop (miniature from the *Keurboek*, register of statutes of the Ypres cloth industry, destroyed in WWI). Chromolithography of the "Société Historique, Archéologique et Littéraire de la ville d'Ypres et de l'ancienne West-Flandre" in 1861 (© Yper Museum, obj. nr. 000396). See also cover image.   55

Figure 2.5   A weaver's broadloom operated by two weavers. In front a young boy is reeling yarn for the weft shuttles (miniature from the *Keurboek*, register of statutes of the Ypres cloth industry, destroyed in WWI). Chromolithography of the "Société Historique, Archéologique et Littéraire de la ville d'Ypres et de l'ancienne West-Flandre" in 1861 (© Yper Museum, obj. nr. 000396). See also cover image.   56

Figure 2.6   Location of *Verdronken Weide* excavation in the 1990s in the former suburb of St Michael, south of the inner city (taken from Dewilde, Ervynck and Wielemans (eds), *Ypres and the Medieval Cloth Industry*, 59; © Vlaamse Overheid, Agentschap Onroerend Erfgoed).   60

Figure 2.7   Wooden plank with holes from the *Verdronken Weide* excavation, probably used to fix woollens on a tentering frame (© Yper Museum, obj. 5622).   62

Figure 2.8   A workshop of dyers in red. A woollen dyed with madder or grain is taken out of the dyer's vat. On the floor near the vat lie woollens that have not yet been dyed in the   67

fabric: white cloth (not dyed in the fibre) and blue cloth (dyed blue in the fibre). Two journeymen (?) are doing the work, while a master dyer (?) checks on the process. White and blue woollens were in the fourteenth century the most common in the Ypres manufacture of greased cloth.

Figure 3.1	City Map of Ypres by Thévelin-Destrée (1564). © Yper Museum, nr. SM 3188.	73
Figure 3.2	Map of the inner city of Ypres with subdivision in four quadrants (which more or less coincide with the later administrative subdivision of the city) and the separate market area (© adapted from Dewilde, Ervynck and Wielemans (eds.), *Ypres and the Medieval Cloth Industry*; © Vlaamse Overheid, Agentschap Onroerend Erfgoed).	76
Figure 3.3	The siege of Ypres in 1383 (map by Guillaume du Tielt, 1610) © Yper Museum, nr. SM 3185.	84
Figure 3.4	Reconstruction of the spatial organisation in the suburb of St Michiel (© Marc Dewilde & Stephan Van Bellingen – Vlaamse Overheid, Agentschap Onroerend Erfgoed).	89
Figure 3.5	Excavation plan of houses and workshops along the Komenseweg (© Marc Dewilde & Stephan Van Bellingen – Vlaamse Overheid, Agentschap Onroerend Erfgoed): light grey area: house, dark grey area: possible workshop.	90
Figure 8.1	Two women behind a broadloom. In the 1470s, when this miniature was painted, it would have been inconceivable for women to operate a broadloom in an urban context without at least the supervision of a master weaver. Before 1300, however, women appear as independent weavers in some Flemish cloth cities. Miniature representing Gaia Cirilla, mother of King Tarquin of Rome, in Christine de Pizan, *Livre de la Cité des Dames* (Flemish translation), Bruges, 1475 (anonymous artist), British Library, Additional 20698, f. 101r.	197
Figure 10.1	Map of the cloth producing towns and villages in the western part of the county of Flanders (© Iason Jongepier, University of Antwerp).	241

Tables

Table 1.1	Ypres cloth types according to the statutes (around 1300): greased woollens (*draperie ointe*)	34
Table 1.2	Estimate of the annual cloth production in Flanders (Dutch speaking parts), in the fifteenth and early sixteenth centuries (fine woollens, *draperie ointe*)	36
Table 1.3	Rented stalls in the Ypres cloth hall (fifteenth century)	39
Table 3.1	Direct taxation in Ypres (construction of the outer ditch), city accounts 1325-6, tax assessments in d. Flemish	78
Table 3.2	Female-led households in the Ypres taxation of 1325-1326	79
Table 3.3.	Occupational analysis, tax roll 1325-1366: textile occupations	82
Table 3.4.	Occupations in Ypres in 1431 (Quarter of Ghemeene Neeringhe) and Bruges in 1436 (guild militia lists)	92
Table 3.5.	Textile Occupations in Ypres 1431 (*Ghemeine Neeringhe*) and of new Bruges citizens (fifteenth century)	94
Table 5.1	Textile occupations in Ypres. Debt contracts: borrowers, 1249-1291 (source: database Martha Howell)	141
Table 6.1	Estimated daily wages in Ypres' cloth manufacture (middle of the fourteenth century)	191

Acknowledgements

The genesis of this book on the cloth industry of medieval Ypres was defined by the covid disturbances in 2020-2021. While I was on sabbatical leave amid the corona epidemic, I had to abandon my scheduled research activities because the measures taken by the Belgian, British and French authorities prevented me from carrying out prolonged periods of research in London and Paris. Using the libraries in those cities for a planned synthesis on the urban history of medieval Latin Europe, the Byzantine Empire and the Islamic Worlds had become impossible. My back-up plan, to begin research for a similarly ambitious plan to write a synthesis of the social history of the great cloth industry in the medieval Low Countries, was equally a non-starter, because most archives in Northern France or even in Belgium had been closed or were imposing severe restrictions on their users, again because of covid.

Almost at the end of this frustrating period, in late May 2021, I decided on another strategy. I had in the meantime looked more closely at the published sources about the cloth industry in Ypres. They are, after the destruction of the city archives at the beginning of the First World War in 1914, all that is left of what once must have been one of the richest medieval archival deposits in Europe. I was intrigued nonetheless by the tireless efforts of many scholars before the tragic events in Ypres of 1914-1918 that had cost hundreds of thousands of lives to make those archival documents accessible to the scholarly community. In the 1990s archaeologists of the Flemish Archaeological Service had also excavated a medieval neighbourhood where textile manufacture had constituted the core of activities. Meeting the head archaeologist of the time, Marc Dewilde, at the beginning of June 2021 in the Yper Museum and afterwards discussing his work, sitting around a table in the Ypres market with good food and good beer, was really the catalyst for this book. I decided to change my plans and to look more closely at the medieval cloth industry of Ypres.

Ypres was, after all, the most industrial Flemish city. In thirteenth- and fourteenth-century Europe the name of Ypres was almost synonymous with woollen cloth. People bought Ypres woollens from Novgorod to Constantinople, from Florence to Valencia, from Lübeck to London. This book is therefore *pars pro toto* of my initial plan to tackle the Low Countries as a whole, but the case study of Ypres, the most renowned cloth city at the time, is also wonderful preparation for that bigger framework. In Ypres we find all elements that made up the success and caused the decline of an industry that defined the urbanisation process of the medieval Low Countries. Cloth has created the dense urban network in which people in present-day Flanders and Northern France still live. The industrial past of the medieval cities is still around us today. We also find here all the political fault lines and social conflicts that rapid industrial growth and the slow decline of a dominant industry caused. Surprisingly, although many scholars – from local historians such as Octaaf Mus to internationally renowned scholars such as John Munro – have tackled the history of Ypres and its industry, no real up-to-date synthesis of this great industry is available, and even less work has been done on the social history of cloth manufacture in Ypres. With this book I want to fill this gap at least partially and look above all at the social consequences of medieval industrial expansion.

Like any other historical work, this endeavour could not have been carried out without the help of many. I am very grateful to Dominiek Dendooven, Hannelore Franck, Jan Decorte and, above all, Marc Dewilde for their initial advice about the archaeological research into Ypres' medieval textile neighbourhood and about the museological representation in the new Yper Museum in the immense medieval cloth hall. Little did they know that our pleasant lunch would trigger me to write this book. They were also very obliging in commenting on the penultimate draft of this book. I am also grateful to Rik Opsommer, the city archivist and a colleague at the Law Faculty of Ghent University, for helping me out with the few medieval documents that have survived the blaze in the archives in 1914. I am, as ever, much indebted to my Antwerp friends at the Centre for Urban History and the History Department, to fellow-medievalists Sam Geens, Jeroen Puttevils and Tim Soens and to Oscar Gelderblom and Bruno Blondé, whom I forgive for having chosen to study other periods, for all their support and advice, and for putting my feet back on the ground occasionally and saving me from my own wild theories. A special word of gratitude also goes to Jan Dumolyn (Ghent), Jelle Haemers and Paul Trio (Leuven and Kortrijk) and to Hugo Soly and Catharina Lis (Brussels) for their very valuable comments on the final manuscript. I am also grateful to the editing board of the Studies in European Urban History series, in particular Anne-Laure Van Bruaene and Marc Boone and the two anonymous reviewers for their comments. Kate Elliot merits all the credits for trying to turn my Flemish English into something that can be understood by English speakers. Finally, my immense gratitude also goes to my partner Inge and our children, Floris, Katrijn and Hannes. I realise that this book and the frenzy with which I have written it have cost them the undivided attention that they would so much have deserved during the summer holiday of 2021, the second corona summer of our lives. I want, therefore, foremost to apologise to them for the fact that medieval clothiers, weavers, fullers, dyers and spinsters from a town far away in Western Flanders were always on my mind during those days.

(Ghent, December 2021)

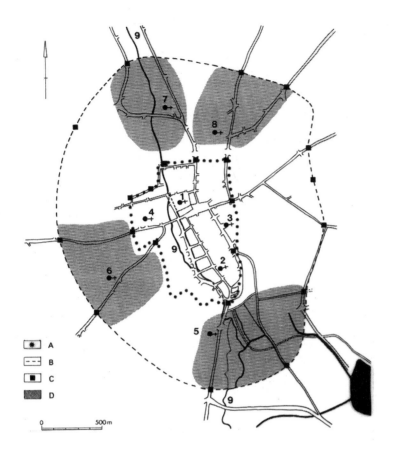

Figure 0.1 Map of Ypres and its suburbs in the 14th century, before the destruction of the suburbs in the 1380s (taken from Dewilde, Ervynck and Wielemans (eds), *Ypres and the Medieval Cloth Industry*, 59; © Vlaamse Overheid, Agentschap Onroerend Erfgoed).
Churches/parishes in the inner city: 1. St Martin, 2. St Peter, 3. St James, 4. St Nicholas / Churches/parishes in the suburbs: 5. St Michael, 6. Holy Cross, 7. Our Lady ten Brielen, 8. St John / 9. Ieperlee; A. 13th-century fortifications, B. 14th-century fortifications, C. city gates, D. surburbs

Money Matters

Medieval sources mostly use money of account, not real coinage, to express value. In Flanders, as elsewhere in Europe, money of account was expressed in pounds, shillings and pennies, whereby £1 = 20s = 240d.

But even the systems of money of account used were often haphazardly. In the late thirteenth century an imitation of the English sterling was much used, in the early fourteenth century Ypres sources often mention £ Tournois besides £ Parisis. The period before and after 1300 was also a period of unstable currency and instability would remain high until the end of the fourteenth century. The count often manipulated his currency to secure income. Gradually £ Flemish is used more and more, for example in the tax list of 1325. Only during the fourteenth century the situation between the various currencies used more or less stabilized and £1 Flemish (= *groot/gros* Flemish) equals £12 Parisis and £40 Payment. The wages in Chapter 7 are expressed in d Fl. (1 *stuiver* (st.) = 2d Fl.) to allow comparison with contemporary builders' wages.

Before that period the relative position of the various currencies used in the county often changed, and because the used currencies are not always indicated, in individual sources it is not always possible to calculate everything to a single standard. Because the present study does not focus on the analysis of quantitative time series, we have therefore maintained the currencies as they appear in the various sources.

Introduction

Growth and Decline of a Textile City

'For the Success of the Industry and the Honour of the City'.[1] Thus begins one of the rulings in the statutes of the Ypres fullers. The honour of the city was to be found in the fact that merchants who dealt in Ypres cloth would find the woollens to be of excellent quality and conforming to their customary measurements as they were used to. To avoid fraud being committed and to achieve the standard quality so desired by the merchants the craft guild of the fullers controlled the production of the craftsmen active in the city. But the guilds were not the only institutions that occupied themselves with the cloth industry. The economy of the city was built on cloth. Both the urban authorities, the bench of aldermen dominated throughout this period by the mercantile elites, and the clothiers (*drapiers*), the true industrial entrepreneurs who were often associated with the craft guilds but who were also a separate group in between the merchants and the craftsmen, had vested interests in cloth manufacture. For far too long, scholars have equated industrial organisation with craft guilds. Instead, medieval industries were playgrounds in which various stakeholders competed. Cloth was the activity in which some could make fortunes and upon which, for most textile workers, sheer survival depended. And cloth was important in Ypres. The city grew exponentially during the twelfth and thirteenth centuries, reaching a population of more than 30,000 at its peak in the late thirteenth century. It was the third city in Flanders, one of the most densely urbanised regions of medieval Europe, after Ghent and Bruges, but substantially larger than those other industrial textile giants in Flanders and Artois, Douai, Arras and Saint-Omer.[2] Most of its inhabitants depended on the success of the cloth industry for their economic well-being, so the industry not only constituted the heart of the urban economy, it also defined the social identity of its citizens.

The medieval history of the city of Ypres can easily be summarised in two brief paragraphs. Starting almost modestly from a comital domanial centre and an adjacent mercantile settlement, as did so many other cities in the county of Flanders, Ypres experienced rapid growth during the twelfth and early thirteenth centuries. The city became a commercial hotspot as one of the main fairs of Flanders. But above all, Ypres became the quintessential industrial city of the European Middle Ages. Its cloth entrepreneurs, fired by the commercial successes of the city's powerful elites, reached customers all over Europe in this period, from Novgorod to Italy, from England to Constantinople, and its woollens were renowned for their quality and desired by consumers to add lustre and prestige to the latest fashion.

---

1 Espinas and Pirenne, *Recueil*, 3, 577.
2 Derville, 'Les draperies flamandes', 353-370.

Growth, however, started to falter at the end of the thirteenth century, and despite many attempts at adapting cloth output to changing demand or at curbing industrial expansion in the countryside and in the smaller towns in its surroundings, Ypres kept losing ground on its traditional markets. In the city itself, the omnipotent political elite of merchants and landowners met with increasing opposition from new entrepreneurs and guild-organised craftsmen. But unlike in Bruges or in Ghent, the other leading cities of the Dutch-speaking part of Flanders, true representation of the commoners continued to be problematic. For the rest of the later Middle Ages the elites retained their dominant position in urban politics, although institutions developed in such ways that some control could be exercised by the count and by the guilds and city districts. The overall economic trend was, however, a decline in both economic success and population size. At the end of the fourteenth century the suburbs were abandoned, and the city retreated to its earlier thirteenth-century defensive perimeter. In the fifteenth century the population had declined even to less than 10,000. Still the cloth industry proved resilient. Output numbers and employment had crumbled while Ypres declined to the size of a midsized town, but Ypres' specialisation in the top end of the cloth market remained the key to continued success. Even in the late sixteenth century, Ypres cloth still remained very much present, with Mechelen woollens, on the luxury market for woollen fabrics in Antwerp. Yet at this stage cloth manufacture had stopped characterising the city. Ypres was no longer a truly industrial city with some regional market function. It became a regional servicing centre for its surrounding countryside (where proto-industrial expansion continued), and it had retained only limited manufacturing capacity.

This true reversal of fortune sets the scene for one of the most interesting historical cities of medieval Flanders, a region characterised from the twelfth century by dense urbanisation. Yet Ypres failed to attract a lot of interest from scholars. While Ghent, with over 60,000 inhabitants by far the largest city in the county, and Bruges, the county's most important commercial centre, kept enticing historians to study one or the other aspect of their social, economic, political and cultural organisation, and the cities of Walloon Flanders (now in the *Département du Nord* in France), Lille and Douai, enjoyed equally great interest from French and American scholars, Ypres withered away in research. While Bruges had the alluring sights of the Burgundian era and its fame was spread across the world by painters, writers and later tourist guides, and while Ghent had the academic culture of its community of historians at the university, the foundations of which were laid by the great Belgian historian, Henri Pirenne himself, Ypres was a provincial backwater in one of the far corners of Western Flanders. Moreover, its late medieval politics were considered by many to be too elitist and too loyal to the prince, and therefore less interesting than those in rebellious and self-conscious cities such as Ghent and Bruges; its industry was decaying anyhow; and even its surrounding countryside was less thoroughly investigated. The little scholarship there was, was limited to some key publications by Henri Pirenne, Guillaume Des Marez and Hans Van Werveke, scholars more known for their work on other Flemish or Low Countries cities, and by local archivists and historians such as Henri De Sagher,

Jos de Smet, Octaaf Mus and some others. Only the Leuven historian, Paul Trio, tries to keep attention on this extremely interesting city alive.

The main reason for this apparent disinterest is, of course, very tangible. What surely must have been one of the most impressive and complete medieval urban archives in the Low Countries has almost completely disappeared. The archives, as did the city itself, fell victim to the destructions of World War I. Because of the short-sightedness of the city's administration and because of personal rivalries, the archives had not been taken into security when Ypres found itself caught in a front line that would almost not move during the four years of this bloody conflict. Moreover, the so-called 'Ypres Salient' was a heavily disputed part of the battlefields of the Great War. Consecutive offensives by German and, later, British troops were all military failures and turned into human catastrophes costing hundreds of thousands of casualties. Many are still buried in the massive war graves that surround the city. Ypres would give its name to one of the deadly gasses that were used to break the deadlock. The war destroyed the whole region, and still today farmers find shells and live munitions every day in their fields. The city was shelled continually, and for the most part it was turned into rubble. The inevitable happened. The archives went up in a huge fire already in the first months of the war on 22 November 1914, and with them also the potential for research.

This does not mean that no medieval sources have survived. Series of city accounts and the accounts of the comital bailiffs (in fact mostly the copies made for the comital *Chambre des Comptes* in Lille) are also preserved in the State Archives in Brussels and a few local chronicles document the city's eventful political history. Yet what most of these surviving sources have in common that they focus on the end of the Middle Ages and they deal primarily with the period of the late fourteenth and of the fifteenth century, the so-called Burgundian era. Accounts, even those kept in the State Archives, from before that period, have been preserved only fragmentarily and the focus of this book lies primarily on the period before the Burgundian dukes became rulers in Flanders.[3] And the same fragmented nature characterises also the notes written down by Arthur Merghelynck and kept at the Royal Library in Brussels. Access to these sources is difficult, and information haphazard.[4] The notes were, because of the difficulties of extracting information not used systematically. Perhaps their systematic analysis may in the future research yield important research results, however.

Ypres may not have attracted the interest of scholars in the way Ghent and Bruges have, but this does not mean that scholars did not realise the enormous potential of its archives before their destruction. Luckily for historical research, some of these treasures have been published or partly analysed. It would be going too far to name all these source publications, but for the topics dealt with in this book the publication of documents about the cloth industry of medieval Flanders (up to 1400) by Georges Espinas and Henri Pirenne (with the help also of the Ypres archivist De Sagher), a selection of *lettres de foire* (IOUs) by Guillaume Des Marez and the oldest city accounts

---

[3] For a survey of Ypres sources, see Trio, 'De bestuursinstellingen', 44-63, Bautier et al., *Les sources*, 192-193 and de Valériola, Le corpus, 5-74. The city accounts were analysed in Merlevede, *De Ieperse stadsfinanciën*.
[4] On the collection Merghelynck, see Papin, 'Gids', 133-145 and de Valériola, 'Le corpus', 13-14.

by De Sagher and Des Marez again are worth mentioning. These source publications have enabled investigations into, for example, urban finance (Merlevede) or, more recently, credit markets (Howell). The Canadian economic historian John Munro has also touched on aspects of Ypres' medieval cloth industry in many publications. But, sadly, this most knowledgeable specialist in textile industries never attempted to write a more comprehensive study of cloth manufacture in Ypres itself.

This is even more of a pity because, as so eloquently described by historian Georges Doudelez, the role of industrial expansion in Ypres was unequalled. The city and its suburbs in the thirteenth and fourteenth centuries were one giant factory, in which 'the aldermen were the administrators, the merchants the CEOs and the clothiers the foremen and overseers of small workshops', literally sweatshops where workers toiled to earn meagre wages.[5] The city epitomised the success of mercantile capital in a world that could not yet achieve economies of scale by building large factories, but that came very close to the industrial capitalistic relations that would define the industrial revolution of the late eighteenth and nineteenth centuries. The city symbolises, therefore, like no other city in Flanders, the essence of urbanisation in the medieval Low Countries, and the very reason why it almost equalled the urbanisation processes in northern Italy.

This book is an attempt to collect the scattered materials of earlier generations of historians and to do justice to the many source collections that were assembled before the destruction of the city archives. But it also wants to go further. Of all the cloth cities of medieval Europe Ypres was perhaps the most significant. While cities such as Florence in Tuscany or nearby Ghent, Brussels, Leiden and Mechelen may have enjoyed similar reputations. Ypres' dominance as a cloth city started earlier, and lasted longer. Moreover, as we shall see, none of these other cities were so successful in very different market segments in the way Ypres had been. In its heyday in the thirteenth century, the city's merchants and entrepreneurs exported cloth to all parts of Europe, and when active trade fell victim to Europe's changed commercial orientation, the city's entrepreneurs were able to adapt their industrial output to these new circumstances, to new customers, new fashions, new competitors. Ypres remained throughout the fourteenth century that vibrant city. Its population may have slowly declined, but this does not mean that its industry lost its sharpness. Ypres is therefore an ideal laboratory for tracing changing social organisation in this most important of medieval industries.

Historiography about the medieval Flemish cloth industry tends to be primarily economic. From Henri Pirenne to John Munro, historians have examined how and why the Flemish cloth industry succeeded in conquering foreign markets. They have looked at the commercial successes of Flemish merchants and at the way foreign merchants in the late thirteenth and early fourteenth centuries themselves came to Bruges to pick up shiploads of woollens and to obtain for themselves wool imported from England. Historians have also charted the industrial cycles and looked at why in particular periods cloth entrepreneurs were forced to change strategy and switch to other market segments and how industrial manufacture shifted from the countryside to the new cities in Flanders, from the large cities to the smaller centres and again to the countryside, and

---

5 Doudelez, 'La révolution communale', 208.

what this implied for the cost of producing woollens and for the identity of the different stakeholders. They have even looked at the technology of cloth manufacture or at how industrial relations defined the struggle for power in the city. But despite particularly perspicuous studies by Hans Van Werveke on entrepreneurship or Martha Howell on the nature of small commodity production and gender, surprisingly little systematic research has been done on the social organisation of the greatest industry in the Middle Ages. The medieval cloth industry is generally considered to be the playground of the craft guilds; its demise is often associated with reckless regulation and high wages; ideology is never far from the analysis, as Marxian historiography tends to focus on the exploitation of the craftsmen by mercantile capitalists and Smithian historians focus on the upward pressure on wages by immoderate craftsmen's associations as the main reason why the Flemish woollens lost ground on export markets.

This book aims, by focusing on one case study but at the same time on probably the most important industrial city of the Middle Ages, to reassess some of these debates. The focus on Ypres allows one, moreover, to bring together the analysis of the industrial cycle, the role of the various stakeholders in manufacture and trade, the changing impact on the urban social fabric and on political relations, the pressures on wage formation and the role of technological innovation. By combining all these different elements, we think we have been able to look at their interaction and assess who stood to gain or to lose from changing organisation.

In the first chapter we draw a picture of the cycle of growth and decline in the industry. Ypres was probably the most important cloth city of medieval Flanders, itself the most industrialised part of Europe. Cloth was everywhere in Ypres, and Ypres cloth was everywhere in medieval Europe. Although we lack quantitative data about exports, Ypres cloth in its heyday of the thirteenth century was primarily dependent upon Mediterranean markets. Ypres merchants exported their expensive heavy woollens and their cheaper worsteds and semi-worsteds to the Champagne fairs, from where Italian traders distributed them further. The same merchants also controlled the flows of raw materials, in first instance English wools. It was a time when production output reached its zenith. The late thirteenth century was a period of difficult reorganisation, a search for a new equilibrium. Unlike in many other Flemish cloth cities, the output of semi-worsteds continued with some success on the Italian markets, and export figures would start to decline really only from the 1320s, but restructuring imposed itself nonetheless and, as everywhere, the focus was on luxury woollens. This meant also targeting smaller but more qualitative outputs. In this Ypres entrepreneurs were particularly successful, partly also because the decline of Mediterranean markets was compensated for by the growing importance of Central and Eastern Europe. Real decline set in only in the last decades of the fourteenth century. In the fifteenth century Ypres gradually lost its export markets and the output figures for woollens crumbled. Yet even as late as the second half of the sixteenth century there would still be some remnants of the once-dominant cloth industry.

In chapter 2 it is the technological infrastructure that receives all the attention. Ypres produced a wide variety of woollens, although during the fourteenth century the focus was mainly on luxury cloth. This required complex manufacturing processes.

Technological change in cloth manufacture is traditionally discussed in terms of industrial innovation and conservatism. While the switch to the broadloom defined further industrial development in urban cloth manufacture, the hesitation to adopt other techniques is said to have jeopardized growth and continuing success. Yet the fact that the fulling mill or even the spinning wheel was adopted only hesitantly or even, in the case of the fulling mill, never accepted was a matter of rational entrepreneurial choices, not just of conservative protectionism. Other techniques and organisational innovations were adopted much more easily if they did not hamper those choices, and the fact that the Ypres cloth industry was able to implement radical product innovation with astonishing ease greatly defined the industry's resilience on the export markets. Moreover, at each stage of production different technological and product requirements also caused workshop organisation to be sometimes very different, affecting size and labour organisation at the level of the workshop.

Chapter 3 looks at the city's social profile. Although the impact of traditional variables such as labour migration or business concentration cannot be known with any degree of certainty, Ypres' industrial development gave rise to specific changes in the urban social fabric. The rapid growth of the industry caused clear spill-over-effects of population to outside the early thirteenth-century walls. In truly industrial suburbs most clothiers, weavers, fullers, both masters and journeymen, lived in relatively open housing, surrounded by fields and close to their employers. Only in the early fourteenth century did a new wall surround the four densely populated suburbs, which contained almost half of the total urban population. The city was characterised by extremely high inequality rates, most likely because, in contrast to other Flemish cities, the middle class of shopkeepers and small artisans was relatively limited. Ypres was, after all, an industrial city, with a small but very wealthy elite and high numbers of semi-proletarianised workers. Inequality was, above all, very high in the inner city. Most single women, active in wool preparation, also lived there. When, because of declining employment and population, the suburbs were abandoned in 1383 after an urban revolt and the failed siege by Ghent and English troops, population was concentrated again within the old city walls and a dramatic population shift occurred. The inner city, the realm of the elites, the middle class and of the finishing industries of textile manufacture, had to readjust again to accepting high numbers of textile craftsmen.

In chapters 4 and 5 we look at the main figures who organised cloth manufacture and the cloth trade, the elite merchants and the cloth entrepreneurs, the clothiers. Historiography about cloth manufacture in Flanders has been haunted by fierce debates concerning the transition of the truly capitalistic nature of cloth-producing in the early stages and the guild-organised economy of the late Middle Ages. In the first, the industry was dominated by mercantile capital, and merchants not only controlled the trade of raw materials and finished woollens, but were also stakeholders in the actual manufacturing processes underlying the urban cloth industries. In the latter, merchants remain important as providers of capital and to link manufacture with international exports; they are seen, however, as absent from the actual organisation of cloth manufacture. It was the clothiers, true industrial entrepreneurs, who coordinated the different production stages executed by both unskilled workers and skilled guild masters. The chronology of this transition is also linked to the chronology of political equilibria, the first stage corresponding to the political control of a limited number of elite families before 1300 and the latter stage with the so-called 'medieval democracies', in which broader groups in society and the guilds could participate in political decision-making.

Despite all caveats because of incomplete data, the Ypres sources nonetheless show that if there was such a transition from merchants to clothiers, it was at best very gradual. The traditional caesura, 1280, when the clothiers gained access to commercial outlets for wool and cloth, did not mean a revolution for the power relations in the city. Because of their hold on capital markets and their commercial know-how, local merchants remained for a very long time yet crucial figures in defining manufacturing relations, and likewise clothiers, who decidedly became more important during the fourteenth century when Ypres started to focus on manufacturing primarily luxury fabrics, had been around in the thirteenth-century industry as well. So, changes were very gradual, but no less important for that. Merchants did indeed lose their hold on foreign markets for wool and cloth from the late thirteenth century onward, and cloth entrepreneurs were the crucial figures in reorienting the industry towards ever more expensive woollens. But despite these long-term economic transformations, political equilibria and the balance of power in Ypres barely changed. The clothiers and the guilds could at best influence local politics.

Chapters 6, 7 and 8 touch upon the organisation of guild economies. Guilds started to intervene in the organisation of manufacture probably somewhere in the second half of the thirteenth century, but the guilds gained momentum with the clothiers, as the industry turned itself more and more to producing high-quality woollens made from expensive English wool. Still, most work in cloth manufacture was situated at the level of wool preparation, and it was unskilled workers, mostly women, who constituted the bulk of the labour force, but from the moment yarn was transformed into fabric the guilds took over. While the cloth entrepreneurs, the clothiers, took care of the production chain, owning the raw materials and the half-finished goods, each manufacturing stage was entrusted to other entrepreneurs, guild masters who ran their own specialist workshops, weavers (very often the clothiers themselves), fullers, tenterers, shearers, cloth finishers and finally dyers. Guild regulation had to ensure the quality of the work and the smooth transition of the product from one artisan to another.

The chain of production was sacrosanct and detailed regulation had to take care of the quality standards throughout the manufacturing process and of the liabilities if something went wrong. But guild regulation was predominantly geared towards organising the labour market and defining the relations between employers and employees, both skilled artisans and unskilled assistants. As a rule, working conditions and wages were negotiated between the different stakeholders, but the few surviving wage data, often preserved only for periods of heightened social tension and rapid industrial change, point to the fact that wage levels were very comparable with the better-known wages in the building industry. Whether wage cycles were equally comparable cannot be known. What is certain, however, is that wages for the typically female occupations in the preparation of wool were substantially lower, lower even than the wages of unskilled assistants. Already before 1300, women had been ousted as independent wage earners in most guild-organised trades. Women lost access to training and lost touch therefore with the highly valued skill of specialist artisans. It was the perfect storm playing against female agency. The quality of woollens was primarily constructed by gender (men) and by institutions that reinforced male entitlement (guilds).

It was also these guildsmen who constituted the revolutionary force in the city. The history of thirteenth- and above all fourteenth-century Ypres was characterised by sometimes very bloody clashes between the semi-proletarianised workers, most of them weavers and fullers, and the mercantile elites. The clothiers often held an ambiguous position in these social and political conflicts. Despite this eventful social history and the importance of cloth manufacture for the urban economy of Ypres, the textile guilds were never able to topple the leading position of the mercantile elites in the political organisation of the city, and repression after a rebellion was often harsh, sometimes attacking the very livelihood of many Ypres textile workers.

The crisis of the traditional urban cloth industry in the large cities is often explained in terms of competition with other production centres in Flanders (small towns and textile producers in the countryside) and abroad (first in other principalities of the Low Countries, Brabant and Holland; later also mainly in England). And indeed, competition drove the structural changes in the Ypres industry throughout the thirteenth, fourteenth and fifteenth centuries. Ypres was, of course, not unusual in this respect. The scale of its medieval industry was probably unequalled in Northwest Europe, in similar ways to the scale of the cloth industry of Florence in Mediterranean Europe; the social tensions that lay at the heart of industrial organisation and the frictions that ensued from these tensions are indicative of the broader patterns that characterise the transition from feudal to capitalistic society. In Ypres a shifting balance had to be found between mercantile capital and the other stakeholders in urban society, not least the guilds. In the end it was that shifting balance that defined the nature of industrial change, allowing or preventing innovation and adaptation, facilitating or impeding social change.

CHAPTER 1

Flemish Resilience?

Cloth and its Markets

In the winter of 1575-1576 the secretary of the city of Antwerp, Jan Gillis, gave the order to establish a list of the current prices for textiles on the Antwerp market. The list was intended to prepare for a new tax on the retailing of textiles in the city.[6] It shows to what extent Antwerp had in the sixteenth century become the leading textile market in the Low Countries. On the list figure a wide range of silks and brocades, of linens, and of says and traditional fine and heavy woollens. Even at this late date the market for heavy woollens of the traditional *draperie ointe* ('greased cloth') was still by far the most diverse, although the volumes of broadcloth were probably easily surpassed by the *draperies légères* (the 'light cloth', consisting of worsteds and semi-worsteds).[7] Yet heavy woollens were clearly still very much part of the Antwerp textile market in the late sixteenth century. Most fine woollens were manufactured in England. Cloth from Coggeshall in East Anglia was by far the most expensive woollen on the Antwerp market, but woollens from Worcester and Castle Combe in the Midlands were also very prominent. Most English woollens were, however, just called 'from England' and they vary from the finest woollens dyed in the most exclusive colours to simple lighter kerseys. Despite the continuing crisis in traditional cloth manufacture that had been taking place since the late fourteenth century, even in the 1570s woollens from the textile cities of the Low Countries were also still quite numerous. The most expensive Low Countries woollens were Mechelen cloth – since the late Middle Ages Mechelen woollens had been particularly renowned for their high quality and high price – followed by those from the small Flemish town of Menen, which even as late as the sixteenth century had experienced remarkable success as a producer of traditional heavy woollens, and by woollens from Lille, Armentières, Bruges, Amsterdam, Nieuwkerke and cheaper ones from other places in Brabant and Holland.[8] But leading the woollens in the upper middle price range was still the traditional cloth industry of Ypres, in this period allegedly assumed to have all but disappeared. At half the price of the most prestigious Mechelen woollens, the red and black Ypres woollens *metten Andries* (branded with the seal of St Andrew) at 61 and 56 *stuiver* per ell figure prominently on the list. Ypres woollens appear also further down the list: a red woollen *met Ons*

---

6 Thijs, 'Les textiles', 76-86.
7 For the impact of the lighter woollen textiles on the Antwerp market see most notably Brulez, 'De handelsbalans', 278-310 and more recently Puttevils, *Merchants and trading*.
8 On Mechelen cloth output see Stabel, 'The Move to Quality Cloth', 159-180 and Mertens 'Changes in the Production', 114-123. The cloth industry of Menen is discussed in Stabel, *De kleine stad*, 131-135. On Lille see DuPlessis, *Lille and the Dutch Revolt*. The Nieuwkerke cloth industry has recently been investigated in van der Meulen, *Woven into the Urban Fabric*.

Lief Vrouwen (a seal representing Our Lady) was estimated at 52 st. And Ypres appears not only as a producer of heavy cloth; worsteds manufactured in Ypres were also still present on the Antwerp market: Ypres bays were priced even higher than the famous Hondschoote says.[9]

So, towards the end of the sixteenth century the cloth industry in Ypres was still alive (although perhaps less kicking). Ypres no longer produced the upper quality range of heavy woollens, but activity in the middle tier of quality woollens was still sizable enough to send woollens to the most important international textile market of Europe. And Ypres was also involved in producing worsteds. This late-sixteenth-century activity must have been quite limited though, and Ypres was certainly no longer leading the textile dance. In the textile region par excellence in the Low Countries, the County of Flanders, the market leaders were, for heavy woollens, the small towns of Armentières and Menen and the (large) semi-urban village of Nieuwkerke and, for worsteds and semi-worsteds, of course, the massive production in Hondschoote, a semi-rural settlement that had become an important town with a population of almost 10,000. Three centuries earlier, the situation had been totally different. At that time, the manufacture of woollen cloth was the result of the industrial power of the large and politically powerful cities in the county, Ghent, Douai, Lille, Bruges and the most industrialised of them all, the city of Ypres.

Ypres Cloth in Medieval Europe

Ypres woollens appear as reputed export products as early as the twelfth century. Although the claim that Ypres woollens were already present on the Russian market in the 1130s is highly doubtful, from the latter part of the twelfth century those doubts start to dissipate.[10] Ypres cloth probably came along with German trade expansion, and very quickly the most prestigious Ypres woollens started to build a reputation as the preferred textiles of the Russian and East-European elites.[11] But the biggest export successes in the early stages of the Ypres cloth industry were undoubtedly achieved on Mediterranean markets. Of all Flemish and Artesian cloth cities, Ypres in the thirteenth century was not just the most important quantitatively; in sheer cloth volumes as recorded, of all cloth cities in the Low Countries it also exported the most diverse range of woollens to Italy, southern France and the Iberian Peninsula: heavy plain-coloured cloth of the *draperie ointe*, from the exclusive scarlets to more mid-range woollens, but also striped cloth (*enforchi, virgati*) and, to a lesser extent, stamforts, usually striped halfcloth (*standvoorden, estainforts, coverturi*)[12] and says, all woollens of the so-called *draperie sèche*, ranging from relatively cheaper fabrics to mid-range qualities. They were

---

9 Thijs, 'Les textiles', 81-85.
10 Pirenne, 'Draps d'Ypres à Novgorod', 563-566.
11 Abraham-Thisse, '*Kostel Ypersch, gemeyn Ypersch*', 125-126.
12 The name stamfort does not refer to the English town of Stamford (although it was also involved in textile industry), but probably refers to *stamine forte* or strong warp, the warp of stamforts being a strong non-greased yarn (Munro, 'Medieval Woollens', 241-243).

exported as coloured woollens, but some were dyed (or re-dyed) in one of the Italian cities, so they must also have arrived as white cloth or blue cloth (undyed or dyed blue in the fibre).[13] There is no doubt that at this stage Ypres merchants' contacts at the fairs of Champagne were crucial in this respect. Ypres merchants belonged to the *Hanse of the 17 Cities* which also controlled the Flemish trade at the fairs.[14]

There were, however, ups and downs which, because of the city's dependence upon Mediterranean markets, must have been felt almost immediately by the textile entrepreneurs and workers at home. The Genoese notarial instruments published by Renée Doehaerd point to a successful period for scarlets and fine woollens in the early thirteenth century.[15] Ypres cloth was exported further to the Levant, Constantinople, Cyprus and the Crusader States. Ypres scarlets, probably dyed with kermes, were the most expensive woollens in these records (408-503s), almost double the price of the normal colours of Ypres cloth (blues were priced between 210 and 300s) and of the striped woollens (*c.* 200s, clearly much more expensive than striped woollens from other production centres). But towards the middle of the thirteenth century Ypres luxury woollens lost ground to woollens from Central France in particular. Although figures apply to individual contracts and may not be representative of the total export volumes, the share of Ypres woollens had been reduced to less than a third of the figures at the beginning of the century. Instead, Ypres sent out more and more stamforts and biffes (*enforchis*), cheaper mixed woollens, many of them also striped with different warp and weft colours (dyed in the fibre or yarn). The latter part of the thirteenth century and the beginning of the fourteenth would be the golden age of Ypres striped cloth. This changing presence of Ypres woollens in Genoa seems to have been a general trend. It is confirmed by similar developments in Siena and Florence, where Ypres luxury cloth remained important until the 1310s. In the Alberti documentation of the early fourteenth century, Ypres scarlets were valued at 80-100 Florins, Ypres whites and blues at 35-47 and Ypres reds (*sanguine*) at 33-41 Fl.[16]

In the second quarter of the fourteenth century the position of Ypres (and of the other traditional Flemish cloth cities like Ghent, Douai, Saint-Omer, Diksmuide and Bruges) started to decline. Striped cloth no longer enjoyed the popularity it had had before and around 1300, and the Italian markets for high-quality luxury cloth from the Low Countries were gradually taken over by import substitution and by cloth exports from the cities in the Duchy of Brabant (Leuven, Mechelen and Brussels). For the Alberti company in Florence, still very active importers of Low Countries woollens in the 1340s and 1350s, Ypres cloth constituted only a tiny part of their turnover, and similarly Ypres woollens became fewer in the business of the Del Bene company. The cheaper Ypres *coverture* fared better and held out somewhat longer in the activities of the big Florentine companies of the Alberti and Peruzzi (but they were clearly poorer

---

13 Chorley, 'The Ypres Cloth Industry', 114-119, id., 'Cloth Exports', 349-379.
14 Bautier, 'Les foires de Champagne', 97-147 and Milgrom, North and Weingast, 'The Role of Institutions', 1-21. The role of the merchant guilds in the organisation of Flemish trade at the fairs is discussed in Van Werveke, 'Hansa' in Vlaanderen', 60-87.
15 Doehaerd, *Les relations commerciales*, vol. 1, and Chorley, 'The Ypres Cloth Industry', 114.
16 Chorley, 'The Cloth Exports', 349-379.

quality products than similarly named woollens half a century earlier and they fetched much lower prices compared to competing woollens from other production centres). The same patterns appear also on other South-European markets, in France, Portugal, Aragon or Castile, all of them serviced by the same Italian merchant companies.[17] When, in the latter part of the fourteenth century, Flemish woollens recovered a little on these Mediterranean markets, this brought little solace to Ypres entrepreneurs. It was the small towns on the River Leie, Kortrijk, Menen and particularly Wervik, that were able this time to recover the falling shares of Brabantian cloth. But the major Flemish cities did not achieve a return in Southern Europe. The Mediterranean markets were lost for good. Instead, the exports from Ypres would have to look to the East. It is symptomatic that Francesco di Marco Datini no longer traded in Ypres woollens around 1400, but turned for Flemish cloth instead almost exclusively to the Leie towns and to Wervik in particular.[18]

In the meantime, however, Ypres woollens became more common on the South-German and on the Hanseatic markets.[19] They had been present already in the latter half of the twelfth century, but growth seems to have become continuous in the latter part of the thirteenth century, at exactly the time when Ypres fine woollens lost their pre-eminence in South-European markets. The fact that Hanseatic trade started to use Bruges as its main commercial hub for Western Europe undoubtedly added to the success of the Ypres merchants. They already controlled wool imports from England; now a steady demand for woollens was nearby and numbers were rising fast. In a matter of a couple of decades we find Ypres woollens becoming almost omnipresent in the 1280s and 1290s. They are recorded in northern and eastern Germany (Hamburg, Stralsund, Lübeck, Breslau/Wroclaw), they are distributed through Cologne to South-German markets (Nurnberg, Augsburg, Regensburg, Lindau) and to Austria and Bohemia (Vienna, Prague). In the early fourteenth century there is no indication of a slump, as was the case in Mediterranean Europe. Ypres cloth outputs remain important throughout the German and Baltic markets. If anything, the frequency with which they appear in the sources is still increasing.

Little can be said about the qualities of the Ypres woollens at this time. In contrast to the typologies on Mediterranean markets, which were very comparable to the nomenclature of woollens in the statutes of the Ypres industry themselves, names of woollens are primarily defined by their colours. But it is certain, that on the German and Baltic markets there was only little room for worsteds or striped woollens; most exports consisted of the fine woollens of the *draperie ointe*. But, as in Italy, exports eastward also seem to have consisted of a wide variety of these fine woollens. The fine prestigious scarlets so coveted by the Russian and Polish nobility tell only part of the story. Ypres catered for princes and feudal aristocrats as well as for bourgeois clienteles. Whether there was a deliberate strategy of downgrading qualities and targeting different consumers cannot be gleaned from the Hanseatic sources. It is clear,

---

17 Chorley, 'The Ypres Cloth Industry', 116; Munro, 'Medieval Woollens', 241.
18 Melis, 'La diffusione', 219-243; Chorley, 'The Ypres Cloth Industry', 115-116.
19 Abraham-Thisse, '*Kostel Ypersch, gemeyn Ypersch*', 125-145.

however, that diversification may have been very effective in attracting customers and stabilising falling exports. Still the strategy was also risky. During the fourteenth century mid-priced fine woollens became the key products of the secondary cloth towns in Interior Flanders. They could probably produce them under more advantageous conditions. Hence, these secondary towns developed a much more flexible infrastructure able to conform to new demands for woollens made with Castilian wool.

Ypres did not, however, experience the same fate as the cloth industry of Bruges. In early fourteenth-century Bruges the focus had been on cheaper woollens, from says to cheaper and mid-priced plain cloth and, unlike those of Ghent and Ypres, Bruges entrepreneurs were less able to adapt their production to the shift away from the Mediterranean, towards the Hanseatic market. As a result, Ypres and that other large industrial city, Ghent, could hang on to a substantial part of their cloth output, while Bruges kept losing markets. So, unlike Ypres, Bruges, also because of the city's role as the commercial hub of Western Europe, became from the late fourteenth century onwards primarily a finishing centre for woollens, with a great number of fullers, shearers and dyers, while weaving lost ground rapidly.[20] Other traditional cloth cities, such as Diksmuide, which did not adapt either, disappeared almost completely from the export market.[21]

The flexibility demonstrated by Ypres cloth entrepreneurs did not, however, prevent exports to southern Germany from starting to dwindle towards the middle of the fourteenth century. Ypres woollens found it harder to compete with the influx of Brabant and Ghent cloth, a clear parallel with the developments in Italy. They did not disappear, however, but, compared to other production centres, they no longer led the dance. The role of Italian firms in the distribution of Low Countries woollens in these regions can probably explain this similarity. But on the North-German and Central-European Hanseatic markets Ypres-produced cloth remained a strong brand. It was strong in the Wendish cities of Lübeck, Luneburg, Hamburg, Stettin and Greifswald, but its presence was even more important in the Prussian (with massive orders from the Teutonic Order in Königsberg), Baltic and Livonian cities. In many cities it was among the preferred gifts to urban officeholders, to noblemen and princes and to high clergymen. Many Ypres woollens were mid-priced fabrics (and some even required local finishing and were therefore probably half-finished fulled cloth or even raw cloth), but the prestigious Ypres scarlets and other fine woollens were still very obvious in elite circles.[22]

During the latter part of the fourteenth and in the fifteenth centuries this trend continued. By now, Ypres cloth had completely lost its Mediterranean markets. The only Flemish woollens to thrive in Italy or the Iberian Peninsula were the mid-priced woollens of the Leie cloth towns (Wervik, Kortrijk, Menen, etc.) and the production centres in the vicinity of Lille (Tourcoing, and gradually also the woollens of Armentières), and the worsteds and semi-worsteds of interior Flanders (bays and says from Den-

---

20 Stabel, *A Capital of Fashion*, forthcoming.
21 Stabel, *Dwarfs among Giants*, 137-157 and id., 'Les draperies', 355-380.
22 Abraham-Thisse, '*Kostel Ypersch, gemeyn Ypersch*', 128-135.

dermonde, Hondschoote, etc.).[23] The older centres of Flanders, Artois and Brabant were more and more sidelined by local Italian woollens and more and more also by imports from England. Cloth exports to France are not particularly well-known, but the traditional cloth cities seem to have lost these markets as well, and in the western and southern parts of Germany they also lost ground. The diminishing production output of Ypres cloth entrepreneurs was certainly caused by these declining markets.

On the other hand, Ypres cloth remained important on the Hanseatic markets, and the popularity of Ypres woollens, and particularly of the more expensive range of Ypres cloth, increased going east. In the account books and letters of the Hanseatic merchant Hildebrand Veckinhusen in the first decades of the fifteenth century and in those of the Teutonic Order, Ypres is, with Saint-Omer and nearby Poperinge, the most important cloth city, far ahead of the Leie cloth towns, the successful secondary centres of Interior Flanders (Geraardsbergen, Aalst, Dendermonde, Oudenaarde) and of other traditional industrial cities such as Ghent.[24] Ypres cloth was also distributed from Cologne to Western Germany, but it is through Lübeck, Riga, Danzig (Gdansk) and Reval (Talinn) that most woollens were distributed to Central and East-European customers. Even in the account books of individual merchants Ypres woollens were often numbered in their dozens, sometimes even in their hundreds. It is very difficult to assess the quality of these woollens. Because of the conservative nature of the East-European cloth market, they were unlikely to be worsteds or semi-worsted, so it is to the traditional heavy cloth that we must turn, and to the higher price ranges. Still within this range there was a wide variety of woollens, from mid-priced to very expensive fabrics. The Veckinhusen firm differentiates no fewer than 21 different qualities of Ypres woollens.[25] In their accounts, Ypres cloth fetched between 32 and 46s Fl., double the price of Poperinge and Tourcoing woollens and substantially more expensive also than woollens from Saint-Omer.[26] But these prices could differ from one market to another. In Russia, Ypres cloth – in this case probably very expensive scarlets – fetched no less than seven times the price of a Poperinge woollen. From the twelfth century onwards, Ypres cloth continued to be the traditional fabric for the Russian boyar elites. Even in the first decades of the fifteenth century, the Lübeck merchant Hildebrand Veckinhusen still sent Ypres woollens primarily to the eastern markets of the Hanseatic world. Although he usually describes the numbers of Ypres woollens he deals in without further specification, sometimes he tries to identify them by their colour: green and *meygron* (may green), blue and deep blue (*sadblau*), red and blood red (*sanguine*), black. Occasionally he mentions *kostel Yperschen* (expensive Ypres woollens). Although Veckinhusen also trades in expensive scarlets, these were often mentioned without naming the place where they were produced (only once is an Ypres scarlet mentioned separately). But Ypres also appears in lookalike woollens: Veckinhusen sometimes deals in Ghent *Yperschen* (woollens manufactured in the Ypres tradition but produced in

---

23 Stabel, 'Les draperies', 355-380 and id. *De kleine stad*, 89-99.
24 Abraham-Thisse, 'Les draps de Flandre', 178-180.
25 Stieda, Wilhelm, *Hildebrand Veckinhusen* (the letter about the problems of selling Ypres cloth, 435). See also Abraham-Thisse, '*Kostel Ypersch, gemeyn Ypersch*', 186-7 citing Lesnikov, *Die Handelsbücher*.
26 Abraham-Thisse, 'Les draps de Flandre', 193-194.

Ghent). But the market for Ypres woollens could also be very fickle. In an undated letter Tideman Brekelvelde, one of Hildebrand's business partners in Lűneburg, warns him to be careful about sending Ypres woollens soon, saying that the cloth sellers in Lübeck do not want them anymore (*in al Lubeke en is nicht 1 wantsnider de an de Yperschen welle*).

Flemish stuffs, with Ypres cloth prominently among them still, constituted the heart of the imports of Hanseatic merchants well into the second half of the fifteenth century, often constituting more than 50 per cent of traded goods.[27] With such market shares, and considering the traditionalism of consumers on these markets, the choice to opt for a standardised and high-quality output was a sure bet, as long as the Hanseatic traders dominated the market. The one-sided nature of exports to Central and East-European markets, however, also had its downsides. It made the industry more vulnerable to fundamental changes in trade routes. Ypres did not give in to Hanseatic demands to produce only particular ranges, unlike some of the smaller centres, such as Oudenaarde and even Poperinge, which started to produce new types of woollens made from Spanish wool for the exclusive use of the Hanseatic traders.[28] The city continued to produce various types of woollens. Yet the Hanseatic focus was fraught with danger, nonetheless. When the Hanseatic merchants gradually started to encounter more competition from Dutch, English and Scandinavian traders from the latter part of the fifteenth century and into the sixteenth century, these traditional markets came under intense pressure.

The scattered data on cloth exports confirm, but also nuance, therefore, the traditional image of the rise and fall of Ypres as a cloth city. It is beyond any doubt that the apogee of Ypres cloth on European markets can be situated in the long thirteenth century. From the late twelfth to the beginning of the fourteenth centuries Ypres was undoubtedly the leading Flemish cloth city, and both in the scope and range of its woollens as well as in the volumes exported, they probably led by far all the other Flemish, Artesian and Brabantine cloth cities. Ghent, Bruges, Diksmuide, Saint-Omer, Douai, Brussels, Leuven and Mechelen came in behind the Ypres production as far as volumes and diversity are concerned. It is no coincidence that the Ypres merchants asked for a cloth hall of their own at the fairs of Champagne, and Ypres cloths were further exported by mainly Italian merchants to various Mediterranean markets from Catalonia in the west to the Black Sea and the Latin Kingdom of Jerusalem in the east.

In the fourteenth century all of this changed. Traditional historiography about Ypres often blames the 'democratic' regime in the late 1320s, and the repression after its fall in 1329, when many textile craftsmen were obliged to leave the city and settle elsewhere.[29] Sources are, however, not consistent enough to corroborate such a sudden breakdown. The loss of Mediterranean markets was a long-drawn-out and gradual process, rather than a sudden change, and Hanseatic markets were not lost. So, the first half of the fourteenth century seems to have been rather a period of adaptation to new market conditions. Ypres had capitalised for a long time on the successes of its semi-worsteds,

---

27 Abraham-Thisse, 'Les draps de Flandre', 186-187.
28 Van Werveke, 'Die Stellung', 296-304.
29 From the older works by Vandenpeereboom (*Ypriana*) to more recent appraisals in Boussemaere, 'De Ieperse lakenproductie' and Mus, *De geschiedenis*.

mainly striped *enforchiés* and increasingly stamforts, in southern Europe. The demand for such woollens declined in exactly this period. As a result, the Mediterranean markets were lost completely, never to be regained. But instead of Italian, Provençal, Catalan and Castilian customers, it is German and Hanseatic merchants who continue to boost in this case primarily the high-quality 'greased woollens', from precious scarlets in Eastern Europe to mid-priced coloured woollens in German and Hanseatic cities. Although volumes cannot be reconstructed, the popularity of Ypres cloth was probably very stable well into the end of the fourteenth and perhaps even the first decades of the fifteenth century, so well after the siege of the city in 1383. Only in the latter part of the fifteenth century did Ypres lose ground on the Hanseatic markets, and this time for good. The Antwerp price list of 1575-1576 still records Ypres woollens, but by this time volumes had shrunk significantly, and Ypres cloth manufacturers were dwarfed by their regional competitors in Armentières, Nieuwkerke and Hondschoote.

Heavy and Light Cloth: A Broken Balance

The short survey of Ypres' cloth exports reveals not only how crucial cloth manufacture and the cloth trade have been for the growth (and for the decline) of the city, but that the city's industry was also characterised by a great diversity of textiles, from very cheap and coarse woollens and says to the top segment of the scarlets dyed in expensive kermes, and everything in between. In fact, this diversity is considered by some textile historians to be particularly unique and much more developed than in any other cloth city of medieval Europe.[30] It gave the merchants and entrepreneurs a great advantage because, depending on the vicissitudes of demand, they could in a matter of months sometimes, if need be, switch to another line of products. This is not to say, of course, that reduced demand for expensive fine woollens could easily be compensated for by switching to cheaper worsteds. It could not. The first required not only much more expensive raw materials (wool, of course, but also more expensive dyes and mordants), but the labour that was necessary to manufacture them was also more diverse and they also required more elaborate industrial processes. Moreover, if Ypres entrepreneurs needed to switch, such change could occur only after some delay, just because wool and dyestuffs had to be ordered well in advance, in this way jeopardizing their business strategies in the short run.

Overall, the Ypres cloth entrepreneurs therefore produced woollens both of the *draperie ointe* (*ghesmoutte draperie*, greased cloth) and of the *draperie sèche* (*onghesmoutte draperie*, ungreased cloth), the difference being that the better quality short-stapled wool of the former was washed and scoured more thoroughly, removing all natural greases from the fibre, while the latter usually lower quality wools kept some of their natural lanolin. After the combing and carding processes the former needed to be greased with a lubricant (usually butter) to facilitate the spinning and weaving

---

[30] Munro, Medieval woollens 181-227; Chorley, 'The Cloth Exports of Flanders', 349-379 and id., 'The Ypres Cloth Industry', 111-124; Stabel, 'Les draperies', 355-380.

processes; the latter did not require that process, but they were, because of the remaining grease levels, also more difficult to dye in the fibre.

Table 1.1 lists all the different woollens that are described in the various cloth statutes from the late thirteenth until the middle of the fourteenth century. This list is certainly not complete. The famous Ypres scarlets, for example, are not mentioned in the preserved statutes, but they were and remained omnipresent on the export markets. We do not know a lot either about the *draps de sorte*, which are mentioned in the late-thirteenth-century statutes. The technical differences between all these woollens and their measurements were very distinct. Customers could recognize the qualities by the cloth boards (*listen*) and by the seals that were added to the finished woollens. Each type of woollen had to be made of a particular range of raw materials (mostly fine English wool), but each also had its technical characteristics in each of the production stages. Most crucial was the weaving stage. More technical details will be discussed in the next chapter, but while preparing the warp beam a fixed number of warp yarns had to be aligned, a specific reed (comb) was needed to beat the weft and to define the width of the fabric, weaving lengths had to be respected (although the length of a woollen was primarily defined in the fulling troughs and at the tentering frames), and the nature of the weft (how warp and weft yarns were crossed) was decided in the harness of the loom. Each element defined the nature of the fabric and its later density after the fulling, tentering and shearing processes, but perhaps nothing was so decisive for the result as the weave. The luxury woollens were woven with a plain 1/1 and 2/1 construction, creating very dense fabrics. The *dickedinne*, the most successful of all Ypres fine woollens (and the scarlets as well), had a plain 1/1 weave; the *derdelinghe* a 2/1 twill weave.

The worsteds (*draperie sèche*) were usually dyed in the yarn (a less efficient method, giving less saturated colours). Striped cloth was, of course, not dyed in the fabric. This would inevitably destroy the colour pattern, but plain worsteds could be dyed afterwards in the fabric, intensifying (or changing) the initial colour. The late thirteenth- and early fourteenth-century statutes, passed when the Ypres *onghesmoutte draperie* experienced its heyday, distinguish between low-quality says, stamforts (*estainforts, standvoorden*), usually half cloths and *Ypersch-Popersche* (a copy of a successful Poperinge worsted). It is, according to De Poerck, also possible that the *enforchiés* belonged to the range of dry woollens. Says were usually woven in a 2/2 construction; stamforts were woven in a 2/1 weave (like the *derdelinghe* fine woollens), a weave that allowed stripes to be brought out in a warp-faced manner (creating strips lengthways). The enforchiés were according to Patrick Chorley a *biffe* (*pijfelaer*) which allowed one to see stripes in the weft (so widthways).

The great variety of woollens produced in Ypres was not only an asset, but it also required scrutiny by the officials and certainly facilitated fraud, the more so because, once sealed, customers did not always have the expertise or the opportunity to check the quality of the raw materials or even the quality of the work. The density of the finished cloth was different for every type of woollen, but qualities were sometimes not that far removed from each other. Hence the Ypres cloth industry required a very strict and complex system of quality control. Removing the seals during or after

Table 1.1 Ypres cloth types according to the statutes (around 1300): greased woollens (*draperie ointe*)

Sources: Espinas and Pirenne, *Recueil*, 3 and De Poerck, *La draperie médiévale*, 1, 293-300. For the measures in Ypres, see Paul Vandewalle, *Oude maten, gewichten en muntstelsels in Vlaanderen, Brabant en Limburg*, (Ghent 1984).

YPRES ELL = 0.697M	N WARP YARNS	WIDTH AT THE LOOM (ELLS)	FULLED LENGTH (ELLS)	SIZE AT THE TENTERING FRAME (ELLS)		FULLING TIME (DAYS)	SIZE (M^2).
1. Dickedinne				length	width		
-small mixed	1,488	2.9	32	41	2.5	3	49.8
-small white/blue	1,584	2.9		41	2.5	3	49.8
-large mixed	1,776	3.5	32	41	3	4	59.8
-large white/blue	1,872			41	3	4	59.8
-boven der kuere				45	2.2		49.2
2. Dueten	1,250	2.7		40	2.7	3	53.4
3. Derdelinghe							
-white/blue	1,488	2.6	30	41	2.2	4	44.8
-(*gherseme*) peckers	1,392	2.6	30	41	2.2	3	44.8
4.(Nieuwe gaernine)[i]	1,080		38		2.1		
5. (Enforchiés)[ii]							

[i] The *nieuwe gaernine* are ranked by Guy De Poerck among the *draperie ointe*, but they are considered by Chorley to be dry cloth (Chorley, *The Ypres Cloth Industry*, 112).

[ii] The *enforchiés* were classified by Guy De Poerck among the light woollens, but Patrick Chorley alleges that because of their price range and quality they must have belonged to the *draperie ointe* (ibid.). For this reason I have added them to this table, but it is likely that the term ('strengthened') refers to a strong warp consisting of ungreased yarn, similar to the stanforts, the difference being the different weave, allowing one to bring the weft yarn forward (see also Munro, 'Medieval Woollens', 229). They are therefore most likely a semi-worsted, with dry warp and greased weft.

the manufacturing process or, worse, using fraudulent seals was severely punished and often led to banishment from the city and the county or to life-long exclusion from activities in the cloth industry. The two brands of the Ypres cloth industry, the greased and ungreased, were not to be mixed at any time throughout the manufacturing process from wool sorting to dyeing – the statutes leave no doubt about this – but also the marketing techniques were rigidly separated. The cloth hall contained stalls for the *draperie ointe* and for the *draperie sèche*. Before 1300 there were 39 stalls for the expensive coloured woollens (with 42 clothiers), but there were also 7 stalls (with 14 clothiers) for the light and cheaper says, 22.5 (with 37 clothiers) for the *enforchiés* and 28 for the half stamforts (with 89 clothiers linked to these stalls).[31] Clothiers and craftsmen could therefore not operate in both branches at the same time. They could switch without a lot of trouble, however, if market conditions demanded change. In 1309 the stalls for *enforchiés* and says were empty, and the infrastructure was reserved for the clothiers dealing in half cloths (stamforts). The continuing popularity of the *coverture*, which were half stamforts, on Mediterranean markets can, however, be noted in the distribution of market stalls until the 1330s, so the overall balance between heavy and light cloth remained very much the same: from 41 per cent in the early fourteenth century to more than 48 per cent in the 1320s.[32] Such data from the latter part of the fourteenth century have not been preserved, but the purchase of leaden seals in this period suggests that light cloth must have been of only marginal importance in the 1370s and 1380s. This should not be a surprise. We have already seen that the markets for light cloth in Mediterranean Europe were gradually being lost, so the focus again came to be almost exclusively on the fine greased woollens that were by this time sent mainly to the Hanseatic world.

An Industry in Continuous Transition

Relatively little is known of the chronology of the ascent of Ypres as a cloth city, or of its decline for that matter. In the next chapter we will see how crucial technological and organisational changes have been to giving Ypres woollens that cutting edge over their competitors, and how very deliberate entrepreneurial decisions lay at the heart of the cloth industry's resilience. But how far the growth of the industry followed trends is not known. It is very likely that Ypres catered at the beginning primarily for regional markets, by turning local wool into fabric. The impact of the domestic market on the further development of the industry must have been important, but no figures have been preserved. In fact, our knowledge about foreign markets is much better. It is very likely that the densely urbanised county of Flanders, and the rest of the Low Countries for that matter, constituted an important outlet for Ypres clothiers and merchants. We only know that many Flemish cities ordered Ypres cloth, particularly fine woollens, to give to their aldermen and other officeholders. Ypres cloth was also consumed at the princely courts in the Low Countries. But the bulk of demand in Flanders and in the county's surrounding principalities must have been generated by the urban elites and increasingly also by the urban middle classes, which in the late Middle Ages experienced a period of rising living standards, their hour of glory.[33] Probably this demand focused on mid-priced fine woollens. We have seen that Ypres gradually lost its hold on the market for lighter cloth towards the middle of the fourteenth century. But this was also the market niche dominated by the smaller towns in the county. How Ypres fine

---

31 Espinas and Pirenne, *Recueil*, 3, 705-707, mentioned in Chorley, 'The Ypres Cloth Industry', 118.
32 Boussemaere, 'De Ieperse lakenproductie', 148-149 and Chorley, 'The Ypres Cloth Industry', 119-120, both referring to Des Marez and De Sagher, *Comptes de la ville d'Ypres*, 2, 425-426.
33 Stabel, *A Capital of Fashion* for Bruges and more general remarks in Blondé et al., 'Living Together in the City', 59-92.

Table 1.2 Estimate of the annual cloth production in Flanders (Dutch speaking parts), in the fifteenth and early sixteenth centuries (fine woollens, *draperie ointe*)
Source: Stabel, 'Les draperies flamandes' and id., '*Dmeeste, oirboirlixste ende proffitelixste let ende neringhe*', 113-153.

	1400	1450	1500	1550
Ghent, Ypres, Bruges	34.1%	24.6%	45.5%	33.3%
Leie towns	28.5%	32.8%	10.9%	28.6%
Scheldt-Dender towns	14,8%	24.6%	20.0%	19.0%
Western, Coastal Flanders	22.7%	18.0%	23.6%	19.0%
Urban cloth (total)	88,000	61,000	55,000	21,000
Rural cloth		3,000	6,000	15,000
Total (urban+rural)	88,000	64,000	61,000	36,000

woollens competed with cloth from the other large cloth cities of Ghent and Douai, with the towns in the river basin such as Oudenaarde, Kortrijk, Wervik and Aalst, or with the lighter woollens in semi-rural settlements such as Poperinge, Langemark, Ronse and later Hondschoote, cannot be known. Competition, not only on foreign markets, must have been quite stiff, given the attention paid by successive Ypres city governments to countering competition in its own hinterland.[34]

If we take one step back and look at the Flemish cloth output at the end of the Middle Ages, a period when the industry in Ypres was already in dire straits (in earlier periods no such rough reconstruction of total cloth output can be made), we see that output figures of the Flemish cloth industry were clearly falling throughout this period, with a rapid overall decline in the first half of the fifteenth and again in the first half of the sixteenth centuries. But this does not mean that there were no changes in market shares, so some cloth towns were hit harder than others. It is striking that around 1400 the big cities still led the field, but that their output was almost matched by those of the smaller towns along the Leie (primarily in Wervik, but also in Comines, Menen and Kortrijk). During the fifteenth and early sixteenth centuries cloth output kept declining, but market shares also changed, sometimes dramatically. The success of the Leie towns in the late fourteenth and early fifteenth centuries, geared towards exports to the Mediterranean, was not continued, and towns like Wervik started to decline in the latter part of the fifteenth century, although at a lower level the success of Menen (and to a lesser extent also Kortrijk) compensated for this trend. The towns in the Scheldt and Dender basin (Aalst, Dendermonde and Oudenaarde in particular) fared better in the fifteenth century, and could hang on, partly because of their successes in the Hanseatic export markets. We find similar stability in the cloth towns of Western Flanders, although this stability hides the decline of traditional cloth towns, among them Poperinge, and the rise of new centres such as Nieuwkerke. The big cities lost

---

34 See the Epilogue to this book.

a substantial part of the cloth output in the first half of the fifteenth century, but they seem to have recovered in sheer output volumes towards the end of that century, but, of course, this has a lot to do with the renewed interest in the big cities (in Bruges, but also in Ghent and Ypres) in light cloth, which had all but disappeared in the first half of the fourteenth century.

This reconstruction dates back only to the period when Ypres cloth outputs had already declined significantly. In the late fourteenth and in the fifteenth centuries Ypres had all but lost its share of lighter and cheaper textiles. But, by now, also its mid-priced ranges felt stiff competition from the 'new draperies' in the towns of interior Flanders (in the Leie towns and in the Scheldt and Dender basin) and in its own quarter of Ypres (Roeselare, Bailleul and, of course, as already from the thirteenth century onwards Poperinge). As a result, the focus on high-quality cloth increased, and with it, evidently, the overall output figures also declined.

Sadly, hard quantitative data establishing the cycle of production are hard to come by. The city accounts mention various indicators, the rented stalls in the cloth hall and the leaden seals that were bought at the city's expense, but the interpretation of these data is very difficult. The leaden seals have been used in literature as a proxy for production output. At each important stage of production (weaving, fulling, tentering, shearing, dyeing) the quality of the product needed to be guaranteed, so in the end a length of woollen was marked by various seals, made either of lead (for the heavy 'greased' cloth) or with wax (for the lighter 'dry' worsted-like woollens). Because the various seals were distinguished in the accounts, they can be used to measure cloth outputs.[35] Many scholars (Henri Laurent, Hans Van Werveke, Jules Demey, Raymond Van Uytven, Patrick Chorley and most recently Pieter Boussemaere) have dealt with this issue since the 1940s and these authors do not always agree on the usefulness of the seals to reconstruct cloth outputs or on the methodology to do this.[36] Estimates of the total production therefore differ substantially. Van Werveke counts about 90,000 woollens in 1318, declining to a mere 34,000 in the middle of the fourteenth century; Van Uytven calibrated the figure to 50,000 in the first decades of the fourteenth century (almost half of the earlier Van Werveke output), while Chorley raised this figure again to 100,000 (this time including also the light woollens).

The methodological caveats are indeed very real. Although they appear almost on an annual basis in the city accounts, the figures do not necessarily reveal the short-term or mid-term cycle of cloth production. Stocks of leaden seals were arranged, from which the clothiers could take what they needed when they needed it; we do not have any idea how many seals were never used. Leaden seals turn up in great numbers during excavations, so every clothier or craftsman probably also had his own stock as well. The

---

35 The purchases have been published in Espinas and Pirenne, *Recueil*, 3, 809-834. For an archaeological and typological analysis of the leaden seals of Ypres: Van Laere, 'Loden penningen', 269-364 and id., 'Loden textielzegels', 257-322.

36 Laurent, *Un grand commerce d'exportation*, 344-345; Van Werveke, 'De omvang van de Ieperse lakenproduktie', 496-508; Van Uytven, 'Technique, productivité et prduction', 283-293; Chorley, 'The Ypres cloth production', 118-119 and Boussemaere, 'De Ieperse lakenproductie', 131-161, which is the most elaborate treatment of this source.

Figure 1.1 Leaden cloth seal from before 1383. This is one of the hundreds of leaden cloth seals that were found in Ypres, most notably from the excavations in the *Verdronken Weide*, south of the inner city. It has a representation of an Ypres cross and was never used as a quality mark (© Yper Museum, obj. nr. 5411).

relationship between the seals and the actual number of lengths of cloth produced can therefore not be known and all earlier reconstructions must be considered maxima. Still the seals may not indicate cycles; they give us an idea of the scale of textile manufacture, the more so because they allow diversification between the various production stages. At every stage the craftsman needed to guarantee both the clothier and the craftsmen who succeeded him that his work had been done according to the standard quality that was required for a particular piece of cloth. So, at the end of the production stage a range of different seals could be found attached to a woollen, before it received final approval at the city press, and the official city seal was attached to it.

The most recent analysis, by Pieter Boussemaere, takes into consideration most of these methodological issues.[37] So his estimates can be considered the most reliable,

---

[37] Sadly, while carefully defining the methodological problems in the work of his predecessor, Boussemaere adds another when he states, without much evidence, that the cloth seals for the fine blue woollens, in other words the fine woollens dyed in blue in the fibre, also include the white woollens, in which case the wool was not dyed in the

Table 1.3 Rented stalls in the Ypres cloth hall (fifteenth century)
Calculated from data assembled by John H. Munro ('Textile Production, Wages, and Prices', published at *The Medieval and Early Modern Data Bank*, Rutgers University (MEMDB https://memdb.libraries.rutgers.edu/).

1400-1410	430
1410-1420	465
1420-1430	405
1430-1440	274
1440-1450	173
1450-1460	91
1460-1470	67
1470-1480	66
1480-1490	17

but they remain, of course, very crude estimates. In the first decades of the fourteenth century Ypres produced about 70,000 to 80,000 woollens per year but lost a substantial part of its output in the 1320s, when output dropped to 50,000 to 55,000 woollens. A direct link with the political troubles in this period, as is suggested by Boussemaere (revolt of Coastal Flanders, democratic regime and its fall in 1329 with the forced banishment of more than 1,000 artisans, although many probably returned shortly afterwards), does not seem likely, however. The decline had already started before these events and seems to be more related to declining exports to the Champagne fairs and the Mediterranean. In other words, decline was structural, not accidental. Throughout this period light woollens represented about half of the Ypres production, but this share decreased rapidly in the 1330s and 1340s. During the second half of the fourteenth century, output figures fell even further, to about 30,000 in the 1350s and even 25,000 in the 1370s and about 12,000 in the eventful 1380s, although Ypres probably recovered a little from this slump, and output figures in the early fifteenth century must have increased. This time production consisted only of expensive, heavy cloth. So, the dropping output figures were probably compensated for partly by higher quality. Considering the longer weaving, fulling and finishing times required for the fine Ypres woollens compared to those of the light cloth, employment, therefore, probably did not drop in a similar proportion.

The data collected by John Munro in the city accounts, amongst them the number of rented stalls in the cloth hall, point to the fact that, at least until the early 1430s, cloth production in Ypres continued with some level of success. It is for this period that we have the best data about exports to the Hanseatic regions, so this relative success was undoubtedly the result of the fact that fine Ypres woollens remained crucial for the business activities of many Hanseatic merchants, and the Veckinhusen firm was

---

fibre (and if dyed at all, the final woollens were dyed only in the fabric (Boussemaere, 'De Ieperse lakenproductie', 131-161).

certainly only one of those. But from the 1430s, however, the number of stalls rented in the cloth hall to clothiers and dyers declined sharply. This is indicative of the fact that by now the Ypres industry was in full decline. In the 1440s, the number was less than half of what it had been in the first quarter of the fifteenth century, and decline persisted in the latter part of the century; it was fewer than 100 after 1450, fewer than 70 after 1460. In the 1480s only a dozen stalls remained of what must have been about 500 a century earlier. But, as we shall demonstrate in the final chapter of this book, at the same time a revival of the manufacture of worsteds seems to compensate for this decline in heavy greased cloth. But even the temporary growth of the *dry* woollens was not able to buck the trend. The cloth industry in Ypres had as such become marginal for the local economy, it seems, and the struggles that continued with neighbouring cloth towns and villages, such as Nieuwkerke, were only rearguard skirmishes, out of despair. This is not to say that cloth became irrelevant in the urban economy. Ypres citizens continued to invest in the regional cloth centres, as they had always done.[38]

Conclusions: Rise and Decline of an Industry

The thirteenth century witnessed a fundamental transition for the great industrial cloth cities of Flanders and Artois. In the course of the twelfth and early thirteenth centuries these two principalities experienced a period of rapid urbanisation because of their industrial expansion.[39] Cloth of all qualities was manufactured in the leading cities of Flanders (Bruges, Douai, Ghent, Lille and Ypres) and Artois (Arras and Saint-Omer) and their woollens reached customers in northern and southern Europe alike.[40] The organisation of the cloth trade was in the hands of Flemish merchants and the so-called 'merchant-entrepreneurs' who, like their archetypical representative Jehan Boinebroke from Douai, used their access to capital to control (some of) the manufacturing stages and the trade in raw materials and cloth.[41] It was the city governments, controlled by merchant and landowner elites, that provided a normative framework and guaranteed standardised export quality, essential for deciding on trade and labour relations,[42] while a far-reaching division of labour – up to 50 different manufacturing stages – had to stimulate labour and capital productivity gains.[43]

From the last quarter of the thirteenth century, the industry, however, changed dramatically. Competition with producers in other regions undermined exports to the Mediterranean markets, which had been the main outlet for Ypres products in the thir-

---

38 Jim Van der Meulen, *Woven into the Urban Fabric*, 65-106.
39 Stabel, 'Composition et recompositions des réseaux urbains', 29-64.
40 Munro, 'Medieval Woollens', 181-227 and 228-324; Laurent, *Un grand commerce d'exportation* and Coornaert, 'Draperies rurales, draperies urbaines', 60-96.
41 Espinas, *La draperie dans la Flandre française* and Van Werveke, *De koopman-ondernemer*.
42 Cauchies, 'Faire Banz, edictz et statuts'.
43 Cardon, *La draperie* and De Poerck, *La draperie médiévale*. Technological aspects are discussed in Endrei, 'The Productivity of Weaving', 108-19 and id., 'Manufacturing a Piece of Woollen Cloth', 14-23.

teenth century.[44] But also elsewhere the Flemish and Artesian fine woollens met with increasing competition from the large cities of Brabant Brussels, Leuven and Mechelen, and later also from Holland and England. And the position of the Flemish worsteds and semi-worsteds, which had experienced their hour of glory before 1300, partly because of the European-wide fashion for striped cloth, was undermined by increasing trade difficulties. General insecurity and increased warfare from the late thirteenth century onwards raised the merchant's transaction costs, which proved to be lethal for these cheaper products.[45] Import substitution in some of the consuming regions did the rest. Moreover, in Flanders itself, the landscape of cloth production also changed. Some small towns, in Coastal Flanders, had in the shadow of the big cities always been active as cloth producers (for example Diksmuide and Aardenburg). Now their number grew significantly; the small and mid-sized towns in the River Basin (Aalst, Dendermonde, Geraardsbergen on the River Dender, Oudenaarde on the River Scheldt and Kortrijk, Menen, Wervik and Comines on the River Leie) did well. In the same way as the big cities, these towns were well connected to labour reserves and trade routes for raw materials, and they started to undermine the position of the larger cities for mid-priced fine woollen textiles.[46]

In such circumstances, Ypres' traditional outlets in continental Europe, at the fairs of Champagne, suffered. Instead, Mediterranean merchants and Hanseatic traders started to go directly to the trade emporium of the Low Countries, Bruges. Cloth entrepreneurs had to adapt swiftly in order to survive. In the large cities they started to concentrate primarily on luxury fabrics, which had probably already been their strength at the start of the period of expansion in the latter part of the twelfth century. As a result, raw materials, skill, increasing market segmentation, higher levels of quality control and carefully managed systems to secure labour markets had already been considered important in the old cloth industry; but now they became critical. This was, after all, a market defined by what John Munro has called 'monopolistic competition', a market where every city tried to individualise its cloth output, but where the different woollens from different production centres were also an alternative option for customers, because differences in quality, cost and fashionability were small.[47] The balance of power in the industry consequently shifted further in the direction of stronger quality control and strict regulation. We will see in the following chapters that this greatly affected the social identity and economic potential of the various stakeholders in the industry, but it probably changed urban society as a whole. Flemish merchants focused on controlling regional trade networks of supply and are said to have abandoned almost completely the control of the manufacturing processes. Clothiers more and more started to deal directly with the foreign merchants. Quality control and human resources management became the demesne of the craft guilds instead. Entrepreneurs were by now recruited

---

44 Munro, 'The Symbiosis of Towns and Textiles', 1-74, Chorley, 'The Cloth Exports' 349-379 and various contributions in Boone and Prevenier, *Drapery Production*. For the smaller manufacturing centres in Interior Flanders see also Stabel, *De kleine stad*, 122-174.
45 Munro, 'The New Institutional Economics', 1-47.
46 Stabel, *De kleine stad*, 215-218; Nicholas, *Town and Countryside*.
47 Munro, 'Urban Regulation and Monopolistic Competition', 41-52.

from within the industry, usually from the core activities of working with the fabric itself. Clothiers (*drapiers*) managed to control these crucial stages, not necessarily by controlling the flows of goods and raw materials, but by setting up manufacturing networks, by organising subcontracting networks and by monopolising skill and expertise.[48] As a result a master weaver or master fuller was not necessarily like any other master. It was in entrepreneurship, as a 'clothier', that real profit could be made. But these were undoubtedly new men in urban society, who also wanted their share of political power. The craft guilds became their instrument for gaining access to polity.

And they were also new 'men'. Women, who, as we shall see in Chapter 8, had enjoyed a significant role in the manufacture before the late thirteenth century, were ousted as independent labourers from the crucial production stages of making and finishing the woollen fabric and banned to the low-paid jobs of wool preparation.[49] Labour relations in the workshops were increasingly formalised as the guild curriculum of apprentice-journeyman-master gradually took hold and guild training schemes became increasingly important as gatekeepers for quality and status. Guild officials started a process of disciplining both labour and quality and in this way helped the still active official controlling system of the 'draperie' organise the city authorities. In the end this movement towards greater involvement of the guilds, which, because of the 'democratic' revolts of the 1290s-1300s and in Ypres in the late 1320s, also had their impact on political representation in most cities of the southern Low Countries, seems to have been a very logical step to take. Besides various social ambitions, it also made economic sense, as the demand for quality cloth agreed with the changes in commercial flows across the continent. The social consequences were, however, not negligible for the organisation of labour itself. The boundaries set by these profound social changes were, however, not just political, but the social position of every stakeholder was also defined as much by economic organisation and social custom linked to the cloth manufacture itself. There was a huge difference between a master dyer and master fuller on the one hand, and a master weaver and a master shearer on the other. It is these changes that will be scrutinised in the next chapter.

---

48 Van Werveke, *De koopman-ondernemer.*
49 Stabel, 'Working Alone?', 27-49.

CHAPTER 2

Of Weaving Looms, Spinning Wheels and Fuller's Troughs

Cloth and Technology

Labour and Textile Technology

Since the 1960s, an important strand of research on the economic history of the Middle Ages has described the long period of economic growth that characterised Latin Europe from the beginning of the eleventh to the end of the thirteenth centuries in terms of a succession of technological revolutions.[50] And certainly, despite the scepticism about technological advance in this period by neo-Malthusian and neo-Marxist historiography, a lot can be said in favour of stressing the importance of fundamental technological change. The turn plough and various systems of crop rotation stimulated agricultural productivity, the introduction of the windmill and improvements to watermills helped to orient agricultural surpluses towards new markets and to a certain extent also allowed a new division of labour in the countryside; new mining techniques helped to fuel the growth of industries and opened up new sources of precious metals that boosted commercial exchange. New business techniques helped the pooling of capital and resources, while institutional innovation at markets and fairs opened routes for securing commercial transactions. Improvements in the transportation system (roads, bridges and new ways of travel overland and overseas) contributed to reducing transaction costs and broadening the scope of commercial exchange. Various fundamental technological improvements gave rise to new and more competitive industries, substituting for the import of luxuries from the eastern Mediterranean and the Islamic World. The era of medieval growth was undoubtedly also an era of technological change and creativity. And perhaps the greatest innovation was not even technological, but legal. The end of the period of feudal anarchy also witnessed the generalisation of more secure property rights, and nowhere were advances in this respect greater than in urban environments. During the late medieval crisis all this changed. The added value of technological change was no longer necessary to supply a much-reduced population and a shrinking economy, and only in trade were new techniques, such as accounting, bills of exchange and other credit arrangements, introduced or improved to compensate for the less secure and unpredictable business environments or reduce the negative effects of bullion famine.

Recently, however, in line with the success of neo-Marxist, in particular of Brennerian economic history and the decline of Smithian approaches in medieval history,

---

50 See various contributions in Beck (ed.) *L'innovation technique au Moyen Âge*, and the literature cited there, most notably the contributions by Braunstein, 'Savoir et savoir-faire', 303-311 and Benoit, 'Au four et au moulin', 293-301.

historians have tended to be more reluctant to point to technological change to explain developments, even to downplay their importance, stressing the importance of overall technological stasis. The attention of researchers seems therefore to have shifted away from what had come to be known as the technological revolution of the Middle Ages.[51] Yet there are exceptions. In a succession of important and successful monographs Joel Mokyr, although primarily targeting more recent periods, has pointed to the added value of new ways of dealing with knowledge; the booming guild historiography has sought attention for the training systems in the economic organisation and its role for the accumulation and transfer of knowledge and skill.[52] No longer do the breath-taking revolutions stand at centre-stage, but rather the slow accumulation and distribution of skill and innovation.

The history of textile manufacture in medieval Europe has followed a similar trajectory. Still, in 2002, the magisterial survey of the impact of textile technology on the development of European textile industries published by the late John Munro tends to describe the causes of change in terms of technological innovation.[53] Strikingly, however, Munro has also stressed the importance of the opposite phenomenon: the refusal to entertain technological innovation in the traditional cloth cities of continental Europe. Munro's approach is much more nuanced than the traditional assumptions by Eleonora Carus-Wilson that technological conservatism led to the disappearance of the fulling mill in some parts of Europe, and most notably in the traditional cloth centres of continental Northwest Europe and Italy, and in a similar vein to the surprisingly slow integration of the spinning wheel in manufacturing processes across the continent.[54] Munro indeed points to deliberate entrepreneurial strategies to safeguard the quality of the end product. So, the adoption of new technologies was made dependent upon commercial goals. In the long run, the divergent attitudes towards technological innovation would lay the foundations, amongst other causes, for the different fates of textile industries across the European continent from the late Middle Ages on, leading to the success of new cloth centres in fifteenth- and sixteenth-century England, Normandy and the Low Countries (Hondschoote) and the demise of the traditional cloth cities in Italy and in the Low Countries (Flanders, Artois, Brabant and even, briefly, Holland). The American specialist in Flemish medieval history, David Nicholas, did not hesitate to conclude that the *drie steden* (meaning Ghent, Bruges and Ypres) 'seemed to have a positive distaste for mechanization and technological innovation', again stressing the refusal to integrate the fulling mill as the prime example of their short-sightedness.[55] Why particular innovations were not taken up has since then been the cause of fierce debate, and we will return to this debate at the end of this chapter.

But not only is the decay in traditional cloth manufacture discussed in terms of technological adaptation (or rather its refusal), the growth of the urban cloth industries

---

[51] The literature about the attitude of particular historiographical traditions towards technological change in the medieval period is discussed in Hatcher and Bailey, *Modelling the Middle Ages*.
[52] Mokyr, *The Gifts of Athena* and Davids and De Munck, *Innovation and Creativity*.
[53] Munro, 'Medieval Woollens', 181-227. See also Roch, 'Innovations et résistances dans la draperie', 46-56.
[54] Carus-Wilson, E.M., 'An Industrial Revolution'.
[55] Nicholas, *Town and Countryside*, 78-79.

is also linked to a remarkable innovation, and one which some have even compared to the English Industrial Revolution of the late eighteenth century: the introduction and success of the horizontal treadle loom.[56] In the following pages we will, of course, discuss the consequences of the introduction of the broadloom for the organisation of cloth manufacture. It is undoubtedly true that no other medieval technological innovation has so altered urban society, indeed society in general, and nowhere as dramatically as in the Northwest European cities of Flanders, Artois and Brabant. It not only enforced a whole new organisation of industry and caused massive transfers of capital, skill and labour from the countryside to the growing cities, but it also in the long run changed the social composition of those cities. It even influenced the political organisation of cities and of feudal states and caused a pace of urbanisation that would bring Flanders, Brabant and to a certain extent also Holland into the slipstream of Northern Italy.

Sadly, however, we do not know that much about the introduction of the broadloom. The horizontal treadle loom operated by only one weaver was introduced probably in the late eleventh century; the broadloom operated by a team of two weavers assisted by additional craftsmen or women for reeling, warping and spooling considerably later, probably somewhere in the twelfth century. But little is known about this early period of urban cloth manufacture, and certainly not in Ypres. The first industrial regulation dates back only to some time after middle of the thirteenth century, and any odd source that documents earlier developments has inevitably been lost during the First World War. At the time when documentation starts, the broadloom was already fully accepted, however, and the social transformations that were caused by it were already in full swing.

In this chapter we cannot, therefore, trace the beginnings of the Ypres industry, nor the fundamental transformations that accompanied the growth of the city and its industry in the twelfth century. When documentation starts, the first troubles were already on the horizon for the Ypres entrepreneurs, and the city and its textile workers would be continually on the defensive thereafter, until the final days of the industry in the late sixteenth century. The preserved (or rather the published) regulations of the industry, in statutes, urban ordinances, wage settings and guild privileges from around 1280 to about 1420, however, are quite revealing of the intricate complexities of industrial organisation in a changing industry and, as we shall see in the next chapters, also in a changing society. They are of course primarily normative texts. They discuss the standards set by urban and guild officials, yet, as is demonstrated on many occasions, regulations also reveal the willingness, indeed the ambition, to change, to transform and to optimise economic organisation. They define, after all, the economic ambitions of the elites, whether they were mercantile or industrial. They are, as such, also revealing of entrepreneurial strategies and of social equilibria that allowed their implementation. Through the minutiae of regulation we will try to unravel in the next pages 1° how the production chain really worked, 2° how the diverse systems of production at each manufacturing stage influenced the social organisation of the workshop and the

---

56 Cardon, 'Des toisons aux étoffes', 35-42.

relations between craftsmen and entrepreneurs in the production chain, and 3° last but not least how the technical organisation defined these systems of production and, therefore, also facilitated or impeded industrial change or product innovation. As we try to unravel these mechanisms, we will follow that chain of production from the fleece to the marketing of the finished woollens in the city itself.

And a chain of production it was. As no other medieval industry, cloth manufacture had given rise to Smithian processes of specialisation. In contrast to rural industries, where division of labour could be implemented only haphazardly and the unit of production, the rural household tended to concentrate all stages of textile manufacture, from preparing the yarn to weaving (only finishing and dyeing were generally left to specialist craftsmen, and mostly urban craftsmen at that).[57] But the central place of the horizontal treadle broadloom in urban manufacture, already with a lot of consequences for the organisation of the pivotal action of the making of the fabric, caused a revolution in the organisation of the other manufacturing stages as well. Primarily, it allowed the emergence of a new textile, the densely woven broadcloth which was fulled, felted and shorn afterwards. But this type of woollen required more complex industrial processes and almost naturally led to specialisation and to complex systems of putting-out. The centrality of the (rural) household where most, if not all, manufacturing stages took place was lost and specialised workers, men and women, many of them urban, started to become integrated into the industrial process, and they started to specialise. As a result, households needed to be integrated into production chains, linking not only various economic units, but also units that were forged by different technological requirements and labour relations. The people who were able to coordinate their collective efforts would play a central role in production.

We shall see in chapters 4 and 5 that these coordinating entrepreneurs, the clothiers and the merchants (and in Ypres also an enigmatic third group, the so-called *upsetters*), would reap most profits from that chain of production, but also at each stage of production, labour and entrepreneurial activity was needed. For all too long, medieval cloth production has been seen only as a process in which capitalistic merchants and/or entrepreneurs used (and exploited) the labour of a semi-proletarianised workforce. The situation was in fact much more complex than that: there was entrepreneurial activity at every level of the manufacturing chain, and the input of labour occurred at various levels of dependence. Moreover, as the success of the Flemish urban cloth industries depended on the careful treatment of extremely expensive raw materials, ending in a product that usually targeted elite consumers, the mass production that was needed to cut manufacturing costs had also to be monitored very carefully, and the responsibility for each part of the production chain carefully allocated. Many things could go wrong, and each time they did losses became inevitable.

Finally, there were also technological requirements. At each stage of the production chain the balance between the input of labour, skill and capital was different, leading to often very different ways of organising production. Some stages were clearly defined

---

57 In Flanders Lille, but also late medieval Bruges, developed into centres for cloth finishing (DuPlessis, *Lille and the Dutch Revolt*; Stabel, *A Capital of Fashion*).

by capitalistic relations between the coordinating entrepreneur and the merchants on the one hand and the labour force on the other hand. This was certainly the case with the stages of the preparation of wool and yarn. Things got more complicated in the weaving, fulling, cloth finishing and dyeing stages. Owning a fuller's or a dyer's workshop not only required serious investment, but it also implied controlling your own workforce directly. The same holds true for the weaving stage, the crucial moment when yarn was transformed into fabric. Although overall weavers tended not to be very wealthy craftsmen, they were able in the thirteenth century to become involved in the monitoring and coordination of the complete chain of production. In Ypres, perhaps more than in other cloth cities in the Low Countries, most clothiers seem to have been weavers (which does not mean that all weavers were also clothiers). Although the guilds often tried to limit the size of individual workshops and merchants also preferred it if industrial concentrations did not grow too large,[58] weavers' and fullers' workshops tended to be complex affairs, involving a lot of input from external labour. The workshop of some textile workers even had to attain a respectable size, only to be profitable. Only at the cloth finishing stage did craftsmen's workshops tend to be small. Cloth finishing took place, however, at the very end of the production chain, when the potential damage caused by error and mismanagement was at its greatest. Cloth finishers therefore needed highly skilled craftsmen, affecting again their position in the production chain. In order to assess the position of all these various workers and entrepreneurs, we must therefore carefully consider how much skill and technological know-how were involved in the actual production process, and how these defined the organisation of the workshop and defined the place of labour. We need, in other words, to look at what exactly textile workers did.

A Mercantile Prelude

The levels of trust in clothmaking were important. They had to be, because fraud and corner-cutting were always a possibility. And they always took place to the detriment of the industry's reputation and therefore its successes on the export markets in the long run. Craftsmen who willingly deceived customers or the craftsmen with whom they worked were heavily fined and were sometimes forbidden further to exercise their jobs. Shearers paid a lot of attention to avoiding deliberate acts of fraud. Fines for infractions were to be raised by 20s in 1280 for all acts done deliberately and with evil intention (*willende quaet*).[59] Guild reputations had therefore to be enforced by control mechanisms. These were organised by the industry itself and guaranteed by the city aldermen. These control measures were focused on the moments of exchange between the different trades. At each crucial stage a leaden seal was attached to the fabric to guarantee to the next artisan in line that the previous stages had been executed correctly and the merchants that the woollen corresponded to the approved standards of the

---

58 Lis and Soly, *Worthy Efforts*, 336-337 and id., 'Subcontracting in Guild-Based Export Trades', 81-113.
59 Espinas and Pirenne, *Recueil*, 3, 455.

industry. At the end of the chain, a seal with the arms of the city (*l'enseigne de le vile*) was attached to the finished woollen.[60] When something went wrong, the length of woollen was taken out of the chain of production; if it was nearly finished, it was degraded to the status of *doucken*, non-regulated textiles, which of course could not be introduced easily into the international commercial networks or which fetched much lower prices on the domestic market.

Sometimes measures were even more drastic. The clothiers' statutes from around 1300 state that fraudulent woollens which were found on the loom (probably made from raw materials that failed to conform to the standards set by the industry) were to be destroyed and the loom burnt (*li ostille sera ars a tout le drape*). Furthermore, both the clothier (the owner of the woollen) and the weaver (in whose house the woollen was found) were to be fined heavily. After been found out three times, clothiers could never again be involved in the Ypres cloth industry. The fullers' statutes fine everybody who did 'hasty work' (*vluchtech werc*) that did not comply with the standards, and if work was found that did not live up to the standard quality it had to be cut in pieces and sold as woollens of lesser quality, while the clothier needed to be reimbursed for his loss. When the flaws could be mended, the craftsmen had to do this at their own expense. Similarly, the clothier had to reimburse artisans for their work if the goods that were delivered to them (yarn or fabric) were not good enough or if they lacked the necessary quality labels, usually leaden seals. At all these occasions, guild or city officials had to corroborate the verdict reached and implement the fines and compensation.[61] Fraudulent woollens found elsewhere were confiscated, and cut into pieces, one piece for the bailiff, one for the city, one for the person who discovered the deceit, and the fourth part was to be burnt. The proceedings of these confiscations were recorded in the accounts of the city and the bailiff, but the documents offer very little detail.[62] It is striking that such a very visual and visible tool for destroying illegal goods turns up again and again in the statutes. The very public nature of destroying (parts of) woollens by fire was there to convince customers that quality standards, and therefore exports on which the industry depended, were taken very seriously indeed, Furthermore, the two weavers who were involved in making the piece would be banned from their weaving activity for a period of a year and a day. It is certainly not a coincidence that a period of one year and a day was also the traditional period for which newcomers had to stay in the city before becoming citizens.[63]

When it was not enough to sanction the goods of clothiers or the work of craftsmen, the person of the cloth producer or the clothier became involved. On 8 August 1375, the city aldermen condemned Frans van Aubegny to 40 days in prison (*gésir en ostage*), in Flanders often an instrument to force people to pay their fines. Moreover, he was

---

60 Espinas and Pirenne, *Recueil*, 3, 460.
61 Espinas and Pirenne, *Recueil*, 3, 572 and 577 (fullers).
62 The surviving accounts of the city are published in Des Marez and De Sagher, *Comptes de la ville*, the surviving bailiff's accounts are kept at the Brussels State Archives (1304-1308, 1336, 1367-1368 and from 1373 continuous): https://search.arch.be/en/zoeken-naar-archieven/zoekresultaat/ead/index/eadid/BE-A0510_000037_002531_FRE (consulted February 2022); see also Nowé, *Les baillis comtaux*.
63 Espinas and Pirenne, *Recueil*, 3, 458-459.

Figure 2.1 Transport and sale at the cloth hall of wool sacks (miniature from the *Keurboek*, register of statutes of the Ypres cloth industry, destroyed in WWI). Chromolithography of the "Société Historique, Archéologique et Littéraire de la ville d'Ypres et de l'ancienne West-Flandre" in 1861 (© Yper Museum, obj. nr. 000396). See also cover image.

forbidden to work as a clothier (*faire draperie*) for a year. During this time, within a month after his release from prison, he had to go on a pilgrimage to Santiago in Galicia. If he did not respect this judgment, his sentence would be doubled. This was surely no laughing matter for the aldermen. No breaches of the city customs about cloth manufacture were. Frans had come to the official cloth press of the city where they were measured, their quality was checked for one final time and where they received the seal of the city. The press was located in the cloth hall. At the press Frans insulted the officials, more specifically one Paul van Passchendaele, who had been there to control the woollens (*moult villaines et horibles paroles sour eaux*). We do not know exactly what had caused Frans's anger towards that one official. Frans accused the officials of being corrupt and alleged that they had taken money from other clothiers (to turn a blind eye to damaged or imperfect woollens?). To make matters worse, Frans had taken Paul by his beard and probably some blows were also exchanged. As proof of his pilgrimage, Frans had to bring letters from Compostela to show to Paul and to the four church masters of St Martin in Ypres. Only after his punishment would the parties to the conflict be at peace with each other.[64] In the same year, another clothier was even banned for life from being involved in the Ypres cloth industry. He was banished from the county and if he returned he would be hanged (*banis … sour le gibet*) because he had used counterfeit seals to replace the seals of the city's cloth press.[65] This case is only one of the many that were recorded in the *Register of Memories* kept by the aldermen, in which transgressions of the city's legal order were recorded. Many of these related to the cloth industry and many also stressed the notion of the reputation of the industry and its craftsmen and entrepreneurs.[66]

Reputation is good; control is better. Quality control was also exercised by the craft guilds. Each guild had its body of 'finders' or 'controllers' (*eswardeurs, vinders*) who followed strict procedure. The shearers, who, as we shall see in chapter 3, worked

---

64 Espinas and Pirenne, *Recueil*, 3, 653-654.
65 Espinas and Pirenne, *Recueil*, 3, 654.
66 De Pelsmaeker, *Registres aux sentences*. Some of the convictions relating to the cloth industry have been published also in Espinas and Pirenne, *Recueil*, 3.

Figure 2.2 The Ypres cloth hall (miniature from the *Keurboek*, register of statutes of the Ypres cloth industry, destroyed in WWI). Chromolithography of the "Société Historique, Archéologique et Littéraire de la ville d'Ypres et de l'ancienne West-Flandre" in 1861 (© Yper Museum, obj. nr. 000396). See also cover image.

primarily in the inner city, divided the city into two parts: a northern and a southern sector (*Nordganc, Zudganc*). In each a group of nine controllers, six masters and three journeymen, had to move around at specific times to look at the quality of the shearing.[67] Shearers were not allowed to put their shearing tables in the backs of their houses; they had to be placed in front, facing the street, to facilitate control.[68] When the output of the Ypres cloth industry declined in the course of the fourteenth century, the number of controllers was reduced to four per sector, three masters and one journeyman, to be chosen by the aldermen. They had to make their rounds twice a day. The mid-fourteenth-century statutes add, ominously, that this function should not be entrusted to beggars. Shearing was clearly not a wealthy occupation.[69] In the fourteenth century the dyers in red had a controlling body of five people, consisting of one cloth merchant, two clothiers and two guildsmen, one master and a journeyman. They had to go each day to all the dyers' workshops to look at the dyeing procedures and the stored raw materials.[70]

---

67 Espinas and Pirenne, *Recueil*, 3, 456.
68 Espinas and Pirenne, *Recueil*, 3, 596.
69 Espinas and Pirenne, *Recueil*, 3, 597.
70 Espinas and Pirenne, *Recueil*, 3, 623.

Wool preparation

The preparation of the fine and short stapled wool involved diverse and complex procedures. The washing and degreasing process to remove impurities and the natural lanolin in the fleece was followed by wool breaking, when the fleeces were beaten so that they disintegrated into loose fibres. Combing and (or) carding separated the fibres and straightened them all in the same direction, so spinning, when the fibres were turned into yarn, became possible, and, finally, for the *draperie ointe*, the spun yarns were greased, usually with butter, to make the weaving process easier. The coarser, long-stapled wool used for worsteds was only partially degreased, and because it retained some measure of the natural lanolin worsted wool did not need to be greased after the wool preparation stages. Some of these complicated procedures were among the most delicate stages of production. Yet because most of these stages were very labour-intensive and often also executed individually, and because they did not require a lot of expensive instruments or raw materials, they were usually not organised in craft guilds. Except for wool beating, where physical force was required to break the integrity of the fleece, most of these manufacturing stages were also traditionally executed by women.

Yet a whole range of regulations was put in place to guarantee the required quality standards. Some authors have associated such policies and their strict enforcement with protectionism, or they have noticed that the ordinances stressed local treatment of wool only in periods of economic downturn.[71] It would be more correct, however, to link them rather to (in this case successful) attempts by the city government to switch to high-quality fabrics, for which the quality of wool was paramount. The measures defined primarily the procedures of transferring the wool from one stage to another and therefore preserved the integrity of the production chain. It was difficult to trace the origin of wool in particular stages, yet the quality of the wool would ultimately define also the quality of the end product. So, mixing different types of wool during the procedure was strictly enforced and fined heavily. But also the equipment used was often well defined: combs were to conform to standards set in the clothiers' statutes.[72]

Most workers in these stages were also women, earning a meagre income from their labour. Moreover, they were also banned from combining their labour with entrepreneurial activities. The clothiers' statutes explicitly forbade female combers and carders from making a piece of cloth.[73] It is not entirely clear what exactly is meant by this decision. It could refer to the fact that some domestic weaving in the city, probably using a vertical standing loom with loom weights, was still common practice around 1300, and clothiers wanted to avoid part of their wool ending up in that domestic production, or perhaps it does explicitly ban these women from becoming clothiers themselves, which would inevitably jeopardize wool quality because different kinds of wool would get mixed up in the women's workplace. Similarly, spinsters were forbidden

---

71 See, for example, the recent work by Jim Van der Meulen on Nieuwkerke (*Woven into the Urban Fabric*).
72 Espinas and Pirenne, *Recueil*, 3, 536.
73 Espinas and Pirenne, *Recueil*, 3, 461.

Figure 2.3 Women spinning (with distaff), carding and combing. These three labour-intensive stages of cloth manufacture were mostly done by women, in Ypres all of them inhabitants of the city. Fragment of miniature representing Gaia Caecilia, wife of Tarquinius Priscus, first King of Rome, from Giovanni Boccaccio, *De claris mulieribus* (anonymous French translation: *Le livre de femmes nobles et renomées*), Rouen, c. 1440 (anonymous artist).
London, British Library, Royal 16 G V, f. 56r.

to have more than three stone of wool in their houses, probably not only to avoid mixing qualities, but also to limit the scope of their entrepreneurial activity. Involving a lot of spinsters who worked with limited amounts of wool prevented them from developing their own entrepreneurial networks.[74]

The ban on combining the preparatory stages of wool preparation and spinning with cloth entrepreneurship was further formalised in the latter part of the fourteenth century. The cloth statutes of the 1360s repeat again and again that the whole range of wool preparing occupations could not be combined with that of clothier: neither the male wool cleaners, wool carriers, nor the female combers, carders and spinsters could be clothiers.[75] It is striking that in these cases carding was directly addressed in the wool preparing stages of production. In many cloth cities of the Low Countries carding was forbidden, because it was said to weaken the yarn for the finest woollens. In Ypres such a ban was in place only for warp yarn, which needed to be stronger and more even

---

74 Espinas and Pirenne, *Recueil*, 3, 461.
75 Espinas and Pirenne, *Recueil*, 3, 518.

because it had to bear multiple tensions on the loom.[76] Weft yarn could, however, be spun from carded wool in Ypres. The suspicion that in the carding process, executed using two boards with short iron pins instead of two combs with long iron teeth as in the combing process, it was much easier to mix less fine wool into the straightened fibres seems not to have been a problem for even the finest Ypres *derdelinghe* and *dickedinne* woollens.

Spinning was, of course, even more crucial. There was a great difference between, on the one hand, the stronger and usually thicker warp yarns, which had to deal with the pressures of the horizontal treadle loom, and the weft yarns, which were generally less strong and thinner because they were not subject to similar forces on the loom. We have already seen that in Ypres carding was forbidden for warp yarns. But spinning with a wheel was also looked at with great suspicion, because it allegedly produced weaker yarn. Before the introduction of the Saxony wheel, which left both hands free for spinning, operating a spinning wheel required the spinsters to use one hand to turn the spinning wheel and the other to draft the yarn. Because the speed of the wheel was less controllable than in the traditional rock or distaff spinning process, uneven and weaker yarn was produced. Warp yarn had to be spun, therefore, using the distaff.

Weaving

Few technological innovations before the industrial revolution have carried so much weight in the historical development of industrial activity as the introduction of the horizontal treadle loom. Without it, textile manufacture would have remained probably a rural and female activity, closely integrated in the domestic economy of rural households and dependent upon the seasonality of agricultural activities. Instead, textile manufacture became urban, certainly for the more complicated and quality fabrics, causing a chain reaction of occupational specialisation in the cities, massive immigration of a new labour force from the (surrounding) countryside and, starting in some regions of Europe, most notably and already at an early stage in Italy and the Low Countries, a process of rapid urbanisation.

It is generally believed that the horizontal treadle loom became widespread from as early as the eleventh century, right at the start of the European urbanisation process.[77] For a long time it was used alongside the standing vertical warp-weighted loom, that continued, albeit increasingly rarely, to be used in domestic settings in the countryside. But there is little doubt that the horizontal loom facilitated the concentration of textile manufacture in urban environments. It turned the central stage of production into a more complex operation. But above all it allowed the manufacture of more qualitative and more standardised products, while stimulating substantial productivity gains. It proved also to be a decisive watershed for gender relations in medieval cities. Medieval

---

76 Munro, 'Medieval Woollens', 200-204.
77 Carus-Wilson, 'Technical Innovation and the Emergence of the Grande Industrie', 359-360. See for a general survey on the differences between the standing and the horizontal loom Munro, 'Medieval Woollens', 192-198. The different weaving processes are discussed in Cardon, *La draperie*.

images that represent weaving activities link the horizontal loom almost exclusively with men, while the domestic vertical loom is similarly almost exclusively operated by women. But because of its advantages the horizontal loom turned weaving, although probably only gradually, into a male occupation. The increasing masculinity of labour probably also facilitated occupational organisation in guilds, and therefore easier quality control. Medieval urban public space was indeed often founded on male sociability.

At what stage the simple treadle loom was replaced by the horizontal broadloom is less certain. By the early thirteenth century the broadloom was already widely present in most urban woollen cloth industries, and probably its generalised use dates to the latter part of the twelfth century. This does not mean that the one-person treadle loom had completely disappeared. Even as late as the 1430s there were in Ypres itself still several weavers of *doucken*, small pieces of cloth that were usually produced in one of the neighbouring villages.[78] Much more than the simple horizontal treadle loom, which could be operated by one weaver, the broadloom required complex labour organisation. It was operated by a team of two weavers, who had to rely on a continuous rhythm to achieve the perfect coordination of movement that was required. Every interruption of the weaving process interfered with this rhythm, and therefore also with the productivity of the weaving team.[79] Experience was therefore paramount in establishing the weaving team and, unsurprisingly, the labour input of apprentices was looked upon with great suspicion.[80] The broadloom, of course, certainly when it was used for the very long and wide woollens that became so typical of the urban industries of Europe, also required a solid structure to allow for the tensions on the loom during the weaving process. It required therefore also a relatively large working space and, because of its weight, the workshop had to be organised mostly on the ground floor.[81]

Furthermore, the process of weaving implied not only the use of the loom, but also the preparation of the yarn for the loom, which involved reeling and spooling (filling the shuttles with weft yarn: *spoelen* in Dutch), warping (winding the yarn in groups of twelve or twenty-four on a large board and measuring their length: *ourdissage* in French and *schering* in Dutch), fixing the warp on to the warp-beam, and fortifying the warp yarn on the loom (by starching it and, which was forbidden in the fourteenth-century statutes, greasing it to reduce friction on the loom).[82] This was a laborious yet very precise process, usually entrusted to young male assistants, apprentices or women.[83] The census of 1431 mentions, however, also two male specialist reelers (*spoelers*) who prepared the bobbins with yarn and also loaded the shuttles. So at least sometimes this work was done by real professionals, rather than by young boys or family members.[84]

---

[78] Pirenne, 'Les dénombrements', 1-32.

[79] Dominque Cardon eloquently describes the rhythm of the weavers as the 'waltz of the shuttles' (*la valse des navettes*: Cardon, *La draperie*, 557).

[80] Dominque Cardon insists on the fact that a team usually consisted of one less experienced 'shuttle-launcher' on the right-hand side of the loom, and an experienced weaver on the left (Cardon, *La draperie*, 542-543. On the role of apprentices in the workshop see chapters 6 and 7.

[81] Cardon, *La draperie*, 506-507.

[82] Espinas and Pirenne, *Recueil*, 3, 580 and 589.

[83] For the technical aspects of warping see Cardon, *La draperie*, 317-390.

[84] Pirenne, 'Les dénombrements', 24.

Figure 2.4 Warping spun yarn (measuring and preparing warp yarn for the weaver's warp beam) was a task often executed by female assistants in the weaver's workshop (miniature from the *Keurboek*, register of statutes of the Ypres cloth industry, destroyed in WWI). Chromolithography of the "Société Historique, Archéologique et Littéraire de la ville d'Ypres et de l'ancienne West-Flandre" in 1861 (© Yper Museum, obj. nr. 000396). See also cover image.

Also, the loom had to be prepared: the warp yarns had to be fixed in their correct length to the so-called warp-beam (*boem, garenboem*) placed at the rear of the loom, and they were to be guided and stretched through the heddle system and the reed (*ros, cam, riet*) so that they did not get confused. Reeds differed, of course, depending upon the type of cloth that was woven: plain cloth, *dickedinne, derdelinghe* or worsteds. The reed was also used to fix and tighten the weft in the fabric. In some cities these reeds could be rented by the weaver, but for Ypres we have no information about such practices.[85] Most Ypres woollens had between 1,400 and 1,900 warp threads and were about 40 to 45 ells long at the loom (28m-34m).[86] The length of the woven cloth of course impacted on the productivity of the weaving process. Warping up the beam (fixing warp yarns on the beam of the loom) took a very long time, so a long piece of cloth saved a lot of labour time, but at the same time a long piece of cloth also tied up the clothier's capital, so the length of the woollen was necessarily a compromise.[87]

The number of yarns was one of the elements that defined the density of the fabric. Treadles operated the heddles through which the warp threads ran, alternating the warp threads according to the desired pattern. The weaving pattern defined by the relationship between warp and weft (one on one or two by two for plain woollens, one by three etc. for more complicated patterns and alternating patterns) was defined by the way the loom harness with its heddles was mounted and by the movement of the weavers and their treadles (two or three per weaver).[88] The weaving pattern also defined the thickness and density of the fabric: dense plain (*plein*) woollens were thicker than the equally dense but thinner *dickedinne*, while striped cloth, popular in the first part of the fourteenth century, was also the result of the weaving process

---

85 Espinas and Pirenne, *Recueil*, 3, 512 and 519 for the *dickedinne* and 507 for the *derdelynghe*. De Poerck, *La draperie médiévale*, pp. 80-81.
86 See table 1.1.
87 Cardon, *La draperie*, 339.
88 A fabric that required three pedals was called in Ypres a woollen 'woven on the third foot' (*weven up den derden voet*): Espinas and Pirenne, *Recueil*, 3, 592 and Cardon, *La draperie*, 452.

Figure 2.5 A weaver's broadloom operated by two weavers. In front a young boy is reeling yarn for the weft shuttles (miniature from the *Keurboek*, register of statutes of the Ypres cloth industry, destroyed in WWI). Chromolithography of the "Société Historique, Archéologique et Littéraire de la ville d'Ypres et de l'ancienne West-Flandre" in 1861 (© Yper Museum, obj. nr. 000396). See also cover image.

that allowed the already dyed weft yarns to be closely woven, so that they hid the warp threads, providing a uniform colour in each of the stripes.[89] Finally, the sley and reed tightened the weft, which was guided through the warp threads using a shuttle (*schietspoel*). Weavers usually used two to four shuttles at a time, speeding up the weaving process. The woven fabric was rolled on to a cloth-beam in front of the loom. The weaving process had to be interrupted every time a warp thread broke, and the damage repaired. The statutes were very strict on this point, because the break would inevitably be visible in the final product.[90] When the woollen was taken from the cloth-beam, it was sealed and became a 'raw woollen' (*raeu, cru*).

This complex procedure not only significantly raised the productivity of weaving, but it also meant that weaving changed gender and that woven fabrics became denser, stronger and, in contrast to the worsteds that were woven on a free-standing loom, apt for finishing procedures like fulling, felting, tenting and shearing. Capital requirements (a complex and expensive weaving infrastructure) and labour organisation (a broadloom was operated by a team of two weavers and required other workers to assist them by warping up and organising the weft yarns in weaving shuttles) moved weaving out of the female domestic sphere into the male public arena, the more so because, as cloth industries were increasingly aiming at export markets, quality control and guild organisation became paramount. This did not happen all at once, as we shall see in chapter 7, and in fact weaving could have remained a female activity, as for example in the silk industry in many Italian cities and Paris. But also, in the woollen industry of Florence female weavers, working on broadlooms, were seen during the entire late Middle Ages. And here too cloth manufacture was equally geared towards

---

[89] On the complicated patterns of medieval weaving see Cardon, *La draperie*, 443-493.
[90] De Poerck, *La draperie médiévale*, 85-86.

export markets.[91] But in most Flemish cities the pivotal action in weaving the fabric (and in finishing the same fabrics, for that matter) became a male prerogative, and so it did in Ypres.

Secondly, the denser, heavier and higher-quality fabrics of the *draperie ointe* also caused the division of labour in textile manufacture to change dramatically. The cloth finishing procedures and the fact that most fabrics were dyed in the fabric (as well as sometimes also in the wool or the yarn) implied that all the elaborate finishing stages needed to be monitored and coordinated. It led to a battleground about who was to control this coordinating function, mercantile capital or industrial capital. The changing relations of merchants and clothiers will be dealt with in chapters 4 and 5, but the result towards the latter part of the thirteenth century was, here as well, a more radical division of tasks. While merchants controlled the flows of raw materials and finished goods, clothiers became responsible for the industrial process, for the chain of manufacture. Although every citizen, man or woman (and a significant number of women did), could in fact become a clothier, clothiers were primarily active in the production chain. In Ypres, perhaps more than in any other city in medieval Flanders for reasons that will be explained later, they were primarily weavers, the pivotal industrial function where woollen yarn was turned into fabric. Hence, we see that weavers were themselves divided into two groups, craftsmen who were also involved in monitoring the production chain and who had access to the significant sums of money that were required to buy the raw materials, and craftsmen who did not have access to enough capital to make investments in raw material and offered their skill and labour, just like all other occupations in the textile production chain, to the former. The census of 1431 in one of the four Ypres districts mentions 195 weavers and clothiers.[92] One third of this number were registered as clothiers. But among the 126 weavers (who were not clothiers), there were 84 journeymen (and 6 weavers of *doucken*, small woollens that did not conform to the Ypres standards), so only 25 master weavers who were not clothiers were registered. If most clothiers were weavers, then only 27 per cent of all master weavers were working only as weavers, and most weavers, therefore, were also or even primarily active as clothiers.[93]

If the figures of 1431 are in any way representative of the late thirteenth- and fourteenth-century organisation of weaving, then a normal weaving workshop with two looms would have required the labour input of three or even four journeymen. A weaver active as a clothier would probably not always be available for the actual process of weaving the fabric. Probably, in order to prepare warp and weft for the loom, the additional input of two unskilled workers, usually young boys or women, was required. An average weaver's workshop required therefore four skilled and two unskilled workers. This was substantially fewer than the next stage in the manufacturing process, fulling.

---

91 Mola, *The Silk Industry* and Farmer, *The Silk Industries* for silks and Franceschi, *Oltre il tumulto*, for the woollens of Florence.
92 The administrative organisation of the city into separate districts is discussed in Preneel, 'Ieperse stadskwartieren', 51-58.
93 See also chapters 3 and 4.

Fulling

Fulling was one of the most complex stages in the manufacture of a piece of (fine) woollen cloth. The clothier, usually the weaver himself, took the raw woollen from the loom with inevitably a lot weaving errors or impurities. The woollen was still very much, despite all the pressures applied on the horizontal loom, an open fabric. Moreover, the fine woollens, but also, because of the remaining lanolin, the worsteds were still quite greasy, so any dyes that would be applied to the fabric were likely to give an uneven result. Fulling had to resolve all these issues. The fulling process consisted of four stages. In the first stage the woven fabrics were washed and scoured, first in a tub or trough with cold water, afterwards with warm water.[94] Fuller's earth (bleaching clay) and sometimes urine were added in the process. The process was also called 'to earthen woollens', because of the use of fuller's earth (*eerden*).[95] Two fullers applied pressure to the woollens by trampling carefully on them in the tub to thoroughly wash them and free them from dirt and other impurities. After this first treatment the woollens were hung up and burled (removal of knots and weaving flaws) and they were given a first felting treatment using teasels. This process was considered crucial, and as the Ypres cloth industry moved towards producing ever more refined woollens during the fourteenth and fifteenth centuries the process was given more and more attention. New and very detailed clauses were added to the fullers' statutes in March 1395, which had to guarantee good practices of burling and felting.[96] After these cleaning and felting operations, the fabrics were folded and returned to the tub for a second, more thorough and more violent fulling operation, to achieve shrinkage and felting (*vullen, upmaecken*). The much more productive fulling mills, which automated the process using water power, were strictly forbidden in all urban cloth industries of the medieval Low Countries because the process was considered too rough for the fine woollens that were the pride of the urban industries.[97] Yet this had not always been the case in Ypres, situated in flat lands which were not particularly suited to building water-powered mills. A fulling mill was in operation in the twelfth century in the inner city, probably at the confluence of two arms of the River Ieperleet in the vicinity of the later Fuller's Street.[98] But later on, any mention of the use of fulling mills disappears. Fulling became a process of purely manual labour. After the fulling process, the fabric was rinsed and taken to the cloth finishers.[99]

This four-stage operation required a sizeable operation. Fullers' workshops tended therefore to be relatively big operations, involving a lot of labour. We have no information in the Ypres statutes about the size of a fuller's workshop. In Douai, a city which

---

94 Espinas and Pirenne, *Recueil*, 3, 570 and 580.
95 Fuller's Earth is a mixture of floridin with hydrous aluminium silicates or kaolinite which, mixed with water and sometimes urine, is used to scour, degrease and cleanse the raw woollen (Munro, 'Medieval Woollens', 204).
96 Espinas and Pirenne, *Recueil*, 3, 580-581.
97 Van Uytven, Fulling Mill, 1-14. The fulling mill, which was introduced as early as in the twelfth century in the Low Countries, would be used more widely only from the sixteenth century onwards.
98 Mus, 'De localisatie', 83-84.
99 Munro, 'Medieval Woollens', 204-205, De Poerck *La draperie médiévale*, 90-112.

produced the same kind of range of high-quality woollens and worsteds, a master fuller had to have at least four and a maximum of eight tubs or troughs at his disposal, suggesting that a fuller's workshop averaged between eight and sixteen workers, not including the master himself.[100] It is not known whether any kind of division of tasks was implemented within one workshop, or whether the journeymen employed took on all tasks. Because the actual fulling, during the third stage, was very hard work, so probably the craftsmen moved from the heavier duties to lighter tasks. There were, however, clearly also limits to switching from one activity to another. Fullers who worked on the expensive 'white' heavy cloth were not allowed to do other work.[101] The textile workshops that were found in the *Verdronken Weide* excavations tended to have troughs reinforced with wood. It is at this moment still unclear whether these were indeed fullers' troughs, or whether these troughs were used to wash and rinse the woollens.[102] It is, however, considering its occupational structure, certain that the suburb of St Michiel contained a great number of fullers' workshops, also because water was very much prominent in this part of the city. It is no coincidence that one of the brooks in the area was called *Vulresbeike* or Fuller's Brook.[103]

The Ypres statutes are very detailed about the fulling process. It was indeed a crucial stage in the manufacture of particularly the fine woollens. The raw materials that were to be used, the amount of labour that was put into the fulling process, the relations between fullers and their workforce were all neatly defined. As we shall discuss in chapters 5 and 6, it was labour relations and not so much the raw materials that were the crucial element in organising a fuller's operation, although fulling of course certainly also required chemicals to achieve the cleaning, shrinkage and felting process and butter for greasing the woollens. Ypres woollens clearly had priority. The year was divided into a summer and a winter season and fullers were not allowed to work on cloth that was not manufactured locally in the summer months. Only in the colder winter months, from 1 October to 15 March, could they work on woollens that came from elsewhere or did not comply with the Ypres statutes.[104]

Two issues were crucial for the end results: the amount of pressure exercised on the woollens on the one hand (and therefore the amount of labour of the two fullers) and the levels of shrinkage that the woollens had to undergo. All depended, of course, on the quality of the woollens. Simple worsteds did not have to undergo a fulling process, but semi-worsteds did. According to the late thirteenth-century statutes of Ypres, stamforts required two days of fulling, half stamforts only one day. The fourteenth-century regulation is better preserved, and for this period we see that large woollens, *derdelinghe* and *dickedinne*, required four days of fulling, the smaller versions of this heavy cloth only three days. Just as in the previous century, semi-worsteds and striped cloth (*standvoord, strijpte, Ypersch Popersch*) required one day of fulling for half cloth and two days for

---

100 De Poerck, *La draperie médiévale*, 101.
101 Espinas and Pirenne, *Recueil*, 3, 572.
102 Marc Dewilde, the chief archaeologist of the excavations of the *Verdronken Weide*, considers the excavated troughs to have been more likely used in the process of manipulating flax (I am grateful for this comment).
103 Van Bellingen and Dewilde, 'De verdwenen Sint-Michielswijk', 149-167.
104 Espinas and Pirenne, *Recueil*, 3, 572.

Figure 2.6 Location of *Verdronken Weide* excavation in the 1990s in the former suburb of St Michael, south of the inner city (taken from Dewilde, Ervynck and Wielemans (eds), *Ypres and the Medieval Cloth Industry*, 59; © Vlaamse Overheid, Agentschap Onroerend Erfgoed).

larger woollens.[105] The work process was continuous. So, the cleansing process in the first fulling was executed at the end of the day for some woollens (probably after a previous set of woollens had been finished: *achter dachwerc*), while others had to be taken on at the beginning of the day (*dachwerc*). It is not clear how long this first cleaning and fulling took (for some of the most expensive woollens like the 'white woollens' the process took one full day, while of other, equally expensive woollens five could be processed in one day), but in essence the process was relatively short. After the burling and teaseling process (*noppen; caerden*), the second fulling was more thorough and probably took most of the overall fulling time for a woollen. This was also the process

---

105 De Poerck, *La draperie médiévale*, pp. 92-93, and Espinas and Pirenne, *Recueil*, 3, 568-569 and 571-572. 10-14 ells of dickedinne could be fulled per day, while a piece of cloth measured 41 ells at the tentering frame; derdelinghe between 12 and 16 ells, semi-worsteds between 15 and 19 ells.

which gave the fabric its density and homogeneity and caused fine woollens to be completely different from worsted or even semi-worsted woollens. The folded fabrics were again placed in a tub or trough (*com*) containing warm water. This time it was not so much the action of the chemicals (although butter was used, urine was forbidden at this stage), but the labour input itself which produced the desired result. It was also a stop-and-go procedure, as the cloth was taken out of the liquid often to be unfolded and refolded and put back into the fuller's tub. Each time the size and level of shrinkage were checked. Only at the last stage was butter added to the warm water to make the fabric more flexible (animal fat or oil was forbidden at this stage).[106] This part of the fulling process took the longest time, at least one or two days for the heaviest cloth. After the fulling one side of the woollen was more felted (*averecht*) than the other (*recht*). Teaseling the wet woollen on both sides using a set of thistles and a first shearing had to prepare the cloth for the finishing stages of the production process. Fullers were, however, not allowed to deal in thistles for carding, either for export to other places or to sell to each other, and they could not possess more than 100 thistles. Apparently, the guild officials or the aldermen feared too much concentration in the hands of only a couple of fullers.[107]

The complete fulling procedure affected, of course, the nature of the Ypres woollens. The levels of shrinkage during the process also defined their thickness. So, the clothiers' statutes repeated carefully the size of the various woollens after fulling and before tentering. In general, the fulled cloth lost about 15 per cent of its width compared to its measurement on the loom. The statutes do not allow us to compare exactly the length of each type of cloth on the loom, but probably the length of a woollen was significantly reduced in the fulling process. In other cloth cities the shrinkage amounted to almost half of the size of the woollen. At the end of the fulling process an Ypres luxury cloth had to measure between 30 (*derdelinghe*) and 32 ells (*dickedinne*) or 20.9m and 22.3m. At the frame the tenterers stretched the cloth again to a length of 28.6m and a width of 1.6 to 2.1m, depending on the nature of the fine woollen, therefore stretching the size of the fulled cloth lengthwise by more than 28 per cent for the *dickedinne* and 37 per cent for the *derdelinghe*. During the dyeing process the woollens again lost some of their size at the frame, a loss of about 5 per cent.

Cloth finishing

After the fulling process, the fuller took the woollens to the quality control for approval. Fuller's seals were fixed to them, and now it was the turn of the tenterers (in Ypres commonly called *uutslares* or *recwachters*) to return the woollens to their desired size. The woollens were for this purpose hung using hooks on large wooden frames (*raem* or *rec, lice*). In Ypres, there were long frames for the large woollens, double half-frames for two pieces of half cloth and half-frames for the smaller woollens. A sign on the frame,

---

[106] Espinas and Pirenne, *Recueil*, 3, 580.
[107] Espinas and Pirenne, *Recueil*, 3, 576.

Figure 2.7 Wooden plank with holes from the *Verdronken Weide* excavation, probably used to fix woollens on a tentering frame (© Yper Museum, obj. 5622).

a double cross (*dobbel cruce*), indicated the desired length and width of the woollens, and whenever a new frame was erected the frame had to be measured and signed off by the *zeghelaers*, the city officials who controlled the city's measures, and anybody who tampered with the right measurements would be banished from the city for a year.[108] A movable crossbar at the bottom of the frame, and a movable pole that could be rotated using a winch or windlass (*boom*) on one end of the frame allowed the cloth to be stretched, in the process sometimes regaining almost 50 per cent of its shrunken fuller's size, both in length and in width.[109] As we saw earlier, the expensive Ypres woollens were stretched lengthwise by about 30 to 40 per cent. In the excavations in the suburb of St Michael what is probably the crossbar of a tentering frame, a wooden board with a lot of holes, was found reused as a wooden reinforcement of the embankment of the Ieperleet.[110] The statutes provide no clues as to where the frames were placed. It was, however, decided in the fourteenth-century statutes of the tenterers that they were to be set up in groups of at least six long or twelve short frames. The frames were also to be erected in open space, without trees or hedges or dykes which could interfere with the procedures. The frames required plenty of open space around them. Trees were even not allowed within a radius of 11m around them.[111]

At the end of the tentering procedure, the large Ypres luxury woollens measured about 28.6m to 1.6 or 2.1m, depending on the type of cloth. It goes without saying that stretching was a delicate operation which had to be carried out very gradually in order not to damage the woollens. In Ypres the desired length was reached only on the second day of the operation, and only in case of frost could the tenterers adapt the procedure.[112] While the cloth was stretched the woollen was also subjected to a more thorough napping process using teasels and small shears to remove the remaining loose

---

108 Espinas and Pirenne, *Recueil*, 3, 584 (for similar arrangements in other cities see also De Poerck, *La draperie médiévale*, 120-121).
109 Munro, 'Medieval Woollens', 209.
110 Dewilde and Van Bellingen, "Excavating a Suburb", 69.
111 Espinas and Pirenne, *Recueil*, 3, 584.
112 Espinas and Pirenne, *Recueil*, 3, 495 (c. 1300), mentioned also in De Poerck, *La draperie médiévale*, 122 and 124.

fibres and to complete the felting process ('wet shearing'). Stretching and the work with teasels were clearly a team effort. An addition to the tenterers' statutes in 1372 mentions a team of three tenterers, one at each end of the frame and one to operate the winch.[113] Dogs probably guarded the tenterers' fields, because the statutes provide for possible damage done by the dogs to people and to the woollens. After these operations and a second control at the frame, the cloth was cut loose and delivered to the shearers for the actual shearing process. Some specific woollens seem to have been sheared when still wet, so before tentering. This was the case for the *dueten*, a less refined version of the expensive *dickedinne*.[114] The tenterers were also responsible for putting dyed woollens on the frames.

The shearers completed the work with teasels, a labour-intensive operation that could take eight hours for a large woollen. In Ypres – and this is exceptional in the Flemish cloth industries – shearers also seem to have done the first shearing (wet shearing) of one side of the woollen (*averecht*) during the fulling stage. The other side (*recht*) was done after the tentering process.[115] But their main activity was to clip and crop the cloth with their large and heavy steal shears or scissors (*c.* 45cm) to remove the last naps and give the piece of cloth a shine by smoothing the surface.[116] Although archaeologists have found scissors in sites that can be associated with the Ypres cloth industry, large shearers' instruments were not among them. Shearing was done on a downward-sloping table (*scherdisch*), and the shearer's table could not be hidden away from view.[117] Similarly shearers around 1300, who also had one or two weaving looms in their houses, had to arrange their houses – they could only work at home – in such a way that the two activities were completely separate, without connecting windows or doors, and people had to be able to reach both workshops in the same house directly from the street, even if the shearing table was placed in the attic. This strange ruling does not necessarily imply that shearers were also clothiers. As we shall see in chapter 4, this combination was strictly forbidden in Ypres. It shows that large houses could be used to accommodate more than one trade, or that shearers could also be weavers. Double guild membership in Flemish cities was very frequent, and, although the Ypres data do not give any more detail, probably this was also the case in the Ypres cloth industry. But such practices, of course, made guild control even more important and they were often felt to be endangering the integrity of the production chain. In the late fourteenth-century statutes it was forbidden for shearers to be active in weaving or fulling.[118]

Shearers also seem to have worked in teams of two or three craftsmen. In order to work together, the movements of the shearers had to be coordinated all the time. In Ypres, only experienced apprentices could work on a cloth, and when they were

---

13 Espinas and Pirenne, *Recueil*, 3, 585.
14 Espinas and Pirenne, *Recueil*, 3, 573, mentioned in De Poerck, *La draperie médiavale*, 116.
15 De Poerck, *La draperie médiévale*, 129-130.
16 Munro, "Medieval Woollens", 209-211.
17 *Quiconques meteroit disch forcheleit, pierderoit 20s* (Espinas and Pirenne, *Recueil*, 3, 475). If found out, the shearer's table was burned.
18 Espinas and Pirenne, *Recueil*, 3, 474; for the late fourteenth-century statutes: Espinas and Pirenne, *Recueil*, 3, 598.

in their first year of training they had to be accompanied by two journeymen at the shearer's table.[119] After several shearings, the piece of cloth was checked for the last small flaws, which were repaired by a specialist group of *lakenboeters*;[120] it was folded, pressed and packed; and finally taken to the cloth hall to be distributed, if necessary, to the dyers. The final stage of cloth finishing was executed by the so-called *lakenreders*. In fourteenth-century Ypres it was strictly forbidden for shearers to become cloth finishers of the most expensive woollens, the *dickedinne*.[121] But whether this also applied to other qualities of cloth is uncertain. In 1280 shearers seem to have been involved in folding at least stamforts.[122] In most cloth cities there does not seem to have been a strict division between shearers and cloth finishers, who also did the last repairs, folding and pressing the woollens.[123] Ypres cloth finishers worked either at home or in the house of the *upsettere* or clothier (for the most expensive *dickedinne* woollens).

Dyeing

After the fabric was completed by the cloth finishers, it could be sold as it was (white cloth, usually says, and striped cloth, which was woven with a colour pattern from dyed wool or yarn), or it could be taken to the dyer's workshop for additional colouring. Dyers could dye in the wool or in the yarn, so weavers could work with coloured yarn, usually dyed with blue woad because this dyestuff did not require a mordant that could damage the yarn (although certainly for striped cloth, wool or yarn were also dyed in other colours that required a mordant) or they could be dyed in the fabric at the end of the manufacturing process. The clothiers' statutes indicate that the most expensive Ypres fabrics, *dickedinne* and *derdelinghe*, existed in both white (undyed) and blue versions. For the former, dyeing took place only in the fabric. Fine 'white woollens' were often used to achieve the famous and exclusive scarlets (*scaerlaken*), where the undyed fabric was dyed with only the most expensive red dyestuff, kermes (*grein*), imported from the eastern Mediterranean. It was forbidden to mix madder dyeing in a first soaking with kermes afterwards. For kermes woollens, the prestigious dyestuff was the only red colour that could be used. The prestige and the cost of kermes were legendary, and the Ypres dyers were even permitted to dye woollens manufactured elsewhere with the most exclusive dyestuff on the market.[124] The so-called 'blue woollens' were probably already dyed with woad in the wool or the yarn and after the manufacturing process were given their final colour in the fabric.

The thirteenth-century statutes distinguish between dyers who use woad (*tainteniers ki taint de waide*) and the dyers who dye in kettles or vats (*tainteniers a le caudiere*)

---

119 Espinas and Pirenne, *Recueil*, 3, 473 (statutes of 1280 and *c.* 1300) and ibid., 599-600 (statutes fourteenth century).
120 De Poerck, *La draperie médiévale*, 142-143.
121 Espinas and Pirenne, *Recueil*, 3, 605.
122 Espinas and Pirenne, *Recueil*, 3, 455.
123 De Poerck, *La draperie médiévale*, 145.
124 Munro, 'Medieval Woollens', 211-217 and more details in id., 'The Medieval Scarlet', 13-70. For the exception to dying woollens from other cities with kermes, Espinas and Pirenne, *Recueil*, 3, 619.

who use madder. In the fourteenth century, the same division applies, but the dyers are called dyers in blue (*blauververs*), who worked primarily with woad and did not use mordants, and dyers in red (*roodververs*), who used madder red, but also other colours and made use of mordants. But besides red and blue, Ypres woollens were dyed in a whole range of other colours which were achieved by adding other dyestuffs (brazilwood for red, brown, and black, weld for yellow and green, gallnut for greys and blacks, etc.). The combinations of dyestuffs were relatively well-known, but every workshop must also have had its own secret recipes.

Dyeing involved complicated chemical processes.[125] To apply woad (*isatis tinctoria*, a biannual plant with yellow flowers) a base of boiled water, bran and grated madder was required, to which the woad and a catalyst (potash ash) were added. After three days of fermentation, this mixture was added to warm water and brought into contact with wool or fabrics. After drying and oxidation, the fibres or fabric became blue. Woad was readily available. It was grown in many parts of Europe, but also in the nearby regions of Picardy, Artesia and Walloon-Flanders, so it was relatively cheap.[126] The other colours required mordants, mostly alum imported by Genoese merchants from Asia Minor (Phocea or Foglia in Italy, hence also the name in the Ypres statutes *fuelge*), and from the middle of the fifteenth century from Central Italy (Tolfa).[127] Woollens were soaked in water with alum and acidic tartar (potassium bitartrate) and boiled, whereby alum adhered to the fibres and made them receptive to the dyestuffs. They were then put in a vat with boiling alkaline water and the dyestuff.[128] The root of the madder plant (*rubia tinctorum*) was used to achieve red. Madder (*crap*) was grown in the coastal regions of Zeeland and Flanders, so, like woad, was easily available to the cloth industries of the Low Countries. The imported and much more expensive brazilwood also yielded a deep red; weld, grown in parts of Interior Flanders, yielded yellow. But the most exclusive dyestuff was undoubtedly kermes or grain, imported from the Mediterranean, which was used only for the most expensive fine woollens.

Together with the quality of the wool, the nature, quantity and quality of the dyestuff was one of the key pointers for defining the quality of a particular woollen. They defined the colour saturation of the woollens and, therefore, also their price. It is not surprising, therefore, for a city that was famed for the quality of its textiles, that the dyers' statutes of Ypres are very precise about all these issues. Markets for dyestuffs were very complicated, with many different qualities that needed to be kept separated.[129] Because of all these complexities, it was difficult to make the market for dyestuffs transparent, and all raw materials that were used by the Ypres dyers had therefore to

---

[125] The clearest survey of these processes can be found in Munro, 'Medieval Woollens', 211-215. See also Langhals, 'Die Farben des Mittelalters', 1017-1024.
[126] Verhille, 'La guède en Picardie', 393-399.
[127] De Poerck, *La draperie médiévale*, 169-170. See also Delumeau, *L'alun de Rome* and Liagre, 'Le commerce de l'alun'. 177-206.
[128] See also Hofenk-De Graaff, 'The Chemistry of Red Dyestuffs', 71-79.
[129] For example Espinas and Pirenne, *Recueil*, 3, 483 (*c.* 1300). There were at least five types of madder, and woad could also be found in many different qualities and shapes (dried, partially fermented, etc.). More details in De Poerck, *La draperie médiévale*, 150-166 for woad and 175-179 for madder.

be rigorously controlled at the market: for example, woad was mixed in their barrels to homogenise the quality of the dyestuffs (*keren*). Forestalling was explicitly forbidden, and the city government tried as far as possible to avoid monopolies and concentration in the hands of only a few merchants or dyers. The quality of some dyestuffs was difficult even for experienced dyers to assess. For woad, buyers usually demanded, at their own expense, a trial sample (*proufcupe*) to check its quality.[130] Also the different colours and the ways to achieve them were often mentioned in detail. These were, of course broad descriptions, allowing each workshop to use its own recipes. They show nonetheless the enormous variety and savoir-faire of an industry which had to adapt continually to changing demand.

The general trends of medieval fashion demanded great alertness from the dyers. The requirements of thirteenth-century fashion with its juxtaposition of long and colourful robes for the elites and lighter tunics for the lower classes, which stimulated markets for a wide range of evenly coloured textiles, were totally different from the much shorter fashion of the late thirteenth and early fourteenth centuries with a preference for patterned woollens and striped cloth that did not require dyeing in the fabric, but featured the greater importance of the dyeing of wool and yarn, and the preference for brightly coloured textiles in the fourteenth century. From the late fourteenth century, medieval fashion changed abruptly to moving away from bright and diverse colouring. Following trends set by the culturally influential royal and princely courts, fashion required bright reds (*vermeil, sanguine*) and blacks. During the fifteenth century red fabrics lost ground, except for ceremonial dress, and blacks started to dominate medieval fashion. Clothiers, merchants and dyers did, of course, have to respond to such general fashion trends, yet there was also geographical diversity with preferences for particular-coloured fabrics often being very different from region to region. The often very catchy names particular colours received demonstrate how nuance and taste made these markets highly volatile.[131] Dyeing the wrong type of woollen in the wrong colours could mean disaster and ruin for clothiers, or dry up the flow of demand for dyers. Stocks of dyestuffs were inevitably very expensive, so risks had to be managed all the time.

To accommodate the market dyers would use a whole array of colours and shades. The Ypres dyers in blue had a whole range of different shades of blue and, of course, also various qualities of colour saturation (amongst others also the famous Ypres *sadblaeu*, a saturated clear blue), and similarly the dyers in red produced various kinds of red, by adapting quality and saturation of madder (by applying multiple soakings), but also by using other dyestuffs such as brazilwood to achieve vermilion red, blood red (*sanguine*) which required more brazilwood than madder, *moreit*, pink, purple, violet, etc., usually also starting from blue-dyed wool. To achieve all these nuances the statutes distinguish between no fewer than six different qualities of woad and five of madder.[132]

---

130 Espinas and Pirenne, *Recueil*, 3, 629 (see also De Poerck, *La draperie médiévale*, 157-159).
131 Monnas, 'Some Medieval Colour Terms', 25-57. For fashion developments, see amongst others Van Uytven, 'De korte rokken', 219-231.
132 De Poerck, *La draperie médiévale*, 167 and 178.

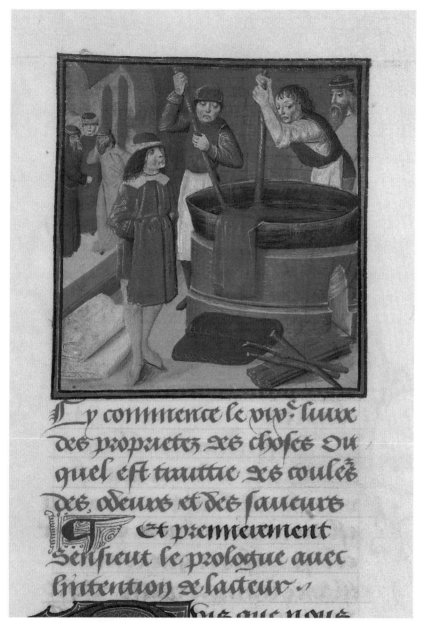

Figure 2.8 A workshop of dyers in red. A woollen dyed with madder or grain is taken out of the dyer's vat. On the floor near the vat lie woollens that have not yet been dyed in the fabric: white cloth (not dyed in the fibre) and blue cloth (dyed blue in the fibre). Two journeymen (?) are doing the work, while a master dyer (?) checks on the process. White and blue woollens were in the fourteenth century the most common in the Ypres manufacture of greased cloth.
Miniature from Bartholomaeus Anglicus, translated by Jean Corbechon, *De proprietatibus rerum* (in French: *Livre des proprietez des choses*). London, British Library, Royal 15 E III, f. 269: *Cy commence le xixe livre des proprietez des choses duquel est traicttié des couleurs, des odeurs et des saveurs*. Bruges 1482 (scribe Jean du Riès; painter Master of Edward IV).

Of course no illegal dyestuffs or additives to speed up the process were permitted (chalk is often mentioned in this respect). The cost of dyeing depended therefore not only on the quality, but also on the saturation of the dyestuffs in the vats; as a rule, the more saturated and the darker the colours had to be, the more expensive the woollens became.

The dyers' statutes are, however, much less explicit about the actual organisation of a workshop and the technical aspects of the dyeing process.[133] Even the physical appearance of dyers' workshops is not known. The archaeological data about the *Verdronken Weide* excavations do not yield a lot of information in this respect. Although traces of weld (a yellow dye) have been found, they could not be linked to a particular workshop. Excavations of dyers' workshops in Bruges (*Verversdijk*) reveal, nonetheless, very complicated arrangements close to an important waterway (*Reie*), with water wells, pits or troughs reinforced with brick, kilns on which copper containers could be heated, traces of wooden vats, provisions for drainage towards the river, and also traces of dyestuffs (weld).[134] The complex procedures of preparing the fermented woad for the dyers in blue or the soluble alum for the dyers in red required an infrastructure, but in particular the kilns and large copper or bronze vats for producing warm water for heating the dyestuffs and textiles and the wooden (or brick) containers (*cupe*) for soaking or cleaning the wool or fabrics must have required considerable investment. So, a dyer's workshop was probably capital-intensive not only because of the expensive raw materials used, but also because of the complex workshop itself that had to be located, like a fuller's workshop, close to a source of water supply or close to running water for removing the waste products and dissolve the unsavoury smells. The workshop was also the place where the master dyer lived. He was not allowed to organise his business elsewhere in the city.[135] Although it was generally forbidden for dyers to organise a joint business, the statutes leave some room for capital pooling: in the late thirteenth century, one, two or three dyers could establish a dyer's workshop together in their houses, but only to dye their own wool and woollens, not to dye for other people.

The statutes communicate precious little detail about the actual dyeing procedures. Dyers were not only active in dyeing the new Ypres woollens, but they also gave fresh colours to second-hand clothing and other fabrics. These could not be mixed into the dyeing process of the woollens.[136] Wool could not be mixed with finished fabrics in a dyer's vat, but warp and weft yarns had to be dyed together.[137] Ypres dyers could dye only Ypres woollens around 1300. At least at that time, Ypres did not cater for the neighbouring cloth industries.[138]

---

133 See also Bove, 'Une sombre affaire', 105-128 for the dyers in Saint-Denis, close to Paris, where the association was not able at all to develop a thorough regulatory framework.
134 De Witte, 'Craft in the Town of Brugge', 115-122 and Hillewaert and Van Besien, *Jaarverslag 2005*.
135 Espinas and Pirenne, *Recueil*, 3, 481.
136 Espinas and Pirenne, *Recueil*, 3, 624.
137 Espinas and Pirenne, *Recueil*, 3, 619.
138 Espinas and Pirenne, *Recueil*, 3, 481.

Soaking textiles in a solution of woad, brazilwood, madder or weld could be a long process. Because work could not continue on festive days or Sundays, the dyers in blue could not start a new batch of woad on a Thursday, because time was too short in that case to finish the dyeing process. Workshops could reach a certain scale: dyers in blue could set up three to four vats of woad per week, using a maximum of 18 measures (also called *vat*) of woad.[139] For this, water was to be warmed in vats or kettles, but the dyeing itself happened in *cuves* or *cupen*, probably wooden containers. Dyers in red could, according to their late thirteenth-century statutes, put up to six woollens in a batch of dye, but no more than two woollens together, in a soaking either of madder or of weld. In July 1385 that number was even reduced to one woollen, but this proved too difficult to enforce and the old maximum of two woollens was restored just two months later.[140] Henceforth only the most prestigious Ypres woollens, the *dickedinne*, had to be dyed separately. Tariffs for dying could differ between the winter and the summer seasons (around 1300 a winter dye cost 30s, a summer dye 27s for each batch). The temperature probably played a role here, but overall dyers could dye only 6 woollens per day in winter, but they were allowed 12 per day in summer (between 2 February and 1 November).[141] A dyer was, however, not allowed to dye striped cloth or worsted at the same time as greased woollens.[142]

Conclusions: technological innovation and the emergence of the 'grande draperie'

Ypres produced a wide variety of woollens, although over the fourteenth century the focus was more and more on luxury cloth. This required complex manufacturing processes. Traditionally, technological change in cloth manufacture is discussed in terms of innovation and industrial conservatism. While the switch to the broadloom defined the further industrial development in urban cloth manufacture, the hesitation to adopt other techniques is said to have jeopardized growth and continuing success. Yet the fact that the fulling mill or even the spinning wheel was adopted only hesitantly or even, in the case of the fulling mill, was never accepted before the sixteenth century was often inspired by rational entrepreneurial choices, not just by conservative protectionism.[143] Other techniques were adopted much more easily if they did not interfere

---

139 De Poerck, *La draperie médiévale*, 165-166.
140 Espinas and Pirenne, *Recueil*, 3, 618.
141 Espinas and Pirenne, *Recueil*, 3, 477-482. In the fourteenth century the number of woollens in winter was raised to 8 (Espinas and Pirenne, *Recueil*, 3, 614).
142 As a rule, striped or mixed (*mellé, gheminghet*) cloth was not dyed in the fabric, to retain the different colour patterns. If striped cloth was dyed in the fabric, it took on the last colour (or showed different shades of colour if, for example, dyed and undyed yarn were used) and the stripes appeared only in the weft of the fabric, not in their colour.
143 In the beginning of the sixteenth century Ypres allowed the use of fulling mills, as did rural cloth industries. It is remarkable that the much more successful cloth industry in Nieuwkerke, associated in literature with cost efficiency, accepted the use of fulling mills only much later, in 1564, a reminder that the fulling mill was not necessarily considered an important variable in the production cost of cloth in the Low Countries even as late as the sixteenth century (see also Van der Meulen, *Woven into the Urban Fabric*, 65-106).

with those choices. Interfering with quality would have threatened the carefully constructed reputation of Ypres woollens, such was the reputation of new technologies in entrepreneurial and commercial circuits. Urban manufacture was defined by guild rules and conventions designed to create a product that conformed to anticipated quality standards. On the other hand, export volumes had constantly to be adapted to changing markets, changing clients and changing fashions. These adaptations always carried the risk that long-term reputation would be jeopardized by the introduction of badly perceived new techniques. So technological adaptation had to be carried out with great care. The English cloth industry, organised mainly in the late Middle Ages in rural contexts, was much less defined by such reputation mechanisms, it seems, and hence could much more easily introduce, for example, the fulling mill, but also the spinning wheel. The requirements of flexible cloth output were just too important. But the only slow introduction of some productivity-raising technologies did not mean that technological innovation was completely absent from the Flemish urban cloth industries. The origins of urban cloth manufacture must be sought in the massive introduction of the horizontal broadloom, leading to new ways of organising the finishing of raw woollens and of adding colour to textiles.

A second important feature is that the technological organisation of cloth manufacture cannot be dissociated from the actual organisation of workshops. These had to be adaptable to changing output. Workshops seem to have catered with astonishing ease for the continual and sometimes radical product innovation that occurred in the Ypres cloth industry. It is this product innovation that has greatly defined the industry's resilience on the export markets. At each stage of production different technological and product requirements, often changing with the different focus on worsteds, semi-worsteds, mid-priced 'coloured' woollens and the famous luxury scarlets, also caused business organisation to change. A greater emphasis on finishing for the 'greased' woollens inevitably affected not only the weavers' workshops, but also the fulling, shearing, cloth finishing and dyeing processes. Flexible labour markets, but also the organisation at the level of the workshop itself, had to solve such structural reorientations of the industry. The focus on imported high-quality wool from England meant that entrepreneurs had to rely on the quality of the work of spinsters, carders and combers. So not only guild-organised workshops but also domestic industrial activity were integrated into the production process.

CHAPTER 3

The Rise and Fall of Industrial Suburbia

Cloth and the Urban Fabric

Urban Change in Medieval Ypres

In the previous chapters we saw how the successes of its cloth industry pushed Ypres into becoming one of the leading cities of medieval Flanders, but also how the monoculture of textiles gradually undermined the city's resilience from the fourteenth century onwards and turned it into a mid-sized town in the fifteenth century. But even then, textiles still made up a substantial part of the urban economy, and Ypres also kept performing well above its political weight. With Ghent and Bruges, two cities with much more diversified economies, the city was still one of the three (later with the rural region of the *Franc* around Bruges of the four) Members of Flanders, monopolising for their hinterland political representation in the governing bodies of the county. We have also seen that the demographic weight of the city rose rapidly with the growing cloth industry in the late twelfth and thirteenth centuries, but was already declining substantially by 1300, with a clear period of crisis, like the other leading cities of Flanders, in the first half of the fourteenth century, when the spatial organisation of the Flemish cloth industry was changed by growing competition from Brabant and England and from the successful secondary manufacturing towns of Flanders, in particular in the Flemish river basins of the Scheldt, Dender and Leie (Oudenaarde, Aalst, Dendermonde, Kortrijk, Wervik, Menen, Comines, etc.). But while Ghent and Bruges were able to recover in the second half of the fourteenth century, Ypres never quite regained its momentum. Certainly, it was still successful on export markets for luxury cloth, yet output figures for woollens must have been significantly lower than in the late thirteenth century and the city's population kept declining to a mere 10,000. The fifteenth century was a period of apparent stability, at this much lower level. The Ypres cloth industry met with increasing problems, however, and it is likely that the overall improved standards of living in town and countryside stimulated the city's regional functions, with servicing industries, fashion and the supply of durable consumer goods decreasing the impact of textiles on the urban economy. Ypres in this period took on the more normal cloak of a regional servicing centre and had shed most of its industrial nature.

These rapidly changing cycles in the late medieval period must, of course, have seriously affected the composition of the urban population, and as such also the nature of urban space. In this chapter we want to look at how the urban fabric developed and how, across these successive stages, the activities related to textile manufacture were spread across the city. Given that it lacked the research infrastructure of a university city like Ghent, and did not have the international allure of medieval Bruges, much less is known about the topographical development of medieval Ypres than about its two Flemish competitors. Yet the broad lines of urbanistic change can be reconstructed, nonetheless.

Revolt and Taxation

In the winter of 1325-1326 a tax was levied. This period must have been among the darkest hours of Ypres' medieval history. Although the city's population had probably already dropped from 30,000 in the middle of the thirteenth century to 20,000 around 1300, there was still a substantial labour potential in the city. But at the same time, there is little doubt that exactly in this period the textile industry met with increasing output problems and that the position of Ypres cloth on export markets changed dramatically as the city's entrepreneurs lost out on markets for cheaper and mid-priced woollens. A decade earlier, the city had been hit hard by the effects of the Great Famine. No less than 10 per cent of the population died from the effects of starvation and malnutrition.[144] Bruges, in this period also a city in crisis, was hit almost as hard, yet in Ypres the losses do not seem to have been compensated for by a subsequent intensification of immigration. Very much to the contrary, at times violent political tension between the craftsmen and the mercantile elites and declining demand for Ypres textiles sharpened the crisis in the city.

The disequilibrium between a still important population and declining industrial outputs had a deleterious effect on unemployment figures which must have been extremely high, and there is little surprise in the fact that political friction in the city itself was exacerbated by this economic downturn. In 1325 the commons overturned the elitist city government. This was only one episode in the continuous struggle since 1302 between the traditional urban elites of merchants and landowners and the commoners, a mixed group of small cloth entrepreneurs (*drapiers*), the textile guilds, the associations that united the important cloth trades of weavers and fullers, and the smaller, non-textile guilds. It is uncertain whether the so-called *poortersneeringhe*, which united capital-intensive trades like butchers and brewers, but also some of the textile trades (and mostly those that were characterised by heavy capital investments in raw materials, the dyers, or labour, the cloth finishers), were part of this commoners' party. But the struggle was also characterised by continually changing positions, and shortly after the 'democratic' revolt of 1303 the elites returned to power. In the meantime plans were made and executed to build a new defensive perimeter. A long ditch of no less than 7.6km was dug and an earthen wall with ten gates was erected, covering a very substantial area, almost quadrupling the area within the defensive perimeter. All suburbs were now located within the 'outer ditch' (*fossé, uuterste veste*).[145] In 1325 a more radical power switch occurred, and many members of the traditional elites were

---

[144] Van Werveke, 'La famine', 5-14. On the regional consequences of the Great Famine, see also Geens, 'The Great Famine', 1048-1072.
[145] Mus and Trio, *De geschiedenis van de middeleeuwse grootstad*, 49.

THE RISE AND FALL OF INDUSTRIAL SUBURBIA 73

Figure 3.1 City Map of Ypres by Thévelin-Destrée (1564). © Yper Museum, nr. SM 3188.

expelled from the city. The traces of this physical removal of substantial parts of the urban elites can easily be detected in the taxation that was organised shortly after the revolt.

The 1325-1328 period, when the revolutionary faction was in power, was not a period of turmoil just in Ypres; all over the county of Flanders revolt brewed. The cities and parts of the countryside in Coastal Flanders revolted against Count Louis of Nevers, exactly at the moment the Ypres revolt had toppled the city elites from power. In this period of unrest, the new regime, initially sanctioned by the count's representative (the count himself had been taken prisoner in Kortrijk), his uncle Robert of Cassel, tried as far as possible to break away from the old regime's policies. Again, better protection of the city's suburbs stood high on the aldermen's priority list, all the more so because the backbone of the regime, the masses of weavers and fullers, lived in those parts, and the outer wall that protected the four suburbs of the city was reinforced.

In the period of rapid demographic growth from the late twelfth century, four substantial suburbs had grown outside the city walls, each with its own parish church (St Kruis, founded in 1277, St Michiel, first mentioned in 1249, St Jan in 1196 and Our Lady ten Brielen around 1200).[146] The inner city filled up, and newcomers were probably forced to settle primarily outside the walls. Even some mendicant orders (Carmelites, Augustinians) were forced to build their friaries in Ypres during the thirteenth century in the unprotected suburbs. Only the Dominicans and Franciscans could find a place in the periphery of the inner city, thanks to the intervention of the countess.[147] The same thing happened to two of the major new beguinages. The growth of the suburbs speeded up in the fourteenth century, and in the latter part probably more Ypres inhabitants lived in the suburbs than in the inner city. As we shall see, a substantial part of the urban cloth industry shifted to the suburbs. The immediate surroundings of the city were characterised by a complex set of seigneuries (the comital demesne of Hofland, the lands of the Templars, Ketelkwaad, the liberty of the collegiate church of St Martin in Ypres, Rolleghem), some of them also with territories in the inner city. Some of these seigneuries would gradually be absorbed by the urban body politic, and some of these were even administered by members of the city elites.[148] A lot of the urban expansion outside the walls therefore took place on lands owned by those city elites (the families Belle, Scattin, Van Scoten, Baerdonc, de Ketelaere), and they were also active as sponsors or founders of religious institutions in the city's outskirts. So, the urban expansion probably also proved to be a very lucrative operation for them, and the intensification of habitation must have stimulated their rental income. The construction of a defensive perimeter may have been an initiative of the commoners who took over political power from the elites; paradoxically the initiative probably did not hurt the financial basis of those elites.

---

146 For the territorial survey of the urbanization process in Ypres, see Mus and Trio, *De geschiedenis van de middeleeuwse grootstad*. More recently the development in Ypres has been compared with other cities in Flanders, Artois and Hainaut, see Bervoets, *Quicumque in villa per annum unum et per diem unum manserit*, 234-290.
147 Simons, *Cities of Ladies* and his survey of mendicant monasteries in the county of Flanders in *Bedelordekloosters*.
148 See Mus, *De geschiedenis van de middeleeuwse grootstad*, 36-46; id., 'L'évolution de la ville d'Ypres', 48-51.

As usually happened with the urban expansion in the years around 1300, ambitions far exceeded the potential for growth. In fact, growth had already been halted for some decades. Because the construction costs could not be borne just by the regular income of the city which consisted of indirect taxes on consumption and trade, direct taxation was also levied. A parchment roll, which was kept at the City Archives before these were destroyed in 1914, mentions 1,646 households, or the equivalent of about 7,410 inhabitants.[149] This means that a substantial part of the population was left out of the tax. The city population was assessed at still about 28,000 even after 1300. The Great Hunger, which had hit Ypres particularly hard, and the acute crisis of the cloth industry in this period must have greatly influenced population figures, but even a very conservative estimate would still amount to probably more than 20,000 in the 1320s, so the tax hit only less than half of the population. It is not clear from the list which part of the population was taxed. The minimum tax assessment amounted to 12d Flemish (or about 4 days wages of a skilled artisan), which represents already a sizable contribution. It is likely therefore that the very poor were exempt, and in a cloth city such as Ypres, with a substantial labour reserve of unskilled labourers and textile workers, a lot of people lived probably at mere subsistence level, certainly in this period of relatively low real wages. There seems to be no geographical limitation, however. All city wards and streets are mentioned, both in the walled city itself and in the suburbs. It is therefore very difficult to use the taxation as a proxy for levels of social inequality. Too many imponderables are weighing on its interpretation.

Still, it is the only tax list we have for this period, so the data must be analysed nonetheless, albeit very carefully. The first striking feature is that the taxpayers in the city itself are only a minority of all taxpayers: 699 households or 42.5 per cent are registered as taxpayers within the thirteenth-century walls, which means that a clear majority of all taxpayers were registered as living in the four suburbs lying between the city walls and the new *uuterste veste*, the outer ditch. The overall Gini-coefficient, which is a number between 0 (complete equality) and 1 (complete inequality) for the city is 0.669, with inequality much more accentuated in the inner city (0.751) than in the industrial suburbs (0.559). So, we see less social polarisation in the suburbs than in the inner city, with, most of all, fewer extremely wealthy people, who skew the distribution of capital to high inequality rates. Taking into account the relatively high tax assessment of even the poorer households and the fact that probably more than half of the population was not included in the taxation because of poverty, inequality rates may even have been higher still, suggesting that the social composition of Ypres consisted of a tiny and extremely wealthy elite, a small middle class, a high proportion of lower middle class to poorer strata, many of them textile workers (wealthy enough to be included still in the taxation) and the majority of the population living from insecure and unstable wage income and overall too poor to be taxed efficiently. From these very rough estimates we can deduce therefore that Ypres conforms to the already established urban typology. Commercial cities and regional servicing towns tend to be

---

[49] The taxation was published in the edition of the city account of Ypres: Des Marez and De Sagher, *Les comptes de la ville d'Ypres*, 2, 498-523.

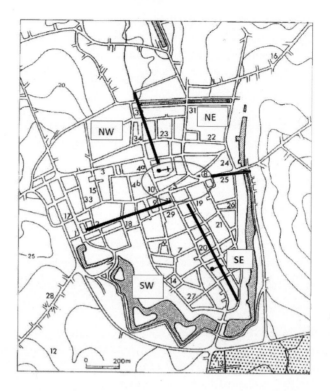

Figure 3.2 Map of the inner city of Ypres with subdivision in four quadrants (which more or less coincide with the later administrative subdivision of the city) and the separate market area
(© adapted from Dewilde, Ervynck and Wielemans (eds.), *Ypres and the Medieval Cloth Industry*;
© Vlaamse Overheid, Agentschap Onroerend Erfgoed).

1. Scottenhoue; 2. Vleeshouwerstraat; 3. Elverdingestraat; 4a. Korte Meersstraat; 4b. Lange Meersstraat; 5. Donkerpoort; 6. Oude Konijnstraat; 7. Voldersstraat = Lombaardstraat; 8. O. L. Vr. Hospitaal; 9. Boomgaardstraat; 10. Kaasstraat; 11. Leerlooiersstraatje; 12. Nieuwendamme; 13. Nieuwe Leye; 14. Zaalhof; 15. Beluikstraat; 16. Lindendreef; 17. Boterpoort; 18. Tempelpoort; 19. D'hondtstraat; 20. Rijselsestraat; 21. Sint-Jacobsstraat; 22. Cartonstraat; 23. Surmontstraat; 24. Kauwekijnstraat; 25. Meensestraat; 26. G. Gezelleplein; 27. Tegelstraat; 28. Dikkebusseweg; 29. Casselstraat; 30. Torhoutpoort; 31. Diksmuidepoort; 32. Boezengepoort; 33. Eigenheerdstraat; 34. Leet

substantially more equal, in particular because of the greater share of urban middles classes of skilled artisans and retailers active in regional and local supply systems. These groups were relatively much less numerous in real industrial cities. Fifteenth-century Ghent and Leiden were therefore substantially more unequal than Bruges, and Ypres, in the early fourteenth century still the quintessential industrial city, clearly fits neatly into this industrial inequality pattern. But the difference between the inner city and the suburbs also points to another phenomenon: inequality could differ substantially from one part of the city to another. We need therefore to look also at neighbourhood and even street patterns.

We have divided the city into four quadrants (Southwest: Rijselstraat, Ieperleet, St Pieter; Northwest: Boterstraat, Elverdingstraat, St Nicolas; Northeast: Diksmuidestraat, Torhoutstraat, Menenstraat; Southeast: Bollingstraat, Bukkerstraat, Hontstraat) and the streets of the suburbs into the four parishes, St Kruis – West, outside Temple Gate, Butter Gate and Elverdinge Gate, OLV ten Brielen North, outside the Diksmuide Gate, St Jan – East outside the Torhout gate and Hangwaert Gate (present-day Menin Gate), and St Michiel – South outside present-day the Lille Gate. Some tax assessments cannot be localised in the urban fabric, they are the contributions of those members of the city elites who had been banished from the city after the revolt of the commoners in 1325; Their tax assessments were paid by their wives or other family members who were left behind. Because during these years of popular government in the city, the political (and mercantile) elites had fled the city, it is not surprising that their assessments were the highest in the city. Possible there was also an element of revenge in their assessment. It was payback time.[150] It is also probable that most of these households lived in the stone houses in the very centre of the city (market and adjacent streets and the vicinity of St Nicolas Church in the western quadrants). It is probable, therefore, that the calculation of the average wealth in these streets, already by far the wealthiest in the city, is a minimum assessment.

Strikingly, the median tax assessment in nearly all districts is very similar, and the lowest assessment everywhere identical. So, despite or, more correctly, because of the highly polarised nature of Ypres society, most inhabitants belonged to low-taxed, low-income or middle-low-income households. This does not mean, of course, that in some quarters there were not also some wealthier households. In the inner city those were concentrated in the central market zone and its adjacent streets (an average taxation of 94d on the market and of 54d in the southwest quadrant, thanks to high tax assessments in Rijselstraat (*Zuudstrate*) and around the parish church of St Peter. The Volderstraat (present-day Lombaardstraat) and Montstraat, both situated near St Peter, yielded high taxess (averages of 139 and 95d). This area can be described as having an utterly bourgeois character, with wealthy elite families living in stone houses making up a substantial part of its population. But even in the southwest quadrants there were also poorer streets, most notably Tegelstraat where, as we shall see further, a great number of textile artisans lived.

It must also be remembered that some of the wealthiest households, those banished from the city after the political take-over of the commons, were probably living in the same central areas. So, these figures probably underestimate the average wealth in these streets. But also in the other quadrants some streets contained households with much higher average wealth. This is particularly true for the surroundings of St Nicolas towards the Butter Gate (Boterpoort) in the northwest quadrant, but also for isolated dwellings in Elverdingestraat and Boezingestraat close to the market. In the eastern quadrants some wealthy households lived, but not only was average wealth lower, but those wealthier households were also much rarer (and located mostly in

---

50 See also chapter 9.

78 CHAPTER 3

Table 3.1 Direct taxation in Ypres (construction of the outer ditch), city accounts 1325-6, tax assessments in d. Flemish
Inner city: Market, Southwest (Rijselstraat, Ieperleet, St Pieter), Northwest (Boterstraat, Elverdingstraat, St Nicolas), Northeast (Diksmuidestraat, Torhoutstraat, Menenstraat), Southeast (Bollingstraat, Bukkerstraat, Hontstraat). Suburbs: St Kruis (W), OLV ten Brielen (N), St Jan (E), St Michiel (S).

	N	MEDIAN	AVERAGE	MAX.	MIN;
Inner City					
Market	29	24	91	960	12
SW	149	24	54	1200	12
NW	277	12	34	720	12
NE	99	12	33	360	12
SE	99	24	35	360	12
Unknown	44	240	645	7200	12
Total	697	24	79	7200	12
Suburbs					
W	250	24	47	960	12
N	219	24	35	480	12
E	109	12	33	720	12
S	369	24	47	1200	12
Total	947	24	43	1200	12
City Total	1644	24	58	7200	12

Diksmuidestraat and Torhoutstraat in the northeast quadrant or in the Clierstraat, present-day Sint-Jacobstraat).

So, in essence Ypres conformed to a traditional premodern Sjoberg-model, with wealth concentrated in the centre of the city and along some of the main thoroughfares.[151] But even though poorer households also lived in these central areas, levels of concentration were extremely high, and the social geography of the inner city has a clear tendency to the segregation of rich and poor. Most streets in the inner city can be described as poor to lower middle class. The sharp social polarisation that appeared in the city's GINI-coefficient of 1325-6 was translated also into polarised urban space. This snapshot of segregation changes dramatically, however, when the populated suburbs of Ypres are considered.

The most striking feature is that on average the suburbs were wealthier than most streets in the inner city (with somewhat higher median and average assessments). Of course, they do not even come close to the central streets and market square of Ypres,

---

151 Sjoberg, *The Preindustrial City*.

Table 3.2 Female-led households in the Ypres taxation of 1325-1326

	N (N widows)	%		N	%
Inner City			**Suburbs**		
Market	5 (0)	17,2	W	14 (2)	5,6
SW	26 (3)	17,4	N	17 (4)	7,8
NW	22 (4)	7,9	E	9 (1)	8,3
NE	13 (2)	13,1	S	32 (4)	8,7
SE	18 (5)	18,2			
Unknown	4 (2)	9,1			
Total Inner City	88 (16)	12,6	**Total Suburbs**	72 (11)	7,6
Total City	160 (27)	9,7			

but the average assessment easily surpasses those in most working-class streets in the inner city. This is particularly true for the western and eastern suburbs (St Kruis and St Michiel). These were, as we shall see, typical industrial suburbs accommodating a lot of weavers and fullers. The northern and eastern suburbs conform more to the northwest and eastern quadrants of the inner city, with almost exclusively low- and middle-low-income households, almost uniformly distributed also in the different streets, with only a few exceptions of streets with wealthier households (most notably in Boezingeweg in the northern and in Groenstraat in the eastern suburb). The pattern in St Kruis and St Michiel is more interesting, with sometimes sharp polarisation between poorer streets and streets where also very wealthy households lived. In the western suburbs these were situated along the main thoroughfares outside Temple Gate and Elverdinge Gate, and in the southern suburb along Zillebeekstraat and Komenstraat, where some households were taxed at almost equal rates to the elite families around the market in the inner city.

A gender analysis shows similar differences between the suburbs and the inner city. There were substantially fewer female-led households in the suburbs than there were in the inner city. Within the city walls, the wealthier a neighbourhood was, the more women led separate households. But also in the less affluent neighbourhoods, single women tended to be numerous. This means that on the one hand in the inner city poor single women remarried less or later, either because they were less appealing on the marriage market because of their relatively fewer possessions or because the inner city offered more possibilities of gaining a separate income through (textile) labour or retail. Wealthy female households in the central market and streets tended to be more numerous, because single women probably had greater wealth or easier access to entrepreneurial or market activities. Some of the differences between neighbourhoods or between suburbs are more difficult to explain. Single women were less obvious in the northwest quadrant than in the other poorer regions, and more obvious in the equally poor southeast part of the inner city.[152] Similarly, it is not clear why in the western suburb of St Kruis single women were even rarer than in the other suburbs. Most single women in Ypres seem to have never married. Widows constituted only a small minority among the single women, which means that (in case of full registration, of course) widows tended to remarry sooner, a pattern that is more apparent in larger cities with an important servicing function and less in industrial cities (where the widow's right facilitated the continuity of the workshop). So, both the relatively important share of single women and the lower number of widows mean that the Ypres market must have provided opportunities for single women in retail or industry. It is tempting to look at the wool-preparing stages of the cloth industry, like spinning, to explain this high proportion of single women in the inner city, while the guild workshop-based economy made the married household a more apt choice for young people in the suburbs.

Textiles in the Urban Fabric

It is very difficult to assess the importance of cloth manufacture before 1325 in each of the neighbourhoods and suburbs. No reliable data have been preserved, yet a taxation on the clothiers from Ypres, probably a report on fines that had to paid after the Cokerulle revolt of 1280, sheds some light on the distribution of cloth manufacture in the city.[153] At this stage, almost 60 per cent of the tax paid by the *drapiers* came from the inner city, with a clear concentration in the parish of St James in the southeast corner of the inner city, but with equally high numbers of clothiers probably located in the parishes of St Nicolas (northwest quadrant) and St Peter (southwestern quadrant). Cloth manufacture seems to have been of lesser importance in the northeast part of the city, although the figures are difficult to interpret because 11 per cent of all taxes were levied in the seigneury of Rollegem, located in this part of the city (Stede-Rollegem) but extending beyond the city walls (Sint-Jans-Rollegem). It is, of course, logical, that concentrations of particular textile occupations seem to be linked directly to the availability of and access to water. Dyers and fullers in particular were dependent upon a steady supply of preferably clean water. The suburbs at this stage are the source of only 42 per cent of all fines, mostly concentrated in the suburbs of St Michael (south) and Our Lady Ten Brielen (north). The western suburb of Holy Cross is not mentioned, but in St John to the east there was also cloth activity. How the fines relate to the actual importance of the cloth trades in each of these districts is, of course, not precisely known.

The already mentioned tax for the construction of the outer ditch in 1325-1326 is much more informative about the location of textile occupations in the urban fabric. The list does not contain many occupational indications, usually only to avoid confusion between homonyms. But because three years after the tax list, when the traditional

---

152 The southern part of the city also contained two small beguinages in the early fourteenth century. The major two beguinages of Ypres were, however, located in the northern and eastern suburbs, but moved into the inner city after the destruction of the suburbs in 1383 (Simons, *Cities of Ladies*, 300-301).
153 Espinas and Pirenne, *Recueil*, 3, 698-699.

mercantile and landowning elites again took control of political power in the city, a great number of artisans were banished from the city and obliged to settle beyond the borders of the county of Flanders, even beyond the River Somme in France, and their names can be compared with those on the list. The names of more than 91 textile workers could be traced in the tax list (which numbers 1,644 households). So, about 5.5 per cent of all taxed households can be linked to cloth manufacture – not an impressive number in a city where probably more than half of the population depended on the industry, but enough to give some indications about where textile manufacture was organised – and because most craftsmen were either weavers or fullers, it is likely that a substantial number of them can indeed be situated on the map of the city.

In sharp contrast to the distribution of fines after 1280, the tax register of 1325-1326 suggests that the centre of gravity of Ypres clothmaking had shifted to the suburbs. Two thirds of all textile cloth-related craftsmen who could be identified lived in the suburbs with strong concentrations in the south (St Michael), north (Brielen) and west (Holy Cross). The easterly suburb of St John seems to have been less characterised by cloth manufacturing. If we isolate cloth weavers and fullers, the shift to the suburb was even more important. All but a few fullers lived and worked in the suburbs, as did 71 per cent of all weavers. Although weavers and fullers were both well represented in what seems to have been the suburb most touched by cloth manufacture, St Michael, fullers seem also to have been active in the northern suburb (downstream of the Ieperleet river), while weavers seem to have preferred the westerly St Kruis suburb. Cloth finishing, on the other hand, was not particularly developed in the suburbs, perhaps to facilitate control in the inner city and also because proximity to water was less an issue.

In the inner city the impact of cloth manufacture in 1325 was completely different. The occupational data show that there was still a significant number of weavers, distributed evenly across the urban fabric, but fullers had been clearly pushed out to the suburbs, and only a few remained within the thirteenth-century city walls. Fulling required proximity to water, but water was also widely available in the inner city, near the Ieperleet and the canals that were dug in the westerly districts. Fulling, of course, involved polluting activities, but whether this was the reason for moving fulleries to the suburbs seems uncertain. Also, dyers both required water and were involved in noxious procedures. Dyeing and shearing remained, however, a typical activity for the inner city, that did not seem to have been expanded much in the suburbs. All this, of course, needs to be considered with great caution. It is primarily a suggestion of trends, rather than hard evidence, because the 1325-1326 taxation touched only part of the population (and we do not know exactly who was involved, but for the fact that the whole urban fabric is mentioned) and, therefore, we can identify only some occupations.

Table 3.3. Occupational analysis, tax roll 1325-1366: textile occupations

	AVERAGE CONTRIBUTION IN D.FLEMISH	TOTAL TEXTILE OCCUPATIONS	DRAPIER	WEAVER	FULLER	SHEARER	DYER	OTHER	LINEN WEAVER
Inner City									
Market		0							
SW	22,7	9		4	1	1	1		2
NW	17,3	9	1	4	1	1		1	1
NE	32	3		1			1	1	
SE	18,7	9		4		3			2
Unknown	60	1	1						
Total Inner City		31	2	13	2	5	2	2	5
Suburbs									
W	56,5	17	3	11	3				
N	26	14		7	6				1
E	18	2			2				
S	23,1	27	1	14	10	1	1		
Total Suburbs		60	4	32	21	1	1	0	1
City Total		91	6	45	23	6	3	2	6

City Walls and Social Segregation

If the trend towards moving the principal stages of cloth manufacture, weaving and fulling, out to the suburbs around 1300 is correct, then a kind of division of industrial activity gradually took place, whereby cloth manufacture itself was done outside the walls (from 1326 within the defensive perimeter of the *uuterste vesten*) and cloth finishing remained largely within the thirteenth-century urban nucleus. The preparation of wool must have been distributed across the whole urban territory, but as these production stages involved a lot of female labour for washing and spinning wool (wool beating was a male occupation), and the tax list of 1325-1326 indicates that single women tended to live in the inner city more than in the suburbs, this input of cheap and female labour was probably slightly concentrated in the inner city itself.

Weavers were very much inclined to organise their workshops in the suburbs. This leaves the question whether industrial entrepreneurship in textile manufacture, which was concentrated in the pivotal figure of the clothier (*drapier*), moved along to the suburbs. As we shall see in the following chapters, Ypres was more rigid than the other Flemish cloth cities in excluding occupations such as those of fullers and dyers from becoming *drapiers*. In theory entrepreneurship in cloth manufacture could be exercised by all citizens, with or without direct links to one of the manufacturing stages. But because of their skill and the possibility of entrepreneurial control, once access to investment capital became possible, some textile occupations were privileged in this respect. The central position of weavers in the manufacturing process gave them an advantage, and in Ypres their pivotal position was strengthened because the statutes of the cloth industry forbade other crucial manufacturing stages from entering the coordinating entrepreneurial activity as clothiers. We are not well informed about the clothiers in the tax assessment of 1325-1326. Here the link with the banishments cannot be used, because these mention only guild-organised occupations such as weavers and fullers, rather than non-guild-organised entrepreneurship. Yet the tax list itself contains some indications: in six cases a person is described as a *drapier*, two taxpayers in the inner city and four in the suburbs (three in the western and one in the southern suburb). Again, this is only circumstantial evidence, but it suggests a trend, which is corroborated, of course, by the relative higher tax assessments in the suburbs than in most districts in the inner city. It seems, therefore, that from the second half of the thirteenth century until at least the middle of the fourteenth the suburbs not only accommodated a substantial proportion of the textile workers, but they also became places where textile entrepreneurship itself was concentrated. As a result, cloth entrepreneurs in the suburbs were even visually separated from mercantile capital within the walls.

Very soon after the construction of the outer ditch, however, the functional division between the inner city and the suburbs must have come under intense pressure. When the output of the Ypres cloth industry started to decline, unemployment must have risen and the attraction of the city to newcomers diminished. As a result, Ypres' population declined sharply in the 1330s and 1340s, and there would be no recovery in the

Figure 3.3 The siege of Ypres in 1383 (map by Guillaume du Tielt, 1610) © Yper Museum, nr. SM 3185.

latter part of the fourteenth century. Most other large Flemish cities experienced similar problems in this period. The decline of textile manufacture could, however, be partly compensated for by the development of a differentiated economy in Bruges from the middle of the fourteenth century, geared towards the production of consumer goods, luxuries and fashion, or by the strategic position in regional trade flows in Ghent and Douai. These two cities, because of their institutional hold on their hinterland, became crucial commercial players in the river basins of the Scheldt, Leie, Scarpe and Dender in this period. Lille also profited from its rich agricultural hinterland. In Ypres, the increase in central functions must have occurred as well, but these central functions could not stabilise the city's population, which had grown artificially because of the textile boom in the previous centuries. Social unrest, revolt and continuous friction between the city elites and the textile workers, with the position of the urban clothiers at the heart of these struggles, were the inevitable result.[154]

---

154 See chapter 9.

In the process, the steady depopulation in both the inner city and the suburbs could not be stopped. How this affected the allocation of textile manufacture in the urban fabric is, sadly, not known. A map representing the siege of 1383 but made, probably with the use of older cartographic materials, only in 1610 is not very informative about the organisation of habitation and industrial activity in the suburbs (or in the inner city for that matter). Some elements on the map seem to be mere fantasy (hydrographic situation, size of the suburbs, the representation of buildings), while other elements have some truthful relationship with the actual situation (the loose habitation along the main thoroughfares).[155] Archaeological evidence suggests that the functional division between the inner city and the suburbs was maintained to a certain extent throughout the fourteenth century, however. Structural adaptation to the population decline did not happen gradually; therefore, it was enforced suddenly. In 1383 the suburbs and the outer ditch were abandoned, and all habitation and industrial activity were concentrated again in the inner city. Gradual depopulation had provided the necessary space for such a deliberate intervention in the urbanism of Ypres.

During the Ghent war of 1379-1385 Ypres was at the centre of the political turmoil. The guild-organised workers, mostly weavers and fullers, sympathised with the Ghent cause against Count Louis de Male, and chronicler Olivier van Dixmude clearly located the commoners of Ypres in the suburbs. When the Ghent militia tried to conquer Ypres in September 1379, they were assisted by the Ypres commoners who, under the command of their *hoofdman* (chief), Jacob van der Berst. came to the Ypres market 'from all sides from outside the gates' to help the Ghent troops. Van der Berst was named warden of the city afterwards.[156] The commoners' victory was short-lived, and quickly the city elites, with the help of the other guilds, were able to regain their position of power in the city. But the balance of power in the county shifted continually, and when the Bruges militia were defeated by the Ghent troops of Philip of Artevelde in May 1382, the guilds again had the upper hand, to lose it again after the defeat of Ghent by the French royal army at Westrozebeke. A military and political stalemate followed the Ghent defeat. English troops invaded under the command of Henry le Despenser, Bishop of Norwich, the county of Flanders to loosen the French hold. They were promptly assisted by the remains of the Ghent militia and started to lay siege to Ypres. The elitist city government remained loyal to the count and decided to abandon the outer ditch. It succeeded in resisting the attacks of the English, who abandoned the siege on 8 August.

During the siege the suburbs were destroyed completely, either by the Ypres defenders themselves or by the English troops. Three years later, in October 1386, the King of France, Charles VI, undoubtedly inspired by his uncle, Duke Philip the Bold of Burgundy, the new Count of Flanders after the death of his father-in-law Louis de Male in 1384, forbade the suburbs from being rebuilt and ordered all inhabitants to

---

55 Vannieuwenhuyze, 'Reading History Maps', 292-321, based primarily on the unpublished work by Marieke M. Moerman, *Diepgaande analyse van twee Ieperse kaarten: het stadsplan van Thévelin-Destrée (1564) ende gravure over het beleg van Ieper van Guillaume du Tielt (1610)*. (Ghent: unpublished Master's thesis Ghent University, 2010).
56 Van Dixmude, *Merkwaerdige gebeurtenissen*, 2-3, cited in Mus, 'Het beleg', 24-25.

relocate to the inner city or move to neighbouring settlements. What was left of the outer ditch of 1325-1326 was abandoned and destroyed. Instead, the thirteenth-century walls were rebuilt at great cost to the urban finances.[157] The prohibition on rebuilding the suburbs was linked by contemporaries to the rebellious nature of the craftsmen who had lived there. In the inner city they thought control of such unruly masses of textile workers would be easier. Whether this was the real reason is not certain. It was certainly not the only reason. The destruction of the outer wards was, of course, also a symbolic way of punishing the revolt, considered as lèse-majesté to the authority of the king, and destruction was a typical reaction to any breach of royal (and comital) power.[158] Moreover, despite its symbolic and political impact, the reduction of Ypres to its mid-thirteenth-century core was to a certain extent also a sensible urbanistic decision. Population decline must have created huge gaps in the urban fabric in the inner city and the habitation in the suburbs must have become fragmented as well. Ypres in the 1360s and 1370s, with its declining population in a huge urban territory, must have looked very much like a rural place. Concentrating habitation in the inner city also restored Ypres' urban nature.

The consequences were, however, considerable. The parish churches of St Michiel and St Kruis had already been demolished in 1384 and an urban ordinance in 1391 specified the royal decree further: all houses were to be destroyed, except those along Rolleweg, to the northeast of the city, but bleach installations and urban cloth frames were still allowed, with their watchhouses and a place where the guard of the frames could live. The craftsmen had been driven away, but business had to continue. Thus, the destruction of the suburbs had, of course, serious implications for the various social groups in urban society. The elites (and the urban religious and charitable institutions) all probably lost some of the rental income they had received from the once densely populated suburbs, yet some of these losses were probably compensated for by rental income from land that was put to agricultural use and from the migration of the inhabitants of the four suburbs into the inner city, which was repopulated. In fact, what we probably see is a process of densification of a declining population in the inner city and, as a result of this process, also the opportunity for landlords to obtain speculative profits. The rental income of, for example, St John's hospital in Ypres from plots of land in the inner city increased after 1383 and the city itself saw its rental income increase as well. Urbanistic interventions, such as breaking open cul-de-sac streets or organising or constructing new connecting alleys, had to solve the problems caused by this greater population density.[159] Moreover, as the households of industrial workers tended to be much smaller than those in middle class or elite families, the nature of living units (large and small houses, apartments, etc.) had to be adapted as well.[160] Paradoxically, despite its overall declining population, Ypres had in the late fourteenth century quite rapidly to adapt its street pattern to acute population pressures. Contemporary observers also

---

157 Mus, 'Het beleg', 27-30.
158 Boone, 'Destroying and Reconstructing the City', 163-186.
159 Mus, 'Het beleg', 32.
160 For the well documented Italian cities see, for instance, Franceschi, 'Famille et travail', 105-108. See also for Flanders: Stabel, *De kleine stad*.

noticed that, because the size of the population in the suburbs was greater than that of the inner city (and certainly by 1325 there are indications that this was indeed the case), a part of the suburban population was even forced to move to neighbouring towns and villages (Langemark, Wervik, Comines, Warneton, Mesen, Belle and Nieuwkerke are mentioned, all of them centres of urban or rural cloth manufacture). Whether a true exodus of craftsmen occurred is less certain. Cloth output experienced a 200 per cent increase in Wervik and Langemark at the end of the century, but cloth manufacture in Langemark was relatively modest, while Wervik woollens, one of the popular export commodities in the trade of Tuscan merchants, were already experiencing a boom before the Ghent revolt and there is no evidence of a direct link with the demise of the Ypres suburbs. It is striking that the production in the surrounding villages, most notably in Nieuwkerke, did not increase significantly in this period.[161] How important this emigration of skilled craftsmen was can, therefore, not be acknowledged. Inter-urban migration was a permanent characteristic of a dense urban network such as the one in the county of Flanders, so probably the phenomenon was not so exceptional, and certainly it was not a fundamental cause of the further decline in the Ypres cloth industry, as is sometimes stated by scholars.[162]

Most incoming craftsmen, usually weavers and fullers (and other polluting craftsmen like tanners), must have settled in the city, therefore. For weavers there were few problems. Most town houses were suited to accommodate workshops with broadlooms on the ground floor. Yet, more complex workshops with more than one broadloom probably required already large dwellings, so they also required much more capital. In 1325 weavers in the inner city seem to have lived primarily in the southern and western districts, less so in the northeast quadrant around Diksmuidestraat and Torhoutstraat. The northwest district around Boterstaat, Vleeshouwerstraat, Elverdingestraat and Boezingestraat became associated with the weaver's trade, while the southwestern quadrant along the Ieperleet with its constant water supply became the preferred zone for fulling. The rental income of Ypres' almshouses and hospitals show the presence of fulleries on the west bank of the Ieperleet, south of the friary of the Dominicans and the comital *Zaalhof*, and the presence of new streets as a result of their arrival in exactly this period: again, a paradoxical dynamic urbanism in a period of declining population. But fullers are also documented in the weaver's district in the northwest quadrant.[163]

The 'Marshy Meadow'

The demise of the Ypres suburbs after 1383 offered archaeologists the ideal opportunity to investigate a medieval textile area. The area south of the Lille Gate, the most southerly suburb of St Michiel, was never again occupied. Its marshy nature, cut across

---

61 Despite only flimsy evidence of a mass emigration of Ypres cratsmen, Van der Meulen (*Woven into the urban fabric*, forthcoming, chapter 4) maintains this traditional image.
62 Stabel, *Dwarfs among Giants*, 127-134 and id., 'Composition et recompositions des réseaux urbains', 29-64. For the impact on the Ypres cloth industry see Mus, *De Geschiedenis*, 48-50.
63 Mus, 'Het beleg', 37-40.

by brooks and canals, prevented its intensive agricultural use. Moreover, bleach fields and cloth frames were better suited to dry land, so the area did not have many new uses. Even the late seventeenth-century Vauban fortifications of the city used it as a flood zone. So, when in the 1990s archaeologists excavated a part of what is now commonly called *Verdronken Weide* ('Marshy Meadow'), they found parts of an almost undisturbed fourteenth-century industrial suburb. The excavation took place in the centre of the suburb of St Michiel. This was not only one of the suburbs of the quintessential cloth city of Flanders; it constituted, if we consider the taxation of 1325-1326, also the quintessential textile neighbourhood in medieval Ypres. The suburbs boasted all kinds of textile occupation, among them a dyer, a shearer, but above all high numbers of weavers and fullers.

The archaeological findings corroborate this picture. Although traces of the cloth industry are very difficult to pinpoint archaeologically, in the *Verdronken Weide* site they are obvious. As the current toponym already indicates, the St Michiel suburb lay in marshy land on both sides of the Ieperleet. Various canals and brooks cut through the area, offering difficult terrain for housing, but giving textile artisans plenty of opportunity to use the water resources for their manufacturing processes. The fullers clearly made use of this natural advantage. The statutes of *c*. 1363 tried to regulate the inevitable pollution caused by such concentrated fulling activity and speak of a 'fuller's brook' (*vulresbeik*) and various brooks in its vicinity that needed to be cleared at regular times by the fullers who lived there. Fullers were not allowed to throw their waste into the water.[164] This does not, however, mean that all economic activity in the suburb was necessarily related to cloth manufacture. Traces of leather industries, another sector that required a lot of water, have also been found.

The excavations covered a substantial area on both sides of the Komenseweg (road to Comines), together with the equally densely populated Rijselseweg (road to Lille), one of two central axes in the suburb, and a stretch of land along the main branch of the Ieperleet, upstream from the inner city.[165] The building pattern along these thoroughfares is surprisingly open. The houses were detached and built on a relatively important plot of land. Most artisans in the suburb also lived and worked in separate buildings, and only occasionally does the workshop seem to have been part of a larger and more complex house with annexes. The material culture found in or near these houses was representative of the lower middle classes. The material culture of artisans was quite diverse (toys, tools, ceramics, furniture, clothing, etc.), which fits with recent evaluations of late medieval urban material culture.[166] Three different types of buildings seem to be present along the Komenseweg and the Ieperleet. There were wooden constructions dating back to the third quarter of the thirteenth century, wooden constructions on sandstone or limestone foundations with central ash-pots

---

[164] Espinas and Pirenne, *Recueil*, 3, 576, mentioned in Van Bellingen et al., 'De verdwenen Sint-Michielswijk', 261.
[165] No complete survey of the excavations and the archaeological findings yet exists. Useful information can be found in Dewilde and Van Bellingen, 'Excavating a Surburb of Medieval Ypres', 57-72 and in various archaeological reports published in the open archive of the Flemish Organisation for Immovable Heritage: https://oar.onroerenderfgoed.be.
[166] Smail, *Legal Plunder*; Stabel, *A Capital of Fashion*.

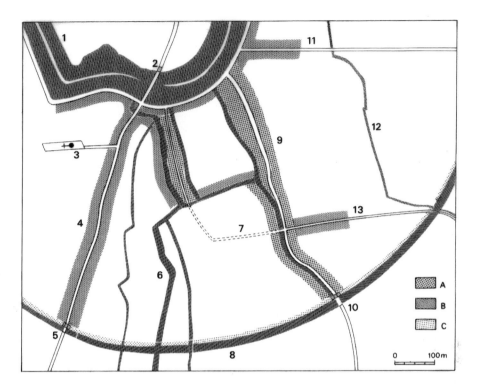

Figure 3.4 Reconstruction of the spatial organisation in the suburb of St Michiel (© Marc Dewilde & Stephan Van Bellingen – Vlaamse Overheid, Agentschap Onroerend Erfgoed).

from the late thirteenth century and half-timbered constructions on brick bases and with brick central fireplaces from the first half of the fourteenth century. These various construction phases are evidence of a very dynamic and changing habitation. It is unclear from the current state of research which artisanal functions can be linked to the individual houses. The sizes of the workshops (separate or linked to the house) fitted, for example, the installation of a broadloom, or sometimes even allowed two broadlooms within the same space (a fourteenth-century workshop at Komenseweg even had a length of no less than 14.8m and was lavishly decorated; another house measured 23m).

Many of the workshops were relatively open constructions, so it is not certain that they would have accommodated weaving activities. The identification of workshops is, however, difficult. Pits or troughs lined with wood can perhaps be linked to fulling activities or to the washing of wool (or fulled cloth). Many objects refer directly to cloth manufacture, but these objects cannot always be linked to specific workshops: iron spikes from wool combs were found, fragments of a shuttle of a horizontal loom, loom weights for fixing warp yarns, even a perforated beam of wood, probably stemming from a frame to stretch the finished woollens. Furthermore, many leaden cloth seals were found. Thistles point to cloth-finishing activities and there were even botanical traces of

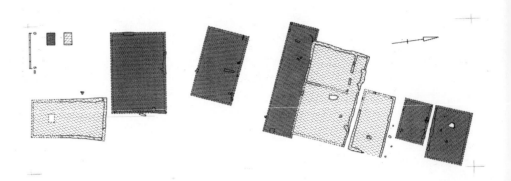

Figure 3.5 Excavation plan of houses and workshops along the Komenseweg (© Marc Dewilde & Stephan Van Bellingen – Vlaamse Overheid, Agentschap Onroerend Erfgoed): light grey area: house, dark grey area: possible workshop.

weld (used as a yellow dyestuff), which would suggest dyeing activities (perhaps in one of the kilns found during the excavations).

Until a more systematic investigation of the *Verdronken Weide* excavations is published, the fragmented findings clearly point to the fact that the suburb of St Michiel was indeed a hotspot for cloth manufacture. All stages from the initial treatment of wool (combing) through weaving to fulling and cloth finishing are documented archaeologically and took place within the same space. There are no indications of spatial concentration of activities in this part of the suburb. Although the proximity of water probably favoured the settlement of fullers, real and unequivocal evidence of fulleries has not yet been identified, although the presence of washing troughs points in that direction, as does the presence of fullers' seals. The only stages of production that could not be traced in the suburb are shearing and dyeing (the botanical presence of weld is only circumstantial evidence and no real proof of the presence of dyers in the neighbourhood). We saw earlier that shearers and dyers seem to have resided for preference in the inner city, although isolated craftsmen were also present in St Michiel.

Towards a Post-Industrial City?

After the integration of the artisans from the suburbs into the inner city, it is less clear how the ever-shrinking industry adapted itself to its new urban environment of dense housing and cramped streets. No large-scale excavations of industrial neighbourhoods in the inner city have been undertaken. The set of censuses, used by Henri Pirenne in his ground-breaking article of 1903 discussed in chapter 2, reveal only a precious few indications of the territorial impact of textile production on the urban fabric.[167] The censuses were probably preparatory documents used for the organisation of direct taxation. They list household size, the number of men that could be used for the city's defence, in the case of the 1431 census also the occupations, or in 1491 the stocks of grain in the city.[168] Although Pirenne had been able to trace the social and even the occupational composition of the city, he did not include the geographical dimension in his analysis. The censuses were organised in each of the four districts and they also listed the streets in which each household lived. Pirenne decided not to include in his article how the households were distributed across the urban landscape, and because the sources were lost in 1914 this information has been permanently lost.

Fifteenth-century Ypres was formally divided into four quarters, probably resembling the four quadrants in which we divided the tax register: the quarter of the *Poorterie* (bourgeoisie), the quarter of the *Draperie* or *Weifambochte* (weaver's guild), the quarter of the *Vulres* (fullers) and the quarter of the *Ghemeene Neringhe* (the common crafts or the small crafts). On 17 July 1389, after the destruction of the suburbs, a clause was added to the fullers' statutes that fullers were henceforth allowed to rinse fulled cloth in the Ieperleet (*in dYpre*), but that they needed to rinse the cloth afterwards in a trough of clean water, suggesting that the water of the Ieperleet itself was not clean enough for the guild.[169] The division clearly also reflected the various social groups competing for political power in the city (bourgeois and *poortersneringhen*, wealthier crafts linked to the bourgeoisie such as butchers, fishmongers, dyers, silversmiths, cloth finishers and mercers, the two major textile guilds of weavers and fullers, and the small crafts, a heterogeneous group of various manufacturing and retailing guilds), divisions that were used to distribute power in the various political bodies of the city (for example in the *Great Council*).[170] But in the fifteenth-century censuses the direct link to social status and occupational organisation was lost, and each of the four quarters had clearly become a territorial organisation, headed by a *hoofdman* (chief).[171] Probably the name was derived from the dominant trade in each of the quarters (after 1383?), yet in the fifteenth century the quarters seem already to be very mixed. As we shall see, the quarter of the 'small crafts' was in the 1430s also dominated by textile trades.

One of the striking features of the censuses is that they show Ypres in the early fifteenth century as a city with an extremely high number of single households. As early as in the 1325-1326 tax register the inner city had been characterised by a substantial number of single women, probably earning a living from retail and textile work (mostly in the preparatory stages of wool treatment), but their share had certainly not decreased in 1412: more than one fifth of all households were single (and more than one fifth was also composed of two people, probably mostly young couples). So we find a very young city, still offering work opportunities probably to singles and households

---

167 Pirenne, 'Les dénombrements', 1-32.
168 Pirenne did not have the registers for each section of the city at each time, so the lists were some kind of jigsaw with various gaps in them (Pirenne, 'Les dénombrements', 7-10).
169 Espinas and Pirenne, *Recueil*, 3, 580.
170 Trio, 'Bestuursinstellingen', 343-344.
171 Trio, 'Bestuursinstellingen', 345.

Table 3.4. Occupations in Ypres in 1431 (Quarter of Ghemeene Neeringhe) and Bruges in 1436 (guild militia lists)

Data from Pirenne, 'Les dénombrements', 23-27 and Stabel, *A Capital of Fashion*, forthcoming.

	MEN	WOMEN	BRUGES 1436
N	539	165	
Textiles	54.0%	43.6%	17.3%
Trade and transport	8.9%	3.6%	11.5%
Food	5.6%	9.1%	10.3%
Government and church	5.2%	0.0%	
Clothing	5.0%	12.1%	26.4%
Construction	4.8%	0.0%	12.5%
Various	4.1%	1.8%	0.7%
Durables	6.7%	1.2%	13.4%
Unskilled	3.0%	27.9%	
Leather	2.8%	0.6%	

starting up. Fifteenth-century Ypres is often described in terms of economic decay, yet despite the shrinking numbers of craftsmen and the ever-worsening position of Ypres cloth on international markets, the demographics of early fifteenth-century Ypres point not only to a diminished population, but also to a city still very much characterised by industrial labour and the job opportunities this implied. Half of all singles were, moreover, women, more or less like the c. 10 per cent of female-led households in 1325 (and almost 13 per cent in the inner city at that time).[172] By 1431 Ypres' demographic composition had changed, however, and the city had only 11 per cent of singles, half of them women (and the share of young two-person households had decreased). So, if job opportunities for starters still existed in the early fifteenth century, they must gradually have disappeared from the late 1420s. The average household size in every quarter also rose from 3.2/3.4 in 1412 to 4/4.3 in the late fifteenth and early sixteenth centuries, a trend which resembles those in more diversified urban economies in Flanders.[173] So the dominance of textiles in the city seems to have gradually diminished and, instead of a primarily industrial city, Ypres was on its way to becoming a more normal regional servicing centre. The declining number of singles suggests that the loss of industrial jobs was not yet compensated for, however, by a proliferation of servicing industries and retail.

In 1412 most people in the quarter of the *Ghemeene Neringhe* were still involved in textiles. The traditional cloth industry still employed more than half of the population, and probably the quarter of the 'small crafts' was slightly less characterised by textiles than, for example, the quarters of the weavers and the fullers. Differences between Ypres

---

172 Stabel, 'Working Alone?', 27-49.
173 Pirenne, 'Les dénombrements', 368-369; Stabel, *De kleine stad*, 69-75.

and Bruges are telling. In Bruges only a minority of the all-male craftsmen (for Bruges the figures indicate the share of each guild in the urban economy) were involved in textiles, while the city's success as a centre for fashion, luxuries and durable consumer goods can be acknowledged in the important share of guilds active in these sectors of the urban economy. In Ypres, the figures relating to the 'small crafts' neighbourhood demonstrate that the overall importance of those small crafts, and therefore of the production and trade in durable consumer goods, dress, luxuries and even food industries, is much less than in a diversified commercial economy such as the one in Bruges.

The Ypres data also allow a gendered analysis of labour markets. Both working men and women were primarily involved in textile manufacture. Women were also very much active in clothing (as laundresses or seamstresses; the guild-organised occupations of tailor or second-hand clothes dealer were exclusively male) and food (again not in guild-organised sectors like butchers, bakers, brewers etc.; but in the non-organised retail jobs of selling fruit and vegetables, dairy produce and pastries). Women were particularly active as unskilled workers in Ypres: 28 per cent of all women with registered occupations were called *wercwijf* (working woman) vis-à-vis a probably very unreliable 3 per cent of all men who were called 'worker'.[174] The Ypres censuses make it abundantly clear that domestic personnel were very numerous (albeit probably less numerous in an industrial city like Ypres than in trading cities) and usually integrated into the household. A later list in Ypres, dating from 1506, mentions 126 living-in female servants (*joncwijven*) and 98 living-in male servants (*cnapen*) or a total of 10 per cent of the population at that time. But more likely, the substantial proportion of single women in Ypres who were listed as 'working women' provided a floating workforce that could also be integrated into the formal guild economy, whenever required, probably also in textile-related occupations.

The textile occupations in the *Ghemene Neringhe* point to the overwhelming dominance of weavers, both clothiers or *drapiers* (who were usually weavers) and the so-called *conventers*, master weavers who worked for the clothiers. There are also a significant number of fullers, but these may be atypical. It is very likely that the 'small crafts' quarters lay in the eastern part of the city, away from water. It is not surprising, therefore, that the district had only a few fulleries. Only four master fullers were listed, but no fewer than 44 journeymen fullers lived in the quarter. We can assume that most of these journeymen worked in the more numerous fulleries in the western districts where access to water was much easier because of the course of the Ieperleet. The more difficult access to water did not, however, prevent dyers from setting up business in this district: five dyers of blue (using woad) with 12 journeyman, five dyers of red (using madder or the more expensive grain) with eight journeymen, and an additional two journeymen dyers were living in the neighbourhood. Also, shearers and cloth finishers

---

[74] The word 'pinere', which literally means 'he who makes the effort (of working)', is used in the sources. In most cities the 'piners' had the much narrower meaning of 'carriers', which constituted a privileged group of workers monopolising the internal transport of bulk goods in the city or having a monopoly of working in the urban port infrastructure.

Table 3.5. Textile Occupations in Ypres 1431 (*Ghemeine Neeringhe*) and of new Bruges citizens (fifteenth century)

	Men	Women	Bruges 15th c.
N	285	71	
Drapers	23.2%	4.2%	
Spinning	0.0%	90.1%	
wool preparation	1.1%	1.4%	
Weavers	40.4%	0.0%	24.6%
Fullers	16.8%	0.0%	18.6%
Dyers	11.2%	0.0%	21.0%
Shearers and finishers	6.0%	1.4%	16.2%
Cleaning	0.4%	1.4%	
linen weaving	1.1%	1.4%	13.8%

are obvious (three cloth finishers, 11 master shearers with two journeymen and one woman active as a shearer, probably a master's widow).

A comparison with Bruges is equally revealing. Data here are for the listed occupations of new citizens (citizenship was, as in Ypres, required for entry into the guild system).[175] Bruges since the middle of the fourteenth century had no longer been a typical textile city, yet textiles were still present, more so even at the end of the fifteenth century when a great number of say weavers acquired citizenship. But even then, weavers in Bruges were much less numerous than in Ypres. It was dyers and cloth finishers (above all shearers) who could find employment in Bruges, while the number of fullers can also be compared with that in Ypres (although the 'small crafts' district may be atypical in this respect). So, if Ypres was in 1430 still a quintessential cloth-manufacturing city, Bruges entrepreneurs had clearly started to specialise in cloth finishing and craftsmen probably dyed and finished woollens that were brought to the city from elsewhere.

The 'small crafts' data also show that the guild-dominated stages of production (from weaving to cloth finishing) were clearly exclusively male, while wool preparation (except for the guild-organised beating of wool) was almost exclusively female. Although Pirenne's data do not allow this to be checked, probably the only women involved in guild-organised activities were widows, who continued the workshops of their deceased husbands. The high number of spinsters is very striking, if we consider that only a minority of the households were identified with their occupational activity: more than 90 per cent of all women in textiles were spinsters (and most of them must have been single women). Some women were also active in linen weaving and in burling the finished woollens (*nopster*), but they were very few. Strikingly, as well as the

---

175 Stabel, *A Capital of Fashion*.

low-status and poorly-paid jobs in the preparation of wool, women also seem to have been active as clothiers (*drapierigghe*), the entrepreneurs who coordinated the various stages of production,. Although the presence of widows may have been substantial in this category too, women's favourable juridical position in the cities of the county of Flanders allowed them to be active as merchants and entrepreneurs without much juridical interference from (male) third parties.[176] Some unmarried single women must, therefore, have taken up this opportunity and become involved in the most lucrative trade in the cloth cities. They were, however, not very numerous. The low figure of merely three female clothiers vs. 66 men proves this. In a cloth-manufacturing city like Ypres the bulk of occupations carried out by single women consisted of the preparation of wool and yarn for the weavers and dyers. Many single women in cloth cities were probably spinning most of the time or used spinning to supplement other sources of income in retail. At the other side of the social divide, a few women probably succeeded, thanks to existing networks of relatives or available capital, in becoming entrepreneurs themselves and in joining the ranks of the economic or financial elite of the city, which consisted of merchants, financiers and drapers.

Conclusions

The impact of the cloth industry on the urban social fabric in Ypres can be studied only with great difficulty. Sources do not do much more than present us with circumstantial evidence, even if Ypres is one of the few medieval cities where a textile neighbourhood has recently been excavated. But despite the difficult sources a picture emerges, nonetheless. It is a picture of extreme dynamism. In the growing city, gradually spatial specialisation emerged. There is little doubt that the industry was initially organised in the inner city. In the southwest and around the market square natural conditions favoured textile production. Water was available via the Ieperleet which crossed the city from south to north, and various canals were dug to protect the urban nucleus or to drain excessive water from the site. But it seems that as the industry and the city grew textile manufacture moved out of the inner city, probably because of the more abundant availability of land and proximity to water for some trades such as the fullers who were dependent upon water supply. It was transferred to the suburbs, which grew at faster rates and around 1300 must have surpassed the inner city as the main nucleus for industrial labour.

Despite difficulties of interpretation, in the first half of the fourteenth century, even when the industry went through a difficult reorganisation and many textile workers found themselves condemned to structural unemployment, a division of labour seems to have been imposed. The main activities of cloth manufacture, weaving and fulling were primarily organised in the suburbs (mainly the southern, western and northern suburbs, it seems) along with other economic activities that required easy access to water or where fire hazard made a location in less densely populated areas safer (leather,

---

176 See, for example, for the cloth city of Ghent Hutton, *Women and Economic Activities* and Nicholas, *The Domestic Life*.

metal). Most other textile activities seem to have been organised primarily in the inner city, and this is true even for the capital-intensive dyers (who, like the fullers, required a steady water supply and caused some degree of pollution). Also, shearers seem to have been active primarily in the city centre and, even more surprisingly, the poorly paid women active in spinning and other stages of the preparation of wool and yarn also seem to have lived and worked primarily in the inner city.

In 1383 everything changed. The forced destruction of the suburbs during the English (and Ghent) siege and Philip the Bold's subsequent ban on reconstructing the suburbs forced weavers and fullers and all other trades active in the suburbs to move into the inner city. In the meantime, the Ypres cloth industry had declined further, and just before the destruction of the suburbs Ypres must have looked like a sparsely populated city, both inside the thirteenth-century walls and in the suburbs. Archaeological research has shown that there was loose and open habitation along the main thoroughfares in the southern suburb of St Michiel. The forced removal increased the density of the urban population in the inner city. Ypres remained, however, a quintessential textile city, offering employment to many craftsmen, but also to many (single) women. Fullers seem to have been relocated primarily to the southwest along the west bank of the Ieperleet. Weavers were numerous in the northwest quarter, but industrial workers seem to have been distributed over the whole urban territory. Even in the quarter of the 'small crafts', which took its name from the presence of the small guilds, textile workers constituted more than half of the population, and in the real textile quarters of the weavers and fullers this share was probably even higher. Only from the middle of the fifteenth century is it likely that this impact of cloth manufacture declined more strongly. A century later, Ypres would become a typical regional centre and lose its dominant industrial features.

Finally, the data on the composition of the Ypres population also give us information about the place of entrepreneurs and merchants in the urban fabric. Ypres in the first half of the fourteenth century was a highly polarised city, with the mercantile and landowning elites living in the city centre in and around the central market square, close to political power and commercial infrastructure in the majestic cloth hall of the city. For the cloth entrepreneurs, those who supervised and coordinated the successive production stages, this seems less obvious. We will see in the next chapter how clothiers, or *drapiers* as they are called in the sources, an enigmatic blend of bourgeois and craftsmen (in Ypres mainly weavers with access to capital), became the pivotal group in industrial organisation. They constituted a new middle class above the normal craftsmen, but dependent also on mercantile capital. The tax list of 1325 clearly suggests that many of those clothiers moved to the suburbs together with the craftsmen they controlled. As a result, the suburbs held the real middle class in Ypres society, and average tax assessments in most suburbs tended to be substantially higher than in the poor and lower-middle-class neighbourhoods of the inner city. In 1383 the *drapiers* moved along with the craftsmen to the inner city and seem to have dispersed themselves all over the urban fabric.

CHAPTER 4

The Boinebrokes of Ypres

Cloth and Mercantile Capital

In April 1277 11 merchants from Ypres, men who called themselves 'merchant-clothiers' (*marchands drapiers*), among them many members of the about 30 elite families that also supplied most of the aldermen of the city in this period, the Belle, de Rijcke, Van Acker and Falais families, wrote a document stating that they rented from the abbey of Lagny, for a yearly sum of £70 tournois, a building with appendant houses and galleries (*voultes*) and with infrastructure that would accommodate their commercial purposes. They would use the building as a cloth hall, a hall where the woollens from Ypres that they had taken along to sell at the Fairs of Champagne, would be stored and presented to potential customers. The lease would last for a period covering the following ten fairs. Lagny-sur-Marne was one of the four towns, the others being Troyes, Bar-sur-Aube and Provins, belonging to the famous cycle of fairs in the Champagne region. It was the meeting place for all merchants exchanging goods, money and information between Northwest Europe and Southern Europe. It was here that Italian, Iberian and Provençal traders met with their counterparts from France, England, the Empire and with many merchants from the cities of Flanders and Artois who brought their woollens to exchange them for Mediterranean luxury goods, silks and spices. The commercial space that the Ypres merchants rented was already called the 'hall of Ypres', so this lease was probably not the first one. The lease also indicates that even in Lagny, not the most prominent of the Champagne fairs, the sales of Ypres cloth were such that a separate commercial space was found necessary.

The 11 merchants did not act on their own; they spoke on behalf of the 'community of merchant-clothiers from Ypres visiting the fairs of Champagne' (*pour toute le communité des marchans drappiers d'Ypre frequentans les foires de Champaigne*).[177] One of the clauses said that the rent would not be paid by the Ypres merchants if the 'merchants of the Seventeen Cities' decided in a particular year not to come to the Champagne fairs. In that case they had to give timely warning to the abbey. So, the Ypres merchants undoubtedly also considered themselves members of the Hanse of the Seventeen Cities, which assembled all merchants at the Fairs coming from several cities in Flanders, Hainaut and Artois, among them Ypres, Douai, Saint-Omer, Bruges and Ghent, the most significant cloth cities in the southern Low Countries.[178] The Hanse was a merchant guild aimed at protecting mutual business interests, at offering security

---

77 Espinas and Pirenne, *Recueil*, 3, 677-678.
78 Most literature about the Flemish merchant guilds focuses on the Flemish Hanse of London, the multi-city guild that organised wool and the cloth trade in England (Van Werveke, 'Das Wesen der flandrischen Hansen', 7-23; Wyffels, 'De Vlaamse Hanze van Londen', 7-30 and id., 'De Vlaamse Hanzen', 3-17). Specifically on the Hanse of the Seventeen Cities: Carolus-Barré, 'Les XVII villes', 20-30 and Nicholas, *Medieval Flanders*, 169 and 174-175.

to its members and representation at the fairs abroad. Traditionally Bruges merchants led the Hanse, but Ypres merchants also figured among its prominent members and, as we can see in the lease, they did not hesitate to act as a separate group as well. This was clearly a document issued by a group of traders with a great sense of self-importance. They represented a collectivity and even belonged to a greater group uniting most, if not all, merchants from the Low Countries. Their direct links with political power at home and their crucial importance for the city's main industry certainly helped to boost such confidence. As we saw in chapter 1, the Mediterranean markets were at this time still the most important outlet for Ypres woollens. So, both at home and at the fairs, they were a group to be reckoned with. Moreover, most merchants active on the Champagne fairs were also members of the Ypres section of the Flemish Hanse of London, which controlled the essential wool trade with England in most of the thirteenth century. Being a member of this Flemish Hanse was in Ypres also a necessity for gaining access to the cloth hall, so merchants often combined wool and the cloth trade, in this way also defining the conditions in which textile craftsmen could operate. Membership of the merchant guild therefore defined the social status, the economic agency and the political power of this group.

The Shadow of Boinebroke

In 1933 the French medievalist, Georges Espinas, published one of the most influential theories about the organisation of the medieval urban economy.[179] Putting one figure, the Douaisien merchant Jehan Boinebroke († 1286), at centre stage, he defined the contours of how mercantile capitalism in the thirteenth century took hold of the industrial urban networks as well, and how this entanglement gave rise to systems of economic dependence that not only shaped urban society, but also fostered the conflicts of the late thirteenth and early fourteenth centuries, when so-called 'democratic' revolutions allowed social groups that had hitherto been far removed from political and economic decision-making processes access to political and economic power: in other words no guild revolution without oppressive mercantile capital.

The story of Boinebroke is known primarily through the problems caused by his death. His will indicated that before his heirs would get access to his holdings all his remaining debts had to be cleared and loans he had provided to others had to be recovered. In a long list therefore appear his debtors and creditors, and through these relations we can reconstruct his complex business relations and other economic activities.[180] Jehan Boinebroke had been a powerful politician, an influential member of Douai's political elite, but he was also a very active businessman. His commercial network included activities in the English wool trade, but he dealt also in domestic wool. He was also active as a cloth merchant, but on a smaller scale than his commercial

---

[179] Espinas, *Les origines du capitalisme I*.
[180] The sources were published in the works by Espinas (*Les origines*) and partly also in Espinas and Pirenne, *Recueil*, 2, 184-208.

involvement in the raw materials for textile manufacture. But besides these mercantile activities abroad, Boinebroke was also very active in and around the city of Douai itself. He provided wool on credit to Douai clothiers and was involved in all kinds of credit operations inside and outside the city. He himself employed workers in the preparatory stages for wool (wool sorters and beaters) and in the finishing stages of the cloth (in the tentering frames that he owned). He also ran an important dyeing facility, where not only his own woollens, but also those of others, were dyed. There is no evidence, however, that he ever supervised cloth manufacture itself. He owned a sheep farm in the surroundings of Douai, probably to supply wool for low-quality woollen fabrics, and he possessed a lot of real property in the city. His houses were rented by the craftsmen he employed and by others.

For Georges Espinas there was little doubt. Here was the perfect example of a wealthy and all-powerful merchant who combined international business ventures with local and regional trade on the one hand and had a strong involvement in the city's cloth manufacture on the other.[181] He reached out for raw materials, wool, to England; he was active with finished woollens on various European markets. But he was primarily involved in textile manufacture itself as a clothier, someone who commissioned and supervised cloth manufacture (*faire faire draps*). And he abused his position of power, economic and political, to interfere in the daily life of his fellow townsmen. He was a landowner with real property in which his workers lived. And in various industrial operations he bound textile craftsmen to him and his business activities by various methods. Like the great Florentine merchants of the late Middle Ages, he was even active as an entrepreneur in the finishing of the woollens that were manufactured for him. He therefore owned the raw materials, the industrial products through the different production stages and the finished commodities, and, thus, the mercantile capital he commanded was entangled with manufacture itself. Jehan Boinebroke traded in raw materials, he organised or controlled textile manufacture and he traded the finished woollens across Europe. He was the ultimate merchant-entrepreneur, a leading mercantile capitalist, and but for the (limited) scale of the many industrial operations he controlled, he could have been almost a true industrial capitalist. In many respects for Espinas the rise of textile tycoons like Boinebroke lay at the 'origins of capitalism'.

Henri Pirenne had followed similar reasoning earlier. There were merchant-clothiers, *marchands-drapiers* and there were artisans, clothiers or *drapiers*, and there was a strict division between the two. The first was a capitalist, the second was someone who 'nourished the trade' of the first. The second was therefore a 'subordinate' of the first.[182] These relations changed only in the fourteenth century when the Flemish merchants lost ground on markets abroad, and foreign merchants came to the Low Countries to be supplied with woollens, at which time the skilled guild artisan became a true entrepreneur. At this time, and only from this time, the clothier became the pivotal

---

81 'Le patricien comme tel, est tout puissant : c'est la conséquence naturelle de l'union de tous les caractères, de tous les pouvoirs précédents qui s'associent et se complètent les uns les autres grâce à ses emprises diverses, il domine et tient la cité et ses habitants' (Espinas, *Les origines*, 216).

82 'Le labeur de l'un ne sert qu'à alimenter le commerce de l'autre' (Pirenne, *Les villes et les institutions*, 382, cited in Van Werveke, *De koopman-ondernemer*, 8).

figure in cloth manufacture. The dramatic change was caused by the urban revolutions of 1302 (and the surrounding years) and the subsequent rise of guild-dominated urban governments. The thirteenth-century capitalists had lost control of the situation and withdrew from a further active role in cloth manufacture itself.[183]

From the 1950s on this model of nascent mercantile capitalism and of a strong involvement of mercantile capital in urban manufacture came under increasing pressure. As more details surfaced about cloth manufacture, the figure of the late medieval clothier came to the forefront. The clothier in the cities of the Low Countries was not a merchant; he (or she) was an artisan who combined his (or her) craft with the organisation of manufacture and the work of others. He or she also bought raw materials, monitored manufacture and sold the finished textiles to merchants or other customers, but the financial scope of his or her business and the output and scope of the enterprise were much more limited than those of Pirenne's or Espinas' merchant-entrepreneur. Hans Van Werveke was the first historian to try to combine the two models of entrepreneurship.[184] Without denying the capitalist nature of merchants such as Boinebroke, or questioning the chronological development from one to the other, in his eyes there was no clear break between this merchant-entrepreneur and the clothiers who allegedly dominated cloth manufacture from about 1300. The two activities had coexisted already in earlier periods, and the chronology was much more complex than initially devised. The strong position of the merchants had in fact already been weakened from 1270, when the active involvement of Flemish merchants in the English wool trade was severely weakened by a trade conflict between the County of Flanders and the English king.[185] Other merchants, mainly Italians, rapidly filled the void. But also, the regulation of urban cloth industries from the 1250s had already weakened the impact of merchants, and this even though the urban political elites consisted in this period exclusively of mercantile and landowning elites. So, pressure from the emerging cloth guilds must have played a considerable role in this changing regulatory framework. As a result, there was a trend whereby the entanglement of mercantile capital and industrial entrepreneurship steadily faded. In Ghent the size of the industrial operations of wool merchants was limited, and in many places there came about restrictions on combining wool and the cloth trade, greatly reducing the all-encompassing hold of individual merchants on cloth manufacture.[186] Often such restrictions were linked to internal struggles for political power among the elites themselves, and sometimes such measures were also reversed. But by the end of the thirteenth century a formal separation was installed in many places between the activities of clothier and of merchant. These new regulations, however, also clearly state that there had already been clothiers before that date, so that the hold of mercantile capital on manufacture had not been complete and was implemented often only indirectly long before 1300.

---

[183] Pirenne, *Les anciennes démocraties*.
[184] Van Werveke, *De koopman-ondernemer*, 1-26.
[185] Lloyd, *The English Wool Trade*.
[186] Van Werveke, *De koopman-ondernemer*, 12-13.

Van Werveke's approach did not completely alter the Pirenne-Espinas model of the merchant-entrepreneur; it was an important addition to it. But in the 1970s the Boinebroke model itself was challenged more fundamentally.[187] In his studies of the cloth industry in medieval Saint-Omer, Alain Derville even refuted the model completely. According to him Boinebroke was a typical merchant, untouchable because of his political dominance and wealth, and used to cheating those around him and abusing his pre-eminence, but he was not a clothier or a textile entrepreneur.[188] He controlled trade flows of raw materials and finished goods, but actual textile manufacture was out of his reach. Instead, it was already the small craftsmen, the weavers, fullers, shearers and dyers, who had become the pivotal actors in textile manufacture. They were active as 'small commodity producers', and it is the artisanal workshop that stands at centre stage in late medieval (and early modern) urban economies.[189] In 1993, Jean-Pierre Sosson could only conclude with satisfaction that although Espinas' ideas were still worth considering, they had been successfully 'exorcised' by Derville and others.[190]

But some doubts remained, and the discussion did not die down. Even John Munro, who also refuted the Espinas thesis unequivocally by claiming that Boinebroke himself was no clothier and so no 'industrial capitalist' – how could he be; before the industrial revolution the essence of capitalism remained mercantile, and floating capital was dominant in business ventures – but just a wool merchant and (to a lesser extent) also a cloth merchant.[191] But still, there is indeed the inescapable fact that besides his important commercial ventures, Boinebroke had also been firmly entrenched in the manufacturing world of Douai as landowner and as entrepreneur. Although these activities did not include the crucial stages of actually making the fabrics or turning them during the fulling process into dense woollens, they did include the treatment of wool and the finishing stages of the woollens (tentering and dyeing).

More recent scholars have, therefore, returned to a more nuanced approach, very much in line with what Van Werveke had already done. Jean-Louis Roch, a specialist in Norman cloth industries, was most vocal in this new approach, stressing the fact that a mighty trade tycoon with political connections such as Boinebroke did not operate as a true clothier but was truly involved nonetheless in industrial entrepreneurship, in the finishing and dyeing of fabrics. He cannot, therefore, agree with the Derville thesis of a strict separation between commercial and industrial entrepreneurship.[192] But Boinebroke was also heavily involved in those industrial operations in which he was not himself directly involved. He swapped (processed) wool for cloth, not only with clothiers but also with other citizens of Douai, men and women. So Boinebroke is not to be considered as the equivalent of the Italian merchant-clothiers, who processed wool

---

[187] Right after its publication Guillaume Des Marez, one of Pirenne's own pupils, had already challenged the model using materials from Brussels (Billen and Boone, 'Pirenne in Brussels', 470-475).
[188] Derville, *Saint-Omer*, 215-222 and id., 'Les draperies flamandes', 538-540.
[189] DuPlessis and Howell, Duplessis, 'Reconsidering the Early Modern Urban Economy', 49-84.
[190] Sosson, 'Conclusions', in Boone and Prevenier, *Drapery Production*, 253.
[191] Munro, 'Medieval Woollens', 219.
[192] Roch, 'De la nature du drapier', 5-7 and id., *Un autre monde du travail*, 99-148.

and woollens in their large-scale *botteghe*, but nor was he a merchant who kept himself and his commercial activities away from manufacturing networks.

The question remains when, if Boinebroke is somewhere between the Espinas and Derville archetypical representations, these merchants with access to political power and a genuine involvement in industrial process appeared, and when they disappeared to make way for the clothiers, people mostly with an artisanal background, who coordinated the industrial process, or is there, continuing upon the remarks by Hans Van Werveke indeed no such succession of different economic stakeholders, no evolution or shift from one stage to another, but rather a development in which both mercantile and entrepreneurial activities followed their own chronology and coexisted for a long time.

The Boinebrokes of Ypres

Whatever the nature of Boinebroke's activities, it is beyond doubt that mercantile capital even in Ypres kept a tight hold on cloth manufacture before 1280 or even 1300, and that even in the fourteenth century the relations between cloth entrepreneurs and mercantile capital were still of the utmost importance. Before 1280, by controlling the trade in raw materials and often similarly of the finished cloth, merchants were able not only to dominate commerce, but also to define to a great extent the conditions in which manufacture took place. But did the Ypres mercantile elites also go further, did they, like Boinebroke, control also the daily life of their workers and did they actually do what clothiers are said to be doing, monitor and coordinate manufacture by systems of putting-out, and shift raw materials and half-finished goods across the chain of production?

To achieve this, merchants did not have to impose close control on manufacture itself, as was suggested by Espinas, but their influence on manufacture was achieved almost exclusively through the capital they controlled. By developing credit relations with artisans, they could impose on the cloth entrepreneurs the conditions and constraints under which the latter had to work. Whether this was achieved in a system of direct putting-out in which merchants retained direct control over some of the manufacturing stages, or through a *Kaufsystem* whereby they sold the raw materials and bought the finished commodities from the true industrial entrepreneurs, the clothiers, who themselves organised the putting out system in the manufacturing stages, does not matter much. Probably, as is suggested by the case of Boinebroke, who had direct control of cloth finishing and dyeing on the one hand and of wool sorting and beating on the other, it was a mixture of both systems. In the greater part of the thirteenth century craft guilds were still embryonic and had little influence on production processes. Regulation was decided and implemented at the level of the industry, so by the city aldermen and therefore by the mercantile elites themselves. But even later, we see that merchants often dealt directly with dyers to give their woollens the desired colour.

There is little doubt that the mercantile elites in Ypres, the *homines probi*, firmly held the reins of political power in the twelfth and thirteenth centuries. A system of co-opting the aldermen gave them the tools to make this dominance permanent. As we shall see in Chapter 9, a lot of the grievances of the commoners, the community of citizens, were directed against this hold by the commercial elites on the administration of the city, and they tried to allow control on the administration of the city and aimed for a higher degree of political participation. The thirteenth-century aldermen also monopolised the implementation of the (probably still very limited) regulation in the city's cloth industry. The tight regulation of cloth manufacture from the late thirteenth century onwards is mainly an indication that control had escaped from the local mercantile elites and was taken over by foreign merchants (who needed such strict standardised quality control for marketing purposes) on the one hand, and by cloth entrepreneurs (clothiers and guild masters), who used regulation not only for guaranteeing quality control but also for strengthening their grip on labour markets, on the other. But in the twelfth and thirteenth centuries, this was not yet necessary, as the impact of the elites on the industry was still quite direct. Moreover, the mercantile elites controlled not only political organisation, but also all other aspects of urban society. It is they who made up the personnel in all other important religious and secular institutions, and defined therefore, often with the active support of the Count of Flanders, the institutional framework in which society and the economy were organised.[193]

The elites primarily controlled trade flows outside the city and were, therefore, paramount for defining the trade flows both in raw materials for the cloth industry and in the finished products, the Ypres woollens, from low-quality worsteds to the expensive fine scarlets. Ypres merchants were, well into the fourteenth century, still active in the English wool trade, but their share of the imports of wool into Flanders (and, of course, into Ypres in particular) before 1270 was dominant. In the last decades of the thirteenth century the Anglo-Flemish trade conflict almost abruptly ousted Flemish merchants from the English wool markets and, although they would never leave completely, their share was largely taken over by local English, Brabantine (supplying mainly the Brabantine cloth cities of Leuven, Brussels and Mechelen with fine English wool) and, above all, Italian merchants (mainly from Lucca, like the Ricciardi, or from Florence, like the Peruzzi or Frescobaldi). The preserved credit contracts that we will investigate later in this chapter show that from this period particularly Italian merchant firms became key players in the organisation of the international trade connections in Ypres. But before the 1270s wool merchants were inevitably from Ypres itself and they belonged without exception to the upper strata of Ypres society.[194] They were all members of the Flemish Hanse of London, the key also to entering the city's political elites. It is less clear that they also controlled the markets for dyestuffs. Their role on the Champagne fairs must certainly have helped them to import alum and the very expensive Mediterranean dyestuffs, not least the exclusive grain or kermes, which was used to give the Ypres scarlets their bright colour. But the more widely used regionally grown dyestuffs, madder, weld and above all woad, were in the late thirteenth century brought in mainly by merchants from the regions where they were grown, for woad mostly merchants from Walloon Flanders and Picardy (Saint Quentin), or from Coastal

---

[93] Doudelez, 'La révolution communale', 196-201, and more recently the survey in Trio, 'Instellingen', 333-360.
[94] Lloyd, *The English Wool Trade*; Mus, 'De rol van Ieperlingen' and Wyffels, 'De Vlaamse handel', 205-213.

and Interior Flanders for madder and weld respectively.[195] There is no reason to assume that this was not also the case before the 1270s.

Ypres merchants not only controlled the flows of English wool, but they also controlled the flows of finished goods. They had a monopoly on stalls in the Ypres cloth hall and banned everyone else involved from marketing finished woollens. In this way they effectively achieved a monopoly, because high-quality broadcloth could only be sold in the hall, and all other stakeholders were forced to deal only in lower quality goods such as half-cloth and low-quality *doucken*. So, in essence, their access to the hall also guaranteed a monopoly on export. As members of the Hanse of the Seventeen Cities, they joined the mercantile elites of other Flemish and Artesian cities to organise trade to the Champagne fairs, in this way opening the crucially important Mediterranean markets. But while they were getting wool in England, they were also involved in export markets of cloth in the British Isles (and probably also in Eastern Europe).[196]

There has been a lot of speculation on the size of the group involved in the wool and cloth trade. Ypres merchants active on English wool markets have been estimated at no more than 10 to 20 in any one year, and only a couple of these were involved in transactions with the crown.[197] Still the few surviving court cases about trade conflicts and taxation records show that most elite families, Belle, Baerdonc, De Brune, Falais, Van Loo, De Waghenare, Van Scooten, Broederlam, Paeldinc, etc., were involved.[198] The estimates of merchants involved in the Champagne trade are even more fraught with uncertainty. The lease of the cloth hall in Lagny-sur-Marne mentions 11 merchants, but they claim to be acting on behalf of many more.

But trade was not the only hold the mercantile elites had on cloth manufacturers. The mercantile elites also seem to have controlled most of the real property in the city. The work by Guillaume Des Marez on real property leaves no doubt that the Ypres elites not only possessed most of the land inside the city walls, but were also firmly entrenched in the surrounding countryside. Hence the growth of the Ypres industry in the four suburbs must have greatly increased the income of families owning or administering the feudal lands surrounding the city.[199] Besides the lands controlled by the Templars (to the east of the city) and those owned by the collegiate church of St Martin, the most important seigneuries around the city (Hofland, Ketelquaet, Upstal) were part of the comital demesne, but they were gradually integrated into the urban territory. A new city wall, granted by Count Ferrand in 1214, surrounded parts of these seigneuries, and arbitration by the successive countesses, Joan and Margaret of Constantinople, later solved various judicial problems and confirmed the urban hold on these enclosed lands, while the juridical rights to the comital lands were transferred to the urban aldermen.[200]

---

195 See also Thoen, 'Technique agricole', 51-67; Verhille, 'La guède en Picardie', 393-399.
196 See also Chapter 1. For England Moore; *The fairs of Medieval England*.
197 Moore, *The fairs of Medieval England*, 69-75, cited in Bell, Brooks and Moore, 'The Credit Relationship', 129.
198 Mus, 'De rol van Ieperlingen', 338.
199 Des Marez, *Etudes sur la propriété foncière* and Fecheyr, 'Het stadspatriciaat te Ieper', 197-204.
200 Des Marez, *Etudes sur la propriété foncière*, 210-211.

We have already seen in the previous chapter how various religious and charitable institutions (hospitals, a leper's house, mendicant houses) were founded on these lands.[201] These institutions were often favoured by the thirteenth-century countesses, but often they had also been founded by the active participation of the city elites themselves, the Baerdonc or Belle families, the same elite families which were also heavily involved in the commercial growth of the city in the late twelfth and thirteenth centuries.[202] The population growth of the thirteenth-century city was absorbed primarily in these suburbs. The elites, who were either involved in the administration of these lands or held them in fief or by customary rent from the counts/countesses, profited from that growth by parcelling them out to craftsmen who paid them rent in return. We have seen in the previous chapter also that by 1300 more than half of the Ypres population lived in these suburbs, so the profits for a city with 30,000 inhabitants must have been enormous. The city archives used to contain lease contracts in respect of these lands. Some have luckily been preserved in source editions, including the lease on 1 July 1270 of a tenting field by Diederik Joseph, a citizen of Ypres, for a period of 20 years from Jan de Brune (a family name linked to the city's mercantile elites).[203] Two months earlier, in May, the same Jan de Brune leased another tenting field outside the Mesen Gate for six years to Luuc van Berghe.[204] On 29 December of the same year another Ypres craftsman, Nicolaes van der Hiedene, bought from Michiel De Brune – the same elite family keeps turning up in these documents – a house with two fulling troughs. Nicolaes also leased Michiel de Brune's land for 20 years. The location is not mentioned this time in the contract, but in this period most fullers were active in the southern suburbs, in the parish of St Michiel along the banks of the River Ieperleet.[205] Eleven years later, fuller Jan Ney rents a plot of land with a pond near the river from Michiel van Cassel, again a name linked to the old city elite, outside the Comines Gate, again in the suburb of St Michiel.[206] Of course, these scattered data provide only circumstantial evidence, but there seems to be a clear trend. The housing and land market in the industrial suburbs was controlled by the same urban elite that was also very active in the wool and cloth trade. Families like Belle, Broederlam, Van Cassel and De Brune always pop up as landowners in the few surviving lease contracts with craftsmen active in these suburbs.

It is therefore the combination of landowning and access to mercantile capital, through the membership of the city's merchant guilds, that entrenched the power of the elite. In short, a limited number of mercantile families had all the means to develop ruthless control of the main source of wealth in the city, its cloth production. They added to this, it seems, also a level of non-economic coercion. Odd remarks in the statutes of the cloth industry seem to suggest that Ypres was, as far as the commercial

---

201 Mus, 'De ruimtelijke ontwikkeling', 36-48. More general remarks in Verhulst, *The Rise of Cities*, 133-148.
202 Des Marez, *Etudes sur la propriété foncière*, 209-214. The Belle hospital was controlled by the Belle family for the remainder of the premodern period, even while other hospitals were run by wardens appointed by the aldermen.
203 Espinas and Pirenne, *Recueil*, 3, 674.
204 Espinas and Pirenne, *Recueil*, 3, 673-674.
205 Espinas and Pirenne, *Recueil*, 3, 675-676.
206 Espinas and Pirenne, *Recueil*, 3, 678-679.

elite's involvement in cloth manufacture and the cloth trade is concerned, almost a lawless city, the 'Wild West' of Flanders, where the elite merchants could do almost as they liked. The first statutes that regulated the actions of the clothiers, when these gained more independence from the mercantile elites in 1280 and the following years, insist on the fact that merchants could no longer use random violence to achieve their goals, implying that they had been used to doing exactly that before. In 1280 the aldermen decreed that sellers of cloth could sell their fabrics at their stalls on the Ypres market in all safety. The merchants were not allowed to just take the woollens away without the permission of the clothiers (*se ce nest par le volentei de celui cui li dras est*).[207] On 1 April 1281 the charter issued by Count Guy repeats this clause in order to remedy the many *griefs et damages*, the wrongs suffered by the craftsmen and the clothiers at the hands of the aldermen and the merchants. As the clothiers were now allowed to sell in the cloth hall itself, the count even broadened the initial meaning of the urban ordinance. Merchants (*barghengneurs, marchans*) could not go to a clothier's stall in the hall and seize his/her woollens against his/her will. They had, in other words, to follow due process, and agree a deal first. They were no longer above the law.[208] But such incidents were clearly not limited to the end product alone. At all stages of production, the elite merchants were apparently used to intervening and taking woollens from workshops without paying the craftsmen first for their labour.[209]

So the mercantile and landowning elites had adopted very similar ways of dealing with their surroundings to the ways the feudal lords were accustomed to use on their estates. A military identity completed their mercantile identity. And this identity not only popped up in their attitude to other urban social groups, it also sometimes exploded in internal feuds. Even the famous Cokerulle revolt of 1280 was largely caused by rivalries among the Ypres elites.[210] It is no wonder that some of the city's elites thrived on owning seigneuries in the immediate surroundings, that they did not hesitate to negotiate with the thirteenth-century countesses to incorporate feudal land into the city's zone of influence and that they profited probably directly from the demographic growth of the city that spilled over into the surrounding countryside with the creation of at least four nuclei of habitation outside the walls, a growth that was the direct result also of their own successes in the cloth trade.

The tentacles of the commercial elites stretched a long way. Their position was so strong that they were able, together with merchants from another Flemish cloth city, Douai, to enter the credit networks of the English king himself. Before 1270, several Ypres merchants supplied the English crown with goods, of course in first instance Flemish woollens, on credit. As such they not only delivered goods, they were also credit intermediaries for the king. The king paid the Flemish merchants on credit for the luxury goods they imported for the royal wardrobe (woollens, of course, but they also imported Mediterranean luxury goods like spices from the Champagne markets),

---

207 Espinas and Pirenne, *Recueil*, 3, 453.
208 Espinas and Pirenne, *Recueil*, 3, 682.
209 Espinas and Pirenne, *Recueil*, 3, 457 (fullers of stamforts).
210 Boone and Haemers, 'The Common Good', 93-117. See also Maire Vigueur, *Cavaliers et citoyens*, and Wickham, *Sleepwalking*, for similar attitudes in the Italian cities.

credit that was used in its turn to purchase wool for the Flemish cloth industries. The profits on such trade were therefore double: the merchants could expect a relatively high price for their woollens (credit on the purchase of goods, which of course involves deferred payment, often implied because of the ban on usury, higher prices. Moreover, by providing credit to the king, they also received his favour and the crown granted them, in exchange for taxes, the privilege of trading on English soil. The Flemish merchants could also use the cash income later to finance their wool purchases in England (on which their profit in Flanders was about 13.5-22.2 per cent).[211] It is striking that, for example, Douai merchants are seen transferring the royal debts or parts of them to other merchants, and Ypres merchants, for example Niclaes Sclinger and Michiel Croc, did likewise.[212] The royal connection was probably lucrative in the first instance, but after 1255 Ypres merchants withdrew from these activities. Kings and princes are, of course, notoriously bad debtors. The Ypres merchants settled for the arrears that the king owed them. After that, direct connections with the crown became only haphazard, and after 1270, with the decline of the active Flemish trade, they stopped altogether.

So, if anything, the nature of commercial capital seems at first sight to have been even more dominant than in Boinebroke's Douai. The statutes of the cloth industry before the Cokerulle revolt of 1280 seem to have taken all initiative away from the clothiers. They were not allowed to enter the cloth hall and were therefore kept away from the main source of wool supply and from the commercial networks for marketing the finished woollens. It is unlikely in these circumstances that they acquired an independent role in monitoring and coordinating the production chain, as they would do in the fourteenth and fifteenth centuries. Even when, in the final decades, the Ypres merchants themselves lost ground on the international wool and cloth market, when they lost direct access to the English wool supply and when the international commercial networks around the Fairs of Champagne gradually dissolved, the clothiers do not seem to have been in a good position to take over the role of mercantile capital.

Then in 1280 everything changed. Clothiers gained access to the cloth hall and many of the restrictions limiting the scope of their commercial involvement started to disappear. This truly must have been a watershed, a social change comparable only to the rise of the city elites during the communal revolt of the long twelfth century. Only from that time could the urban middle classes start to emancipate and some of them become merchants in their own right. The figure of the classical merchant-entrepreneur was born: they were relatively well-off artisans who ventured also in trade and combined the role of clothier with that of merchant. But the scope of these new merchant-entrepreneurs was not that of the thirteenth-century merchants like Boinebroke. They no longer ventured on foreign markets in Champagne, by now in full decay, or in England, where the wool trade was gradually being taken over by Italian

---

11 Bell, Brooks and Moore, 'The Credit Relationship', 123-145 and Munro, 'Wool-Price Schedules', 125.
12 A case is mentioned involving a Jakeme Boinebroke, undoubtedly related to the already mentioned Jehan Boinebroke (ibid., 130-131).

merchants and where, because of the English king's attempts to establish staple markets for wool (in Saint-Omer in the 1310s, in Bruges in the 1340s and 1350s and finally more permanently in Calais form 1363), active wool trade was no longer a viable business.[213]

A Hostile Take-Over?

In the latter part of the thirteenth century, therefore, the dominant position of the landowning and mercantile elites came under great pressure. As a result, internal feuding probably became more intense (as is shown in the Cokerulle revolt) and new wealthy groups, most of them also with a commercial background, tried to gain access to the commercial circuits of the city, internal and external. But, more importantly, the guilds, which slowly became organised in exactly this period, became more important in the political and economic equilibria of urban society.[214] In the same vein the clothiers, the entrepreneurs who coordinated the manufacture of cloth by the different craftsmen, manifested themselves as the new pivotal figures in the cloth industry. In Ypres this shift is traditionally linked to three important political events.

In 1270-1274 the Anglo-Flemish trade conflict undermined the active trade of Flemish merchants in England, and, therefore, also their direct access to English wool suppliers. Instead, foreign merchants (English, Italian, West-French and Brabantine) started to compete with Flemish wool merchants and quickly ousted them from the markets for raw materials. From being active traders in Europe, Flemish merchants entered a period of passive trade. Some cities would profit from this change, not in the least Bruges, of course, that became the hub of international trade in the late Middle Ages, but other cities, among them Ypres, lost ground as trading cities. The groups that were involved in commerce had to look for alternatives. Because of the rise of Bruges as a permanent market, the cycle of Flemish fairs had become less important, the fairs in Champagne lost much of their attraction after 1300 because of overall insecurity in Europe, and as a result of direct foreign competition the Ypres merchants gradually started to abandon their activities outside the county. It must, however, be noted that this change was neither abrupt nor complete. Even in Bruges, where active foreign trade had been even more important in the thirteenth century, the connections of local merchants and brokers with the incoming foreign merchants remained close and intense. A new symbiosis of local and foreign mercantile capital started to develop.

Ten years later, in the difficulties surrounding the Cokerulle revolt in 1280, the aldermen were obliged to grant the clothiers access to the Ypres cloth hall, opening to them the market for the high-quality woollens that were exported abroad. On the other hand, the clothiers could now supply themselves with raw materials; English and other wool they could buy not only from the mercantile elites in Ypres itself, but from all merchants on this side of the channel (meaning in continental Europe). The intermediate role of merchants, who supplied the wool and marketed the finished

---

213 Lloyd, The English *Wool Trade*, 209-210.
214 Blondé et al., 'Living Together in the City', 59-92.

woollens, was therefore no longer a monopoly position, and their influence on the manufacturing process must have diminished sharply as a result. A comital charter confirmed this decision a year later, on 1 April 1281, and it became irreversible. As we shall see in the next chapter, the clothiers were certainly not a new group. They had been active as organisers of cloth production probably throughout the thirteenth century. This time, however, they became more independent of mercantile capital. The question remains how far this independence really went, and what consequences this entailed for the organisation of manufacture. Mercantile capital, necessary to acquire the raw materials, was very much still in the hands of the Ypres elites. So the process of becoming independent of mercantile capital could be achieved only by clothiers with ample access to credit (in its turn probably delivered by the elites) or by a reduction in the scale of operations. Both mechanisms were probably set in motion.

Finally, when after 1300 the bench of aldermen was slowly opened to newcomers from the urban middle classes, the decisive influence of the traditional mercantile elites on urban politics and economic regulation was over altogether. Henceforth, regulation of the industry would come about in close association, even cooperation, with other stakeholders, the clothiers and the craft guilds. Control of the industry was to a certain degree also outsourced by the aldermen (and therefore by the traditional elites) to those stakeholders. Yet, in Ypres the so-called 'democratic revolution' of the early 1300s never took hold completely. Despite some violent political changes in the fourteenth century, the guilds never gained as much influence as in Ghent or Bruges, so the new equilibrium was always fragile and continually contested. Ypres would experience a very troubled fourteenth century.

These three decisive political moments affected the very heart of the economic organisation in the city and undermined the position of the city's elites; foreign competitors entered the market for raw materials and finished woollens in Ypres itself, the intermediaries in cloth manufacture became crucial stakeholders in the process, developing their own levels of agency, and the political hold on economic organisation was taken partly out of the hands of the mercantile elite. This was indeed a three-stage hostile take-over that must have shattered the economic resilience of the elites and altered their class identity as the untouchable *homines probi*. Yet, the importance of these three key events must not be exaggerated either. They were undoubtedly true catalysts for rapid change. They were, however, also part of a slow process in which the mercantile elites' position of strength was slowly eroded. They were therefore mere highpoints in a gradual process that took more than half a century and would continue well into the fourteenth century. Already from the middle of the thirteenth century the direct wool trade of Ypres merchants in England had started to evaporate. In 1255 they stopped lending important sums of money to the royal wardrobe, and although merchants from Douai would linger on for a longer time, in essence the English kings started to rely on Italian credit, leading eventually even to the famous bankruptcies of the largest Florentine firms of the Peruzzi, Frescobaldi and Acciaiuoli in the 1340s.[215] But their wool trade also started to decline in this period. Nor did the trade conflict in

---

15 Hunt, *The Medieval Super-Companies*.

1270 mean the complete end of the Ypres wool trade in England. Export figures from Boston, the main export port that Ypres traders used, in the 1290s still exceeded 1,300 sacks; around 1300 they amounted to more than 1,000 sacks, declining to 700 sacks around 1310 and 500 in the early 1320s. In the meantime, Ypres merchants also moved their trade to London. So there was inevitably a decline in active trade involvement in England, yet it was a slow and gradual process, not as sudden as is suggested by the English-Flemish trade disruption. Ypres merchants did not disappear suddenly from foreign markets, and the same is probably true at the Champagne fairs. We saw in chapter 1 that the striped stamforts remained popular in Italy until the late 1320s. Although these woollens were traded by some of the large Italian companies with direct links to the Low Countries, in Bruges and elsewhere (Del Bene, Alberti), it is likely that some of the exported volumes were still catered for by Ypres merchants at the Champagne fairs, which remained important until the early fourteenth century.

We can conclude therefore that change came sooner than suggested by the three political events, but that the Ypres mercantile elites were also much more resilient than is generally acknowledged and disappeared from active trade only in the early fourteenth century. It is therefore also probable that they did not give up their pivotal position in the wool and cloth trade in Ypres itself so easily. There is one source that can highlight this pattern: the impressive collection of chirographs that was preserved in the city archives dating from the latter part of the thirteenth century.

In a sweeping analysis Martha Howell has recently discussed credit relations in thirteenth-century Ypres. Her information is based on the thousands of debt contracts, IOUs or obligatory bills that were preserved in the City Archives of Ypres before 1914.[216] The contracts or, more correctly, a substantial and probably highly representative sample of these contracts from the 1249-1291 period (about 5,400 of a total of about 7,000 documents preserved in the city archives before World War I, most of them dating back to the period after 1266) involved almost one third of the total population of Ypres, and a great number of foreigners as well. It is unclear what part this formal circuit of credit arrangements, registered before the city aldermen and given as chirographs to the parties involved, would have represented of the total number of formal and informal credit relations. We will return to this issue in the following chapter, but, undoubtedly, the contracts would have constituted a major part of the high-profile credit contracts, involving parties that did not come from Ypres, and involving also higher sums of money. The security given by an official registration by the highest court of justice in the city in these cases constituted significant added value for the parties involved. The contracts were saved from destruction because Guillaume Des Marez transcribed a number of them for the study of what he somewhat misleadingly called 'fair letters' (*lettres de foire*). In fact, many contracts had little to do with the Ypres

---

216 Howell, 'Credit networks and political actors', 3-36; id., 'Un réseau de crédit', 19-40. See also for a more source-related assessment De Hemptinne and Howell, 'The "lettres de foire" of Ypres', 133-152. Some of the calculations in the following pages are my own work, for which I was able to use the database that was assembled under the supervision of Martha Howell. I am very grateful to Martha who was so kind as to allow me to use it.

fairs, although probably those concerning the largest amounts probably did.[217] This material has yielded information only haphazardly,[218] yet Martha Howell's new analysis demonstrates quite convincingly how complex credit relations had become in the late thirteenth century. They constituted an essential building block of urban society.

Howell has focused primarily on the middle strata of Ypres society, on the rise of the craftsmen in a period when they were emancipated also politically. Yet, of course, the more important credit contracts illustrate primarily how the traditional Ypres elites operated and what kind of relations they developed with foreign merchants, who at this time entered also the local Flemish commercial circuits in greater numbers at their expense. In this way, Des Marez' description of the contracts as *lettres de foire* in which the payment for goods was arranged at a later date was not completely wrong. They were intended primarily to arrange the financial implications of transactions in wool, cloth, dyestuffs and various other luxury goods (spices, silks) and bulk goods (wine, timber, leather, metal, etc.). It is striking that most high-profile transactions were negotiated between foreign sellers (lenders) and Ypres merchants as buyers (borrowers). They were there for settling the accounts, usually after a period of a few months up to one year, but occasionally the period could be extended for much longer than a year from the initial contract.[219]

It is striking that in most substantial credit arrangements foreign merchants lent money to Ypres merchants, who were either members of the traditional Ypres elites or merchants that were otherwise documented as being active in international trade. On average a credit arrangement involving an Italian merchant (from Florence, Lucca or Piacenza) amounted to £68.7 sterling, almost the same amount as in the case of merchants from Cahors in Southern France, Saint-Jean d'Angély on the French Atlantic coast, or the Hanseatic city of Lübeck. Figures were even higher in the case of English merchants (almost £100). Merchants from La Rochelle on the French Atlantic coast lent on average £34.5 St Lenders from northern France and from elsewhere in Flanders were involved in much smaller sums of money, resp. £14 and £3.6 St., almost equal to the average of contracts among inhabitants of Ypres.[220] It is clear, therefore, that high-value transactions, in many cases probably concerning (English) wool, were taken care of by a limited group of foreign merchants: 47 contracts of merchants from Florence, 36 from Lucca, 25 from Piacenza, 16 from Cahors, 18 from Lübeck, 11 from St Jean and no fewer than 51 from La Rochelle. Most borrowers (buyers) belonged to the Ypres elites. It is clear from these data that while Ypres merchants gradually lost hold of wool imports in the late thirteenth century, they were still the favoured commercial partners for the Italian, French, German and English traders who started to import wool to Flanders. In other words, certainly in this period, the elites did not abandon their crucial role in the wool trade at all, and they probably also continued

---

217 Des Marez, 'Lettres de foire'. Guillaume Des Marez also made short summaries of most contracts and these were published long after his death by Carlos Wyffels in the series of the Royal Commission of History (Wyffels, *Analyse des reconaissances de dette*). See also for a recent assessment of the sources de Valériola, 'Corpus', 14-32.
218 Coppejans-Desmedt, 'Handel en handelaars', 69-88.
219 Howell, 'Credit Networks and Political Actors', 9.
220 Data from Howell, 'Credit Networks and Political Actors', 17-19.

their commercial dominance of the supply chain of raw materials. It is not clear whether this situation continued into the fourteenth century.

But there were also fundamental changes among the foreign wool suppliers. The data assembled by Des Marez allow one also to make a chronological assessment of their involvement in the Ypres industry. The first foreign merchants to enter the Ypres fairs with significant credit arrangements with the local elites were merchants from La Rochelle. They were present already in the 1260s and thrived particularly in the 1270s and into the 1280s. Their compatriots from Saint-Jean d'Angély were much slower to come to Ypres and appear in great numbers in the early 1280s, to disappear rapidly afterwards. Merchants from Cahors were numerous in the late 1270s but became less prominent from the 1280s. Similarly, merchants from Lübeck were numerous in the late 1270s, also to disappear later. English traders appeared in the late 1270s and were particularly numerous in the early 1280s, but they also almost disappeared in the late 1280s. Finally, Italian merchants entered the Ypres credit arrangements relatively late: hesitantly in the early 1270s, but Florentines and merchants from Piacenza, on the banks of the River Po south of Milan, became more numerous in the 1280s, never to disappear again. In the early 1280s they were joined by merchants from Lucca. This suggests not only that merchants bringing in the most essential of raw materials for the Ypres cloth industry were in first instance French traders from cities on the Atlantic coast, Hanseatic Germans and, of course, English merchants, only later from the late 1270s to be overhauled by Italian merchant companies, dominated from the 1280s by merchants from Florence and Lucca. It also suggests that because of this changing identity, the Ypres elites were probably necessary to provide continuity in the supply systems. Foreign merchants often seem to have come only once or on a limited number of occasions, so they were probably not able to connect to the supply system of wool without the experience and know-how of the Ypres merchants (and of the Ypres elites in particular). Even if the same merchants return in the debt contracts, they do so often in the same year, and only exceptionally do we find them returning to Ypres for several years in a row. Even the big Florentine merchant firms, the Peruzzi, Bardi and Frescobaldi, who were present at the Ypres fairs almost permanently, were represented by different merchants. Again, this rapid turnover probably strengthened the pattern of continuity in Ypres itself. The local elite merchants continued in the late thirteenth century, even after the Anglo-Flemish trade conflict in 1270 and the opening of the wool market for clothiers in 1280, to be the pivotal figures of the Ypres wool supply.

There are exceptions, though. Jean Benoit from Cahors appears in six contracts almost on an annual basis between 1277 and 1281, but his compatriot, Pons Elye, contracted five debts, all in the same year. The presence of merchants or financiers from Cahors is striking for other reasons as well. They were, of course, heavily involved in moneylending in the county of Flanders during the twelfth century, besides the "Lombards", originating mostly from Piedmont, and from the city of Asti in particular. But the merchants from Cahors had a completely different role, it seems, than the Lombards at the Ypres fairs. It is striking, that besides active merchants from Piacenza, located on banks of the Po River in Emilia-Romagna, who were not that much involved in as moneylenders in the Low Countries, none of the traditional "Lombards" seem to have acquired a significant position on the Ypres financial market related to cloth manufacture.[221] It is, on the contrary, merchants from Tuscany, also involved in dealings with the English crown and therefore directly involved in the wool trade, that start to appear massively at the Ypres fairs. It is therefore the involvement in the (English) wool trade, not the quasi-permanent presence as financiers in Flanders, that constitutes the main catalyst for getting involved in the financial networks in Ypres in this period.

The continuing privileged position in the wool trade of the Ypres elite is very marked in the case of English and Italian merchants. English traders arranged credit contracts with representatives of the Balgh, Cauderlier, de Canne, de Mont, Piet de Soile and Van Cassel elite dynasties and also had dealings with the equally strong merchant families of Raboud, Slingher and Van Dixmude. The Florentine, Placentine and Luccese firms dealt with representatives of the Broederlam, De Brune, Cauderlier, Croeselin, de Waghenaere, Piet de Soile, Paeldinc, van Loo and Vilain families. But also among the customers of merchants from Cahors we find representatives of the elite families of Waterbalgh, Paeldinc, Bru(n)man and Van Scoten. Only in loans from merchants from La Rochelle, who were among the first to enter the Ypres market, do we find fewer familiar names. Probably at this very early stage of the transition in the 1270s, the Ypres elite still tried to trade directly with their English suppliers. It is striking that merchants from Lübeck, who also came in at this early stage, traded more with the Ypres elite than with those from the French Atlantic coast. Among their customers there are again the traditional elite families of Balgh, Baerdonc, de Brune, Van Cassel, Croeselin, Paeldinc and Piet de Soile.

All these elite families in their turn were lending money to fellow citizens of lower status.[222] It is not clear what share of these relations was part of the regular wool supply system in the city. We will see in the next chapter that perhaps the formal obligatory bills were not essential to supply the clothiers with wool continuously. We will suggest that this transfer of raw materials was organised mostly through the informal and personal relations of the elite merchants and the clothiers, not through formal letters passed before the aldermen. These arrangements were regular, happening each year or several times per year even, they were long-standing and involved relations of personal reciprocity. But nonetheless, for other, less regular debt arrangements, which are probably more likely to be written down in a formal IOU, the elites were acting as main suppliers of credit to the rest of urban society. They may in the last quarter of the thirteenth century have lost their direct commercial access to international trade, but their strong position in international finance and their experience in accessing business networks beyond the County of Flanders remained. It will be no surprise therefore, that this period also saw the confirmation of their pivotal role in all kinds of credit arrangements which defined urban life, both in the cloth industry itself, but also in urban society at large. In the short run neither the take-over of the international trade by foreign merchants, nor the partial take-over of local trade networks by rising middle

---

221 On the groups involved in moneylending in Flanders, see Kusman, *Usuriers publics* and Bigwood, *Le régime juridique*.

222 Howell, 'Credit Networks', 23-24.

groups truly threatened the leading role of the traditional mercantile elites in the city's leading industry. Their position of power in the city was, therefore, not fundamentally altered in the decades before 1300. It would require the slow ascent of other forces in urban society to do just that.

How did Woollens Find their Way to International Customers? Merchants and Brokers

In order to disentangle the mechanisms with which merchants, whether they be local or international, controlled export markets for woollens, we need to look at the ways in which woollens found their way to markets abroad. In Chapter 2 we already saw that a lot of the regulation was intended carefully to define the transfer of the product from one production stage to another. This was, of course, necessary to make work a manufacturing process that was defined by successive stages of production carried out by different craftsmen or women. It was the clothier or (in the case of the first and last manufacturing stages) sometimes the merchant who was responsible for monitoring the whole process. It should not come as a surprise, therefore, that the transfer from the manufacturing to the marketing stage was also carefully described and the activities of all those involved, clothiers and merchants, officials, brokers and customers, well defined.

The statutes of the cloth merchants, dating back to the late thirteenth century, are therefore very detailed in describing the different woollens of the Ypres industry, their measurements and seals and the way they should be marketed in the Ypres cloth hall or in the fairs of Flanders and Champagne. It seems, even as late as 1300, that it was still standard for merchants dealing in Ypres cloth, the target group of these statutes, to come from Ypres itself. Regularly it is stated that merchants were not allowed in specific circumstances to associate themselves with foreign merchants.[223] The statutes share the same aversion to non-monetised trade that we also encountered in the industrial regulation of Ypres. It was explicitly forbidden for merchants to just barter (*bareteir*) wool or dyestuffs for cloth with foreign merchants within the jurisdiction of Ypres, but during fairs no such prohibition existed, while other marketing techniques were also more relaxed.[224] And there were also limits as to the volumes of trade. The nature of elite trade was to a certain degree redistributive within the group: no merchant could trade more than 86 woollens in each of the Champagne fairs, even if he was associated with other merchants. An addition to the statutes in 1289 provided for a maximum of 80 woollens in one of the Flemish fairs (in Ypres itself, twice, in Torhout, Mesen and Bruges). Merchants could not circumvent this clause by using their servants or assistants (the statutes mention *vallès loych* or 'paid servants'). These could take no more than two 'blue woollens' (expensive fine cloth) to the fairs in Central France

---

[223] Espinas and Pirenne, *Recueil*, 3, 498 and 500: *nus estraingnes peut gieter sort avoec bourgois d'Ypre pour esteir avoec draes dessous le courtine d'Ypre, ne en Champainge, ne en Engletiere, ne aillours* and *nus bourgois ne ait part ne compaingnie avoec homme estraigne en marchandise.*

[224] Espinas and Pirenne, *Recueil*, 3, 497.

in Champagne and Burgundy (Chalon-sur-Saone).[225] Implicitly these statutes from around 1300 suggest, therefore, that active trade in Flanders and in Champagne was still very much an option for the Ypres merchants. But something had changed, of course, and the regulatory framework was also used to adapt to change.

As long as the local mercantile elites had completely controlled the trade flows of raw materials and finished woollens, trade could be organised in relatively very straightforward ways. Of course, credit relations were ubiquitous and delivery problems of wool and cloth probably at times very unpredictable, but the patterns of trade in the city were familiar to everyone. Both merchants and their customers came from the city, and most would have had long experience of dealing with individuals or groups of individuals. This changed, of course, dramatically when the local elites were pushed aside or retreated from active trade in raw materials and woollens. The merchants taking care of both were now foreigners, who very often would have been less familiar with the networks of production, or even with the different types of woollens and colours that were manufactured in the city.

Quality assessment was probably the easiest to deal with for these newcomers to the city. Quality was guaranteed by the cloth seals of the city and controlled by city officials, who had everything to gain from keeping a tight leash on things. The successive manufacturing stages were also controlled by guild officials or mixed commissions of merchants and guildsmen. It was the suppliers themselves that posed most problems for the merchants. The woollens sold to the city militia in 1302, which were registered in the city accounts, offer a good insight into these difficulties. It is possible that in this troubled period – in contrast to Ghent, Ypres participated with great enthusiasm in the Bruges-led revolt against the French – the aldermen aimed as much as possible to be inclusive and ordered woollens from most, if not all, clothiers. But the list nonetheless contains the names of hundreds of clothiers and craftsmen, who sold one or two woollens to the city. All these clothiers controlled, therefore, only a very small volume of cloth output. So, merchants who wanted to buy a substantial number of Ypres woollens needed to contact a lot of clothiers or dyers to achieve some result. Ideally, they also needed to know what kind of woollens the clothiers had made, at what time these could be delivered, at what price and under what conditions they were prepared to sell. Trade was usually organised in the cloth hall, which already solved some of these issues, because the fixed times of trade on one location brought all stakeholders together, yet some information issues could not be solved so easily, and merchants would want to know a lot of other things before they even entered the cloth hall. In other words, they needed to invest heavily in research and information costs.

The trade system of the medieval Flemish cities provided a solution to these trade difficulties. Brokers or hostellers-brokers (when the brokers also provided accommodation and storage facilities, as well as some simple banking services) started to act as middlemen between merchants and between merchants and entrepreneurs. In late-thirteenth-century Ypres there were local brokers, men or women (*ostelier bourgois, ostelière bourgoise*), and brokers who were not from the city (*ostelier forein*: apparently,

---

225 Espinas and Pirenne, *Recueil*, 3, 498.

in this case, these were all men). A broker needed, however, to work from a house in the city or to store woollens in that house, *ou on a fait seurteit* ('where he had financial pledges'), so his clients could always be sure that they would be reimbursed if anything went wrong.[226] During the fourteenth century, according to the statutes dating from the middle of the century, foreign brokers were no longer allowed to be active on the Ypres market, except during the days of the Ypres fair. For the rest of the year, all brokers had to be citizens of Ypres.[227] These brokers did not come out of the blue. Brokers were already active when the Ypres merchant class still dominated the wool and cloth trade. The fairs in Ypres and the cycle of Flemish fairs in general had already attracted foreign traders in the twelfth and thirteenth centuries, and they needed to solve similar issues, not only to buy industrial goods manufactured in Flanders, but also to sell their own wares, usually luxury commodities like silks, jewellery and spices, and perhaps already at this stage also some wool.

But when Ypres merchants slowly abandoned the wool and cloth trade, the function of middlemen became more urgent and their role more comprehensive. Foreign merchants needed reliable intermediaries and the Ypres elites, still controlling the urban government, probably wanted to protect their own interests as well and, if possible, also their income, so the brokers also became the subject of complex political equilibria. Strict regulation became necessary and very quickly, already in the 1280s, new statutes were issued. Of all statutes related to the cloth industry, these were probably the most dynamic, it seems, with additions in 1286, 1287, 1292, 1294, 1300, 1302, and each year between 1306 and 1309. Almost continually, therefore, (sometimes contradictory) clauses were changed or complemented.[228] This seems to have been very much a process of trial and error, surely the result of the very sensitive issues involved, whereby the power position of various Ypres stakeholders, merchants, clothiers and craftsmen alike, were very much at the heart of things. The transition from active to passive trade was not something that was taken lightly.

The way brokers operated in late medieval Flanders is particularly well-known for late medieval Bruges.[229] They not only solved the research and information problems for foreign merchants, but they also in many cases provided room in inns for the merchants themselves and for their goods and acted in the fourteenth century as links with the financial services of the Bruges moneychangers and in the fifteenth century as bankers themselves.[230] The surviving accounts of the late-fifteenth-century hosteller Wouter Ameide reveals how through his double-entry bookkeeping systems (Italian) merchants and (Flemish) clothiers bartered cloth for wool.[231] The Bruges brokers

---

226 Espinas and Pirenne, *Recueil*, 3, 493.
227 Espinas and Pirenne, *Recueil*, 3, 639.
228 Espinas and Pirenne, *Recueil*, 3, 486.
229 Van Houtte, 'Makelaars en waarden te Brugge', 1-30 and 177-197; Greve, *Hansische Kaufleute, Hosteliers und Herbergen*; and for cloth brokers also Mus, 'De verhouding van de waard tot de drapier', 156-218.
230 Murray, *Cradle of Capitalism*.
231 Verbist, *Traditie of innovatie?*; Stabel, 'Entre commerce international et économie locale', 75-100 and id., 'Ambachten en textielondernemers', 79-98.

figured among the wealthiest and politically most influential groups in Bruges society.[232] For Ypres such information is sadly not available, but the statutes do reveal how the clothiers operated in the changing cloth market around 1300.[233]

It is not surprising that their activities were particularly important during the period of the Ypres fairs. But the Champagne fairs remained in this period also an important time for clearing accounts. The brokers had to make sure that all woollens bought at the fairs by foreign merchants were duly paid for within eight days after the fair. There was a general suspicion about sales on credit. Brokers were not allowed to have credit relations with their customers. One of the early additions to the statutes, dated 4 October 1287, even forbids any basic credit transaction without proper security.[234] Clothiers had to be paid once the woollens left their houses (*osteliers qui achatent draes a payer tantost sec, que il les fachent payer anchois que on les enmaine hors de lor hosteil*).[235] Trade was not without risk, and when customers were not paid within 15 days, the broker's own assets and these of their securities could be seized to compensate the cheated traders. An addition to the statutes of 1294 states that this rule was not binding on everyone, however. For merchants from Spain and above all from Germany (the German Hanse?) other rules applied. Brokers had to be able, in other words, to guarantee to their customers that they had enough capital or access to capital to reimburse them for damaged goods, delayed deliveries, or to guarantee the clearance of the accounts. The brokers constituted therefore a buffer to limit risk. Preferably they would be liable with their own capital. There was even a strange clause discouraging citizens of Ypres from pledging themselves as security for brokers (*nus bougois d'Ypre soit pleges de aucun courretier d'Ypre*).[236] It is not clear why such a clause was added. It is unlikely that it was ever implemented. What else should the broker turn to than capital that was present in the city itself? Was it to protect the property of Ypres burghers in a market fraught with risk in this transitional period, or was it to stimulate Ypres merchants not to venture too far into a new role as intermediaries, rather than investing their capital in true commercial ventures abroad? The clause disappears from the later fourteenth-century statutes. The services that the brokers provided for the foreign merchants in Ypres also included storage. Merchants could temporarily store their goods in their brokers' houses (*osteil*). Various clauses dealt with possible damage to the woollens during this period of storage.[237]

Crucial in the statutes are the barriers between the different stakeholders. Brokers could in no way participate in a commercial transaction without being fined and losing their right of brokerage. Brokers were not even allowed to accept a gift of wine from clothiers or merchants. No suspicion about possible collusion could be raised.[238] In

---

232 Stabel, *A Capital of Fashion*, forthcoming.
233 Espinas and Pirenne, *Recueil*, 3, 486 ff. See also De Pelsmaeker, 'Le courtage à Ypres', 439-484.
234 *Nus courretiers, ne bourgois, ne forains acache draes encontre bourgois de le vile d'Ypre à créanche, s'il n'ait fait seurteit* (Espinas and Pirenne, *Recueil*, 3, 490-491).
235 Espinas and Pirenne, *Recueil*, 3, 489.
236 Espinas and Pirenne, *Recueil*, 3, 490.
237 Espinas and Pirenne, *Recueil*, 3, 493.
238 Espinas and Pirenne, *Recueil*, 3, 491.

order to avoid conflicts of interest, brokers, or members of their household, were not allowed to be active in trade or to sell goods for the merchants they worked for. They would lose their licences if found out a third time. We know from the Bruges case that there was often a very thin line between brokering and commercial activities, and brokers sometimes operated as merchants' real local agents. An addition to the statutes dated 1 April 1300 states that brokers and members of their household were forbidden to be active as moneychangers or bankers, but, probably like in Bruges, they could link the merchants they helped with the local money-changing system. The addition probably indicates that in fact they were used to doing this.[239] But brokers (as well as merchants) were also forbidden to go to the workshops of the clothiers and dyers to do direct business there, or they could not use the money that was put in their trust by merchants to finalise cloth transactions for other purposes, not even to pay dyers. Everything had to be arranged in full transparency in the cloth hall.[240] Even market niches were separated. There were brokers of wool and brokers of cloth, and the two activities could not be done by the same broker, nor by any other member of his household.[241]

Conclusions

A merchant in the middle of the fourteenth century or later would probably have looked with some envy at his colleague living in mid-thirteenth-century Ypres or before. Before 1250 representatives of the Baerdonc, Belle, Scattin or Van Scoten mercantile dynasties were, in the manner of their Douai equivalent Jehan Boinebroke, almost untouchable. They controlled political power completely at the local level and their will was, at least formally, uncontested. In collusion with the counts and countesses, or sometimes at odds with them, they extended their power beyond the boundaries of the city by absorbing the surrounding feudal lands and making a huge profit from the spectacular growth of the city by parcelling out plots of feudal land to migrants and textile workers. They even seem to have adopted some elements of the feudal order, when there was a profit to be made or when their position was to be defended, by using violence, even random violence, to enforce their authority over all social and economic transactions. But primarily they controlled, more or less uncontested, the main economic activity in the city, the cloth trade. As merchants they managed the imports of wool from England, where they engaged in financial relation at the highest level with the royal administration, and they marketed the finished woollens all over Europe, and, of course they held the crucial outlet at the Champagne fairs under close supervision. By controlling trade and finance they also dominated the cloth industry itself.

---

239 Espinas and Pirenne, *Recueil*, 3, 487: *Nus courretiers, ne sa femme, ne si vallet, ne meisnie de courretier change, venge, ne n'achate monnoie par aucun engien, sour 50 lb.*
240 Espinas and Pirenne, *Recueil*, 3, 488.
241 Espinas and Pirenne, *Recueil*, 3, 490.

Although we do not have the materials to prove active engagement in actual cloth manufacture, their monopoly on the trade in raw materials and the finished products, a monopoly that was secured by their political dominance, made them also the dominant figures in the industry. The clothiers, who organised manufacture, were not much more than their employees. They were completely dependent upon the wool supply and upon the merchants' hold on the markets for finished woollens, and so they had little choice but to follow the instructions of their mercantile superiors. Henri Pirenne's assessment that the subordinate craftsmen, in this case the clothiers, 'nourished' the mercantile dominance was very correct in this respect. Moreover, guilds did not yet exist or they were just present embryonically, nor probably did the detailed regulation of cloth manufacture define the position of all stakeholders in the industry. This was truly an industrial system dominated by capitalists, who encountered little resistance from the other groups in urban society. It was the merchants therefore who defined the contours of trade and industry, it was they who held the reins of financial and political power.

In the middle of the fourteenth century a lot had changed, and at first sight the dominance of the mercantile elites of politics and industry had significantly diminished. As we shall see in chapter 9, politically they had become anything but untouchable. Three major revolts, interspersed with industrial conflicts, had shown that their monopoly of political power was not secure, although they always maintained control of urban government. But primarily their economic position had changed drastically. In 1280, a relatively minor revolt had swept away their monopoly on trade. It had been an attack on two fronts, on the one hand they lost almost at once their hold on international markets. Instead, it was now foreign merchants, gradually mainly Italians, who brought the English wool to Flanders and Ypres. The disappearance of their active involvement in the marketing of woollens was less immediate, but the decay of the Champagne fairs and the new role of Bruges as a commercial hub linking Mediterranean and North-European trade meant that Hanseatic merchants for the northeast European markets and Italian merchant companies for the Mediterranean markets for woollens did, in the end, take over from the active trade of the Ypres merchants themselves.

With the loss of active trade, the clothiers, whose position had been strengthened in 1280, had more alternatives for obtaining supplies of wool or for selling their woollens. Their complete dependence on mercantile capital in Ypres itself had, at least theoretically, disappeared. In the same vein the coming of age of the (textile) guilds created a new platform for the regulation of both quality standards and labour markets. It was also what the industry needed, now that the focus of cloth manufacture came to be more and more on the production of expensive high-quality cloth. The craft guilds, which had played a crucial role in political dissidence, became the carriers of a new value system aimed at respectability and reputation. The guilds were also the vehicles for mobilising against the mercantile hold on political power. This was truly a dramatic change, and one the merchants would have felt not only in their purses, but also in their political and social clout: no more non-economic coercion without sanctions, no more treatment of subordinate workers and entrepreneurs as if they were their own employees.

Yet, despite all this structural change, it would be wrong to overestimate the impact of change from 1250 to 1350. Despite often bloody revolts, the political landscape in Ypres did not change all that much. Artisans, retailers and small entrepreneurs could claim some victories. Most notably they could penetrate and influence decision-making in the new city councils, in the neighbourhood institutions and, of course, in the guilds themselves; but as a rule the mercantile and landowning elites continued to dominate the bench of aldermen and, therefore, city government. Their regional hold increased even as Ypres was an undisputed part of the College of the Three Members of Flanders, consisting, besides Ypres, of Ghent and Bruges, and the city was allocated strong fiscal powers over its quarter, including some of its main textile competitors like Poperinge. The mercantile elites may have lost their grip on international markets and were in danger of being sidelined as the clothiers could attract more entrepreneurial agency. They remained, thanks to their financial clout, however, true spiders in the financial web of Ypres, and were therefore still essential for all who wanted to get access to raw materials. If they had perhaps lost some of their political, commercial and industrial power, their financial power kept them very much at the centre of things. But a new balance had to be found with the other stakeholders in the industry nonetheless, and it is the relationship with the clothiers that was paramount in a new industrial power equilibrium.

CHAPTER 5

The Clothiers' Century

Cloth and Entrepreneurship

In his 2019 book on the growth of the woollen industry in medieval and early modern England, John Oldland discussed the importance of the long sixteenth century as the crucial era when English fabrics started to outcompete textiles manufactured in continental Europe. It was the clothiers who managed the industrial expansion in rural boroughs which produced all kinds of qualities of woollen cloth. They acted as intermediaries between rural cloth manufacture and the commercial (and cloth finishing) infrastructure in the provincial towns, and particularly in London itself.[242] Cloth was then exported by the English 'Merchant Adventurers' to the markets and fairs in Europe, above all to the fairs of Brabant and more and more also to Antwerp itself, where another layer was added to the cloth-finishing process to adapt the woollens to continental taste.[243] But it was the rural clothier who managed the production process and the transportation networks to the urban commercial hubs. Recently John Lee's in-depth study confirmed this image of the English clothier.[244] The clothier was a rural entrepreneur, in many cases stemming from the class of yeomen. He became the pivotal figure in the success of the English cloth industry in this period. From this time, the cloth industry – even the manufacture of high-quality broadcloth – was no longer an urban affair, as it had been in so many other parts of Europe. It became a rural activity, with rural weavers and other textile workers, assisted by high numbers of operating fulling mills and with loose and often direct links to the urban markets, and most notably to London, from which cloth merchants sent in their orders or communicated information about the latest fashions. But it was the rural clothiers themselves who constituted the heart of the industry. And many of the successful entrepreneurs accumulated wealth. They built impressive mansions in their rural centres or in small market towns, and some institutionalised their success by becoming landowners and members of the regional gentry. Here was a clear path to social advancement. The long sixteenth century was indeed truly the clothiers' century.

In the southern Low Countries no such dramatic developments occurred in the final decades of the Middle Ages. The triumph of the rural industries in the county of Flanders from the late Middle Ages into the early modern period was not based

---

242 Oldland, 'The Clothiers' Century', 1-22 and id., *The English Woollen Industry*. For the older studies of the English woollen industry see in particular Munro, 'Medieval Woollens', 243-244 and 269-275.
243 Thijs, *Van werkwinkel tot fabriek*. For the role of the English Merchant Adventurers at the Antwerp market, see Sutton, 'The Merchant Adventurers', 25-46. The commercial headquarters of the English in sixteenth-century Antwerp were located in one of the patrician palaces in the city, the "Hof van Liere", now owned by the University of Antwerp.
244 Lee, *The Medieval Clothier*.

on producing high- or middle-quality broadcloth; it was targeting completely different markets for cheaper textiles, cheaper woollens in the western parts of the county (Hondschoote and many other villages in the Flemish hill region, primarily in Nieuwkerke), cheaper linens all over the interior of Flanders and Hainaut into Holland, and cheaper tapestries in the countryside between Oudenaarde and Geraardsbergen. Always the upmarket versions of these textiles were produced in cities – linen in Kortrijk, woollens in the older cloth cities of Menen and Ypres – and in new urbanising centres such as Armentières with its famous *outrefin* woollens, and tapestries in Tournai and Oudenaarde.[245] Proto-industrial development in the countryside built on cheap labour, local or regional supply lines of raw materials (for flax and linen), and on systems of putting-out defined usually not by rural entrepreneurs, but by urban merchants using, if necessary local middlemen (*kutsers*). In England, on the other hand, all these systems existed for cheaper woollen kerseys and for linens, yet rural proto-industries, much more than their counterparts in the southern Low Countries, also targeted quality fabrics, where skill and expensive raw materials had to be combined in more complex arrangements. As we have seen, the rural clothier had been crucial in this process. He had no equivalent in Flanders.

But, of course, clothiers existed in Flanders as well. But unlike the rural *kutsers*, who distributed flax and linen in a *Kaufsystem* in the Flemish countryside, acting often on behalf of urban merchants, clothiers in Flanders were not rural, they were urban.[246] They coordinated, as did their English colleagues, the manufacture of woollens, distributed raw materials and took the finished goods to their commercial outlets, but they did this not in a rural, but in a very urban environment. At best they integrated rural labour in the manufacturing process for the labour-intensive stages of wool preparation (most notably for spinning). We saw already in chapter 2 that in Ypres the integration of rural labour in the urban process was not allowed, certainly not for those woollens that required the more expensive English wool. The monitoring activity of clothiers involved also the possession of the raw materials. Clothiers had to invest primarily in the expensive wool, not only in the actual monitoring costs. Urban craftsmen like weavers, fullers, tenterers, shearers and other cloth finishers (dyers constituted a separate category of labour relations because they were not necessarily supervised by the clothier) were not as such their employees, as is sometimes wrongly stated in literature, but they did little other than supply their labour, their tools of the trade (broadlooms, tenterers' frames, shearing tables and scissors, fullers' workshops) and their skill. Sometimes some of the raw materials were also included in the process: fullers had to provide the ingredients for the fulling process (fuller's earth for scouring, ammoniac liquids etc.). They provided, in other words, a service rather than a product, the bulk of which consisted of labour, and it was the clothier's task to coordinate this succession of services in order to safeguard the integrity of the production chain.

---

245 On these developments: Lis and Soly, 'Subcontracting in Guild-Based Export Trades', 81-113, and on the urban dimension of industrial change in fifteenth and sixteenth-century Flanders: Stabel, *Dwarfs among Giants*, 156-158.
246 Holbach, *Frühformen von Verlag*, 51-78.

Clothiers were therefore not necessarily craftsmen, although very often they were. The activity was in most Flemish cities open to all citizens, men and women (with a few exceptions, usually merchants active in wholesale trade, brokers and specific craftsmen in the production chain who were allegedly at risk of suffering from conflicts of interest between their trade and being clothiers, usually fullers, dyers and wool beaters). Still the old image of the clothier as the archetypical artisan-entrepreneur who had followed in the footsteps of the thirteenth-century merchant-entrepreneur persists. In the previous chapter we already downplayed the fact that there was such a clear-cut transition before and around 1300. The hold of the mercantile elites on the Ypres industry continued after 1300, and we will see in the following pages that perhaps also the so-called independent position of the clothier was not necessarily free of interference from merchants. Most money in the late medieval Low Countries was still to be made from active involvement in commercial ventures. Despite the rapid growth of a guild-organised middle class in Flanders during the fourteenth and fifteenth centuries, documented for Bruges, merchants were still leading the fiscal hierarchies.[247] The ringleaders of the many revolts in the fourteenth century were often merchants (or people who had ascended the commercial ladder). Some of the most famous leaders of urban revolts in this period were still from mercantile families. Even Jacob van Artevelde, the famous leader of Ghent in the 1330s and 1340s, was a wealthy cloth merchant before he started leading the anglophile party in Ghent.[248]

But clothiers were not necessarily new men. Although their social position and status undoubtedly changed in the final decades of the thirteenth century and they became more prominent, also as political figures, in the fourteenth century, they had been around before as well. In the previous chapter we saw that the position of merchants in the cloth industry was challenged in the final decades of the thirteenth century. Although they do not seem completely to have lost their hold on the cloth trade (and on the trade in raw materials), they met with increasing competition on the one hand from foreign merchants, mainly Italians, who took over much of the English wool trade. The decline of the fairs of Champagne for the wool and cloth trade proved fatal. Economic agency in the cloth business inevitably moved to the clothiers. In Ypres, clothiers appear already in the earliest surviving statutes of the cloth industry just before the Cokerulle revolt in September 1280. But there is little doubt that the function of clothier, of a middleman between industrial workers and merchants, was already in existence long before then. Throughout the late medieval periods the clothiers managed and coordinated the successive stages of manufacture. When, from 1280, they could buy wool for the Ypres cloth manufacture everywhere except in England, they could organise their activities more independently, it seems at first sight, of the mercantile elites in the city.[249] Whether they truly imported wool into Ypres is less likely; the wool that was used in the urban industry was still imported by merchants, now more often

---

47 Stabel, *A Capital of Fashion*, forthcoming.
48 In this sense Pieter de Coninck, one of the leaders of Bruges in the events surrounding the battle of Kortrijk in 1302, who was a weaver with modest origins, seems to have been the exception, rather than the rule (Dumolyn et al., 'Social groups', 148-150 and Van Werveke, *Jacob van Artevelde*).
49 Espinas and Pirenne, *Recueil*, 3, 453-454.

foreigners than Ypres-based merchants. But there is no doubt that their ways of securing a wool supply had been greatly diversified, and the risks involved in having that wool turned into cloth had also been greatly enhanced, as the protective shelter of mercantile capital under which they operated started to fall away. The potential gains, of course, also increased significantly. The clothiers had that wool turned into fibre and yarn; in many cases they also organised the dyeing of the fibre (or, less frequently, of the yarn). They sent the yarn to the weavers' workshops (which in many cases in Ypres they owned themselves), gave the raw woollens to the fullers, after the fulling process they took the felted fabrics to the tenterer's frame, from there to the shearer and from the shearer's workshop they either sent the finished woollen to the cloth hall for quality control and to sell to merchants or retail sellers of cloth, or they had them dyed in one of the city's dyeing workshops, taking them to a second tentering process and finally to the cloth hall.

From merchant entrepreneurs to clothiers: a social revolution in 1280?

In Ypres there is even a fixed date for that social transformation. In order to curb the tension in the social unrest surrounding the Cokerulle revolt of 1280, the mercantile city elites were forced to grant new groups in society better access to economic entrepreneurship. In a game-changing agreement the new group of clothiers could enter the cloth hall as independent economic actors. The clothiers could now invest in the most expensive raw materials for the industry, wool (and the fine expensive wool from East Anglia and the Midlands at that), at the start of the production chain, and they were able to sell the finished cloth at the end of it, retaining complete control of the production process in between (and they remained, in fact, the owners of the wool and woollens throughout the production chain). Hence, they were responsible for monitoring the production chain. It was this coordination task that would constitute the essence of their social role in the two centuries to come, and that turned the clothiers in Ypres from playing a subordinate role in the thirteenth century into an influential social group which, no longer satisfied with the passive role they had been given in the urban political system that was still dominated by the traditional elites, would be one of the driving forces for political dissent and economic change in the following decades, or so the traditional narrative goes..[250] It is also thanks to their efforts that the drive in Ypres towards ever more luxury cloth was implemented. Their central role was therefore also a necessary step for the flexibility the industry showed during the difficult late Middle Ages.[251]

Yet the clothiers remain an inscrutable group. Where did they come from? Who were they before the alleged revolution of 1280? Did they constitute in fact only one group? Where did they get the necessary financial means to acquire so rapidly a central

---

250 Howell, 'Capital Networks and Political Actors', 14-15 and 34.
251 Munro, 'Medieval Woollens', 244-249.

role in the distribution of raw materials to the textile workers? Wool was extremely expensive, certainly the wool used in the *draperie ointe*, so acquiring it required substantial financial means. What was the average size of their enterprise or, in other words, how many working women and textile craftsmen were dependent on them? Certainly, the already mentioned lists of 1302, in which hundreds of clothiers sold individually only very limited amounts of cloth to the city officials, suggest that a clothier's operation was usually only very small. So it is likely that around 1,300 clothiers employed only a limited number of people. What was their relationship with the actual industrial operations of guild masters: were they in fact themselves part of the production chain at this early stage? And why were the merchants apparently so easily persuaded to leave their dominant role as central coordinators of textile manufacture? Before we start answering some of these questions, let us turn first to the already numerous studies about the Ypres industry that deal with the rise of the *drapiers* in the late thirteenth century. Literature, hardly surprisingly considering the nature of the preserved sources, tends to focus on political relations. It is a story of sometimes bloody confrontation, of political emancipation and a struggle for political participation at various levels of urban society. This political turmoil will be dealt with in chapter 9, but through the story of political struggle, historians have also pointed occasionally to the social (and sometimes economic) identity of these new political stakeholders.

For Georges Doudelez, the most important historian of the social revolts in medieval Ypres, things were relatively simple. The Ypres clothiers had grown as an important group during the rise of the Ypres cloth industry in the thirteenth century. Alongside the textile guilds of the weavers, fullers and shearers, they had been emancipated from the overall control of the mercantile elites, and from the 1280s they were also able to develop their own institutional arrangements to facilitate their hold on the production chain. This change seems to have been very sudden in Ypres. In the period just before the Cokerulle revolt of 1280-1281 the mercantile elites started to lose their grip on the political organisation and on the cloth industry itself. They first tried in September 1280 to find allies among the other textile guilds, the fullers and shearers, by granting them advantageous wages at the expense of the clothiers (who had to pay these higher wages), and when this did not work – the fullers and shearers participated in the *Cokerulle* revolt, just like the clothiers – the elites were forced to grant the clothiers themselves new advantageous privileges. Indeed, only a couple of weeks after their attempt to seduce the shearers and fullers, the clothiers were given access to the market for raw materials outside Ypres (but not in England), and they were able to enter the cloth hall as traders of all finished products (before, they could only trade in cheaper textiles outside the hall). From this moment on, the mercantile elites lost their monopoly on the wool and cloth trade. Suddenly, the clothiers were able to cut themselves loose from their dependence on the merchants, which had stifled their business potential before that date and had kept them, to use Pirenne's description, in a subordinate position. Despite the (relatively easy-going) repression after the revolt, the clothiers' privileges were maintained and later confirmed by the Count of Flanders, Guy of Dampierre, in April 1281.

This interpretation of the events, adopted by many historians ever since, needs, however, to be looked at more carefully. As we will show in Chapter 9, the attempts of the mercantile elites in September 1280 to find allies among the textile craftsmen, more precisely among the fullers and shearers, are only a matter of speculation. Nothing in the two wage settings of 1280 suggests that they were issued to appease the textile workers. They could just as well have been very restrictive and therefore issued at the request of the clothiers or the merchants. We do not know what the wages were like before the September wage setting. Nothing even suggests that clothiers were at this stage what they would become in the fourteenth century, the central figures in the organisation of the production chain. Furthermore, it is highly unlikely that the fullers' and shearers' wage settings, allegedly negative for the clothiers, and the clothiers' statutes, assumed to be very positive, which are only weeks apart, imply a volte face on the part of the elites. After all the *Cokerulle*, which happened only many weeks later, was also an internal elite conflict that was transposed on to a social conflict involving the broader urban community, and the textile guilds in the first instance.[252] The wage settings primarily fixed the rewards for the journeymen's efforts and point therefore in the first instance to internal friction within the guild between masters and journeymen. Moreover, the so-called restrictive measures against the clothiers were aimed primarily at fighting abuse and were repeated in almost all later statutes, when the clothiers were already a force to be reckoned with.

What is certain, however, is that the clothiers started to come to the forefront of industrial organisation in exactly this period. They were, however, already around before the 1280 and 1281 rulings, but from these dates, despite or perhaps thanks to the social unrest, they could operate more independently of the mercantile elites, and they obtained access to the commercial tools that allowed them to adapt more flexibly to changing economic circumstances. So we must look at both the circumstances in which this social change occurred and the conditions in which clothiers worked before and after the reforms of 1281.

Following Espinas and Pirenne, Doudelez also points to the master weavers as the main group from which the clothiers were recruited. As a result of their dominance in the weavers' guild, the weavers who appear in the guild statutes of the late thirteenth century were even usually in fact only journeymen; it was the clothiers themselves who were the entrepreneurs leading the weavers' workshops. They were therefore the guild masters, and their activities were primarily ruled by the clothiers' statutes, not by the weavers'.[253] As already mentioned, in the fourteenth and fifteenth centuries this assimilation of weaving and cloth entrepreneurship was certainly not general, and we have no indication that that was the case in the earlier period either. What later came to be known as *conventers*, master weavers who were not (able to become) clothiers, seem to be present in the latter part of the thirteenth century as well. In

---

252 In the literature, from Doudelez to very recently Bervoets, this aspect of the revolt is underestimated and the cokerulle is a pure class conflict between the elites and the textile workers (see Bervoets, *Quicumque in villa per annum unum*, 413-415 with an overview of this traditional interpretation).
253 Doudelez, 'La révolution communale', 205, a representation taken over by Van Werveke, *De koopman-ondernemer*.

the debts, recorded in the so-called *lettres de foire*, master weavers (*tisserand, tellier, tillier*) borrowed on average 150d sterling, while clothiers (who were sometimes also master weavers, of course, but whose economic interests were primarily served by their activities as clothiers) borrowed on average more than 1,900d.[254] The former probably had to invest only in a workshop with one or two broadlooms, a once-in-a-lifetime investment, while the latter also had to arrange such an investment, but they had to be able primarily to gain access to capital continually in order to buy the necessary raw materials and pay for the overheads of monitoring production. As 'makers of cloth' (*faisceurs de draes*), the clothiers were therefore small businessmen (and, unlike the master weavers, also businesswomen), but because they controlled the flows of raw materials and the product in its successive stages, their entrepreneurship exceeded the scope of a mere master craftsman, and they became as such a group in between the mercantile elites and the small commodity producers (although, as master weavers, they were also such small commodity producers), a real middle class in the true sense, a class in the middle of things. At all times, from the start of the production chain with the preparation of the wool to the final product when the finished woollens were taken to the cloth hall, they remained the owners of the wool or woollens. So, in fact, they were the organisers of a complex outsourcing chain.

Doudelez does not, however, mention where their starting capital came from, and how exactly the new relations with the merchants originated.[255] It is likely, in light of the many restrictions on their operational independence (they had to buy wool in Ypres from the merchants and sell the woollens again to the merchants, which put them, of course, in a position of complete dependence), that the clothiers before 1280-1281 were indeed very much like foremen in an industrial operation, wage earners in all but name. Whether money changed hands already at the beginning of the process or whether clothiers were engaged in credit relations with the Ypres merchants, the lack of alternative and the fact that they could not deal with other importers of wool or with other exporters of cloth meant that they were in fact employees of the merchants and their independence was only theoretical. It is likely in such circumstances that they developed privileged relations with specific merchants and that in this way true economic clienteles were established. Clothiers could only follow the social and economic choices enforced on them by the merchants. Although it was the clothier who monitored the industrial operations already in the thirteenth century, it is likely that the merchants themselves were also involved in the industrial process, and in the same way as Boinebroke in Douai. The same mercantile elites were also landowners who, directly or indirectly as administrators of charitable institutions, rented (or sold) the properties in the centre of the city and in the industrial suburbs, in which the textile workers, the clothiers included, lived, and, as we saw in Chapter 2, in the early dyers' statutes they were also still very important in the late thirteenth century for giving commissions to dyers.

---

54 See also Chapter 4.
55 Doudelez, 'La révolution communale', 201-208.

In 1280-1281 all this changed. Instead of facing operational restrictions, clothiers could henceforth operate more flexibly and, at least in theory, independently of the Ypres mercantile capitalists. This had everything to do with the changed position of the merchants themselves. In successive trade difficulties with England, the Flemish merchants lost their hold on the English export market for wool. Instead, wool was increasingly imported into Flanders by English, Hanseatic and primarily Italian merchants. The pressure to loosen their grip on the wool trade must have been enormous, certainly in market conditions in which English wool became more important than wool of other origins. In the same vein, export markets changed as well, and the Flemish merchants turned away from exporting the woollens to Europe. The risky commercial operations in much less predictable market conditions were exchanged for more secure regional commercial systems. In the thirteenth century the Low Countries had become one of the densest urban systems in Europe, offering mercantile capital many alternatives. For many this change was successful. Merchants remained, in the urban societies of the late medieval Low Countries, by far the richest and politically most influential group. In late fourteenth-century Bruges, the average wealth of regional merchants in wool, cloth, grain, wood etc. by far exceeded that of those who, as middlemen, were involved in international trade (brokers and hostellers).[256] Moreover, the abandonment of international trade was never complete and Flemish merchants were also much engaged in financial arrangements with foreign merchants. The most intense financial operations in late thirteenth-century Ypres were those between Italian financiers and Ypres merchants.

It is therefore much more the changed strategy of the Ypres mercantile elites, rather than the social and political emancipation of the clothiers themselves, that generated the social shifts in society. The social change was therefore in the first instance driven by economics, rather than by politics. It was therefore also a slow and gradual process, rather than a sudden revolution in 1280-1281. The success of the clothiers after their legal status changed in 1281 was also not immediate. They led the other textile trades, certainly (they probably already did long before 1280), but their share of the £500 art. that had to be paid to the Count of Flanders, Guy of Dampierre, by the craft guilds in the aftermath of the *Cokerulle* revolt amounted to only £92, more than the other textile guilds (fullers and shearers had to pay £60 each), but not significantly more.[257] This already shows their different financial strength from regular guild entrepreneurs like master fullers or shearers, but it does not show the economic dominance of a wholly separate middle group, which is described by Doudelez and adopted by many other historians.

There is little doubt, however, that from the 1280s they acquired a significant role in urban society. The charter itself, given by Guy of Dampierre in April 1281, is a strange mixture of measures defining the clothiers' role in the industry, but it also contains general measures securing urban government in general.[258] It was meant, therefore, to

---

256 Stabel, *Capital of Fashion*, forthcoming.
257 Espinas and Pirenne, *Recueil*, 3, 681.
258 See also Chapter 8.

ease the tense situation in Ypres, and perhaps the fact that in the end the sanctions the city received were relatively mild, certainly compared with those after the events of 1303 and 1329, can probably be interpreted in the same way. But not only had the social position of the clothiers changed slowly, those of the elite merchants had as well. After the trade difficulties between England and Flanders in 1270-1274, they gradually lost hold on the catalyst of their leading position in the industry, their control of the wool supply or, rather, the English wool supply for the fine woollens. Although English customs accounts are difficult to interpret, the reconstructions for the late thirteenth century and early fourteenth century suggest that imports by Ypres merchants from Boston, their main point of access to the English market, declined steadily from about 1,300 sacks in the 1290s (which must have been already substantially lower than before the 1270s) to about 500 in the 1320s. Moreover, besides the traditional elite families, already a substantial number of newcomers, sometimes called *marchands-drapiers* (in this case perhaps entrepreneurs with mercantile activities, rather than the other way round), figure among the Ypres tradesmen in England and at the fairs of Champagne.[259] The social composition of the mercantile class changed in the same period from a closed mercantile elite consisting of a limited number of families that monopolised political power to a more open group, consisting still overwhelmingly of mercantile capitalists, but counting among its numbers also new families which had risen from the city's middle classes. It is not certain, however, that before 1280 the clothiers were among these newcomers (or that, if clothiers achieved mercantile success, they held on to their industrial activities). So the gradual decline in active trade after 1270 may not have been that critical for the economic dominance of the merchant class. As in so many other cities, the elite was opened to some newcomers, and the internal frictions within the elite during the Cokerulle events – the revolt was financed and led by new wealthy families – seem to be an indication of this.

The social changes in the late thirteenth century, with the growing importance of a mercantile role for clothiers in the city itself after 1280, were certainly facilitated also by the changed economic environment. They were not necessarily decided by deliberately altered strategies of the Ypres mercantile class completely to abandon international trade yet. Exactly in this period, as the share of foreigners in the wool trade in Ypres grew, English wool exports were more and more also concentrated in London. But Ypres merchants still demonstrated a willingness to go with the flow and they moved to London from smaller port towns such as Boston. So they appeared to be still reacting swiftly to changing trade flows.[260] They remained active for another couple of decades also at the Champagne fairs, before finally these lost their European-wide importance in the early fourteenth century. And Ypres cloth output did not yet change dramatically. The production of says, worsteds and semi worsteds, of the *enforchié*-woollens suffered in this period and overall output declined, but at the same time the late thirteenth and early fourteenth centuries were also the golden age for striped half-cloth, the stamforts with a dry warp yarn and made (partly) from wool imported from elsewhere. These

---

[259] Mus, 'Het aandeel van de Ieperlingen', 322-355.
[260] Nightingale, *A Medieval Mercantile Community*, 102-107.

covertures started to dominate exports to Mediterranean markets and compensated for the lesser appeal of the other worsteds and semi-worsteds. But the trends in the Ypres cloth industry after the 1320s nonetheless moved inevitably towards a greater share of greased luxury cloth, and thus a greater share of the finest English wool (in Ypres usually coming from the Midlands).

In the longer run, however, the Ypres merchants' abandonment of the English wool trade was probably also an abandonment of wool supply and control of the cloth output altogether. With this the mercantile elites inevitably started to lose their strongest instrument for controlling the industry. This was more likely to have been a gradual process than a shock in 1280. But fourteenth-century cloth manufacture would not be dominated by merchants; this would be the century of the clothiers.

Access to Entrepreneurship

Flemish clothiers are still very much enigmatic figures. Traditionally associated around 1300 with skilled textile artisans, and therefore with guildsmen, they cannot be defined only in those terms. Craft guilds in medieval Flanders, and the textile guilds most of all, were bastions of male entitlement, where women were kept from the training schemes and could not therefore aspire to gaining access to the guild curriculum. So, except for specific cases (widows of master guildsmen and very rarely also masters' daughters), no women appear in regular guild manufacture. As a rule, guild entrepreneurship outside the protective shelter of the master's household (as wives, daughters and domestic servants) was therefore not possible for single women or women acting independently of their husbands, fathers or guardians. Yet there were women among the clothiers in most Flemish cities, and this was also the case in Ypres.[261] The fact that during the whole late medieval period dyadic strings (men clothiers and women clothiers: *drapier ende drapierigghe*) were used is telling, as most other female occupations tend to disappear from the cloth industry's statutes around 1300 (except for the preparation of wool: spinners, combers and carders who are addressed often by female occupational titles only).[262] The statutes do not provide any impediment to women being active as cloth entrepreneurs, therefore, despite the fact that they were kept out of the important manufacturing stages organised by the guilds. Before assessing who clothiers really were, we need therefore to take a close look at the regulation, and how this regulation changed over time.

In theory, all Ypres citizens could become clothiers, yet there were also specific incompatibilities. Because the broker was the intermediary between the Ypres clothier and the foreign merchant, he had to be trustworthy and avoid potential conflicts of interest. To achieve this, Ypres clothiers were not allowed to become wool or cloth brokers. But other wool and cloth craftsmen were also excluded from becoming clothiers. This was the case for the (usually wealthy) dyers, their journeymen and members of

---

261 See also chapter 8.
262 Stabel, 'Working Alone?', 27-49, and for Douai Kittel and Queller, 'Whether Man or Woman…', 63-100.

their households, and certain cloth finishers as well. The most important group to be excluded was, however, the guild of the fullers. In order to be successful entrepreneurs, master fullers had to run a sizable operation with a substantial number of employees and involving access to sufficient capital. So they were, in theory, just like the dyers, also well placed to become clothiers. But the preparatory stages of wool treatment were also excluded. Wool washers, wool carriers and (female) carders, combers and spinsters, all of them belonging to the much poorer strata in Ypres society, were not allowed to become clothiers either. But their lack of capital probably prevented them from being active as cloth entrepreneurs anyway, although a strict ban which was repeated in the clothiers' statutes from around 1300 suggests that perhaps some tried nonetheless. If these women were found in any association with a clothier or to be monitoring cloth manufacture themselves, the woollens would be confiscated.[263] It is not particularly the gender of these workers that was at stake (other women were permitted to become clothiers), but rather the danger that illegal wool would be used. Moreover, outside cloth manufacture in the strict sense, all tradesmen dealing in various greased goods were forbidden to become clothiers as well. Grease constituted, of course, one of the crucial ingredients for the treatment of woollen fibre, yarn and woollen fabric (for spinning, weaving and fulling operations), and they were the source of a lot of anxiety about the quality of the products (butter was allowed; animal grease and oil in many cases disallowed).[264]

As always, regulation about access to the position of clothier was cumulative, and restrictions were built on other restrictions. All craft activities were forbidden in the clothiers' charter of 1280: clothiers were not allowed to practise any craft. But restrictions were eased in the middle of the fourteenth century, when Ypres became primarily a producer of luxury cloth. Henceforth all Ypres citizens, men and women, were allowed to become clothiers, except for the occupations already mentioned: brokers, dyers, dyers' journeymen, wool cleaners, wool carriers, fullers, combers, carders, spinners and all who dealt in greased goods or sold goods as retailers (*alle die scuppe houden van vettewaren of van van clenen penewaerden te vercopene*).[265] So in practice only the making of cloth was allowed, in this way restricting access to entrepreneurship in the Ypres cloth industry to all citizens who were not craftsmen, with the exception of the 'makers of woollens', the weavers (*tant comme il face dras*). Shearers and cloth finishers are not mentioned. So, from the original ban on simultaneously executing another occupation while being a clothier, it became impossible for many specific tradesmen to become clothiers. The married partners of clothiers could, however, continue another craft that was considered to be incompatible. As guild-organised crafts were usually restricted to men, this clause points to the fact that not only could women become clothiers, because their activity did not constitute an impediment to their husbands continuing their craft, but it was even encouraged for women to become clothiers, because a household could

---

[263] Espinas and Pirenne, *Recueil*, 3, 461.
[264] Espinas and Pirenne, *Recueil*, 3, 516.
[265] Espinas and Pirenne, *Recueil*, 3, 518.

otherwise not continue its activity in cloth entrepreneurship when the husband was also a member of one of the excluded guilds.[266]

These incompatibilities were refined and even sharpened in the following decades. Gradually all kinds of other associations between clothiers and craftsmen that went beyond their professional relations were forbidden. In the fourteenth century fullers could no longer engage in financial relations with clothiers. They were forbidden not only to invest directly in clothiers' operations, but they were also not allowed to act as financial pledgees for them.[267] Access to cloth entrepreneurship was reduced further. Not only were guild members (except weavers) considered unsuited to becoming clothiers, but also other activities in cloth manufacture that were not organised into a guild were targeted more and more.

Around 1300 the dyers were also removed from having a coordinating role in the production chain. They were formally banned from being active as clothiers. The separation between clothiers and dyers was completed with other rules. Clothiers could not even give instructions to dyers to dye their woollens; it was merchants who had to do this.[268] This initial limitation of the clothier's activities disappeared quickly, however. It was probably impossible to maintain in the fourteenth century, when merchants gave up direct involvement in textile manufacture. In the early fourteenth century the statutes of the dyers in red state that dyers could dye the woollens of *upsetters* or clothiers. The strict prohibition on dyers being active as clothiers remained, of course.[269] But apparently it was not impossible for dyers to own woollens that needed to be dyed. As it is not very likely that these woollens would be for their own use, it seems that the combination of a dyer's workshop and a merchant's activity was not unthinkable. Dyers more and more obtained therefore the privileges of merchants and the institutional distance from the other main textile trades of weavers and fullers increased. The dyers' guild in Ypres did not belong to the traditional textile trades, but to the citizens' trades. The two lines of activity were, indeed, however, separated completely.

In fact, almost everywhere in Flemish urban cloth manufacture the most frequent combination of a guild-organised trade and entrepreneurship in cloth was probably the weaver-clothier. It was in the end the only occupational combination in cloth manufacture that was formally mentioned in the statutes. Weavers, even master weavers, were, however, never among the big earners in manufacture. Even among the textile trades, their average income was paradoxically relatively low, and in contrast to those of fullers and dyers the average size of their workshops was small. Still entry to the weaver's guild was an option for ambitious citizens. They saw here a chance to gain additional leverage, not because of the weaving activity itself and the income it generated, but because weaving constituted the crucial link between wool preparation and cloth finishing. Weaving was undoubtedly the most strategic stage in the production chain. So, although cloth entrepreneurship also came within reach of other artisans

---

266 Espinas and Pirenne, *Recueil*, 3, 453-454. See also chapter 8.
267 Espinas and Pirenne, *Recueil*, 3, 579.
268 *Nus ki fait taindre draes puet faire faire draes. Et nus ki fait faire draes peut faire taindre draes* (Espinas and Pirenne, *Recueil*, 3, 481).
269 Espinas and Pirenne, *Recueil*, 3, 621.

in the urban economy and although in fact all citizens with easy and cheap access to capital could become clothiers, the weaver's guild was bound to be the main entry into cloth entrepreneurship. And, probably, most master weavers were in fact primarily clothiers who also ran a weaver's workshop. A training in the weaver's guild was a ticket for those Ypres citizens with the potential to mobilise a certain amount of capital into entrepreneurship in the woollen industry, without the actual weaving activity necessarily providing a solid income base for thriving as a weaver. This is surely the major organisational anomaly in the leading industry of the medieval Low Countries.

The tax registers for late fourteenth-century Bruges show that weavers were a socially very heterogenous group, with most artisans belonging to the poor and lower middle-class population of the city, yet also with very wealthy representatives belonging to the higher middle classes and even to the city elites.[270] There is little doubt that their wealth did not come from the actual weaving activity. It was the combination of the position of master weavers in the production chain and their guild membership on the one hand with the income generated from being active as clothiers that gave them this privileged position in the wealth distribution. A similar pattern is very likely for Ypres as well. In other words, the fact of being a weaver gave the clothier an advantage in his/her competition with other clothiers. Controlling a weaver's workshop allowed him/her to reach out to both ends of that production chain. The combination of weaver and clothier was so ubiquitous that sometimes the two occupations were mixed up in the terminology of the statutes. In the statutes of the cloth measurers it is stated that the clothiers are responsible for 'weaving the seal' in the raw cloth themselves, something a clothier who was not a weaver could, of course, not do. He had to rely on the master weavers for this. But this is not mentioned in the statutes.[271]

Yet there were also limits to the combination of weaver and clothier. Not all clothiers were weavers, and not all master weavers became clothiers. According to the clothiers' statutes of Ypres of the late 1380s, when the city's cloth output had already diminished considerably and most of the manufacture was now geared towards exclusively high-quality woollens, active weavers (*wever metter hand*: literally meaning weavers 'who work with their hands') were not allowed to combine their trade with being *upzetter*, cloth or wool merchants. This was clearly a new ordinance, because statutes provided rulings for those weavers who had been active as merchants or *upzetters* before that date.[272] *Upzetters* were also cloth entrepreneurs, but they controlled only parts of the production chain, and their role was usually limited to coordinating (not executing) cloth finishing and dyeing.[273] This ruling shows that during the heyday of the Ypres cloth manufacture in the late thirteenth and first half of the fourteenth centuries it had become possible for craftsmen and guildsmen to combine the cloth trade with cloth manufacture. Were these the *marchands-drapiers* in some of the Ypres sources: merchants active in cloth manufacture and disposing of larger amounts of

---

270 Stabel, *Capital of Fashion*, forthcoming.
271 Espinas and Pirenne, *Recueil*, 3, 525.
272 Espinas and Pirenne, *Recueil*, 3, 549-550.
273 Demey, 'De Vlaamse ondernemer in de middeleeuwse nijverheid', 143-156.

capital than the artisan-clothiers? But it also shows that the combination of commerce and manufacture was gradually looked at with suspicion. It is perhaps the drive towards more quality that separated these functions again. From the 1380s it was stated formally that merchants who were active in cloth finishing and dyeing were not allowed to become involved in any of the other manufacturing stages ('in the way of the clothiers'). Merchants, in other words, continued to cherry-pick in the most lucrative manufacturing processes, but the thresholds for clothiers to become involved in trade were raised. It is probably no coincidence that exactly in this period access to the political institutions of Ypres was again limited to the mercantile elites.

Monitoring Cloth Manufacture

Clothiers held a crucial monitoring position in manufacture, but their position vis-à-vis the craftsmen, certainly in the last stages often guildsmen with their own workshops and employees, and therefore also with their own access to capital and economic initiative, was not necessarily always the same. As a rule, except for the labour-intensive stages of production and perhaps some of the equally labour-intensive finishing jobs, where in the former women and in the latter men primarily sold their skill and labour, these craftsmen offered what can be described as an all-in outsourced service in the production chain. As we saw in Chapter 2, weavers (if they were not clothiers), fullers, dyers, tenterers and shearers were entrepreneurs in their own right. As guild masters, they headed workshops of their own, integrating labour and sometimes also raw materials (fullers and dyers) in the production process. The clothiers therefore operated in a market where long-term and reciprocal relations between clothiers and craftsmen were important certainly, but where there was always an alternative option, for both the clothier and the craftsmen. They operated, in other words, in a competitive market, where the price for goods and services could change and evolve in function of relations of scarcity. Although the clothiers owned the wool and the fabrics in the production chain, the market position of the clothiers could therefore vary.

This was considered probably as a possible threat for the continuation of the industry, so the relations between clothiers and their craftsmen were well defined and described in a complex and evolving regulatory framework. Its main concern was to stabilise economic and social relations and make them more predictable in order to safeguard the standard quality of the products and the continuity of the industrial relations. So regulation dealt 1° primarily with the phases of transition, when a product had to move to the next link in the production chain, 2° with reimbursement for the services rendered (what was to be paid when and for what, who paid for the tools and raw materials of the operations, what the labour relations on the work floor were and how these affected the position of the monitoring clothier), 3° with the timing of manufacture (how long particular operations took, when and in which circumstances the product was transferred to the next production stage, how the successive stages could be coordinated efficiently), and finally 4° with possible liabilities if something went wrong (when there was damage to the product, when time limits were not met, when the end-consumers, the merchants, were not pleased with the overall result, quantity or quality).

A smooth and reliable transition from one stage of manufacture to another was the key element for the success of the industry, and of the clothier. Delays were costly and, considering the limited scope of a clothier's business, badly monitored quality was potentially lethal for his or her economic survival. The clothiers had to make sure that before the woollen finally received its official seal at the cloth hall, all the different seals were attached to it at each stage of the production chain, at the loom, after fulling, before and after tenting and shearing, or when woollens were, because of fundamental flaws, removed from the production chain, that they were duly cut up and not reinserted into that chain. Such discarded woollens could not be sold in the regular marketing system, in the cloth hall or before the hospital (*voor tgasthuus*).[274] The clothier was the person merchants could turn to if something went wrong, so clothiers were allowed to sell only woollens they had monitored. In fourteenth-century Ypres commercial concentrations were not allowed at the level of clothiers. Being a clothier was after 1280 directly linked with having a stall in the cloth hall (or at the central market square for the cheaper woollens). Commercial concentration and economies of scale therefore clearly remained a prerogative for merchants.[275] There was only one exception to this rule. Clothiers were during the fourteenth century allowed to buy woollens and have them dyed for resale. The dyers, the very last stage in the production chain (which, in contrast to all other operations, did not necessarily have to be executed in Ypres itself), were as always, the exception in the strictly defined transition of the product in the chain.

The scale of a clothier's operation was also limited regarding the wool supply. Those who dealt in wool *in groots* ('in large quantities') were not allowed to be active as clothiers, nor to have clothiers working directly for them. After 1280 the direct involvement of the merchants in cloth manufacture was indeed abandoned. Nor were clothiers (or weavers) allowed to sell wool in the city (except when they had fetched that wool from England and Scotland themselves). The clean separation between industrial and commercial activity was imposed at great expense (a fine of £50) to those who did not abide with it. Clothiers could therefore not create hierarchical networks. In other words, they were not allowed to buy raw materials for other clothiers.[276] It has been established that in the late-fifteenth-century cloth industries of the Leie towns (Menen and Kortrijk) wealthier clothiers planned with Florentine wool and cloth merchants to barter woollens for wool. Those clothiers distributed that wool among other clothiers, creating in fact hierarchical supply systems and mutual dependencies among clothiers.[277] In thirteenth- and fourteenth-century Ypres these hierarchical networks of clothiers were clearly not yet tolerated. Still, we see that some fourteenth-century clothiers sold woollens outside the city, at the fairs of Flanders or even beyond the

---

74 Espinas and Pirenne, *Recueil*, 3, 519-520.
75 Espinas and Pirenne, *Recueil*, 3, 539-540.
76 Espinas and Pirenne, *Recueil*, 3, 541.
77 Stabel, 'Ambachten en ondernemers', 79-98.

borders of the county. The expression used in the statutes was 'across the sea and beyond the River Somme' (*over zee of over Somme*), the river that divided the county of Artois from Picardy.[278] So, while true economics of scale could not develop at the clothiers' level, the statutes gradually allowed some room for broadening the scope of clothier businesses, nonetheless.

Regulation is much less developed regarding reimbursement for the services the craftsmen rendered to the clothiers. Most wage regulation was aimed at defining work relations in the workshop, and therefore dealt with wages for journeymen, which as a rule were to be paid by the master craftsman as the head of the workshop, not by the clothier who dealt in principle only with the guild master. Still some issues also touched on the activities of the clothiers themselves. Specific price settings at some key moments defined the costs clothiers had to pay to the master craftsmen. Around 1280 there were wage settings for fullers and shearers. These concerned not only the wages of journeymen, but also the price the masters would receive for shearing or fulling particular qualities of woollens. In the middle of the fourteenth century a similar wave of price settings can be found back in the statutes. So, in key periods, when the overall structure of the industry underwent dramatic change, price and wage settings pop up; in other periods they do not. How long these settings were effectively implemented is a matter of conjecture, but their scarcity points nonetheless to the fact that overall prices and wages were normally left to normal market conditions.

The statutes do, however, pay attention to the conditions of payment. In the shearers' wage setting of 1280 it is stated that shearers should be paid by the clothier every two weeks (*a le quinzaine*).[279] Clothiers should also pay all the masters in full, even when they had taken the commission away from them after having agreed a deal, and then taken it to a competitor.[280] When, because of a flaw or a missing seal in the woollen delivered to them, craftsmen were not able to continue their work, the clothiers had to reimburse them for the time for which they could not work. It was the clothier's responsibility, after all, to check whether at each stage everything had been done to secure the integrity of the production chain. But when such a woollen was found at the fuller's premises, without him having declared the flaw or missing seal, not only was the clothier fined but also the fuller himself.[281] If clothiers complained, however, about the quality of the work, they could remove their woollens, even when they still

---

278 Espinas and Pirenne, *Recueil*, 3, 542. The expression probably refers to the border with France and with England or, more generally, even with France and the Empire and with the British Isles, so everything beyond the borders of the County of Flanders. It is striking that the River Somme border was often used as a point of reference in the Ypres cloth industry. The craftsmen who were banished in 1329 also had to settle beyond the River Somme. The County of Artois, even before the Burgundian dukes took hold of it, was not always considered as a very different principality, although its counts had only occasionally also been counts in Flanders (and not in this period), so it is placed at an equal level with Flanders itself. In this period, the middle of the fourteenth century, Walloon-Flanders, with the cities of Lille and Douai, was also not fully part of the county as it was in the direct possession of the French King (on the border questions, see also Dauphant, *Le royaume des Quatre rivières*).
279 Espinas and Pirenne, *Recueil*, 3, 455.
280 Espinas and Pirenne, *Recueil*, 3, 570 (for relations with a master fuller), 600 (for the shearers), 607 (for the cloth finishers) and 626 (for the dyers).
281 Espinas and Pirenne, *Recueil*, 3, 577-578.

owed the craftsmen their wages. Clothiers should in this case pay half of the arrears within three months, and the other half in the next period of three months.[282] In no way could the clothier pressurise the craftsmen he had contracted with to speed up the work or cut corners by various 'subtle means' (*subtylheiden*). But this was also a two-way relationship: master fullers were not allowed to refuse a commission from a clothier when one of their fuller's troughs was still empty. But the main concern was, of course, payment for the finished woollen: the price the clothiers got for all their investment and efforts. Brokers seem to have had a crucial role in this. They had to register carefully how many woollens were sold, what kind of woollens and their price, whether the parties were liable directly in each transaction (*droghe ghelt*) or for which pledgees had given security for full payment (*ter bortucht*). In the first case full payment had to be arranged within eight days or before the woollens left the broker's inn. The payment delays when a local security was involved (probably a member of the local mercantile elite) were to be negotiated between the clothier and the buyer of his woollens (*also ze staet*).[283]

In all this the clothier was responsible for the quality of the product. A personal token was to be attached to sets of woollens that were sold in the cloth hall or at the fairs of Ypres. In a later addition it is stated that the clothier's name and his personal sign should be written on a small piece of paper (*brievekin*) and attached to the woollens.[284] At the peak moments when a lot of foreign cloth merchants were present in the city, clothiers were allowed to sell only from their stalls in the hall or at the market, and only clothiers or *upsetters* could run such a stall. As a rule, the stalls in the cloth hall were raffled, so that everyone had an equal chance of having a good location in the cloth hall.[285] Woollens that were sold had also to be registered in the cloth hall with the names of the clothiers and the buyers. Brokers had to make sure of this. Sadly, none of this detailed administration has survived. It was to be checked whether the right kind of wool had been used. Traceability was of the utmost importance. In the oldest surviving general statutes of the clothiers from around 1300 it is stressed that, if there was any suspicion about the quality or the provenance of the wool, the clothier could swear that indeed the right wool had been used. Trust and personal reputation were strong elements in the construction of quality. The clothier could 'purge himself by his oath' (*purgier par son sairement*).[286] The clothier remained, however, liable for all shortcomings that were found in cloth with regard to the size or quality of the woollen and, as a rule, if the fault did not lie with the craftsmen, he or she had to make amends for such shortcomings and pay for injury suffered by the merchants. Moreover, consecutive shortcomings could eventually lead to banishment from the trade, and even from the city. If the shortcomings were, however, the result of the operations of the craftsmen, clothiers could refer to them for reparations: fullers could be forced to full the woollen again, and others had to pay for the damage if a woollen no longer complied

---

82 Espinas and Pirenne, *Recueil*, 3, 633 for the dyers.
83 Espinas and Pirenne, *Recueil*, 3, 546 and 549.
84 Espinas and Pirenne, *Recueil*, 3, 543.
85 Espinas and Pirenne, *Recueil*, 3, 539 and 590.
86 Espinas and Pirenne, *Recueil*, 3, 462.

with the standard quality and it was consequently downgraded (by cutting it in two or more smaller fabrics etc.).

But sometimes both the craftsmen and the clothier were punished for illegal practices. It was strictly forbidden for dyers in red to dye woollens, in this case scarlets, with grain (kermes) after they had been dyed with madder. Grained woollens were, of course, the famous scarlets, the top quality of Ypres, and therefore a very sensitive issue. Putting a layer of kermes on a layer of madder was much cheaper than dyeing a white or blue woollen only with kermes. It must have been tempting therefore for dyers to do this, as it was probably very difficult for any customer to detect such practices immediately. The aldermen probably thought that in this case the clothier must surely know of such deceit, and he was fined like the dyer the huge sum of £50 and sentenced to the confiscation of the (expensive) woollen.[287] The problems, of course, started when a flaw was detected only at a later stage, after other operations had taken place, when a merchant had a woollen dyed after he had taken it from a clothier, and a previous fault was detected during the dyeing process for instance.[288]

Clothiers fulfilled a crucial role in establishing the trustworthiness of the Ypres woollens. In the case of a scarlet, the top-end woollen of the Ypres cloth industry, damage to the reputation of the industry could be fatal. Flaws in woollens that did not fundamentally challenge their overall quality were allowed, but these flaws had to be communicated to the merchants who wanted to buy them. In short, the clothier was at the same time the person who supervised the manufacturing process, but also the guarantor of the transparency of the manufacturing and marketing procedures in Ypres itself. Only when the cloth was in the hands of the merchants, duly paid and exported, did his responsibility for the reputation of the industry end.[289]

Access to Capital

In her already mentioned recent research about the Ypres credit contracts, Martha Howell also discusses – how could it be otherwise – the crucial role of Ypres' cloth industry in these financial relations.[290] Her conclusions are very clear. She acknowledges the rise of an urban middle class led by craftsmen in the second half of the thirteenth century. They had carved out a substantial position in the Ypres credit markets both as lenders and as borrowers, although the capital they supplied or took up did not even come close to the important sums of money the merchants were involved in. The catalyst for this growing importance of the middle class, and particularly of the clothiers, had been the events surrounding the Cokerulle revolt. Following Georges Doudelez's

---

[287] Espinas and Pirenne, *Recueil*, 3, 521. On 23 June 1367 Jan Stockin, a clothier, was condemned to a fine of £100, half of the fine for having indeed dyed grain on top of madder, the other half for returning eight woollens that had been dyed in Wervik to a dyer's workshop in Ypres (Espinas and Pirenne, *Recueil*, 3, 649).
[288] Espinas and Pirenne, *Recueil*, 3, 496.
[289] See for instance Espinas and Pirenne, *Recueil*, 3, 497 and 509 for the middle of the fourteenth century.
[290] Howell, 'Credit networks and political actors', 3-36 and id., 'Un réseau de crédit à Ypres', 19-40. See also chapter 4 for a presentation of the source materials.

argument, the opening of the cloth hall to all Ypres citizens, who did not belong to the mercantile elite, gave small producers direct access to buyers of cloth, and at the same time the clothiers were given access to the market for wool (on this side of the English Channel), allowing them to deal directly with the Italian merchants who took over of the major part of the wool trade with England.[291] As a result, slightly more than 10 per cent of all borrowers (and 3 per cent of all lenders, mostly for small amounts) were identified as craftsmen, many of them active in textile manufacture mostly as dyers or clothiers (although the latter were not necessarily craftsmen themselves, of course), less often as weavers, fullers or cloth finishers. And probably many more of the unidentified parties belonged to the group of craftsmen. The financial market was therefore more or less inclusive. At any given time one third of the city's population was involved in it, surprisingly in a Flemish city where women enjoyed often secure property rights almost all of them men. Some of these borrower-craftsmen were involved in credit arrangements with Flemish, Artesian and Picard traders: more than a quarter of the credit contracts with these merchants involved craftsmen. An even greater group was involved in smaller credit contracts with people with backgrounds like their own.

Craftsmen were much less involved with borrowers from the region of Ypres itself, however, and they were almost uninvolved in dealings with merchants from France, Germany, England or Italy.[292] So these craftsmen were on the one hand probably involved in business transactions, and their credit arrangements were initiated for occupational reasons, but on the other hand they do not seem to have become involved in commerce, or in landownership in the region of Ypres, the traditional activities of the Ypres mercantile elites. And although the merchants and the old elites remained the dominant figures in distributing credit over the rest of urban society, the new middle classes of craftsmen and small entrepreneurs started to acquire an important position in credit relations, nonetheless. On the other hand, very few craftsmen dealt directly with foreign merchants. In this respect the old mercantile elites and some new merchants remained the financial spiders in the Ypres web. The position of the clothiers follows these trends, and 1280 does not appear in this material to have been a significant caesura. Although it was only after 1280 that people who did not belong to the merchant class and who had been active on the formal credit market already from the first moment for which we have documentation were engaged in (a limited number of) credit operations with foreign merchants – they were probably operating as clothiers and engaged in the credit contracts in order to acquire wool or other raw materials – no significant relative rise in contacts involving textile craftsmen or clothiers can be noted before and after 1280: the proportion of clothiers among the Ypres craftsmen rises only from less than 1 per cent to about 1 per cent (in real numbers from 4 to 31 contracts). For the dyers even less seem to have changed; their relative share even declined after 1280. Martha Howell confidently concludes therefore that the presence of the craftsmen in the debt contracts suggests that 'they were hardly dispossessed

---

[291] Howell, 'Credit networks and political actors', 14.
[292] See also de Valériola, 'Corpus', 44-50. The distribution of the artisans over the various economic sectors, most notably textile production, is however quite awkward in this contribution.

artisans fighting for their economic and social lives'. Here therefore is a confident group with vested interests in the financial market.[293]

Some of Howell's findings, however, need closer scrutiny. The conviction with which Howell uses financial relations to dismiss the impact of class relations, indeed of class struggle, to explain not only the social relations within the cloth industry, but even the reasons for and dynamics of revolts and social struggle, will be dealt with in Chapter 9. In this section we are dealing primarily with the relative economic position of the clothiers in the contracts. Considering the importance of cloth manufacture, they must be, after all, the flame carriers of the rising middle groups, the first group in the industrial cities of Flanders and Artois that had been able to carve out a central position in economic organisation, and henceforth also in the social and political networks in the Flemish cities. According to Howell, craftsmen, and therefore also the clothiers, were very much engaged in the financial market in Ypres. This is, of course, a logical assumption. Clothiers had to purchase the raw materials for the production of cloth, and they had at regular intervals to pay the unskilled women and the guild workshops that worked for them on their raw materials. Only at the end of the long production chain involving at least 20 to 30 different stages of production and at least ten different craftsmen and women, would they have been able to recover their investment at the cloth hall. So they had an urgent need for hard cash, the more so because we have seen that the guilds insisted very much on cash transactions, rather than on barter trade. Credit must therefore have been an essential instrument in the hands of the clothiers. The flexible financial markets in Ypres were there, of course, to supply this. And clothiers indeed also appear in the Ypres IOUs almost naturally as borrowers (so in essence as buyers of the raw materials or as borrowers needing cash to pay their workers) to collect the financial means for them to conduct their operations.

A closer look at the debt transactions, however, points to a very different pattern. What is most striking about the clothiers is not that they appear in debt contracts. They do, and they also seem to be appearing in similar numbers in the documents other than debt contract that were registered by the Ypres aldermen in this period. It is striking, however, that, for a new ambitious group in urban society, they do not appear all that often.[294] Howell counted seven clothiers before 1281 and 34 after 1281 in a total of almost 6,000 debt contracts, and only about 1 per cent of all transactions involving craftsmen.[295] That they appear so infrequently is remarkable, considering the capital-intensive nature of their business. Of all craftsmen in the city, they needed the largest amounts of cash just to operate. Certainly, a lot of the names in the debt contracts are not identified by their occupations, but this is of course true for all occupations in the city. Their importance is even dwarfed by the impact of another textile-related occupational group, the dyers. Both groups required to purchase expensive raw materials, of course, so they are, up to a point, very comparable. The capital-intensive nature

---

293 Howell, 'Credit Networks and Political Actors', 31-34.
294 Howell, 'Credit Networks and Political Actors', 34.
295 Similar figures in de Valériola, 'Corpus', 47-48, who counts about 50 clothiers, but many more other artisans active in textile industries, among them, although not mentioned separately, many dyers.

Table 5.1 Textile occupations in Ypres. Debt contracts: borrowers, 1249-1291 (source: database Martha Howell)

		LENDERS TOTALS	BORROWERS TOTALS	BORROWERS, FIRST PARTY	DEBT CONTRACTS IN D ST (AVERAGE)
Clothiers	Clothier	13	48	34	1,982
	Marchand drapier		3	1	3,491
Craftsmen	Wool sorter		3	3	273
	Wool beater		6	5	1,206
	Weaver	4	12	10	151
	Reeler		1	1	109
	Fuller	5	55	45	990
	Cloth finisher	6	5	4	910
	Shearer	2	22	20	287
	Dyer	43	279	253	2,383
	Linen weaver		3	3	631

of both their businesses is beyond doubt, yet dyers appear much more often in the credit contracts than do clothiers, some dyers even with great frequency, while most clothiers usually appear only once. The dyers are also engaged in debt contracts for larger amounts of money, and they are more likely to have been in business with foreign merchants. A great number of the lenders in the debt contracts of dyers are in fact merchants from those regions that produced the madder, weld and woad that they required. The numbers of merchants from the Picard city of Saint-Quentin are staggering. This city is located in the middle of a woad-producing region, so these debt contracts are probably in fact arrangements of delayed payment for the raw materials that the dyers needed. Whether the Ypres dyers, like their Florentine counterparts, also engaged in stable partnerships with their suppliers of woad cannot be known. The credit arrangements suggest that there was no system in the credit arrangements between suppliers from Saint-Quentin or dyers from Ypres.[296]

The fact that so many more dyers appear in the late-thirteenth-century debt contracts is even more striking because the total number of dyers in the city was much smaller than that of clothiers. Although reliable census figures are available only from the early 1430s, these suggest nonetheless that for every dyer there were at least two clothiers. In the 1430s the Ypres industry was focused primarily on very expensive woollens, made of the most expensive raw materials, while in the latter parts of the thirteenth century Ypres produced all kinds of qualities, and many worsteds and semi-worsteds were only dyed in the fibre or in the yarn, while many of the luxury

---

[296] Wyffels, *Analyse des reconnaissances de dettes*, passim. For the partnership between Florentine dyers and their suppliers from outside the city see Goldthwaite, *The Economy of Renaissance Florence*, 335-336.

woollens were exported as white (= undyed) or blue (= dyed with woad in the fibre) woollens to Italy, where many received a final dyeing in the fabric locally. So the clothier-dyer ratio must even have been much higher, as much as three to four clothiers per dyer probably around 1300. Furthermore, the capital requirements of clothiers were supposedly much greater than those of the dyers; while investments in dyestuffs could indeed be significant, and the frantic activity of the dyers on the Ypres debt market certainly suggests this, wool still made up the bulk of the cost of raw materials in any woollen of whatever quality. All this suggest that the capital requirements of clothiers were significantly higher than those of dyers. Yet they appear more infrequently and with substantially smaller amounts of money involved in the Ypres debts.

Another feature is that most clothiers appear only once in the debt transactions, and even similar family names are rare. Moreover, the identity of the lenders is in no way like that of the people the dyers borrowed money from. If in most cases the dyers used their debt contracts to prefinance the purchase of dyestuffs, mostly woad and madder, and the people they borrowed money from were mostly merchants who came from the regions producing those dyestuffs, clothiers borrowed money from other citizens of Ypres. Moreover, those moneylenders did not seem to belong exclusively to the mercantile elites, foreign or local. There were certainly lenders to clothiers who were members of the prestigious families in Ypres. Clothier Nicolaas Herbert borrowed £6 Sterling from Lotin Balgh in December 1286 or Pieter de Medem £4.3 from Christiaen Scattin in September 1271 (long before the clothier privileges of 1280 were issued) – the Balgh and Scattin families being prominent members of the mercantile and political elites – yet other representatives of the elite families appear only haphazardly among the lenders. Most other clothiers borrowed from Ypres citizens or even from other Ypres craftsmen: Pieter, son of John, 'who makes stamforts' borrowed £1.5 Sterling from Jan van Lo, a dyer, in January 1285, and similarly Michiel van Reninghe (one of the few clothiers to appear twice in the debt contracts) borrowed £0.6 St from Willem van Hendom, a baker, in the same month or Jan van Rode £4.8 from brewer Jan van Vlamertinghe in June 1284. Strikingly, the amounts of money involved in these debt contracts were smaller when the lender was a craftsman, suggesting that the other Ypres lenders must have been more well-to-do citizens, without direct connection to either the elite families or the world of crafts.

The different textile craftsmen show a very mixed pattern. The most substantial amounts of money were taken up by the dyers, of course, and surprisingly also by the wool beaters (*brisieres de laine*), who seem to have had a similar profile to the clothiers themselves, each appearing only once and for amounts ranging mostly between £3 and £8 Sterling and who were probably, directly or indirectly, also active as clothiers. In the middle we find the labour-intensive trades, in first instance fullers and cloth finishers (*c.* £3 to £4 St.). Most fullers appear only once among the debtors, but occasionally a fuller seems to have used the formal credit market more systematically for the organisation of his workshop: Willem van Marcke appears three times as a debtor for sums ranging from a mere 25d to £6 St between 1283 and 1286, Jan Mente twice (but in the same year 1284) and Hendrik van Passchendaele also twice in 1287, Nicolaas *li Rous* (de Rode?) twice, but in 1283 and 1285 (but only for very small amounts of 218d and 109d). All lenders to fullers were Ypres citizens, and sometimes even members of the mercantile elites (Jan de Brune, Christiaen Baerdonc, Wouter Vilain). Also, cloth finishers (*appareillier, feutrier*) have a similar profile. It is striking that both groups also seem to have been embedded in local financial networks as borrowers and lenders, but that the financial relations did not extend beyond the city and probably not beyond the urban middle classes either. This was also the case for most clothiers themselves. Finally, the other textile trades borrowed money only occasionally at the formal credit market and usually only smaller amounts. Strikingly, the cloth weavers, described as *teliers* (the French equivalent, *tisserand*, is only used for linen weavers: *tisserand de toile* or *toilier*), appear on only a few occasions and only for very small amounts (between 40d and 316d St), very different from the clothiers, who were, as we have seen, often weavers themselves. It is not clear whether these weavers were masters (*conventers*) or journeymen. It is unlikely that in these cases this money was used to pay for their workshops or looms, which must have come at a much higher price.

My conclusions are, therefore, almost the opposite of what Martha Howell has suggested recently. While it is true that the presence of Ypres ordinary citizens and craftsmen is remarkable, this is much less true for the textile craftsmen, the most numerous occupational groups in Ypres, and it seems to be even less true for the clothiers, even though these needed large amounts of cash to keep their businesses going. If we take the atypical dyers out of the constellation with their many mercantile contacts outside Ypres, their capital-intensive trade and their ubiquitous presence on the formal credit market, textile craftsmen and the leading textile entrepreneurs, the clothiers are, if anything, under-represented at the market for formal debts in Ypres, and so are the textile craftsmen. The craftsmen are involved only in small credit transactions and they appear only once or twice in the surviving data. They do not seem, therefore, to have systematically used the legal instrument of the IOU for starting up or broadening the scope of their textile workshops. There can be no other conclusion than that the necessary cash must have been procured by other means. The same holds true for the clothiers as well. They usually appear only once in the IOUs; they do not seem to have entertained systematic relations on the formal credit market with the mercantile elites, nor with the foreign merchants, and therefore they were not involved in any kind of formal credit relation with their main suppliers of wool. So, at best the money that was accessed through the IOUs was used only occasionally, probably for specific purchases that may or may not have been related to their trade.

Information about the Flemish financial markets is rare for this period. Recently I have argued for early fifteenth-century Bruges that the credit market for ordinary Bruges citizens consisted of three major circuits. The first was a formal circuit that made use of mortgages (*renten*). This market, of course, targeted people who already had access to real property or it was used for people acquiring real property (that was mortgaged right away). The second, quantitatively much more significant circuit consisted of formal credit arrangements: obligatory bills (IOUs) sanctioned by the city aldermen. The data for late-thirteenth-century Ypres are similar to this second circuit. The third circuit, probably even more important, consisted of more informal credit arrangements, founded on trust and reputation and sanctioned by local notables or members of the parochial clergy. While the formal market brought together people who were not always familiar with each other, the latter informal arrangements built upon social capital present in the neighbourhoods, in the fraternities or in the guilds. They were arrangements between people who knew each other, who had regular social, cultural or professional dealings with each other.[297]

It is tempting to look at the credit relations in Ypres one and a half centuries earlier along similar lines. One of the striking features of the regulatory framework of the cloth industry in Ypres is the focus on hard cash. All payments in kind were looked at with great suspicion or were banned. Similarly, barter trade was strictly regulated and limited to specific periods or transactions. Everything was done as far as possible in money. This focus on cash transactions (direct or through credit arrangements) cannot but have relied on strong and regular credit relations. Still the artisanal world and even the leading cloth entrepreneurs almost do not appear in the contracts, and if they do it is only haphazardly and never systematically, the only exception being the dyers. If the world of cloth could not do without credit, then credit must have been arranged differently, and the only alternative, for which we have sadly no information at our disposal, is the informal credit relations. The fact that even in the formal IOUs craftsmen are primarily linked to each other or to ordinary citizens suggests that this was only the tip of a giant iceberg of mutual dependencies, most of them probably arranged informally.

This web of financial interdependencies does not, however, suffice to explain the position of the clothiers. Clothiers needed much higher amounts of cash to finance their operational costs than guild craftsmen. English wool came at a very high price. Before the clothiers could be active as buyers of wool and sellers of cloth in 1280, they had to deal almost exclusively with the mercantile elites of the city. In this sense this dependence turned them almost in foremen of the city's elites. After 1280 their agency was strongly enhanced. Instead of relations with the mercantile elites, they could now market the woollens themselves in the cloth hall, and we see them occupying the stalls there almost immediately. Moreover, they could buy wool outside the city of Ypres (but not yet in England). This certainly must have broadened the scope of their activities and widened the networks within which they could work. Therefore, the apparent absence of clothiers as systematic users of the formal credit market in Ypres is even more surprising. Of course, not all transactions were registered, and not all registered transactions have survived – what we have is, however, a large selection made by DesMarez, which is according to most scholars highly representative for the total collection of documents preserved in the archives before 1914. So, the scarcity of references to clothiers is more than just a coincidence. Their need for capital was, however, urgent in order to allow them to develop their business activities. They therefore required an alternative and, given the nature of financial relations in this period, this alternative was surely informal credit relations. Such informal relations were, however, very difficult to arrange with foreign wool merchants. Many Italian merchants operated already in the context of larger firms, not least the famous Florentine firms of Bardi

---

297 Stabel, *Capital of Fashion*, forthcoming.

and Peruzzi, but the identity of their representatives changed frequently, so it was difficult to build long-term relations of trust with the large number of clothiers present in Ypres (and in the other Flemish, Brabantine and Artesian textile cities). So unlike the dyers, the clothiers did not develop long-standing financial relations with their mercantile partners, and they did not use systematically the formal capital market in Ypres as it appears in the chirographs. There was only a limited array of alternatives open to them. And the role of local financiers was necessarily always paramount for these alternatives. Recently Claire Billen and David Kusman have revealed for Tournai, how a local financial tycoon, Jehan Biérengher, was able to build a wide array of credit relations with a large group of citizens.[298] The importance of such local financiers active as professional providers of credit cannot be excluded for Ypres, but for the moment data to investigate the importance of such figures is not available. But there was another, an even more obvious route for the increasingly independent clothiers to mobilize capital in the final decades of the thirteenth century, and obtain access to hard cash for their investment: the local mercantile elites possessed the capital required, and they had the tradition of investing in the industry anyhow.

Very few traces of the formal credit relations of clothiers and Ypres merchants are registered in the contracts. So these credit arrangements must have been informal. If this was the case, 1280 did not change all that much in the end, and it certainly did not change things suddenly. The clothiers gained independence, but were probably tied in by their capital requirements, which forced them, at least in this period, to turn to the Ypres elites. From being semi-independent foremen of the merchants, the clothiers became their semi-independent agents. If the level of agency of the clothiers in the Ypres cloth industry certainly must have increased, as did their responsibility vis-à-vis the textile craftsmen, the central role of the mercantile elites did not stop immediately. At least until 1300, as the main providers of capital they kept control over the industry and its workers. The long fourteenth century may have been the clothiers' century; it did not stop still being the merchants' century, too.

Conclusions: A Dance of Capital and Labour

The clothier has in Ypres been a key figure to explain the development of the cloth industry. He (or she) was the pivotal figure around which the industry was organised. His (or her) skill and expertise allowed the efficient adjustment of raw materials and skilled labour for producing the desired woollens, which were in demand on changing and increasingly adverse markets from the late twelfth to the late fifteenth centuries. As such, they became the intermediaries between commerce and manufacture, between the capitalistic merchants and the guild-organised craftsmen. As in England, it is this role that allowed for industrial flexibility and for adaptation of the industry to these market conditions. They added a layer of creativity and flexibility to the industrial development for which the other stakeholders, merchants and craftsmen were less

---

98 Billen and Kusman, 'Les affaires', 41-70.

suited.[299] According to Richard Goldthwaite, it is this relative independence of cloth entrepreneurs that gave the northern cloth industries a competitive edge over the Italian, or more specifically the Florentine cloth manufacturers, who were more under the direct control of mercantile capital.[300]

This does not mean, however, that the medieval Flemish and Ypres clothiers were the same figures as the mostly rural clothiers of late medieval England. The financial scope of the English clothiers and the wide-ranging industrial networks that they controlled were much greater than the scope of the urban clothier in the Flemish textile cities. And this is also true for the Ypres clothiers. Both may have organised their trade in similar ways and their industrial function was not that different. But the English clothiers, and certainly the successful English clothiers, were much more independent of merchant interference, and much freer to develop their own strategies and networks. In Flanders, and in Ypres in particular, the financial clout of the clothiers was much less, their direct dependence upon mercantile capital much greater. Clothiers never really became part of the urban elites, and the few *marchands-drapiers* who did were able to enter the financial elites of cities because of their mercantile involvement, probably much less because of their industrial entrepreneurship. As such, and certainly in Ypres, they were intrinsically tied to the guild-organised trades, rather than to mercantile capital. The clothiers grew out of the ranks of the textile workers, and although other segments of the Ypres population were certainly also involved, many were independent weavers, who complemented the meagre earnings from full-time weaving with the profits clothiers could make while executing their coordination and monitoring tasks. They did not reside in the urban palaces and mansions in the district of the central market square of Ypres, but rather in the neighbourhoods where the craftsmen also lived. Many clothiers, therefore, must have lived among the people they employed, in the suburbs of the thirteenth- and fourteenth-century city. But in order to have sustainable enterprises, the clothiers also required access to capital and, therefore, equally close relations with the mercantile elites, who wielded that financial power. Because social positions evolved in medieval Ypres, it seems that the changing position of clothiers must therefore be explained by this relationship with mercantile capital.

There seem, therefore, to be three periods of cloth manufacture. Probably in the late twelfth and in the major part of the thirteenth century trade and manufacture were dominated by merchants, who also oversaw cloth manufacture through middlemen who were probably also dependent upon them through various credit relations. These intermediaries were already the clothiers. The Douai model, with Boinebroke as its most outspoken model, was present to a certain extent, while manufacturers were primarily proletarianised workers, not or only loosely organised into associations. The clothiers were dependent upon the merchants not only for their raw materials, but also for marketing their cloth. Although we have no information in this period about the position of these intermediaries, clothiers were probably tied to mercantile interests through credit arrangements. Whether the merchants also continued to own the raw

---

299 See also DuPlessis and Howell, 'Reconsidering the Early Modern Urban Economy', 49-84.
300 Goldthwaite, *The Economy*, 281.

materials and supervise the processing of woollens cannot be known. But what is certain is that the mercantile city elites also controlled much of the land. It is likely that, with the growth of the industry, textile workers were gradually pushed to the suburbs outside the walls, suburbs which would be integrated in the second circle of (earthen) walls of the early thirteenth century.

From the middle of the thirteenth century onwards things started to change. Technological and organisational change was inspired by changing outlets, as Ypres started to target more and more export markets for high-quality cloth, striped semi-worsteds (stamforts) and for its more expensive greased fabrics (*dickedinne, derdelinghe,* scarlets). Quality control and a thorough assessment of manufacturing procedures led to a greater importance of standardised procedures with constant checks on the quality of raw materials and due process. Guilds, and their ability to control, came forward as pivotal organisations. The survival of the normative documents from the 1280s may have been linked to archival traditions and political friction, but undoubtedly regulation in this period became more crucial for the success of the industry as well. It is therefore probably no coincidence that most regulation dates from the pivotal decades before 1300 (when clothiers became centre stage) and from the third quarter of the fourteenth century when the drive towards luxury cloth made the role of the guilds as guarantors of quality control even more important. And with increasing control and the rise of the guilds came the guild masters, the small entrepreneurs who, with limited access to capital and limited production capacity, were able nonetheless to start coordinating the manufacturing stages more independently of mercantile involvement. Clothiers in this period were no longer foremen of the merchants, they were operating as intermediaries with the merchants, but probably at this stage personal ties became looser as they were offered more alternatives. Merchants, however, retained control of the markets for raw materials and finished goods because of their hold on capital. The coordination charges, however, were much more lucrative than manufacturing itself, and many weavers became clothiers, leading to polarisation within the (weaver's) guild between entrepreneurs with access to the means of production, entrepreneurs without much access to capital and wage-earning skilled artisans or journeymen who just offered their labour and skill to the guild master or clothier. It needs to be acknowledged that the tensions linked to such social relations, and the social ambitions of the successful group of clothiers who were kept out of city politics by the traditional mercantile and landowning elites, provided the backdrop for the continual political conflicts from the latter part of the thirteenth to the end of the fourteenth centuries. But infra-guild relations also became more important.

As always there was a backlash. The elites in many cities regained access to political power during the fourteenth century and either the influence of the manufacturing guilds was limited or a new equilibrium was found between the city elites and the guild elites of small entrepreneurs (for example in Ghent). Fourteenth-century conflicts, we will see in chapter 9, focused on controlling access to entrepreneurial initiative and on political participation, whether it concerned the sometimes bloody internal conflicts between weavers and fullers (for example in Ghent) or the struggles to gain a foothold in the urban political institutions. Hence, scholars tend to describe late medieval revolts primarily as struggles for political power. They were, however, much more than this and were founded on profound social and economic contradictions and frictions in urban society. In Ypres the rigid distinctions about access to economic entrepreneurship in the 1370s and 1380s are therefore not just a struggle between conservative mercantile or rentier elites and guilds, but they are also struggles within and between the guilds about access to entrepreneurship in urban society. When the merchants gained the upper hand, they tried to sever the link between trade and manufacture; when the latter were successful these links were strengthened. Ypres held a median position: the links between trade and industry were severed only partially, to contain the clothiers in their traditional role, but also to keep open mercantile initiative in the lucrative finishing stages of production. With cloth manufacture geared towards high quality, high price and fashion, preparing woollens for the market involved controlling the colours and the finishing they received.

The continuous friction and competition about entrepreneurship are therefore not just political, but even primarily economic. Hence the statutes of the weavers of the 1380s, when the traditional elites had gained the upper hand again in Ypres and when, also because of the city's demographic decline, the suburbs were abandoned, are very strict in limiting commercial activities in the cloth trade for the weavers-clothiers. They could not become *upzetter* (and focus their entrepreneurial activities primarily on the finishing stages of manufacture), they could not be active in the wool trade (except for trade in some types of low-quality wool that was probably for domestic use and was not suited to making the prestigious Ypres export woollens). But, logically, wool merchants, members of the city elites, could similarly not become involved in cloth entrepreneurship, nor in any other guild-organised trade.[301] Even the commercial organisation was segmented as wool merchants could not also become cloth merchants.

Why Ypres in particular was very reticent about allowing craftsmen to gain access to the markets for wool and finished woollens is not entirely clear. Similar restrictions also existed elsewhere, yet Ypres had experienced a clear embourgeoisement during the fourteenth century. The declining output figures of cloth manufacture and the increasing specialisation in very expensive high-quality woollens had changed the city's population dramatically, from a highly polarised industrial city to a more balanced economy of services and textiles. Even in Ypres, although much less than in Bruges or Ghent, the middle classes must have profited from the occasion, and the proportion of cloth manufacturers plummeted towards 1400. The long decline of the industry had begun.

So, from at least the middle of the thirteenth century and probably even before, throughout the later Middle Ages, the direction the Ypres cloth industry took was defined by the interplay of two groups in urban society. Within a changing equilibrium the mercantile elites of the city and its clothiers supervised, coordinated and steered the commercial and industrial processes that decided what was produced, how it was produced and to what commercial ends it was produced. There were sometimes staggeringly important decisions to be made. When the market for Flemish cheaper

---

301 Espinas and Pirenne, *Recueil*, 3, 549-550 and 552-554.

textiles, says and worsteds collapsed towards the end of the thirteenth century, Ypres merchants and entrepreneurs held on with great success to producing mid-quality striped stamforts, marketed in the Mediterranean as *coverture*. In the meantime, the very highest qualities, scarlets, *dickedinne* and *derdelinghe*, remained the core of the Ypres production, and when in the 1330s the Ypres stamforts also lost their appeal to Italian, Portuguese and Castilian consumers (and Mediterranean markets were lost for good), the switch to high-quality luxury cloth intended for German, Central-European and East-European elites was made almost instantly.

But these entrepreneurial choices had shattering consequences, of course, for the producers, for the craftsmen who worked on the Ypres woollens. The demand for labour must have been significantly reduced, first in the 1280s, later also in the 1330s, even if the transformations of the industry were relatively successful. Moreover, the change to luxury cloth and highly expensive raw materials, and to more saturated colours, like deep blacks and shiny reds, also involved a qualitative change, in which the demands for expertise and skilled labour did not suffer similar downward trends in employment. It must also have changed the financial basis of a clothier's enterprise. More expensive raw materials forced them to require more capital even to get started. It must have raised the financial thresholds for activity as a clothier or strengthened the financial dependencies om the mercantile elites. It is tempting to speculate, as we will see in Chapter 9, that the Ypres clothiers were not quite the revolutionary group defined by Doudelez and Howell. The fourteenth century, with its industrial transformations and social frictions, may have been the clothiers' century, as they became pivotal figures in adapting the cloth output to changing demand, but the clothiers' position did not remain the same, and it is paradoxically the greater emphasis on luxury cloth that also made clothiers more vulnerable. The shift from quantity to quality also defined their social identity. The return of the mercantile elites to the political scene over the fourteenth century probably also entailed a renewed centrality of capital, and therefore of the mercantile class, in the economic infrastructure of the city.

But clothiers and merchants, despite their hold on manufacture and capital, were far from being the only stakeholders in the Ypres cloth industry. They may by their entrepreneurial decisions have influenced the overall demand for textile labour, they did not necessarily directly control the labour markets in the more prestigious and better paid stages of cloth manufacture, from weaving to dyeing. In fact, even the clothiers who were master weavers, as many were, had only a limited direct impact, as they ran relatively small workshops of max. two broadlooms, employing at most four journeymen and several young or female assistants for warping and reeling activities. Weavers were, after all, with the shearers, relatively poor, in comparison to the much larger and capital- or labour-intensive workshops of fullers and dyers. Only for coordinating wool preparation did clothiers have direct control of the workforce. For all other stages of the production, it was with guild masters that they had to negotiate, guild masters who themselves employed workers from skilled and guild-trained journeymen to unskilled adult assistants and young boys and girls. Enter the world of the guilds.

CHAPTER 6

The Rules of the Game

Cloth, Labour and Guilds

Craftsmen and Guilds

When exactly the Ypres cloth workers started to associate into guilds must remain uncertain. Most craft guilds in Ypres developed towards the middle of the thirteenth century as fully fledged craft organisations. It is not clear whether this early guild development was directly related to earlier devotional groupings around a patron saint, or whether the administrative and military organisation of the city – the craft guilds together with the neighbourhoods, as in most Flemish cities, constituted the core of the mobilisation system of the city militia – was in any way connected to early craft organisation.[302] In most cities it was not particularly the textile trades that started to become organised first. Food trades in particular, like butchers, bakers and fishmongers, organised themselves very early into craft guilds, but the textile guilds followed their example shortly afterwards.

It is also not clear how the appearance of the guilds changed the industrial landscape of cities like Ypres. The development of a massive cloth industry had predated guild formation, yet, because sources relating to the organisation of the textile crafts start to appear only from the late thirteenth century, it is impossible to assess how early guild formation changed industrial relations between the various stakeholders in the industry. We have seen that by 1280, when the clothiers were emancipated at least partly from merchant control, guilds were already clearly representatives of the craftsmen, and that they even had legal status. The fines that the count of Flanders imposed on the city in 1281 were to be paid by some of the textile guilds, and in the earliest charters – the wage settings for fullers and shearers in 1280, drafted during the Cokerulle turmoil – the guild curriculum of masters, journeymen and apprentices was already well established.

What is certain, however, is the increasing impact guild organisation had on textile manufacture. From the moment guilds came of age, regulation of the industry seems to have become more palpable and the regulatory framework within which the industry was organised denser. This was also a cumulative process across the late thirteenth and fourteenth centuries. The sense of detail and the ambition of guild regulation to be comprehensive were by no means a coincidence, nor did they mean that before 1250 craftsmen could do just as they liked. Even before 1250 cloth manufacture must have been a highly specialised activity with clearly defined protocols for the organisation of manufacture and well-defined industrial processes at each stage of production. The

---

302 Wyffels, *De oorsprong der ambachten*, 85-142; see also more recently the remarks in Blondé et al., 'Living together in the city', 59-92.

guild regulation that survives did not appear out of the blue. Ypres' complex and highly diverse cloth output required careful coordination of manufacturing stages, and already before 1250 the cloth trades were highly specialised occupations. When guilds came of age and the craftsmen themselves became independent stakeholders in manufacture as small commodity producers, regulation became even more important. While around 1200 the growing industry thrived on asymmetrical power relations and mercantile elites seem to have been crucial in defining the rules of the game within the industry, from the moment guilds came of age the actual organisation of manufacture was outsourced to the guilds themselves. They were the new guarantors of due process. In these circumstances the power relations within the guild, between entrepreneurs and employees, between on the one hand the masters and on the other hands their skilled and unskilled workers, became even more critical. Hence a complex hierarchical system of merchants, clothiers as cloth entrepreneurs, masters as manufacturing entrepreneurs, journeymen as skilled workers and a whole range of unskilled workers emerged. As guild masters usually (but not always: see for example the master dyers) carried less clout than the hierarchical superior merchants and clothiers, they started to rely on the craft guilds and on their own hold over those craft associations as an instrument to control labour markets. Thus, guild regulation was of paramount importance in achieving these goals. Regulation was therefore not only intended to control standard quality in an ever more specialising and changing industry, but it was also and perhaps principally intended to control labour relations. And because the industry did well and was already highly diversified before guild regulation came of age, it was perhaps even primarily intended to give masters the instruments to monitor manufacturing relations in the workshops. In other words, guilds were perhaps more than is usually admitted in recent historiography: institutions defining class relations.[303]

Guilds were, however, institutions that defied simple categorisation, even in the same city or in the same sector. First and foremost, not all textile guilds had the same importance, nor were they organised is similar ways. Cloth manufacture in Ypres was clearly dominated by the weavers, but many master weavers were in fact primarily clothiers, and as such they controlled not only a weaver's workshop but the whole chain of production of a piece of cloth. Weavers who were not clothiers tended to be mere wage-earners. In the early statutes these so-called *conventers* were not even separately mentioned. In the eyes of the authorities the guild consisted of the clothiers (*drapiers*) and of journeymen (*valès, cnapen*), wage-earning skilled workers who were employed by the clothier-weavers. Only in the later statutes are the conventers mentioned next to the clothiers. And because of the clothiers' special position, the count and the urban authorities in the wake of the Cokerulle revolt even addressed only the journeymen in the weavers' guild, implying that all masters were in fact clothiers.[304] Despite this

---

303 On the nature of medieval guilds in the Low Countries see Soly, 'Political Economy' and Stabel, 'Guilds', 187-212. For more general remarks, in particular about the late medieval and early modern period see De Munck, *Guilds, Labour and the Urban Body Politic*. The traditional view of guilds as rent-seeking institutions serving group interests is amply discussed in Ogilvie, *European Guilds*.
304 Doudelez, 'La révolution communale', 204-205 mentioning the charters by the aldermen and by Guy of Dampierre in 1280 and 1281.

ambiguous position, the weavers' guild enjoyed a central position in the guild landscape of Ypres. Just like the fullers they had a separate position in the guild landscape as crafts of the cloth industry. All other textile crafts were hierarchically below these two most numerous guilds. In the corporate political system they were also part of groupings of other guilds, mostly ones which had little to do with the dominant cloth industry: the shearers and dyers belonged to the 'citizen crafts' (*poorterneringhe*), others to the 'common crafts' (*ghemeene neringhe*). This hierarchical difference also impacted on internal relations in the guilds. In the thirteenth century the officials of the shearers' guild were appointed from within the guild, but they had to be approved by both the aldermen and the weavers' and fullers' guilds, while the two separate textile guilds of the weavers and the fullers had purely internal controlling mechanisms. Even the wealthy dyers did not escape external control.[305]

Guildsmen were, of course, associated with the skills they mastered. Nearly all cloth statutes mention the quality of labour and the product as defining the very reason for the guild's existence. They insist therefore continually, directly or indirectly, on the levels of training and the acquired expertise of the guildsmen. The shearers' statutes of 1280 are very clear in this respect: all shearers and all others involved in the trade could not do their jobs in Ypres without being *forces et estanchie* ('capable and established').[306] These skills were, however, in the right circumstances sometimes also exchangeable, from one place to another and also, as we shall see further, from one trade to another. Guild entrepreneurs could hire foreign employees only if these were trained properly in recognised craft guilds in other cities (and, it must be added, if and when local employment was not available). There was an element of reciprocity in this recognition, as it had to be mutual. Ypres entrepreneurs could hire someone from the same trade in Ghent or Douai only if Ypres craftsmen could similarly be hired in Ghent or Douai. Immigrant guildsmen who wanted to move permanently to Ypres could also be accepted into the Ypres guild without much problem if they could prove that they had been properly trained in a recognised city and could do the required tasks 'with their own hands' (*metter hant*).

Guild masters were, of course, dependent upon international commercial exchange. Normally investments in raw materials constituted the major part of the production costs of any guild workshop. In the medieval cloth industry this was not (or not necessarily) the case. As regards woollens, merchants and clothiers remained crucial in delivering them to the local producers. Thus, the guild masters were primarily 'takers' in the network and their operations can be compared to traditional outworking systems which were ubiquitous in rural industries. The guild masters did not control the raw materials, nor had they to invest in them. Relations with merchants and clothiers were therefore primarily based upon the labour and skill the guild workshops provided. It was the clothiers who, from the 1280s but probably also more indirectly before that date, supplied them with the raw materials. But clothiers had, by definition, a very ambiguous position. They were as clothiers not necessarily guildsmen; yet many clothiers were also

---

[305] Espinas and Pirenne, *Recueil*, 3, 455.
[306] Espinas and Pirenne, *Recueil*, 3, 454-455.

master weavers and as such belonged to the weavers' guild. So, some masters in the weavers' guild therefore invested in raw materials, while others, the so-called *conventers*, were members of the same guild and enjoyed a similar master status, yet did not or were not able to raise the amounts of money necessary for them to become actual cloth entrepreneurs. As a result, systems of financial and economic interdependence between masters with a lot of economic agency and masters without those levels of agency inevitably became important within the same guild.

The accounts of Wouter Ameide, a Bruges cloth and wool broker from around 1500, show that clothiers from the smaller cloth-producing towns on the River Leie, Kortijk and Menen, used hierarchical networks to purchase English wool in Bruges from the Florentine merchant companies of the Frescobaldi, Gualterotti and Altoviti, and to sell them their woollens. In fact, wool and cloth were bartered through Ameide's account books. Some clothiers from Menen bought and sold quantities of wool and cloth that far exceeded the scope of their own production. Some clothiers therefore bought wool for other clothiers and sold woollens produced by other clothiers as well, in this way creating financial dependencies and entrepreneurial hierarchies in the cloth-producing town itself.[307]

There is no reason to assume that such relationships of dependence between merchants and entrepreneurs and between entrepreneurs and other craftsmen were new in the fifteenth century. Whether they were similar, however, is not entirely clear. The Ypres statutes of the cloth industry were very insistent upon the fact that all transactions, between guild entrepreneurs and their workforce, between guild masters and the clothiers, and between the clothiers and the merchants could not be arranged in kind. Neither services nor goods were to be bought with other goods or services. Hard cash had to be exchanged at all levels and on all occasions (or credit arrangements involving cash had to be set up). Only the dyers' statutes mention that clothiers and merchants could pay dyers not only with money, but also with Ypres woollens, but all other payments in kind were strictly forbidden.[308] And, likewise, relations between the clothiers and guild masters were also strictly controlled on any other type of payment than hard hard cash. Clothiers were not allowed to pay the guild masters for their services in any way in kind and possible collusion between clothiers, like the hierarchical networks in the Menen cloth industry, had to be secret, if it existed at all.[309]

The obligation to use hard cash does not, however, preclude complex credit arrangements being made and some leverage while postponing or advancing payment or delivery being available. That credit arrangements were crucially important for the supply of raw materials is beyond doubt. It is, however, not easy to pinpoint the consequences of such relations. Furthermore, the dyers, for example, did not always have themselves to acquire all the raw materials they used. When making arrangements with merchants to dye high-quality woollens, merchants for every batch of six woollens to use an amount

---

307 Stabel, 'Ambachten en textielondernemers', 79-98.
308 Espinas and Pirenne, *Recueil*, 3, 625-626.
309 Espinas and Pirenne, *Recueil*, 3, 575, fullers: *Item, dat gheen meester vulre moet ware nemen jeghen eneghen drapier, up ene boete van 3 lb. par.*

of alum of a well-defined quality.[310] For the dyestuffs themselves, mostly madder and woad, no similar arrangements could be found. That such practices strengthened the hold of mercantile capital on local and regional manufacturing systems is, however, certain.[311]

Clothiers and their Workers

As we have seen, the clothiers were the main coordinators of the manufacturing process. This means, at least from the 1280s onwards, that they owned the most important raw materials in that process, wool and woollen yarn, and that during the whole manufacturing process they also owned the woven fabric. It is not surprising, therefore, that most of the statutes of the Ypres cloth industry dealt directly or indirectly with the way in which the basic materials were transferred from one manufacturing stage to another and with the quality of the product at each stage. This defined the way in which the clothiers could allocate the input of labour and skill in each of the manufacturing processes. As we saw in the previous chapters, some of the manufacturing stages were executed by guild-organised craftsmen, while others were given to non-guild labour, very often also women. Because the raw materials and the fabric at the different manufacturing stages were distributed to the workers, who usually executed their tasks at home or in the workshop of a guild master, and direct control by the clothier was therefore difficult and sometimes even impossible, it was crucial that the procedures of exchange and the execution of the manufacturing processes were as standardised as possible. The relations between the clothiers on the one hand and the guild masters on the other were therefore crucial. The statutes had to ensure equilibrium between all these stakeholders. Clothiers did not at this stage concern themselves with the actual labour input, which was within the realm of the guild master himself, so relations tended to be described in terms of reaching quality standards, of organising the required labour input, and of controlling mechanisms.

It is paradoxical, therefore, that the manufacturing stages that were not controlled by the textile guilds, and where connections between the clothiers and labour input were much more direct, are the least documented. We are for Ypres particularly badly informed about the preparatory stages for the wool: wool-beating (executed by men), combing and carding (both executed primarily by women). The spinsters' statutes of the middle of the fourteenth century, however, go into some detail about this exchange and control.[312] There were two ways in which the loosened and straightened fibres

---

10 Espinas and Pirenne, *Recueil*, 3, 618.
11 See, for example, the trade in alum and the distribution of that product in the textile cities (Dumolyn and Lambert, 'A Chemical Compound', 238-258, a contribution that is, however, not very precise in describing the industrial relations that ensued). Alum, accessed in the Mediterranean, constituted one of the staple goods of the large Italian firms and gave rise to close links with the political authorities both in the cloth and trade cities of Flanders and at the level of the county. For the role of the Medici, and of their principal agents in the Low Countries, see in particular Boone, 'Apologie d'un banquier', 31-54.
12 Espinas and Pirenne, *Recueil*, 3, 535-536.

reached the spinsters. Either the spinsters themselves went to fetch the fibres at an agreed place, or *uutdraghers* ('deliverers') or *wulledraghers* ('wool carriers') took the fibres to the spinsters who had to return the yarn, well spun and conforming to the anticipated weight of no less than 4lb. warp yarn for each stone, an anticipated loss of one third (a pound of wool – in Ypres 0.43kg – was one sixth of a stone of wool).[313] Warp and weft yarn had to be twisted in different directions and yarn should be ready for reeling (so moistened, greased and combed). The yarn was not yet wound on to spools by the spinsters. This took place in the weaver's workshop.

There were maximum amounts of wool fibre the spinsters could take on and they had to finish everything before taking in a new load of fibre. Different qualities had to be kept separate. But, perhaps most importantly, all wool was to come from only one clothier, so the latter had complete control over volumes and quality. It is likely that similar arrangements existed for the combers and carders. Also at this stage there was a real risk that different wool qualities and different batches owned by several clothiers or wool merchants would be mixed up. Foreigners were not allowed to interfere in the process, and Ypres spinsters could not even take on spinning work from clothiers from elsewhere or fetch spinning work from outside the city. This was supposed to be a closed circuit to avoid fraud concerning wool qualities as far as possible. No wage rates for spinsters have been preserved, nor do the spinsters' statutes give any more detail about the organisation of workshops and relations with clothiers.

Running a Textile Workshop

Much more is known, of course, about the guild workshops. The statutes of the cloth industry in Ypres give a lot of detail about the quality of the woollens, the way they had to be marketed or who was to be involved in their manufacture, but they give comparatively fewer details about the actual organisation of workshops. Most guild regulations deal with apprenticeship, the transfer of skills within the trade and the socialisation of new guildsmen, yet few deal with the size of a workshop, the number of employees a master could hire, the contribution to the labour effort to be made by domestic staff, non-skilled staff or family members. Some of these rules must have been self-evident in an economy restricted by limitations on craftsmen accessing capital or coordinating their own manufacturing activities with the input of other workers in the workshop. But the fact that so little was said also suggests that guild masters could experiment with the size of their workshops and the levels of profitability that a workshop could achieve. The only condition set by the city officials was that all workshops should be equipped with the relevant tools and that all manufacturing stages should take place in Ypres itself.[314]

Skill was, of course, a necessary precondition for any master to start up a business. In the fourteenth century fullers had to have received training as apprentices for a

---

313 Vandewalle, *Oude Maten*.
314 Espinas and Pirenne, *Recueil*, 3, 576 (fullers).

period of at least three years, and they needed also to have additional experience as a journeyman, a wage-earning assistant. The shearers' and dyers' statutes stipulated that before becoming masters, craftsmen had to work as journeymen for at least one year after their apprenticeship ended. Only after this period could they be tested by the guild officials (*gheproufi*) to see if they really were fit to run a workshop and become masters.[315] Sons of master dyers or trained apprentices who married a dyer's widow were exempted from this obligatory year as a journeymen according to the statutes of 1416. They could become masters in the guild right away. The continuity of the workshop was in such cases considered to be more important and in itself a guarantee of good work. Apparently, in this period of industrial decline it was much harder to persuade people to be active in an Ypres textile workshop.[316]

Financial collusion with hierarchically superior clothiers or with the hierarchically inferior journeymen was looked at with great suspicion. Master fullers could in no way set up in partnership with clothiers. They could not even become financial pledgees for the clothier's activities. But there were also limits on financial collusion with journeymen. Journeymen fullers could engage as security for their masters for only a short period, less than a fortnight. Engaging themselves in true partnerships to start up a business thus became impossible for journeymen. There were sometimes also other limitations on starting up workshops. In the beginning of a workshop's lifecycle, fullers could recruit only the labour input of skilled journeymen. They could not employ any inexperienced apprentices or unskilled workers in their first year of operation.[317] Of course all new masters in the guilds of the weavers, fullers, shearers and dyers or any other trade in textiles had to be citizens of Ypres, just like the clothiers themselves.[318]

Ypres entrepreneurs manufactured a wide range of various qualities in the thirteenth and fourteenth centuries, and the few indications of output in the latter century also suggest that the relative share of each of these products could change dramatically over time, according to the demands of the market. New types of woollens were introduced, some with success and others less successfully, and although weavers were often not allowed to mix specific types of woollens – the distinction between the heavy *draperie ointe* and the lighter dry woollens in particular was strictly maintained – they could decide to opt for one or the other type when the market required this. A lot, of course, depended on the scale of operation of each master and the possibility that chains of production could be arranged by coordinating the output of of various workshops. Various kinds of collaboration between workshops of the same trade or in the form of formal subcontracting, arranging workshops hierarchically, were probably ubiquitous. The fact that in 1431 in the quarter of the 'Small Crafts' 25 weavers are described as *conventers* (independent master weavers who were not clothiers, but the list also mentions

---

15 Espinas and Pirenne, *Recueil*, 3, 579. Whether this 'test' was really a true "masterpiece", which would appear in most cities of Flanders only in the Early Modern Period, is not certain, however (see De Munck, *Guilds, Labour and the Urban Body Politic*, 133-138).
16 Espinas and Pirenne, *Recueil*, 3, 603 (shearers) and 615-616 (dyers in red): the exemption in the dyer's guild was also for *cnapelinne kinderen*, so also for the sons of journeymen.
17 Espinas and Pirenne, *Recueil*, 3, 578-579.
18 Espinas and Pirenne, *Recueil*, 3, 465 (1280).

no fewer than 66 male clothiers, many of them probably master weavers themselves) demonstrates that many weaver-clothiers probably oversaw and coordinated the chain of production while also using other master weavers' workshops with spare capacity as subcontractors for their own activities. It is almost impossible to calculate from these figures the exact ratio of weaver-clothiers and *conventers*. If the 84 journeymen weavers who lived in this district had worked only in their own district, and weavers' workshops had on average 1.5 broadlooms (implying a steady workforce of an average of two journeymen for each workshop), the district would have had 42 weavers' workshops, 25 of them *conventers'* workshops. From these calculations it can be hypothesised that only 17 workshops would have been run by clothiers themselves, and that only one quarter of all clothiers would have been master weavers, a figure that seems, however, much too low. But it points nonetheless to the fact that master weavers did not have a monopoly on being clothiers.

Similarly, although many of the 44 journeyman fullers probably worked for workshops other than those of the four master fullers in the same district, the skewed relations between numbers of masters and journeymen indicate that a master fuller must have employed many more skilled workers than a weaver's workshop and, therefore, that the average size of a fuller's workshop must have been significantly bigger than a weaver's or dyer's workshop, which operated with fewer skilled workers (but dyers, of course, required more capital for raw materials). So, the scale of operations was often very different, not only within the same trade, but also more structurally from one textile trade to another.

On occasion, guilds intervened more directly in the actual organisation of the workshop. Fullers were, for example, not allowed to run a workshop open access to which from the house where the master lived was possible, probably to avoid masters being able to bring fabrics into the workshop or take processed fabrics away from the workshop in an uncontrolled manner without at least being supervised by their competitors. This may explain why, for instance, many workshops excavated in the suburb of St Michiel, a fullers' neighbourhood, had separate housing and workshop infrastructure.[319] In the fourteenth century it was also forbidden for two master fullers to live together in the same building, unless the two different businesses were clearly separated by fences or walls (*tusscheloken*).[320]

The profitability of a guild workshop depended primarily on its turnover, and therefore on its size and the number of people working in it. The minimum size of an Ypres fulling workshop was a master and two journeymen. Liability for damage to the cloth they worked on was to be divided equally between the master (the entrepreneur who owned the means of production) and his two wage-earning and skilled workers.[321] But most fulleries were probably much bigger in order to be profitable. There seems not to have been a fixed limit to the size of fullers' workshops. And tenterers, too, were not

---

319 *Et doi mestre ne pueent manoir en une maison, se li maisons et li mestier ne sont entre clos* : Espinas and Pirenne, *Recueil*, 3, 457-458 (1280). See also Van Bellingen and Dewilde, 'De verdwenen Sint-Michielswijk', 149-167.
320 Espinas and Pirenne, *Recueil*, 3, 572.
321 Espinas and Pirenne, *Recueil*, 3, 513.

limited as regards the maximum size of their frame fields. There was only a minimum of six large frames. This was very different in other textile trades. Surprisingly, the most capitalistic activity in Antwerp's cloth trade, cloth finishing, was probably the least so in medieval Ypres. The maximum size of a shearer's workshop was limited to two shearing tables, and a shearer could employ only four people (excluding an apprentice in his first year), and the size of the workshops of master cloth finishers was strictly limited. A cloth finisher could employ only one journeyman and one apprentice.[322]

The dyers in red fixed the number of journeymen by reference to the number of woollens that needed to be dyed: two woollens required one journeyman, three woollens two journeymen, five woollens three journeymen and so on, up to the maximum of 12 woollens per day, for which six journeymen were required. So, depending on the scope of the activities, a dyer's workshop employed, besides a master and possibly also an apprentice, between one and six journeymen in summer and one and five journeymen in winter (when the number of woollens was limited to eight per day). In 1416 the summer number was also limited to eight.[323] Dyers in blue also had their limits. The size of their venture was limited by the number of *zettinghen* they could start each week (soaking tubs of woad): three to four with a maximum of 18 vats of woad per week.[324] Although subcontracting was more rule than exception in a manufacturing system defined by putting-out relations, the scale or size of a workshop was looked at with great attention. Guilds tried to control workshop size by imposing a (relatively high) limit on employees, but also by the physical restrictions of the workshop, for example the number of troughs a fuller could use. Fullers were not allowed, for example, to rent additional fullers' troughs linked to another fuller's workshop. This would inevitably mix work of different workshops and make quality control more difficult.[325] Real subcontracting did not create that problem, because it was the subcontracted master who was controlled, not the master who employed him.

Starting a Guild Career: Apprenticeship

Skill was, of course, paramount in the guild, and so was the transmission of skills. Yet attitudes to apprentices were also highly ambiguous. In recent scholarship it has been stated that apprenticeship defined the most important functions of a guild because it guaranteed the continuity of skill and the induction of future guild members into the guild system. But apprenticeship also constituted one of the cornerstones of guild identity. It guaranteed the social integrity and continuity of the guild system, but the process of 'learning with your eyes' on the shop floor also allowed future masters to master the art of product innovation (and, to a lesser extent, process innovation) and,

---

[322] Espinas and Pirenne, *Recueil*, 3, 605-606 (cloth finishers, fourteenth century).
[323] Espinas and Pirenne, *Recueil*, 3, 614 and 623.
[324] Espinas and Pirenne, *Recueil*, 3, 630 (middle of fourteenth century).
[325] Espinas and Pirenne, *Recueil*, 3, 573.

therefore, it facilitated flexible reaction to changing market circumstances.[326] Despite the great flexibility of individual negotiation processes, guild members also had to abide by some basic rules. The cloth guilds of Ypres required all masters and apprentices to obtain the approval of the guild officials. Foreigners could not be trained in Ypres, so before the apprenticeship started the apprentice had to become a citizen.[327] Many guildsmen also primarily trained their own children.[328] According to the statutes of the Ypres clothiers of *c.* 1300, weavers did not have to pay a fee to do this.[329] There was flexibility also as regards other issues. Guildsmen were able to switch surprisingly easily from one trade to another. In the middle of the fourteenth century sons of weavers or sons of fullers could learn the trade of the other guild for a modest sum of only 10s and the additions to the weavers' statutes stipulate that citizens of Ypres who were the children of members of another guild could learn the trade of weaver by paying the same fees as master weavers' sons; sons of citizens who were not guild members had to pay the usual entry fees of 30d Fl. for an apprentice, 20d for a journeyman and 40d if they wanted to become clothiers.[330] Probably the century-long decline in cloth output and the accompanying structural unemployment for many skilled artisans led guilds not only to adapt cloth output to changing markets, but also to react by stimulating relatively flexible labour markets.[331]

This did not mean that this relatively open access resulted in great numbers of apprentices throughout the period. If the better data for the Bruges craft guilds are anything to go by, only a small minority of masters had apprentices in their households for the whole of their careers, thus training young people almost continuously.[332] For them, besides an educational calling, apprentices also constituted part of their business model. The fees paid by the parents and the fact that apprentices could be integrated as normal employees in the operations of the workshop, certainly towards the end of their tenure, at often cheaper rates than others in the same workshop provided for additional income or influenced profit margins. The few surviving medieval apprenticeship contracts testify to the complex financial arrangements that were made. In 1283 Isabella van Dixmude, who had a dyeing workshop, received £13 Artois for training Arnoud Spaeignaert to dye with kermes, a sum she could use as she wanted but which would be returned to Arnoud after the training period. In the meantime Arnoud received board and lodging at Isabella's home. In the same year fuller Jan van Parys received £2 Artois for training Boidin Bouderis for a period of two years.[333] The master did not always receive a sum of money for training a young apprentice, however. A shearer, called Cornelis promised, again in 1283, a Hanin Hourier that he would train him for

---

326 See Epstein and Prak, *Guilds, Innovation and the European Economy*, Epstein, 'Craft Guilds in the Premodern Economy', 155-174 and Ogilvie, 'Whatever is Right?', 649-684.
327 For the weavers: Espinas and Pirenne, *Recueil*, 3, 563.
328 Stabel, 'Guilds', 187-212.
329 Espinas and Pirenne, *Recueil*, 3, 462.
330 Espinas and Pirenne, *Recueil*, 3, 565.
331 Espinas and Pirenne, *Recueil*, 3, 576.
332 Stabel, 'Apprentices', see also id., *A Capital of Fashion*.
333 Espinas and Pirenne, *Recueil*, 3, 689-690.

three years. He would not receive money, but Hanin was to serve him loyally during his apprenticeship in exchange for board and lodging. The same contract was negotiated between shearer Geraerd de Mesmaekere and his apprentice, Andries Keutaert, in the same year. But in this case, the contract was renegotiated as little as a year later: Andries's service was probably much appreciated by his master, and a clause was added that master Geraerd would also give his apprentice clothing (a pair of stockings every year).[334] Sometimes, the statutes wanted to limit the freedom of individual negotiations. In 1280 master shearers at the beginning of their contract with their apprentices had to receive a sum of 3 marcs for a training period of three years and apprentices could be paid a wage only after one year. Similarly weavers in 1282 received 32s Artois for training an apprentice.[335] A contract could not be broken, so apprentices were not allowed to leave their workshops, nor were masters allowed unilaterally to stop the training.[336] But, as a rule, it seems that the detailed arrangements between master and apprentice remained a matter of personal negotiation, rather than general rulings.

Relations between the guild entrepreneur (the master who ran a workshop) and his apprentice were sometimes viewed with great suspicion. In late medieval Bruges not all masters were involved in training young apprentices. While some never had apprentices in their workshops, the great majority of masters seem to have been involved in transferring skills to the next generation only occasionally, once or twice in their careers. There were also formal limits to the number of apprentices in a workshop at any given time. Fourteenth-century guild masters in Ypres could train only one apprentice at a time, and sometimes there were further restrictions. The *conventers*, weavers who were not clothiers, could, according to the additions to the weavers' statutes of 1403, train only their own children or brothers. Apparently the aldermen (and the clothiers) feared that *conventers* would be able to broaden the scope of their enterprises with the use of cheap labour and as such endanger the integrity of the raw woollens, or they intended that this rule would make access to becoming a clothier more difficult, in this way preserving the operational scope of the clothiers themselves.[337] When an apprentice left his post, the cloth finishers did not allow the master to replace him immediately.[338] In the fullers' guild, training had to last for a minimum of two years, and the same learning period is mentioned in the statutes of the cloth finishers and the dyers. Yet in other textile crafts this apprenticeship period was three years. Individual contracts could always depart from the prescribed period, however.

Apprentices also had to be of irreproachable reputation and they were certainly not allowed to become involved in a revolt or a strike.[339] As has already been said, in all fourteenth-century statutes apprentices were required already to be citizens of Ypres and needed the approval of the guild officials before they could start their training pe-

---

334 Espinas and Pirenne, *Recueil*, 3, 693-695.
335 Espinas and Pirenne, *Recueil*, 3, 462.
336 Espinas and Pirenne, *Recueil*, 3, 455.
337 Espinas and Pirenne, *Recueil*, 3, 566.
338 Espinas and Pirenne, *Recueil*, 3, 572 (fullers); 475 (shearers), 606 (cloth finishers).
339 Espinas and Pirenne, *Recueil*, 3, 464-465.

riod.³⁴⁰ According to the very detailed regulations for apprentice shearers, apprentices had to be at least 15 years old (only a master's son or stepson could be trained at the age of 14, but in that case the three-year training period would be extended by a year). So most trained apprentices entered the market for skilled labour at the age of 18. In 1377 the entry fee to the guild was fixed at £5 parisis. (= 100d Flemish or the equivalent of about 20 days' work), to be paid to the guild officials of the 'four crafts' (the crafts that were united in the so-called *poortersneeringen* or bourgeois crafts: amongst them also the shearers and dyers). Apprentices in the cloth finishers' guild paid only £3 around the same period.³⁴¹

Apprentices, of course, also played an important role in the organisation of labour at the level of the workshop. Sadly, complete lists of apprentices and their masters in Ypres have not been preserved. But the reservations against using apprentices as full-time workers were clearly also felt in the textile guilds. When the apprenticeship finished, the personal relationship had to come to an abrupt end. The apprentice had immediately to leave the house of his master and find another place to sleep. Journeymen could not find accommodation in their masters' houses or workshops under any circumstances.³⁴² Certainly for cloth finishing, when possible irreparable damage could be inflicted on the almost completed fabric, such concerns were tangible. The earliest shearers' statutes from 1280 forbade masters from employing apprentices to shear woollens before they had received their initial training for a period of at least one year. In that first year apprentices could also not earn their own wage. These measures seem to have been considered very important. Masters risked not only a (heavy) fine of 20s, they also risked losing the permission to continue their trade for one year.

Training was a personal affair that relied on mutual trust. The clothiers' statutes of September 1282 were very insistent on the fact that master weavers had to train their apprentices themselves. Even journeymen in the master's workshop were not allowed to weave together with an apprentice who had not served his fixed term of apprenticeship of three years. Learning on the job came at the risk of the weaver himself. If anything went wrong, it was the responsibility of the master to reimburse the clothier for any damage to the woollen in the master weaver's care.³⁴³ Weaver apprentices could work the loom only in their third year of training. Before that time, apprentices were only allowed to execute other tasks in the weaver's workshop (reeling, warping etc.), and always under the supervision of the master or a skilled journeyman. In 1374 it was even added that an apprentice could work a loom only together with the master, so in fact before apprenticeship had formally ended apprentices could form a weaving team only with the master himself.³⁴⁴ Shearer-apprentices could not work in their first year without the assistance of two journeymen (a shearer's table was normally operated by two skilled craftsmen, so in fact the apprentice was always under close scrutiny). In 1393 it was even added that a starting apprentice had to keep himself at a distance

---

340 Espinas and Pirenne, *Recueil*, 3, 599 and 602 (shearers).
341 Espinas and Pirenne, *Recueil*, 3, 602-603 and 607.
342 Espinas and Pirenne, *Recueil*, 3, 599.
343 Espinas and Pirenne, *Recueil*, 3, 462.
344 Eqpinas and Pirenne, *Recueil*, 3, 564-565.

from the shearer's table, so he could execute only other tasks and in the meantime learn the crucial operations using the large scissors only by observing them. When the first year had passed, the apprentice could, however, start working for the two remaining years of his training period, and he would then receive his own wage.[345] In the weavers' guild, too, experienced apprentices gradually got more freedom to work independently. There was even room for taking new initiatives in the workshop. According to the late fourteenth-century statutes weaver apprentices could start a piece of cloth on the loom (*upsetten*), but only if they were allowed to do so by their master (in this case called 'governor': *governere*).[346] In this case, the distinction between a trainee and a skilled worker started to disappear.

The Rewards of Skill: Journeymen and Unskilled Workers

Apprentices were an asset for the future of the guild and they guaranteed the continuity of the trade. On occasion, they were also integrated into the organisation of the guild workshop. They were never, however, a crucial factor in the labour effort of a guild workshop, probably not even for those few guild masters who were training all the time. Guild masters could not build their output on apprentice labour alone. The input of trained journeymen's skilled labour was the crucial factor in organising manufacture. Their role can also be assessed in the various guild statutes. At least until the first half of the fourteenth century, journeymen still stood in high regard in the guild. In the thirteenth-century shearers' guild one third of all controlling officials in the guild (three, as compared with six masters) had to be journeymen.[347] Later, journeymen seem to have lost this input into the official controlling bodies of the guild.

But many masters also had to provide for less skilled tasks in their workshops: weavers needed people to warp and reel the yarn before it was put on a loom, fullers not only had to organise the shrinking and felting processes in the troughs, but also had to arrange the labour-intensive napping, washing and felting processes, and of course all non-guild-organised manufacturing stages was taken care of by unskilled workers (or, rather, workers who had not been trained in the guild). So the workshops of master craftsmen were not populated only by skilled journeymen or occasionally also apprentices. A substantial part of the labour market consisted of unskilled workers, often called working women (*wercwijf*), servants (*cnecht*) or working boys (*gaersoen*). In weavers' workshops they were responsible for the warping and reeling operations. In fullers' workshops unskilled labour could be brought in for washing and napping operations, while scouring, fulling and wet shearing were reserved for skilled artisans. In the finishing stages of production, however, when the expensive cloth could be damaged, skilled labour was not so easily replaced. Furthermore it is, of course, very likely that the members of the household, the wife, children and domestic servants, also

---

345 Espinas and Pirenne, *Recueil*, 3, 599-600.
346 Espinas and Pirenne, *Recueil*, 3, 563.
347 Espinas and Pirenne, *Recueil*, 3, 456.

played their part in the daily activities of the workshop. Some trades built in limits as to the number of external unskilled workers that could be hired. Master fullers could employ only one *gaersoen*.[348] But this does not mean that unskilled labour in a guild workshop did not have to comply with similar arrangements to those governing the skilled journeymen. Working boys – and these were not necessarily apprentices – could not leave their master's workshop for other employment unless they had served the time they had agreed with their employer.[349] But as a rule the statutes are almost silent on the impact of child labour on the industry. There is little doubt, however, that it was very important. Guild masters did not train all the time, and some probably never did, but their workshops required the input of less skilled and cheaper workers, women and children.[350]

The impact of unskilled labour remained, however, relatively small. It was journeymen who constituted the bulk of the labour force in manufacturing and finishing woollen fabrics. All journeymen had, of course, either been apprenticed either in the guild of Ypres, or had enjoyed equivalent training in another privileged cloth city. Master fullers were, for example, severely fined when they hired journeymen who had not been trained for two years in a privileged city.[351] Journeymen also had to be members of the guild and citizens of Ypres. As a rule, masters were not allowed to employ foreign journeymen if there were still journeymen of Ypres available on the labour market, and if they were obliged to turn to foreigners they had to ask permission of the guild officials.[352] Entry to the guild required the payment of an entrance fee, a kind of licence fee for offering one's labour. It was surprisingly cheap, compared to the fees that were to be paid by starting apprentices (between less than £1 and £5 Parisis). In the shearers' guild, it amounted to only 12s par. in 1377 (= 12d Fl. or about two days' wages). A master paid the equally modest sum of 20d Fl. for his entry into the guild. When the master abandoned his workshop and wanted to become a journeyman again, he had to pay another 20d.[353] So, overall entry fees in the textile guilds of Ypres were quite low. The necessity for an abundant labour supply was paramount.

Journeymen were important in all guilds, but perhaps in none more so than in the fullers' guild.[354] As already stated in chapter 2, a fuller's business had to reach a certain scale before it could be profitable. So master fullers tended to employ more journeymen than other crafts in the industry. As a result the relations between master and journeymen were better defined than in other textile guilds. Ypres journeymen could not leave the city to work elsewhere unless they had the permission of the guild officials, and even when such permission was given they could not return before the time that had been agreed.[355] Labour supply was crucial to keeping wages under control,

---

[348] Espinas and Pirenne, *Recueil*, 3, 572.
[349] Espinas and Pirenne, *Recueil*, 3, 571.
[350] See also for the *fanciulli* in Florence an Siena, Franceschi, 'Famille et travail', 113-115.
[351] Espinas and Pirenne, *Recueil*, 3, 572.
[352] Espinas and Pirenne, *Recueil*, 3, 606 (cloth finishers).
[353] Espinas and Pirenne, *Recueil*, 3, 603.
[354] See also for Ghent and other Flemish cities : Van Werveke, *De medezeggenschap*, 12-15.
[355] Espinas and Pirenne, *Recueil*, 3, 571.

so potential workers were discouraged from going elsewhere. Journeymen were also not allowed to leave their posts and look for another employer before the agreed work period was over. They were heavily fined in such cases, and even imprisoned in the city jail for 14 days when found out a third time. Masters also were obliged to declare this infraction by their employees.

The relationship between a master and his journeymen was defined hierarchically. It was the master who decided whether a journeyman's work was good enough, and journeymen could not leave their posts before the master had approved of their work.[356] Disobedience to the orders of the employer often led to the loss of a day's wage. When work was not executed properly, the master could have it redone by someone else at the expense of the journeyman at fault.[357] When work arrived in a fuller's workshop the master fuller decided on which cloth he would work himself and the other operations would be distributed among the journeymen present. Journeymen sometimes drew lots for who was to do what kind of work, and the outcome of that could not be altered.[358] Journeymen could also not refuse to work with another journeyman, unless that man had been convicted of an infraction by the guild officials or the city aldermen.

There was a radical separation between the private spheres of masters and of their journeymen. The independence of the journeymen, and as a consequence their availability on the labour market, had to be guaranteed. Of course privileged relations must have been quite normal. The crucial rhythm of a good weaver's team depended upon their knowing each other well, and previous good or bad experiences must also have influenced the choices masters and journeymen could make when offering or accepting work. But this is how far the guild statutes wanted it to go. In the thirteenth-century shearers' guild journeymen were not allowed to sleep or even eat in the workshop of their current employer (*la u il oevre*) on pain of a stiff fine of 60s. Similar arrangements existed for the weavers (*c.* 1300), who, however, made an exception for family members (*sil nest parens au maistre tellier*).[359] Fullers were more relaxed about this rule. More than any other textile craft, fullers usually employed a great number of journeymen and work could not be interrupted at any time. So like in any other guild, journeymen were not allowed to sleep in their master's house, unless they were related to him, but a ban on eating in the master's house was not imposed.[360]

The cloth guilds were particularly anxious to frustrate all possible entrepreneurial activities of journeymen or partnerships between masters and their journeymen. Journeymen fullers could not advance important sums to a master for a delivery. Investing in the workshop was strictly limited to the masters themselves.[361] But journeymen also had to show initiative on the work floor. Normally journeymen had to deliver their work themselves to the clothier at the market, in his workplace or at the inn from where the clothier organised his or her business, and they were not permitted to give

---

56 Espinas and Pirenne, *Recueil*, 3, 582, addition of March 1395 to the fourteenth-century fuller's statutes.
57 Espinas and Pirenne, *Recueil*, 3, 571 for the fullers.
58 Espinas and Pirenne, *Recueil*, 3, 574.
59 Espinas and Pirenne, *Recueil*, 3, 462.
60 Espinas and Pirenne, *Recueil*, 3, 574 (fullers).
61 Espinas and Pirenne, *Recueil*, 3, 571.

it to anyone else. They could certainly not go to the place where journeymen were recruited to mingle with their colleagues while doing this. All work had to be delivered, in other words, before they could offer their labour again on the market square to another master.[362] Journeymen could not work on woollens of different clothiers at the same time, again probably to avoid different work being mixed up.[363] Additions to the fullers' statutes in 1395 reiterated that journeymen needed to finish the woollen they were working on before taking on another commission.[364] In the dyers' guild the journeymen had less responsibility. The late thirteenth-century statutes even clearly forbade journeymen from having in their own house any infrastructure for dyeing wool or yarn, and their wives were also not allowed to do that.[365]

Not all regulations were aimed at the organisation of labour relations. As skilled workers, journeymen were, as much as masters, the living signboard of the guild and they had to embody the guild's reputation and respectability. This also implied a respectable lifestyle. The Ypres statutes deal less with the moral values that were ubiquitous in, for example, the Bruges guilds.[366] According to the fullers' statutes of the middle of the fourteenth century the clothes of a journeymen had to be worth at least 10s. The fine for a breach of this ruling, 5s, had to be paid by the employing master, who could, however, recover his costs from the poorly dressed journeymen.[367] These ruling are strangely reminiscent of similar ordinances around the same period for textile workers in Mechelen, that other city in the Low Countries which targeted the manufacture of high-quality cloth, although in Mechelen these clothing rules were embedded in a moral framework of clauses regulating the personal lives of the guildsmen. Why these were not particularly prominent in Ypres must remain a matter for discussion. The moral standing of the guildsman was weaponised by the guilds themselves to boost their status in urban society. Perhaps the lack of political participation that the Ypres guilds could muster, and which was surprisingly less far-reaching than in the other large cities of Flanders, caused Ypres guilds, or at least the cloth guilds, to pay less attention to guild identity (and perhaps more to regulating the labour relations themselves).

Hiring a Labour Force

If apprentices, unskilled workers and family members constituted a natural reserve for taking up some of the less specialised tasks in a textile workshop, the crucial factor that defined the workshop's size and profitability was the skilled journeymen. This was particularly true for the textile guilds, because unless they were also clothiers guild masters did not have to invest in raw materials, just in the hardware (the tools) and the software (an efficient input of labour in order to achieve the set goals of production) of

---

362 Espinas and Pirenne, *Recueil*, 3, 573-574.
363 Espinas and Pirenne, *Recueil*, 3, 575.
364 Espinas and Pirenne, *Recueil*, 3, 582.
365 Espinas and Pirenne, *Recueil*, 3, 481, repeated in the fourteenth century, 619.
366 Stabel, 'Guilds in late medieval Flanders', 187-212 and Carlier and Stabel, 'Questions de moralité', 241-262.
367 Espinas and Pirenne, *Recueil*, 3, 573.

the workshop. Journeymen were hired by the master craftsmen, they were put to work in their workshops and paid either time or piecework wages. As we saw earlier, trained journeymen could also come from outside the city, if the labour supply in Ypres itself fell short. But whether local or foreign journeymen were concerned, the procedures of hiring them were standardised, and in order to provide equal access to labour or employment they also had to be transparent, like any other market exchange in a guild economy in order to avoid information asymmetries and, as a result, inequalities of opportunity. Labour markets also had to be flexible and adaptable to short-term changes. Most labour contracts between master and journeyman were negotiated for short periods, which fact, however, does not rule out the chance for long-term relations of reciprocity between employer and employee to develop. Manufacturing cloth was also a matter of trust, so long-standing relations between employer and employee could be an asset for the success of a workshop and a guarantee of income for the employee.

Perhaps the most striking development in the regulation of labour in the late medieval Flemish cloth industry was the attention specific guild statutes started to pay to the process of hiring workers. In the proto-guild period, before the middle of the thirteenth century, the hiring of skilled workers was probably left to the stakeholders themselves. No detailed regulation by either the cloth industry itself or the city authorities has survived.[368] In the guild era, only the bigger cities and some smaller manufacturing centres focusing on luxury cloth, such as Kortrijk and Oudenaarde, seem to have developed a regulatory environment that controlled the market for skilled labour. In the smaller towns, even those marked by cloth manufacture such as most of the Leie towns, details of such regulation have not survived, or the normative framework was not developed as such. In Ypres, the weavers' statutes of the second half of the fourteenth century stipulated that journeymen had to be hired at the customary place on the central market square (*ter plache*). All negotiation had to be done after the labour bell had tolled and before it announced the end of the proceedings. After this all employers, employed craftsmen and those who had not found employment should leave the market as soon as possible. Journeymen who had already had found work and masters who did not need workers were not allowed to attend the market at all; and those who had been hired had to leave the spot immediately after an agreement had been struck. Transparency of the labour market was all-important. Journeymen for hire had to stand at a particular spot when the labour market opened (*tharer rechter stede binder eerster clocke ludens*). Foreign skilled artisans could be hired only when Ypres-based journeymen were no longer available.[369] Once the deal was struck, the journeymen had to go speedily to the master's house and be present there when the second bell (*tweder clocke*) rang and the working day could really begin. The weavers' statutes identify the

---

68 Only in Douai has some aldermen's legislation survived for this early pre-guild period. Elsewhere it is only from the late thirteenth century onwards that the guilds and the urban authorities alike started to regulate where, how and when masters, the new key players in the organisation of the industry, could hire their labour force (Stabel, 'Labour Time, Guild Time?', 27-54).
69 Espinas and Pirenne, *Recueil*, 3, 562 (1362-1405).

employers as clothiers, but there is no reason to assume that the other master weavers were not involved. Also the *conventers* needed the input of journeyman labour.[370]

The labour exchange on the central market square was also the meeting place for employers and employees in the other textile guilds. The fullers stood in front of the *Den Busch* ('The Wood') house, separated from the unskilled workers who sought employment in a fuller's workshop, who stood in front of the *Den Staf* (The Staff) house.[371] If anything, journeymen were even more important for fullers than for weavers, so the labour exchange for the fullers was held every day (even on Sundays, work days and festivals). Employed journeymen were to stand apart from those who were looking for work. Unemployed journeymen could be forced to come to the labour exchange and offer their services to any master who wanted to hire them. It was not permitted to refuse offers of work in that case.[372] When hired, journeymen needed to go immediately to their master's workshop, and when they left after a day's work (*dachwerc*) they could not work for wages for anyone else.[373] Similarly journeymen shearers were not allowed to work if they had refused a previous offer of employment that day.[374]

Guild statutes were also very specific about the origin of workers. Ypres-trained journeymen were clearly favoured. This, however, did not always lead to the exclusion of 'foreigners'. According to the shearers' statutes of 1280 non-Ypres journeymen could be hired to work in Ypres, but they had to be well-trained artisans. So the guild officials could forbid anyone they thought was a 'bad journeyman' (*mauvais vallet*) from working for an Ypres master. In essence, only those journeymen who could produce 'letters from their city' testifying that they were well-trained journeymen and of good reputation (*sans blasme*) and that their period of training had been, as it was in Ypres, at least three years.[375] A century later, foreign journeymen could be employed by shearers or cloth finishers only when they received permission from the guild officials.[376] Clothiers, however, could hire foreign cloth finishers without such restrictions, but these had to work on the premises of the clothier and only on woollens that belonged to him.[377]

The Bells of Labour

The detailed regulations on the procedures for employing journeymen were not the only ones to receive a lot of attention in the regulatory framework of the Ypres textile guilds. The regulation of labour time itself was also among the prime concerns of the craft guilds. Labour time regulation in medieval cloth cities was essentially dealing with

---

370 The new weavers' statutes of 1403 repeat many of these prescriptions for journeymen (Espinas and Pirenne, *Recueil*, 3, 567).
371 Espinas and Pirenne, *Recueil*, 3, 574; Vandenbussche, 'De huizen van de Ieperse Grote Markt', 32-33: for De Staf: 42 and Busch: 46-47).
372 Espinas and Pirenne, *Recueil*, 3, 573-574.
373 Espinas and Pirenne, *Recueil*, 3, 582.
374 Espinas and Pirenne, *Recueil*, 3, 598.
375 Espinas and Pirenne, *Recueil*, 3, 455-456.
376 Espinas and Pirenne, *Recueil*, 3, 593 and 606.
377 Espinas and Pirenne, *Recueil*, 3, 606.

two issues: 1° planning the day and the role of labour in it, and 2° preserving free days in accordance with the festive calendar of the Church and the city. In all cloth cities it was the liturgical calendar that decided the division of the year into working and festive days and of the day into working hours and leisure time.[378] The central issue was, of course, as in the case of the labour market, uniformity: therefore, preventing one entrepreneur from taking advantage in a manner considered unfair to his or her competitors. The central guild adagio of fairness and equal opportunity amongst guild members seems to stand firm in the late Middle Ages, yet it is striking to see that regulation does not seem to change drastically during the course of the thirteenth century, when guilds came of age and when they gradually started themselves to define the organisation of labour. Before and after the guilds, the labour bells continued to follow the rhythm of the church (and of the stomach for the midday meal).[379] The earliest examples of labour time regulation in Flanders stem from the early thirteenth century and they appear with the first surviving sets of regulations. As such, they predate full guild development by several decades.

For Ypres, sadly no such early regulation has survived. The earliest statutes of the textile industry pay no particular attention to time regulation. Only from the late thirteenth century do the more detailed statutes start to mention such issues. By then, however, guild organisation had appeared in full strength.[380] Journeymen weavers could not start working in their masters' workshops before the working bell had tolled, and when the evening bell rang they had to stop immediately according to an addition to the 'keure' of 1309.[381] Once the morning bell was struck they even had to hurry to their work stations (*tantost ke li clocke laisse sen son pour aleir à oevre, ke il soient sour leur ouvrage*). If they were late, the clothiers would have the right to reduce their wages accordingly *al avenant quil monteroit de le defaute de le dite journee*. Most journeymen weavers were paid for their time rather than for piecework. It is also one of the first times in Flemish and Artesian cloth towns that the working bell is explicitly called the 'bell of the workers' (*clocke des ouvriers*). The Ypres statutes were less strict about night work than those from its Artesian or Walloon-Flemish competitors. Certainly, cloth finishers were not allowed to work at night, but in particular periods, in particular in the winter period around Christmas, they could nonetheless work in order to accommodate the clothiers and the merchants.[382]

For weavers working hours seem to have been regulated most carefully. But the statutes for the shearers and dyers also stipulate time control, with an explicit ban on night work and emphasis on the importance of their own 'bell of the workers'. The

---

78 Le Goff, 'Temps de l'église', 417-433. More general observations on the liturgical calendar: Taft, *The Liturgy of the Hours*.
79 The soundscape of bells and the introduction of clocks in public areas have been a much debated issue since the seminal study by Jacques Le Goff. The significance of the medieval time 'revolution' for later periods is discussed in Cipolla, *Clocks and Culture* and Landes, *Revolution in Time* and various contributions in Haverkamp et al., *Information, Kommunikation und Selbstdarstellung*. For the Low Countries see in particular Leroux, *Les cloches et société médiévale*.
80 Espinas and Pirenne, *Recueil*, 3, 461.
81 *Que nus vallés … ne puissent tistre devant le clocke des ouvriers ne apriès le clocke* (Espinas and Pirenne, *Recueil*, 3, 462).
82 Espinas and Pirenne, *Recueil*, 3, 473.

fourteenth-century weavers' statutes explicitly forbade night work and work on Sundays and religious feasts. They also demanded that on working days all craftsmen should respect the hours of the working bell and no weaver should be at his loom before or after the bell or during a lunch break (*no tusscen den clocken*). But during working hours craftsmen should work hard and fast or ensure that people working for them did so.[383] Ensuring that this regulation was obeyed was probably not an easy task. The statutes of 1403 were particularly resolute about guild officers who failed to sanction infractions of the working hours.[384] The statutes of the shearers (1377-1408) and dyers of blue (1363-1403) also mentioned working hours, but they were much less detailed than the weavers' statutes. The shearers' privileges asked all craftsmen to respect the working bells in the morning and the evening and the traditional festive days, while the dyers' statutes were more concerned with setting up new tubs of cloth to be dyed, rather than with actual working hours.[385] These were not regulated at all in the second half of the thirteenth century, but the amount of fabric they could dye depended on the season. In winter, because of shorter days, the number of woollens that could be dyed in a day declined significantly. The dying process, of course, could not always be limited to one day, so the statutes explicitly mention night work (*le jour ou le nuit ke il tainderont draes*).[386] The luxury cloth of late medieval Ypres demanded careful dyeing, so dyers were not allowed to set up a new set of woollens after a Wednesday (when the working bell struck in the evening) – otherwise, work would become necessary on a Sunday – but on the other hand night work was allowed on a Saturday to finish the cloth.[387] Pragmatic solutions for resolving work-related issues seem to have been considered normal. Surprisingly, time regulation concerning Ypres fullers has not survived for this period: only the amounts of time the journeymen had to work on the woollens were stipulated in great detail.

Conclusions

Sketchy and impressionistic as the analysis of the normative framework may be, some general tendencies have become clear. Regulation of the labour market developed casuistically, but there is little doubt that it constituted the heart of guild organisation in medieval Ypres. While the statutes of the clothiers and of the cloth industry in general secured the changing balance between entrepreneurial and mercantile interests and guaranteed the required standard for the ever-changing cloth output of the city, the guild statutes focused much more on the relative position of the different stakeholders in the organisation of labour. Thus, regulation was practical, dealing with daily issues, because it was passed cumulatively with all its inconsistencies and contradictions. It was meant to provide clarity, where necessary, but it also defined very flexible labour

---

[383] *Maer al ander werc moeten zie wel spoeden ende doen spoeden* (Espinas and Pirenne, *Recueil*, 3, 562).
[384] Espinas and Pirenne, *Recueil*, 3, 567.
[385] Espinas and Pirenne, *Recueil*, 3, 604.
[386] Espinas and Pirenne, *Recueil*, 3, 482.
[387] Espinas and Pirenne, *Recueil*, 3, 631.

markets. The labour market may have been segmented and the various guild statutes may have been intended to create a hierarchical system in which small-scale entrepreneurs, the guild masters, could deal more securely with the uncertainties of adapting the scale of workshops to changing demand, it also, through the seemingly rigid guild hierarchies, allowed integrate labour from outside the guild (within the household or coming from outside the household as unskilled workers), while maintaining control over quality. The nexus of skill was guaranteed by complex training systems during apprenticeship. Young guild members were socialised in often narrow relations with the guild masters. But perhaps more importantly, the training systems guaranteed the constant availability of skill through the labour input of journeymen. This constituted the strength of guild manufacture. It facilitated a level of flexibility with which the artisans could incorporate new products or change almost overnight from one type of woollen to another. Finally systems of trust could seamlessly linked the work of one workshop to that of another in a smooth production chain. All these features combined constituted the essence of guild economies and allowed the division of labour and the ensuing productivity gains. It was, in short, the guilds, by defining the pivotal position of the guild masters in the industrial process, that also provided the framework in which merchants and clothiers could develop their entrepreneurial strategies.[388]

Cloth manufacture was already well entrenched in the period before the guilds came of age in the important industrial cities of Flanders and Artois. But guild formation allowed regulation to become more refined and more intense during the early fourteenth century. In a period when the industry moved towards more quality cloth, and greater economic agency came to lie with the clothiers and the guild masters who had to guarantee that quality, guild regulation proved instrumental in adapting the small workshops to changing output and finetuning the labour market to the scale of the workshop operations. The focus was on the relationship between masters as employers and journeymen as wage earners. Measures dealing with the hiring of journeymen, with the transparency of the labour market, with the organisation of the journeymen's working day, and with the exclusivity of relations between hired journeymen and their master-employers became much more widespread. So if the traditional organisation of the labour market was probably already in place before the guilds, the measures were increased when the guilds got hold of the actual organisation of the workshop.

The focus on skill and division of labour, and the need for flexible workshops that could adapt to changing demand cycles (and therefore depended on flexible markets for skilled labour) necessitated more complex and complementary regulation. Hence large cloth cities such Ypres, but also Douai and Ghent, developed complex systems of guild regulation, while smaller towns often did not. This does not mean that regulation

---

[388] This is not the place to discuss more thoroughly the opposed views about the efficiency of guild economies, which are considered to have been harmful (from the traditional but also very nuanced views of liberal historian Henri Pirenne to Herman Van der Wee and more recently Sheilagh Ogilvie) or necessary in the context of the economy of scarcity which was prevailing in the premodern world (with recent scholars such as Larry Epstein and Bo Gustafsson who mostly stress the importance of market continuities and problems of asymmetries in information flows, innovation and human capital). For a more thorough description of my own position with bibliographical references, see Stabel, *A Capital of Fashion*, and the survey in id., 'Guilds in Late Medieval Flanders', 187-212.

was as strictly organised in all manufacturing stages. Weavers, fullers and the various cloth finishers were always at the heart of regulation. But for other groups such as the dyers the regulation of the labour market was less thorough. This did not mean that quality was less of an issue, but that labour relations were less dominantly at the heart of business decisions. It is no coincidence that, unlike most other guild masters in cloth manufacture, dyers also had to invest in raw materials. In this the clothiers were in an awkward position. They had to make arrangements with both guild masters and unskilled workers. For the former, regulation became crucial; for the latter, this was less the case, and only clothiers' statutes do not go into much detail regarding labour relations with the female spinners, carders and combers or with the male wool beaters. Many (but not all) clothiers were also guild masters. Their changed economic position meant that they needed more firmly to control the various production stages and adapt the scope of the enterprise to changing demand. For the preparatory stages power relations were such that they did not require much regulation. But for weavers, the mere survival of their workshops depended also on the flexibility of the labour markets.

CHAPTER 7

All in a Wage...

Cloth and its Rewards

Historical research tends to divide the manufacture of textiles in premodern society into two very separate methods of production. On the one hand, there is the cottage industry, since Franklin Mendels' research often described as proto-industrial development because of its alleged (and not always existing) links with the industrialisation process of the late eighteenth and early nineteenth centuries.[389] As a rule, proto-industrial development is located in the countryside. Peasants are active in particular industrial occupations, textile manufacture, shipbuilding, dairy etc., to complement the income from their farms, which in many cases had by reason of alienation (though inheritance or indebtedness) become too small to sustain the household by themselves. This is usually, but not always, necessarily market-oriented labour. Historians tend to describe proto-industrial organisation often in terms of a survival economy.[390] The industrial goods that are produced are usually of poor quality, requiring few specialist skills, although supply systems for raw materials (for example flax or wool in textiles) and for finished goods could be complicated and capital-intensive. Typically a rural weaver would not use a broadloom, which required complicated labour arrangements, but would use a small horizontal loom (or, in some peripheral regions of Europe, even a standing vertical loom). Workers were usually the owners of the means of production (tools and raw materials) in a so-called *kaufsystem* or, in the case of more expensive textiles, were active in a more normal outworking system, where the entrepreneur or merchant retained control over the raw materials and products. In Interior Flanders it was primarily linen weaving that constituted the main activity in the countryside, but in Western Flanders some villages specialised also in simple woollen cloth (usually called *doucken*). Sometimes cottage industries could be integrated into more complex industrial processes. This was the case for the rural tapestry weavers in the southeast of the county of Flanders, who worked for Oudenaarde tapestry entrepreneurs. The essence of proto-industrial development is, of course, that prices and wages could be kept low because the industrial income constituted only a part of the household income and that there was no real craft guild development.

The other type of industrial development is not rural, but urban. Here, the link with agricultural activity was usually severed, although, because of recent research into, for example, gardening and urban agriculture, this may have to be reviewed in the near future. This type of industrial development was organised within the framework of small (and occasionally also sometimes larger) workshops. Workers or craftsmen could

---

89 For more general remarks on rural proto-industries see Ogilvie and Cerman, 'Proto-industrialization', 227-267.
90 Thoen and Soens, 'The family or the farm', 195-224.

combine several jobs (retailing, industrial, ...) but, as a rule, these jobs did not include substantial agricultural activity. Productivity gains were achieved primarily through specialisation and division of labour, to compensate for the lack of non-industrial income. In most crafts industrial labour was complemented with retail activity, but in the more important industries, such as textiles, chains of production were organised without retail activity. This did not stop artisans, of course, having other jobs that could include retail activities. In late medieval economies, multiple jobs and even membership of multiple guilds were by no means exceptional. In most cities, and in the Low Countries there were only a few exceptions (Leiden, Douai), many craftsmen involved in industrial manufacture, and in cloth manufacture in particular, were organised into craft guilds which primarily regulated labour conditions and quality control. In urban cloth manufacture, systems of quality control were also organised by the city authorities. Such control was the cornerstone of the continued success of a product that depended on export markets. Moreover, urban cloth manufacture usually made use of expensive raw materials, so skill was also of the utmost importance. If something went wrong in the production process, the damage could be significant and costly. So, tight guild control was necessary, and such tight control could be organised only within an urban context.

These two archetypical types of premodern industrial organisation have long been considered to be irreconcilable. The former was a rural phenomenon, the latter an urban. Yet the development of the woollen industry in late medieval and sixteenth-century England already shows that elements of the one are not necessarily absent in the other. The English cloth industry was from the fifteenth century onwards primarily a phenomenon of the countryside. Old cloth cities such as Norwich lost ground, and were replaced by highly successful cloth manufacture in rural boroughs, such as Coggeshall and Castle Combe. Moreover, these rural industries produced the finest and most expensive woollens that could be got on the Antwerp market, suggesting that in the right circumstances – that is, directed by specialist clothiers and with close links to urban finishing industries and commercial infrastructure – quality production and quality control could be organised in non-urban environments too. Ypres was of course a very urban environment, one of the largest cities in Northwest Europe, and it not only boasted about the high level of participation of its mercantile capital in industrial activities, it had all the urban characteristics, with high levels of guild organisation, maintained, as we have seen in the previous chapter, to regulate labour markets and assess the quality of the industrial process.

But the question remains whether all textile workers fitted neatly into those two broad categories. Many were specialists, of course, and we saw in chapters 2 and 6 that their work was closely defined in order to protect the merchants and entrepreneurs' activities and safeguard their profit margins. But were textile workers also fully employed in the industry? Was industrial activity their only source of income? These questions are even more urgent for Ypres, because most textile workers lived in the suburbs before the English siege of 1383. We know from archaeological research that they lived in separate housing, small wooden houses, often with a separate building for their artisanal activities. But this loose habitation implies that around the houses there was also a lot of space that could be used for agricultural purposes. Moreover, habitation was concentrated in four sizeable suburbs, so in between those suburbs space was readily available for other purposes as well. Sadly we have no idea how this empty space was used, and by whom. What is certain, however, that this urban periphery, outside the inner city but within the outer wall, was an ambiguous part of the city, with a different occupational identity and with mixed agricultural and industrial activity.[391] We have already seen that in the large seigneuries surrounding the city, which were theoretically owned by the count, but in fact had become part of the city jurisdiction in the course of the thirteenth century, a lot of land was held in customary rent by the elite families of Ypres. It was often they who parcelled out the land for the textile workers in the four suburbs.[392] But the religious and charitable institutions of Ypres also held a lot of land in these areas which they had given in customary rent to private citizens, or which they leased out to individuals. The income from these holdings was registered in rentals, some of which have survived in the archives of those institutions.[393]

Sadly, fourteenth-century rentals, when the suburbs were still in existence, were not that numerous. For the main leper hospital in the city, *Hoge Zieken*, located in the northeast suburb of St Jan, a lease of 1340 gives not many details beyond the name of the person or persons who held a particular plot of land or house in customary rent (or who leased it), the sum that he or she needed to pay to the hospital, and a rough indication of the location of the property (street and location in the inner city or in the suburbs).[394] No occupational titles were added, nor was any specific information given about the nature of the land (agricultural land, house, garden etc.). So information is scarce. Cross-referencing the names in the rental with the tax list of 1328 and the list of textile workers who were temporarily banned from the city in 1329 did not yield many hits. But the results are telling nonetheless. Almost no names in the suburbs appear in the list of rents in the inner city. The property of the hospital in the suburbs included 214 separate plots of land or farms/houses for which 188 different individuals paid rent, meaning that at least 16 people held more than one plot (between two and four plots). Some of these individuals had family names that were identified in 1328 as those of textile workers. One of them was probably a clothier. It is not possible to carry this analysis much further without a true prosopographical study, which not only is beyond the scope of this book but for which only flimsy evidence has survived. Other fourteenth-century rentals, by the almshouse of Nazareth (1358-1364) and that of Sint Jan (1364), reveal similar patterns: only a small minority of the plots of land were held by the same persons and most rent holders had only one plot.[395]

---

91 On the ambiguity of these urban peripheries, see Clark and Menjot (ed.s), *Subaltern city?*, with many case studies throughout premodern Europe.
92 See chapter 4.
93 The archives of the charitable institutions of Ypres, now kept in the City Archives, have miraculously partly survived the destruction of World War I. They were at the time not yet in the possession of the city archives and escaped the fate of those archives in 1914. For the rich contents of these archieves see Mus, *Inventaris van het archief van de Commissie van Openbare Onderstand*.
94 City Archives Ypres, OCMW, 660.
95 City Archives Ypres, OCMW, 494 and 267 (Sint Jan had been founded by one of the members of the city elite, Pieter Broederlam, in 1280).

The presence of a limited number of people paying rent for several plots suggests that a number of people, some of them probably textile workers in the Ypres suburbs, might indeed have held, besides the plot on which they lived, agricultural land as well (or they might have held plots where other textile workers lived). They were, therefore, in a position to complement their textile earnings with either rental or agricultural income. The evidence is, of course, not very strong – circumstantial at best – but, together with the archaeologically documented loose habitation in the suburbs, it suggests that the separation between an urban 'guild' method of manufacture and a rural 'proto-industrial' method, was perhaps not that absolute for a minority of textile workers. Proto-industries, if supervised by a strong entrepreneurial framework, were fully capable of producing high-quality textiles (fine greased woollens in some regions in England and tapestries in Interior Flanders), while research becomes increasingly aware of the fact that many town-dwellers had direct access to land and the food or rents that such land yielded. Even the flimsy evidence for inhabitants of the Ypres suburbs, most of them linked to an urban textile industry that was capable of producing the finest and most expensive scarlets on the European market, suggests that at least some textile workers had access to land, and therefore access to a different kind of income or direct food supply. In other words, their income was not necessarily based only on wage or entrepreneurial income from textile manufacture. But this 'proto-industrial' pattern concerns only the tiniest minority of textile workers in the suburbs. Most textile workers did not own or use land to gain direct access to food supply. It is likely, therefore, that even in the less densely populated suburbs wage income from textile work was the main source of income. Even in Ypres' suburbs the alternative systems of income were just not there.

Labour and Cloth

When the finished and dyed broadcloth entered the cloth hall, ready to be sold to a merchant, at the beginning of the fifteenth century it cost about £5 to £6 Fl., or the equivalent of 120 to 150 daily wages of a skilled craftsman. For Ghent, John Munro was able to calculate the input of labour. For a Ghent *dickedinne*, which fell more or less into the same price range as an Ypres *dickedinne*, the price of the fine English wool amounted to 60-75 per cent of the total cost, dyeing would, if the regional dyestuffs, madder, woad or weld, were used, amount, depending upon the quality of dyestuffs, to 10 to 15 per cent (rising exponentially to over 30 per cent when kermes was used), leaving no more than 10 to 15 per cent for labour costs and the entrepreneurial costs of clothiers and the various craftsmen through whose hands the woollen had passed.[396] Because

---

396 Munro, 'Medieval Woollens', 216 and id., 'The medieval scarlet', 13-70: the data for Italian woollens differ when these were made from cheaper Mediterranean or Spanish wool, but seem to have been similar for woollens made from the finest English wool (Melis, *Aspetti della vita economica,* 487 and more recently Ammanati, 'Francesco di Marco Datini's Wool Workshops', 489-514). Goldthwaite, *The Economy of Renaissance Florence,* 338-339 estimates the cost of the raw materials for an equally fine woollen from Florence in the fifteenth and sixteenth centuries at 40% of the total production cost, while dyeing (which also includes other stages of finishing cloth) takes up 22%.

the cost of raw materials was relatively beyond the control of cloth entrepreneurs, it is the input of labour, modest as it was, that became the crucial feature of the price of a woollen. Because of the competitive nature of markets for woollens, there was a constant downward pressure on wage levels.

It is extremely difficult to measure labour input. The great specialist in textile technology, Dominique Cardon, has been very reluctant to engage in such reconstructions, calling it, like the Datini specialist Federigo Melis, pure conjecture.[397] Other specialists have been more forthcoming with calculations of labour input, most notably the Hungarian scholar, Walter Endrei.[398] For a mid-range quality woollen (the type manufactured in Armentières in the early sixteenth century), he calculated that the wool preparation (mostly spinning) took 622 working hours, 503 hours for spinning, 23 for combing and 46 for carding. In the luxury industry of late medieval Ypres the proportion of combing probably far exceeded that of carding. These were all operations executed almost exclusively by women. Another 50 hours should be added for wool breakers. Weaving an Armentières woollen required about 130 hours (80 for the actual weaving process and 50 for the assistants' operations for warping and reeling). Fulling took 150 hours and cloth finishing 131 hours (eight hours for tenting, 80 for napping during the fulling and tenting process, 40 for shearing and four for dyeing). This means that 60 per cent of all labour input was invested in the preparation of the wool and yarn, 13 per cent in weaving, 15 per cent in fulling and 12 per cent in cloth finishing, or 17.7, 3.8, 4.3 and 3.7 hours (of a total of 29.5 hours) per square metre of cloth. These are sometimes, of course, very rough estimates, because operations like dyeing, tenting or even fulling often concerned a significant number of woollens at the same time, while others required all attention to be focussed on one piece (weaving, most wool preparing activities, shearing). It is likely that, because of longer fulling times for the higher share of expensive fine woollens in the city, labour input for an Ypres cloth must have been slightly higher.

The conclusions from these audacious statistics are very clear nonetheless. Labour constituted only a minor part of the total cost structure of a fine woollen. This part, of course, increased significantly for cheaper woollens and worsteds for which cheaper wool and cheaper dyeing procedures were used; it decreased when only the most expensive English wool was used for luxury woollens (which also required a more expensive dyeing process). The proportion of labour costs in the overall cost of the woollens was therefore important in the thirteenth and again in the late fifteenth century, when Ypres produced worsteds and semi-worsteds; it was relatively low in the

---

So most labour in wool processing, spinning and weaving can be estimated at 38% (if we deduct the cost of fulling, shearing and tenting form the end stages), labour costs amounted to probably 45%, so substantially more in relative terms than in Flanders or in other Italian estimates.

97 Cardon, *La draperie*, 570-571 citing Melis, *Aspetti della vita economica*, 627.
98 Endrei, 'Manufacturing a Piece of Woollen Cloth', 14-23 building on his own earlier work 'Changements dans la productivité', 1291-1299, 'The Productivity of Weaving', 108-119. A further division of labour can be calculated on the basis of De Poerck, *La draperie médiévale*. The most recent calculations for the Low Countries can be found in Hutton, 'Organizing specialized production', 387-388, who uses the same method as Endrei, but adds the somewhat misleading notion of working weeks of 40 hours to calculate the number of workers involved, without taking into account the real weight of particular operation in the complete process.

fourteenth and early fifteenth centuries when all attention was on expensive heavy cloth. But because entrepreneurs had little control of the markets for raw materials, it was the proportion of labour that they could use to influence price formation. At the same time, manufacturing a fine woollen also required a lot of labour.

This was a perfect Catch 22 situation for all those involved in the process of manufacturing woollens. As organisers of the production chain and as those who had to invest in the expensive raw materials, the clothiers were confronted with small profit margins which, because of upward pressure on wages especially in the latter part of the fourteenth century after the Black Death, were continually threatened. Workers had to be pressured, therefore, into being satisfied with relatively low wages. As we saw in chapter 4, the mercantile elites gradually withdrew from cloth production around 1300. Henceforth, it was the clothiers who took on the coordinating role of manufacture; it was they therefore who had to manage wage costs. The clothiers were often themselves craftsmen, who possessed their own workshops and lived in the same neighbourhoods and streets as their employees. Labour relations were therefore crafted among groups with probably opposing visions of what constituted a fair wage in textile manufacture who also lived in close proximity to each other. The data on the financial market show that this proximity often resulted in strong financial links as well. If craftsmen and clothiers were involved in debt arrangements, these were more likely to take place, not with the elite merchants, but with people with similar backgrounds. The dyers constituted the only exception. But in order to identify which factors defined a textile wage in Ypres, let us first look at the data.

A Textile Wage: What is in a Name?

In the previous chapter we looked at the organisation of the labour market. It was considered essential for the success of the Ypres cloth industry to define precisely not only the successive stages of manufacture, but also the labour relations between the various stakeholders, and there were a lot of them. Labour relations in textile manufacture have been described in recent literature in often overly simplistic terms. In short, there were on the one hand long-distance merchants: in the beginning local, but more and more also foreign merchants, mostly from Italian cities, who were able to capture the flows of English wool and dyestuffs and also particular types of finished woollens, and the Hanseatic merchants, who distributed the high-end Flemish woollens in Central and Eastern Europe. On the other hand there were the cloth producers, who were dependent upon the merchants in a kind of capitalistic relationship. They were, whatever their status, described primarily as wage-earning craftsmen.[399] In the previous chapters, we have seen that the actual labour relations are much more complex, with wage earning, commercial profit and entrepreneurship at various levels of the manufacturing process. The majority of regulations were indeed geared towards dealing with such complexity. So, instead of putting up thresholds to entrepreneurship or of

---

[399] Most recently Dumolyn and Lambert, 'A Chemical Compound', 238-258.

creating monopolies, regulation was intended more as a security net. The expectations of everyone in the process were carefully drawn up, but again not so carefully that economic activity and innovation were stifled. Without it the complex production chain and commercial process could not take place in transparent and therefore durable circumstances. And the same goes for the rewards each of the stakeholders was to get: wages and profits.

These rewards were defined by the position of each and everyone in the production chain. Merchants had to rely on the quality of the fabrics that had to be guaranteed by both the clothiers and the urban institutions because they lacked the means to check that quality immediately. Defective weaving or unsaturated dyeing often appeared only when the fabric was used as clothing or for other purposes. Hence the need to control mechanisms such as standardised quality labels and packing, but also standardised and qualitative labour input. It was those elements that defined the profit margins; it was, as we saw in chapter 4, also those concerns that returned when something went wrong, when the quality was not as anticipated, when colours did not conform to what was ordered, etc. The risks for merchants unable to sell particular textiles at a profit to consumers or to retail systems were intrinsically linked to product predictability and cost control. The clothiers, the real organisers of production from the middle of the thirteenth century onwards, needed to trust the labour effort of the craftsmen involved in the successive stages of manufacture, but at the same time they often combined their activities as clothiers with their own weaving workshops and, as such, they needed to be able to adjust their own industrial activity to the coordination activities of a clothier, who might be another clothier. The master craftsmen, usually but not always small-scale artisans, needed not only to define the quality of the product at the beginning and at the end of their part of the production chain, but they also needed to attract labour in circumstances that allowed their own workshop not only to be profitable, but at the same time also to continue. Labour input needed, in other words, to be both flexible and readily available, and guild masters needed workers to be willing to come and work in their workshops whenever clothiers had a number of woollens to produce. Finally, workers, wage earners in the strict sense, whatever their status (they could be skilled journeymen, apprentices in training or unskilled workers, men, women or children), had to sell their labour to the small-scale entrepreneurs and make a living, as comfortably as possible, which meant adjusting their own labour input to the market conditions, and also organising, in function of their earnings, the trade-off with personal leisure preferences. That said, there was, of course, a huge difference between a guild indentured and skilled artisan working for a guild master, usually adult and male, and a non-guild-associated worker, sometimes male but often also female, without fine-tuned and predictable working conditions.

But it was not only social difference and the level of activity in the production chain that differed; conditions in which to organise labour input and adjust the strategies of the various stakeholders to each other could alter as well; and from the middle of the thirteenth to the end of the fifteenth century they changed dramatically, with labour readily available in the medieval period of growth during the twelfth and thirteenth centuries, with labour becoming more scarce and, as a result, also more expensive in

CHAPTER 7

the latter part of the fourteenth and the early fifteenth centuries. Wages which, in the medieval mind, were the logical result of market conditions but also had to conform in the moral economy of the medieval period to ideas of fairness and the conditions in which they were established changed as a result of this long-term switch.

All these elements came together in the setting of wages. Now it is well-known that real data on wage levels in the medieval textile industry are extremely rare, and this is even more true for the textile industries in the Low Countries. At best, some information is available from normative sources that allows us to assess wage levels, rather than paid salaries. The ordinances and privileges of the textile guilds in particular circumstances, it must be added, often contain clauses that limit wages for journeymen, so we have an idea of wage levels, but still comparison with the one group in urban society for whom we have more data, the building craftsmen, remains very difficult, and we have no idea whatsoever about wage differences or wage volatility in the short run. But textiles in the cities of the Low Countries were by far the leading industry, in cities such as Ypres, Douai or Ghent employing easily more than half of the population. It is necessary therefore, to present at least an impression of particular practices and trends.

The first major problem we encounter is the idea of what constitutes a wage. Wages change through time. They depend on attitudes towards manual labour, and they depend, of course, also on the type of work done. There is a considerable difference between time wages and piecework wages. The first remunerate the active investment of effort in a particular task. As a rule, they do not or not always imply a level of productivity, although in textiles quality inevitably comes into play, because when the goods were damaged or particular tasks not carried out as expected, some kind of arrangement had to be worked out to compensate for this. Moreover, slow and sloppy workers were, of course, always at risk of not being hired another time, so time wages also indirectly involve labour productivity. Piecework wages are defined not by effort but by end result, and therefore also do not necessarily imply productivity, although in reality, of course, piecework wages also have a time element to them, because the wage earner had to be able to live off his wages. Such differences can also be traced back in the surviving Ypres wage regulations. The shearers' statutes of 1280 use the world *loier*, while the dyers' statutes of the fourteenth century describe wage labour as 'dyeing for hours' (*vaerwet omme heure*).[400] In both instances this implies the idea of hiring labour for a specified period of time. An artisan, whether a journeyman or an apprentice, hires out his own labour to an entrepreneur, who hires him or her and who is often, like him- or herself, a craftsman. The cost of the *loier* is defined in this case by the quality of the woollens the shearer works on, not by the length of time he works on them (although both are, of course, intrinsically linked).[401] In the same period fullers draw a distinction between the master fuller, who is reimbursed not for his work but for his 'cost' (*pour son coust*), thus for his own investments in his workshop and his workers, while the team of fullers is reimbursed for the 'price' of their work or effort (*ke il aront*: what they will

---

[400] Espinas and Pirenne, *Recueil*, 3, 619.
[401] Espinas and Pirenne, *Recueil*, 3, 455.

get for the fulling of particular woollens).[402] The two systems of piecework and time wages therefore co-exist and elements of both are often present in the same wage: both contain notions of effort and quality.

The difficulties in assessing wages and their repercussions on standards of living are increased by the fact that most wages in textiles were piecework wages, where the time element is less well defined. As we have seen from Endrei's reconstructions of labour input, most labour was needed at the level of wool preparation, and most even for spinning (substantially less for carding and combing), work that was executed by poorly paid and low-skilled women. It is important to note that both distaff spinning and spinning using a wheel needed a lot of skill for the end-result, an evenly spun yarn (and a stronger and thicker warp yarn), to be good. These women were skilled workers in all but name, yet the work itself was executed outside the guild system and done by women (and often also single women), because it did not enjoy similar status to the male-dominated and guild-organised manufacturing stages. The women worked on limited and contractually agreed quantities of wool in order to limit the scope of their work and protect the interests of the entrepreneur, so it is next to impossible to calculate the investment of time. But the boundaries between piecework wages, time wages and entrepreneurial profit (of the guild master and the clothier) were often blurred as well. Moreover, sometimes it is not clear that the actual wage setting really included the whole of the reward given to the worker. The following reconstructions are therefore not much more than tentative assessments of wage differences and tell us more about wage practices than about wage levels, let alone living standards.

Wages often do not also completely represent the earnings of premodern people. A monetary wage can be supplemented by rewards in kind (food, drink, accommodation, etc.). The dyers in blue in particular seem to have made use of an arrangement that included these extras. The wage setting of 1375 not only changes the weekly rate for wages paid to journeymen, but it states explicitly that on top of this rate journeymen also received customary reimbursement for their 'customary costs occurred during their working days' (*ende haerleider costen up den dach dat sij werken na dat ghecostumeird*).[403] For the other crafts no such extras are mentioned. It is noteworthy that the wages of journeymen dyers were significantly lower than those for weavers, fullers and tenters, so the extras were there probably also to compensate the journeymen for this lower rate.

What we do find, however, in the statutes of all crafts is the importance of the money wage. Except for the dyers, wages in kind do not seem to have been used. Sometimes they were even strictly forbidden. This repugnance could mean that even the 'costs' of the journeymen dyers were probably also paid in money. The Ypres guilds were very reticent about wages in kind. The shearers' and fullers' statutes of 1280 mention explicitly that wages had to be paid in cash, and not in food or commodities (*sans denrees ne ware a donner et a prendre*). Journeymen who did accept wages in kind were also heavily fined, as were the masters who paid them.[404] And these restriction were repeated

---

[402] Espinas and Pirenne, *Recueil*, 3, 457-458.
[403] Espinas and Pirenne, *Recueil*, 3, 631.
[404] Espinas and Pirenne, *Recueil*, 3, 455 and 458.

in all fourteenth-century statutes, from the weavers' to the cloth finishers'. Probably for similar reasons some journeymen were not permitted even to sleep or eat in their employer's workshop.[405] Fullers were more relaxed about this rule, however. More than in any other textile craft, fullers usually employed a great number of journeymen and work could not be interrupted all the time. So journeymen were only not allowed to sleep in their masters' houses unless they were related to them; but having a lunch break on site was apparently no problem.[406]

Wages were to be paid at agreed times. The fullers' guild decreed that all employees, both skilled journeymen and unskilled workers, had to be paid by the master at the end of the week, before Sunday evening and before a new work week began.[407] The usual period a journeymen was hired for was set at one week, yet other periods were also used. All depended, of course, on the chain of payments that started at the entrepreneurial level of the clothiers and the craftsmen who worked for them. Some kind of formalisation was, however, necessary. These temporalities were not the same in every trade. The shearers' statutes of 1280 inform us that master shearers were paid by clothiers for their work every fortnight (*a le quinzaine*). This payment prompted a chain of other payments. Master shearers could, after they received their payment from the clothiers, pay their journeymen.[408]

The official labour market in the city, where skilled and unskilled workers were hired by masters, as we saw in the previous chapter, was held in Ypres on Mondays in the central market square. Only the fullers could hire labour on other days as well. In the fourteenth century, when the textile guilds were well established, these provisions became more detailed and intrusive. In Ypres, the weavers' statutes of the latter part of the fourteenth century are not in any way unclear about how wage labour should be hired. The labour market was, as we have seen in the previous chapter, a collective venue, where all employers, the guild masters, and all potential employees, the journeymen who had not yet been hired by another master or had no further obligations to any other entrepreneur, came together at a particular time and place in the market. All work arrangements had to be decided before the last bell was tolled (*eer dat de laeste clocke verlaet*). In the event of disregard for time and place, both the employer and the employee were fined (by almost the amount of a day's wage).[409]

Finally, it must not be forgotten that labour came in many forms. Even in the most rigid and formalised textile trades there was always room for improvisation and flexibility. There was more than wage labour in a guild household. The family workshop was the central unit of production, and labour was naturally embedded also in the household and in all of its members, the guildsman's (or his widow's) family. Moreover, the household was not a closed entity. It was, on the contrary, always available to be invaded by domestic staff, by hired unskilled labour (male and female), by apprentices who were trained by the master, and by skilled labour (domestic and, in the event of

---

405 Espinas and Pirenne, *Recueil*, 3, 462.
406 Espinas and Pirenne, *Recueil*, 3, 574.
407 Espinas and Pirenne, *Recueil*, 3, 575.
408 Espinas and Pirenne, *Recueil*, 3, 455.
409 Espinas and Pirenne, *Recueil*, 3, 562-563.

labour scarcity, also foreign). Yet there were limits to this openness. In order to protect the training of apprentices (and to avoid masters using apprentices as cheap labour and in this way creating unfair competition with other masters) master weavers could not train more than one apprentice at a time and fullers could employ only one unskilled worker.

Wages in Ypres

a. The preparation of wool

Except for those functions that required a significant amount of physical force (wool breakers beat the fleeces with large sticks so as to break their consistency as a preparation for combing or carding), most non-guild wages at this stage were paid to the many women involved in the preparatory stages for weaving. These were also the most numerous group of workers in the city. In order to supply a weaver no fewer than 12 spinsters were necessary, and an additional comber and carder (or at least two combers for woollens for which carded wool was banned). We have already seen that, both in the taxation of 1325-1326 and in the census of 1431, the city of Ypres had a lot of single women. It is beyond doubt that many of these women were indeed active in preparing wool for weaving.

The statutes of spinsters are, however, usually silent about the wages paid to spinsters and their working conditions. They were there to protect the merchants' and clothiers' interests, so they were primarily targeted at guaranteeing the integrity of the wool fibre that was entrusted to the spinsters. As a rule profits, usually in the form of piecework wages, for spinsters were low, and because of the expensive nature of the raw materials risks could be high as well. Spinsters in Ypres had to pay for the damage when the yarn was not up to standards. In particular the stronger warp yarns were crucial in this respect. As a result spinsters were given only piecemeal quantities of wool. The mid-fourteenth-century statutes in Ypres specify that spinsters had to make at least four pounds of warp yarn from every stone of wool (losing only 2/3 of the weight of wool), and when they did not meet this output they had to reimburse the clothiers or merchants at the rate of 4d per stone. Spinning, even on the spinning wheel which was only slowly introduced in the Low Countries, was a delicate operation nonetheless, with warp and weft twisted in different directions and warp yarn needing to be thicker and stronger than weft yarn. Certainly in the cloth cities focusing on high-quality fabrics, spinning was tightly controlled and usually monopolised by local women. In Ypres spinsters had to be citizens, and they could take only a limited quantity of wool from the same clothier or merchant to turn into yarn.[410] Mixing various qualities and origins of wool was sacrilege and heavily punished. The women had to deliver the yarn to the clothier or the merchant at the agreed time, again on pain of severe penalties of they did

---

10 Espinas and Pirenne, *Recueil*, 3, 535.

not. Timing and security were of the utmost importance and labour had to be supplied when it was required. In Ypres spinsters were forbidden to work outside the city.[411]

The Ypres statutes do not go into any detail about the going piecework rates. This was clearly left to market forces. Detailed data on piecework wages for spinsters are not available for the cloth cities of the Low Countries, but we can assume that as a rule they were extremely low.[412] In late medieval Italy the wages of spinsters and similar female workers were usually set at 50 per cent of the wages of unskilled male labourers, apparently more the result of custom than of scarcity.[413] If this was the case in Ypres, estimated daily wage rates must have hovered around 1.7d Fl. in the middle of the fourteenth century (an unskilled fuller's assistant was paid 3.3d), which compares to the 5d of a skilled fuller or 4d for a skilled weaver around the same time. A wage that low does not, however, seem enough to allow women to live as single households, so probably the rates were a little higher in Flanders (than they would be in Italy). Women tended also to have a much more advantageous legal situation in the Low Countries, with more secure property rights. But it is likely that spinning, carding and combing women did not reach the wage levels of male unskilled textile workers. So probably a wage rate of between 2 and 2.5d Fl. seems a likely hypothesis for the middle of the fourteenth century, the more so because similar rates were paid also in later periods.

Only for the Early Modern Period do we have more reliable data for the Low Countries. In Leiden, the most important textile city of the Dutch Republic, spinners, both male and female, could earn about 60 to 80 stuivers per week in the late seventeenth century (which means in a six-day working week, probably less than 12 stuiver per day). But these figures seem to have been a maximum. Single women in poor relief in the town of Zwolle earned on average only 5 stuiver a week. But these earnings made up only half their income, so they could probably earn through spinning as much as about 10 stuiver, or less than 2 st. per day, which is considerably less than in Leiden, but Zwolle was, of course, not a typical cloth city like Leiden. The average wage of a male fuller or weaver was about 18 to 20 stuiver, so at least in Leiden a female spinster could earn about half the wages of a skilled craftsman.[414] Similarly spinning wages in England in the same period were much lower. Craig Muldrew points to a pattern whereby married women earned about 40 per cent of what their male unskilled companions earned.[415] So, all in all, the estimates that in medieval Ypres female spinsters earned a little more than half the wages of unskilled workers seems quite plausible.

---

411 Espinas and Pirenne, *Recueil*, 3, 536.
412 Verlinden, *Dokumenten voor de geschiedenis van prijzen en lonen*, vol. 4.
413 De La Roncière, *Prix et salaires á Florence*, 439 mentioned in de Pleijt and van Zanden, 'Two Worlds of Female Labour', 611-638.
414 Van Nederveen Meerkerk, 'Market Wage or Discrimination?', 176-179 and van Zanden, 'The Revolt of the Early Modernists', 623.
415 Muldrew, 'Th'ancient Distaff', 509-511.

b. Weaving

If the female spinners outnumbered all the other groups combined in the required labour force, the most crucial stage in producing a piece of cloth was, of course, weaving. A substantial number of master weavers also succeeded in becoming clothiers and had to find the capital to invest in raw materials or pay wages to other craftsmen. There is no way of knowing how the income of a craftsman as a clothier related to his income as a master weaver. Private accounts have sadly not been preserved. Master weavers were paid by the clothier (if they were not himself, of course) at piecework rates. Sadly the price for 'raw woollens' is not mentioned in the statutes, so, unlike for other stages in the manufacture of a woollen, we have no idea of the total cost of weaving. The time a weaver spent on a specific amount of cloth depended, of course, upon the density of the cloth (the warp and weft counts), its size (increasing width and length reduced the time spent on setting up the loom and therefore increased weaving productivity) and on the quality of the spun yarn. It depended therefore on the type of cloth on the loom. The price of weaving also included the cost of warping and reeling/spooling, two activities that were intrinsically linked to the weaver's workshop and entrusted to lower skilled staff (or family members). To work at a broadloom a weaver had to employ at least one skilled journeyman, and three if he owned two looms, besides two unskilled workers (usually a family member was among these unskilled workers for warping up, and a young boy for reeling operations).

No wage rates for journeymen in the thirteenth century have survived. But the statutes nonetheless contain an article about apprentices' rewards. This is a rare feature; wages paid to apprentices are only rarely discussed in the cloth statutes of the Low Countries. There seems to have been little willingness among the guilds to regulate them. According to the clothiers' statutes from around 1300, weaver apprentices received 12d Art. for each woollen they helped to weave. It is not clear from the text that their task included mainly reeling, or that it actually also consisted of weaving on the broadloom itself, in this case probably as an assistant to the master himself. This will undoubtedly have depended upon the apprentice's experience and previous training.[416]

Only in the mid-fourteenth-century statutes (dated before 1363) do we find information about journeymen's wages. According to these statutes, journeymen could be paid no more than 4d Fl. per day, nor were they allowed, if asked, to refuse a job for that wage.[417] This was surely a maximum wage, and it is probably linked to clothiers' concerns about possible upward pressure on wages in the wake of the Black Death, so if this measure was truly enforced it probably approached more or less the real wages paid at that time. Weavers' wages were, as we shall see in the next section, slightly lower than fullers' wages.[418]

---

[416] Espinas and Pirenne, *Recueil*, 3, 462.
[417] Espinas and Pirenne, *Recueil*, 3, 564.
[418] See also Billen and Boone, *Bans et édits*, 41-45.

c. Fulling

Very different arrangements were in operation for fullers.[419] In 1280 the price of fulling a stamfort was set at 52d (for a one-day fulling) and 72d for a two-day operation.[420] It is important to note that the wage setting took place in the context of the troubles before the Cokerulle revolt, and it may have fitted into an attempt by the city elites to appease the workers. These amounts were to be divided between the master and his journeymen. For a one-day fulling the two journeymen received three quarters of this sum, the master for his infrastructure and for the costs of supervision (*pour son coust*), of the raw materials and of coordination one quarter. For a two-day operation, involving fewer raw material costs, the journeymen's share was 83 per cent and the master's 17 per cent. In this case, the possibility that a master might participate in the actual labour of fulling was not even envisaged; but of course he could, and in that case he probably received his share of the journeymen's wage. He could, however, according to the mid fourteenth-century statutes, not work in more than one fuller's trough (*keitele*), just like his journeymen, probably so as not to interfere with the continuity of work on the other cloth.[421] But, of course, the fulling process also involved other stages like washing, napping, felting, folding etc. that had also to be completed on a fuller's premises. So a full-blown operation with two to four fulling troughs required probably at least three to seven journeymen and the labour input of the master. In this case the master fuller's profit easily exceeded that of a master shearer. With an operation of three troughs in full employment, the earnings of a master equalled those of a team of probably two journeymen, which means that his earnings were double those of his journeymen. But fulling of course also required a serious investment in infrastructure and raw materials (not least a sizeable property, but also materials such as fuller's earth, urine, …). So, scale was even more important for a fuller's profitability than for a shearer's. This also explains the relatively uneven ratio of numbers of masters and journeymen in the census of 1431, which lists only a few masters and many journeymen.[422]

The fuller's wages were regularly revised. One of these wage settings, dating from after the middle of the fourteenth century, sets the wage of journeymen at 5d Fl. per day, winter and summer, for high-quality greased woollens, and at 4d Fl. for (semi-)worsteds. A master was allowed one unskilled worker on his premises. A *garsoen* ('working lad') earned one third less than a journeyman fuller, so 3.3d Fl and 2.7d respectively.[423] According to an addition of 1395 to the fullers' statutes, masters received 3d Fl. for a large woollen and 2d for a small woollen more than a journeymen for his entrepreneurial costs.[424] An earlier arrangement just mentions 2d Fl. above the journeyman's wage. In this case, it seems likely that master fullers also worked in the fulling process. For any fulling trough in action they therefore received 3d when a

---

419 See also Brand and Stabel, 'De ontwikkeling van vollerslonen', 203-222.
420 Espinas and Pirenne, *Recueil*, 3, 457-458.
421 Espinas and Pirenne, *Recueil*, 3, 572.
422 Pirenne, 'Les dénombrements', 23-24. See also chapter 3.
423 Espinas and Pirenne, *Recueil*, 3, 575.
424 Espinas and Pirenne, *Recueil*, 3, 578 and 582.

large fine woollen was fulled, and 4d for two smaller woollens. The price of worsteds is not mentioned here, because in this period the Ypres cloth industry focused on fine woollens almost exclusively. Fulling prices therefore amounted to 43d Fl. for a large woollen (four days of fulling by two craftsmen for 40d and 3d for the master's costs); a small piece requiring three days of fulling work would have cost 32d Fl. (30d for the journeymen and 2d for the master). A master working six tubs or troughs, therefore, if he divided his work between large and small woollens, would earn on average 6.25d for his infrastructure (3*3d/4 and 6*2d/3) and a wage of 5d, or 11.25d per day in total, more than double the day's wage of a journeyman. A master working four fuller's troughs would receive an entrepreneurial bonus of 4.2d and, with his wage of 9.2d per day, almost double the daily wage. A journeyman, of course, received only his wage of 5d per day. There was, therefore, with the increasing production of luxury cloth, a tendency for masters as industrial entrepreneurs to see their share of the income increase if and when they could maintain the scale of their operations (in essence the number of fulling troughs in operation) at the same level.

Using these figures the hypothetical turnover of a fuller's workshop can be calculated. If we take the most profitable labour composition in a workshop that was allowed by the guilds, a master would employ himself, one apprentice, one unskilled worker or *garsoen* and, in the case of four troughs five more journeymen (when six troughs were in use, nine journeymen, and when the Douai maximum of eight troughs were in use, 13 journeymen). The overall daily turnover when half of the troughs were used for small and the other half for large woollens would then amount to 40d Fl. for four troughs, 62.1d for six and 84.1d for eight troughs, and the master fuller's earnings to 9.2, 11.25 and 13.3d respectively, or 23, 18 and 16 per cent respectively of the total revenue. The declining profit margin is, of course, caused by the fixed daily wage for the master of 5d Fl. per day.

d. Shearing and cloth finishing

According to a couple of wage statutes dating from the final decades of the thirteenth century, Ypres' shearers received a wage that was comparable to the quality and size of a particular piece of cloth. In 1280 a master shearer received a wage of 12d for shearing one side of a stamfort (semi-worsted), for which a journeymen received 10d (or half for half a cloth). The other side paid 10d and 8d. For wet shearing, usually at the fuller's premises, the tariffs were 6 and 5d respectively. Large and expensive woollens were of course paid at the higher rate of 26d (and 6d for wet shearing), while a journeymen received 22d and 5d.[425] A new wage ruling from 1308 gives only the different piecework wages masters received, without further specifying the wages for journeymen.[426] So we see a fixed arrangement between the master and his employees. A master employed skilled journeymen who received about 15 to 17 per cent less in

---

[425] Espinas and Pirenne, *Recueil*, 3, 454-456.
[426] Espinas and Pirenne, *Recueil*, 3, 474 mentions 20s for the expensive blue woollens, 18s for striped cloth, 14s for two half-cloths.

wages than the master. This must have been the master's profit. So a master's income consisted of his own work, to which 15 to 17 per cent had to be added for every journeyman he employed. The profitability of a workshop, therefore, also depended on its size. But the fourteenth-century shearers' statutes make clear that a shearer could have only two shearing tables and a maximum of four workers (four journeymen or three journeymen and an experienced apprentice).[427] A master with three journeymen could increase his profits by almost half compared to a workshop with only the master himself. The shearer's compensation seems to have changed in the fourteenth century. The statutes indicate that at that time a master shearer could take 25 per cent of the wages of his employees to pay for the cost of his infrastructure (*over hare alame*).[428] A contemporary wage setting describes the various piecework wages shearers would receive for their work (for example 5d Fl. for a dickedinne, 4 d. for a small dickedinne, smaller amounts for wet shearing), but sadly the amount of work to be invested in each type of cloth is not mentioned.[429] These figures do, however, allow one to measure the master's input. A master with two shearing tables and employing three journeymen (which was full capacity, when he worked with the journeymen) earned 43 per cent of the workshop's income; a master employing four journeymen would earn, of course, only 25 per cent for his infrastructure. We have seen that the statutes take into account the fact that shearers could possibly also be weavers, so a shearing business on the side, employing four journeymen, supplied an additional skilled artisan's wage income to the entrepreneur.

Tenters wages are more difficult to interpret. They are typical piecework wages. We know that tenting involved a process of at least two days (for stretching the woollens). During that time the woollens were also cleaned and felted with teasels, yet we have no idea how many woollens could be dealt with simultaneously. Cloth frames were grouped together in groups of at least six large frames, but how many teams of three tenterers were active in such a frame field is unknown. The tenterers' statutes in 1372 stipulate that tentering large woollens cost 4d Fl. and small ones 8 *ingelschen* (or 2.7d Fl.), and the cost of guarding the frame was calculated at 8d par. (or 0,66d Fl.).[430] A six-frame tentering field would therefore yield 24.66d Fl. or 12.3d per day. At this rate, it seems likely that only one tentering team was responsible for at least six frames, as the set rate yielded a daily wage of 4d Fl. per person, but that profitable frame fields probably had more than six frames.

Similarly cloth finishers (*lakenreeders*), who were allowed only one assistant journeyman, received 5 to 6d Fl. for large fine woollens and 4 to 5d for small ones. Again the actual time the work took is not known, but finishers must have been able to process more than one large woollen per day.[431] Cloth finishing, at the very end of the production chain, was considered to be a very sensitive operation. Unlike with fulling or dyeing, damage could often not be repaired, and the damaged woollen would be taken

---

427 Espinas and Pirenne, *Recueil*, 3, 597.
428 Espinas and Pirenne, *Recueil*, 3, 598.
429 Espinas and Pirenne, *Recueil*, 3, 601.
430 Espinas and Pirenne, *Recueil*, 3, 584-585.
431 Espinas and Pirenne, *Recueil*, 3, 607.

out of the production chain and at best downgraded to a lower quality woollen. It was therefore considered risky to use apprentices in the operations. The cloth finishers were not allowed to pay their apprentices a wage or any other kind of financial reward.[432]

e. Dyeing

Dyers' wages are also difficult to assess. The statutes of the dyers in red set the price for dyeing at 4.5s in summer and 5s in winter, but do not mention wages paid by the master to his journeymen. In the fourteenth-century statutes dyers in red who dyed for a clothier, an *upsetter* or someone else had to put an adequate amount of good dyestuff in the process and had to be paid 21s for this for each woollen (if they did not receive the dyestuffs from their commissioners). If they did take the dyestuffs from their clients, however, they could at that time no longer sell alum, madder, bresilwood or weld.[433] In an addition of 1402, the amounts for the dyers in blue were divided up according to the quality of the woad used.[434] Dyers could not be paid in kind, and journeymen were therefore always paid a monetary wage, nor could the master himself receive from the merchant or clothier anything other than a monetary reward for his services. Dyers in red also had to be paid by the merchants per quartal.[435] It is crucial in this respect that the figure of the clothier seems not to be mentioned in the statutes of the thirteenth century, appearing only from the fourteenth century onwards. Apparently in the late thirteenth century, once the woollens were delivered to the cloth hall, the clothier's role ended and the merchants took over, dealing with the dyers themselves.

Only the dyers in blue have left a trace of wage settings. According to the additions to the statutes of 6 August 1375, journeymen had protested against the traditional wage of 15s par. per week which they received from the masters and which amounted to less than 3s (or 3d Fl.) per day and unspecified extras covering the costs of work. It is not clear what is meant by this. Does it refer to their tools or to the food and drink they received over and above their wages? It was decided by the aldermen that this was indeed not enough, and the wages were set anew at 20s par. per week, or about 3.3d Fl. plus the costs. In the same statutes it was confirmed that masters should employ journeymen from the city itself and that only when there were not enough Ypres journeymen could they turn to journeymen from elsewhere.[436]

Textile Wages and Builders' Wages in the Fourteenth Century: a Comparison

The importance of wage labour in the medieval textile cities cannot be overestimated. Premodern urban economies are sometimes described in terms of small commodity

---

[432] Espinas and Pirenne, *Recueil*, 3, 606.
[433] Espinas and Pirenne, *Recueil*, 3, 621-622.
[434] Espinas and Pirenne, *Recueil*, 3, 632.
[435] Espinas and Pirenne, *Recueil*, 3, 480.
[436] Espinas and Pirenne, *Recueil*, 3, 631-632.

producers, in essence guild masters, who make up the bulk of the urban middle classes and who organise their small-scale production only with the help of a limited number of wage-earning assistants. At best it is to networks of subcontracting that more imaginative entrepreneurs turn to increase the scale and size of their manufacturing operations. This is without doubt not the image presented by the great medieval cloth cities of Flanders. In Ypres a substantial part of the manufacturing economy consisted of waged labourers, who were paid an exclusively monetary wage (at time or piecework rates, and sometimes a mixture of the two). While some operations may indeed have been small-scale (shearing and cloth finishing), others can be described as mid-sized (weavers, tenters, dyers) or even had to attain a certain size (fullers) to achieve profitability. In this sense the cities of Flanders were indeed true 'sweatshops', operating for long-distance traders and more modest local entrepreneurs.

But does this also mean that the other (and older) traditional image, of Flemish proletarianised textile workers without access to the means of production succumbing to the political coercion and economic power of the mercantile elites without (before the 1280s) or with (after the 1280s) middle-class middlemen, the clothiers, is still valid, meaning that all textile workers, from wage-earning journeymen and self-employed masters to the isolated spinsters in their domestic workspaces, were in fact dependent on a small number of entrepreneurs unilaterally setting low wages in an unbalanced power relationship that was only slightly modified in the tumultuous fourteenth century.[437]

The wage data available for the Ypres cloth industry inevitably disappoint when addressing these issues. They leave little doubt that wage labour in textiles, both male and female, dominated the labour market. As such, medieval wages, traditionally known through the remuneration of building trades, from master carpenters and bricklayers to their skilled assistants and from unskilled diggers to specialist stone carvers, constitute only a very minor part of the overall labour market in the Flemish textile cities. But, sadly, no wages series are available and the haphazard incidence of wage settings in the guild statutes are all that we have. No changing standards of living can be pinpointed and we must assume that the trends that appear in builders' wages are also valid for textile workers. So we can assume a relatively high wage around 1300. Because of changing industrial relations, a downward pressure on wages was probably felt after 1300, resulting in a continuous decline of real wages in the first half of the fourteenth century, a recovery after the Black Death, initially after 1350 very slow and in cities in particular not very important, but speeding up from the 1370s, announcing the true golden age of the wage-earning craftsman at the end of the fourteenth and the first half of the fifteenth centuries, a golden age that was brutally terminated from the 1470s onwards.[438]

---

[437] Pirenne, 'The Stages of Capitalism', 494-515, Van Werveke, 'De Koopman-ondernemer', 1-26, Thoen and Vanhaute, 'Pirenne and Economic and Social Theory', 323-353.
[438] For the overall development of the real wage in Flanders see recently Geens, *A Golden Age for Labour*; Munro, 'Builder's Wages'; Sosson, *Les travaux publics*.

Table 6.1 Estimated daily wages in Ypres' cloth manufacture (middle of the fourteenth century)

	IN D.FL.
Spinsters	(2-2.5)
weavers (journeymen)	4
fullers (masters)	(11.25)
fullers (journeymen)	4-5
fullers (unskilled)	2.7-3.3
tenterers (journeymen)	4
dyers (journeymen)	3 (+ costs)

Although wage settings are not necessarily the actual real nominal wages that are paid, they nonetheless bear some resemblance to reality. They can be found in the statutes in periods of social unrest and adaptation. As such they are often linked to the entrepreneurs' or city authorities' reactions to wage demands put forward by the wage earners themselves. When in 1375 a new maximum wage was set for dyers, it was at the explicit request of the journeymen who were no longer prepared to work for 3d Fl. per day as before, and were granted a rise of 11 per cent to 3.3d. Again, this raise was, of course, a political compromise to avoid social conflict in a period when labour markets were heating up because of declining population, not necessarily a representation of true wages. But in order to work, this new wage setting had nonetheless to approach real wages.

Table 6.1 gathers together all the maximum wages in the third quarter of the fourteenth century, the period for which we have the best information. It shows that, despite some discrepancies, most notably the higher wages received by fullers, on average the nominal daily wage of a journeyman, a skilled artisan in textiles, amounted to 4d Fl. Unskilled male workers received about 3d and (unskilled) women 2 to 2.5d. The household income of a skilled artisan with a working wife and perhaps also a child would therefore have amounted to 6-7d Fl. (with the wife and child contributing three quarters of the male wage to the family income).[439] A master fuller in a sizeable workshop earned about 11d to 12d Fl. per day, but this also included his investment in raw materials. We have no contemporary wage data for Ypres builders, yet in nearby Bruges a skilled master carpenter or mason earned in this period between 6d and 8d Fl., a builder's assistant or journeyman 3d to 4d Fl. So we can safely assume that wage levels in textiles and in building are quite similar, and that guild masters, once they could achieve a certain scale of operations (with many fullers' troughs, several weavers' looms, shearing tables or dyers' vats), could earn more than the average master builder. Yet, also in building, of course, most profit lay in contracting for larger projects, so also here the scale of operations mattered. It must be remembered, however, that the operational

---

39 These figures are very similar to those for contemporary households in Florence (Franceschi, 'Famille et travail', 118-119).

scope for craftsmen in textiles was generally small, limiting (except for fullers) the scale of their operations and, therefore, also their profitability. In Ypres only the weavers, and only those who were also clothiers, and perhaps some dyers and fullers were able to overcome these limitations.

CHAPTER 8

'Whether He or She'

Cloth and Gender

On 20 August 1368, Mary, the widow of Hendrik de Rike, came before the aldermen of the city of Ypres. She had complaints about the behaviour of Clays van Ghelewe, a broker. She had sent a woollen to 'her fuller' (*haren vulre*), Jan van Calone, to improve its quality in the way fullers were used to doing (*also men vulres pliet te doene*). Jan was, however, burdened with debt. Out of despair, he pawned Mary's woollen without Mary's knowledge. When Jan fled the city to escape from his creditors, the pawnbroker sold the woollen and it ended up in the possession of Clays van Ghelewe. Mary, of course, wanted the woollen to be returned to her. The aldermen decided that because it was custom that the goods that were given to fullers or indeed to any other craftsman to work on remained the property of their original owner, these goods could not be pawned by those craftsmen. As a broker, Clays should have been aware of this. He did not check carefully enough whether he was entitled to buy the woollen at the pawnshop and, therefore, he had to return the woollen to Mary, its lawful owner.[440] The case shows not only that women did indeed enjoy secure property rights in Ypres, but also that male guild craftsmen were not allowed to use for their own purposes the goods that were entrusted to their care. They had, in other words, to respect the contract that was agreed between them and their client, even if that client was an independent woman.

But the case also shows that women were indeed active as clothiers. Mary entrusted her raw woollen, i.e. a woollen that had come off the loom, to a specialist craftsman for the next phase in its manufacture. She acted, therefore, as an independent clothier. It is possible that she was continuing in this way the business of her deceased husband, Hendrik de Rike, but she may, as we shall see in the following pages, also have been a clothier in her own right. Women were not allowed in late fourteenth-century Ypres to enter one of the textile guilds as masters, journeymen or apprentices. Even in a region characterised by a relatively advantageous judicial status for women, Flemish guilds remained true institutions of male entitlement. But women were citizens of Ypres nonetheless and, as citizens, they were also allowed, just like any other citizen, to act as entrepreneurs, and therefore they were able also to become clothiers in the city's main industry, free from any male interference. There was, once a woman was of age, in such cases no need for a male supervisor, husband or guardian. Clothiers were, as we saw in Chapter 4, not members of one of the textile guilds, although many clothiers were indeed master weavers. So, every Ypres citizen, on condition that he or she was not a member of one of the city's leading textile guilds (with the exception of the cloth

---

[440] Espinas and Pirenne, *Recueil*, 3, 650-651.

weavers), could become a cloth entrepreneur and be active, as the statutes so eloquently describe it, as *faiseurs de dras*, those who organised cloth manufacture. And, therefore, so were women.

Women, Guilds and Entrepreneurship

While in traditional domestic settings across medieval Europe the world of textile manufacture was primarily associated with women, and weaving was even considered a female activity, this pattern is thought to have changed dramatically with the introduction of the horizontal loom, and certainly of the broadloom. As textile production was taken out of the domestic sphere in the urban textile industries, men started to dominate the crucial manufacturing stages. In the larger cities, where cloth manufacture quickly became oriented towards export, the operations required a horizontal broadloom at which a team of experienced weavers had to coordinate their movements. Moreover, the fulling process for the new woollens (woollens woven with a standing loom were as a rule not fulled) required a lot of physical strength (and was mostly done naked) and the attention to detail and the responsibility for shearing or finishing an expensive woollen fabric with the odd chance of serious damage were considered to be highly skilled, and as such male activities. Wool preparation, when possible damage to the cloth was still repairable or when the prestige of skilled male artisanship did not yet weigh on the end product, could be left in women's hands – all the more so because the combing, carding and spinning stages required most labour input, and preferably cheap and female labour. For the other operations this was much less the case.[441]

Yet, recent research has questioned the exclusively male identity of urban clothmaking in the medieval city, or the inevitability of male artisanal dominance. In other textile branches, most notably silk weaving, women played a more active role, not just in spinning and reeling, but also in weaving and in the finishing activities.[442] In some Italian cloth cities women retained an important role in cloth weaving as well until well into the late Middle Ages. And also in linen production traditionally women had been very active. In fourteenth- and fifteenth-century Bruges, a city where women traditionally played only a very minor role in the guild-organised economy, nearly all linen sellers in the city's main commercial hall were women.[443] The manufacture of woollen cloth therefore constituted the exception, but in light of the dominance of the wool industry in the urban economy it was a crucial exception. Women are said to have been banned from the early days of the industry to combing, carding, washing and spinning, all labour-intensive production stages, but also stages that yielded inevitably low-status, low-wage jobs.

The last decades this representation has started to shift. In 2000 mediaevalist Ellen Kittel and French linguist Kurt Queller published a study on the much-neglected use

---

441 See for more details, chapter 2.
442 Farmer, *The Silk Industries*.
443 Stabel, *A Capital of Fashion*.

of gendered dyadic references in the city and guild ordinances of the medieval cloth city of Douai in Walloon-Flanders, 60km south of Ypres. Most textile occupations were called by their male and female titles, except for the wool-preparing stages (all female) and fulling (all male). Dyadic reference, naming both male and female actors, gives status to both members of the dyad, and in the Douaisien case it implies that, at least until the late thirteenth century but probably until well into the fourteenth, the social and economic participation of women was perceived as normal and 'virtually on par with that of males'. Kittel and Queller even go as far as stating 'that the city did not reckon its population in terms of patriarchally headed households, but rather in terms of individual workers'.[444] This period of inclusion of the feminine gender in the use of official language is, however, followed by a period of hegemony of masculine usage, which gradually became institutionalised in the course of the fourteenth century. Kittel and Queller looked at dyadic reference in the first preserved ordinances of the Douai urban authorities in the thirteenth century and compared these documents with the decades around 1400. In the thirteenth century, from 1231 onwards, dyadic reference was omnipresent, and it became the default expression for referring to the population at large or to specific occupational groups. Around 1400, decades of what they call the influence of 'French (royal) norms and practices' displaced gender-inclusive usage. After the political conflict around 1302, the Flemish city of Douai came under the direct rule of the French king until it was reunited with the county when in 1369 Philip the Bold, duke of Burgundy and the French king's brother, became the son-in-law of the Flemish count, Louis de Male. According to Kittel and Queler, the French linguistic and administrative practices in this period triggered the disappearance of Picard dyadic reference. Yet this explanation is not totally convincing. As we shall demonstrate below, the disappearance of dyadic reference did not happen only in the French-dominated parts of Flanders; it also took place in the Dutch-speaking parts of the county, which remained under the direct control of the Count of Flanders. Change, therefore, cannot be explained just by linguistic or legal, political and administrative change. It is rather at fundamental change in the organisation of the labour market and at the social organisation of the city that we need to look.

The most used dyadic expression in Douai was 'whether man or woman' and 'he or she' (*home ne feme, cils ne cele*, etc.), but the dyadic formula is also used when the civic status of citizenship is addressed (*borgois ne borgoise*), implying little difference for the aldermen as to the rights, responsibilities and activities of male and female citizens. The most important findings for our purpose are, however, related to the use of dyadic occupational references like clothier, male or female (*drapier, drappiere*), baker, male or female (*boulengier, boulengiere*), etc. The first important conclusion relates to chronology. Occupational dyads are very numerous in Douai in the second half of the thirteenth century, but they all but disappear around 1400. Not all occupations, however, followed the same pattern. Some, already in the thirteenth century, were very much gendered and were considered to be feminine (carder: *garderesse*; spinner, *fileresse*, etc.) or masculine (fuller: *foulon*; and all official functions regarding product

---

44 Kittel and Queller, 'Whether Man or Woman', 63-100.

control). Other occupations appear only in their masculine form (the most notable being cloth weaver: *telier*), but this masculine description is then followed by the omnipresent he/she dyad (*homme ne femme*).

In 1400 the situation had completely changed. Already by 1350 the general dyads (*borgois/borgoise* and *homme/femme*) had all but disappeared in official documents and ordinances. The important city ordinance of 1403, sanctioned by the Duke of Burgundy himself, makes only occasionally some dyadic references for merchants (*marchans ne marchande*), dyers (*tainterier ne tainteriere*), clothiers (*drappiers ne drappiere*) or unskilled workers (*laboureur ne labouresse*), and sometimes also the more general he/she dyad appears in the documents, but these dyadic expressions appear only haphazardly and unsystematically. What is more, when they appear it is usually in very restrictive measures by the authorities.[445] Women seem by now to have been banished to specific low-status occupations such as unskilled workers, spinsters, combers and carders. As a rule, more prestigious and onerous occupations, like merchants and guild occupations, such as weavers, fullers, butchers, tanners, etc. appear all to have been exclusively male.

As already mentioned, both authors point to the incorporation of Walloon Flanders in the French royal possessions. Hence it was standardisation, political centralisation, the growing influence of royal justice (and Roman Law) and simple pragmatics (the convenience of male singleton meaning in listing occupations, etc.) that caused dyadic expressions to disappear. As such their claim that this caused male citizens to have acquired the role of public representatives for their women is very convincing. Kittel and Queller are equally persuasive in blaming French (royal) influence when addressing changes of vocabulary. In the case of the weavers the French exclusively masculine title *tisserand* replaced the Picard dyadic string *telier, home ne feme*. It becomes clear that there was a process, stimulated by state authority, across the fourteenth century to shift the centre of gravity of the ideological construction of labour in the thirteenth century from the worker to the male-dominated household as the fundamental unit of social and political control.[446] Martha Howell's argument about the rise of the Douaisien companionate household, built on newly formulated ideas about love and affection and joint control of assets, was, therefore, a step towards a new system of patriarchy, rather than a construct offering greater opportunity for women. Women were depersonalised and integrated into a household where, as a rule, the man possessed most, if not all, agency.[447]

Kittel and Queller's implicit conclusion, however, is that the occupational activity of women in late fourteenth- and early fifteenth-century Douai need not have changed much; only that their activity was henceforth merely hidden, thanks to a change in political and institutional organisation. In my view this is too timid a claim. Gender relations and gender inclusivity (or exclusion) are not only the result of the framework of government and power, they are also the result of large-scale social, economic and

---

445 Kittel and Queller, 'Whether Man or Woman', 77-79 citing Espinas and Pirenne, *Recueil*, 2, 317-345. See also for the ordinances of Philip the Bold: Bonenfant et al., *Ordonnances*.
446 Kittel and Queller, 'Whether Man or Woman', 83-86.
447 Howell, *The Marriage Exchange*, 196-228 and id., *Commerce before Capitalism*, 93-144.

Figure 8.1 Two women behind a broadloom. In the 1470s, when this miniature was painted, it would have been inconceivable for women to operate a broadloom in an urban context without at least the supervision of a master weaver. Before 1300, however, women appear as independent weavers in some Flemish cloth cities. Miniature representing Gaia Cirilla, mother of King Tarquin of Rome, in Christine de Pizan, *Livre de la Cité des Dames* (Flemish translation), Bruges, 1475 (anonymous artist), British Library, Additional 20698, f. 101r.

cultural shifts. In fact women's position in late medieval urban industries had changed considerably, as had the cloth industry itself, Douai's leading economic activity. The economic position of single women was changed most of all. The thirteenth-century ordinances imply that there were no legal objections to women (single or married) performing most occupations as independent workers. Only some specific functions involving political authority (functions of control within the guilds or guildlike institutions)[448] or occupations that breached particular moral codes of decency (fullers did their job partly naked) seem to have been monopolised by men, while other occupations that referred to women's traditional role in the household (spinning, carding) seem to have been monopolised by women. None of the other key phases of the industrial process of cloth making (weaving, dyeing, shearing, etc.) show any exclusion based on gender. At the time the cloth industry in the big cities of the Flemish and Artesian region, in Douai and certainly also in Ypres, had developed into a massive enterprise, involving highly articulated levels of specialisation and division of labour. It was the era of Boinebroke and the urban industries employed thousands of (mostly badly organised) workers, but only relatively few high-flying cloth entrepreneurs and merchants.[449] The industry was geared almost everywhere to manufacturing all qualities of woollens

---

[448] Howell, 'Achieving the Guild Effect without Guilds', 109-128.
[449] See chapters 1 and 5 and the remarks in Van Werveke, 'De koopman-ondernemer', 26 and Espinas, *Les origines du capitalisme*.

both for domestic markets and for export through the Champagne fairs and other commercial outlets across Europe.[450]

From the late thirteenth century onwards, however, textile entrepreneurs in the big cities gradually started to specialise in luxury woollens, rather than capitalising on a whole range of cheaper textiles. This happened in Ypres, but also in Douai. It caused substantial shifts in the supply side of the industry. Mercantile and entrepreneurial activities were divided between merchants on the one hand, who still controlled most aspects of the flow of raw materials, capital and finished goods, and clothiers on the other hand, who now took control of the production cycle. At the same time the guilds or, in the case of Douai, guildlike institutions became ever more important in order to define and guarantee product quality.[451] As a result, in some manufacturing stages textile producers, who hitherto had been proletarianised textile workers, became small commodity producers in their own right. They were better able to organise production, define and guarantee quality, and adapt cloth output to changing market circumstances. Guild masters were even able in many Flemish cities around 1300 to gain access to real political power, or at least they were able to develop institutions that could compete for influence with the traditional patrician organisations of landowners and merchants.[452]

There was, however, a downside to this development in gender relations, and women paid the price. Hierarchically structured labour markets that functioned within a guild system increasingly defined the social position of all economic actors in the city. Guilds became guarantors of quality, but industrial guilds became most of all guardians of hierarchical labour markets.[453] Masters were, after all, just small commodity producers with only limited leverage themselves to control the 'free' journeymen, the privileged skilled workers who had received training in the guild system. Apprenticeship became a necessary tool for gaining access to the formal economy. And, finally, 'unfree' or non-guild workers acted as a reservoir for periods of labour shortage or were used for unskilled tasks in the workshop. As guild masters and their workshops were able to strengthen the position of middle groups in urban society, the household (under the control of the guild master), rather than the individual, became the focus for the organisation of labour markets. As a result women were gradually (sometimes only partly) banned from (guild) training, and therefore also from access to independent entrepreneurship within the guild system.[454] The only chance for women to enter the formal economy organised by the manufacturing guilds was as widows, when they could

---

450 Espinas, *La draperie dans la Flandre française*; Chorley, 'The Cloth Exports', 349-379 and Munro, 'Industrial Transformations', 110-148.
451 Munro, 'Wage Stickiness', 185-297 and Howell, 'Achieving the Guild Effect', 109-128. General remarks on the role of quality for guild economies can be found in Gustafsson, 'The Rise and Economic Behaviour', 69-106 and Epstein, 'Craft Guilds, Apprenticeship', 684-713.
452 Henri Pirenne's ideas about the late medieval "democracies" in the cities of the Low Countries (*Les anciennes démocraties*) were nuanced by a host of empirical research studies in the past five decades (by a.o. Van Uytven and Blockmans, and more recently Boone, *A la recherche d'une modernité civique*). For Douai, there is little evidence of guild worker resistance to municipal authority after 1280 (Dumolyn and Haemers, 'Patterns of Urban Rebellion', 369-393).
453 See chapter 6.
454 Stabel, 'Guilds', 187-212.

continue to run their deceased husbands' workshops. There were some exceptions (but they typically involved retail, rather than manufacture). As a rule women were ousted from the guild-organised economy as independent economic actors. In this situation, labour opportunities for women were increasingly organised within the household, and the independent involvement of women in the labour market, certainly in those cities that thrived on textile production, was limited to those low-status and badly paid jobs of preparing the wool for weaving in tightly controlled systems of putting-out.

Gender Inclusivity in the Ypres Cloth Industry

The frequency of gendered dyadic strings not only occurred in the cloth city of Douai, of course. In fact such dyadic strings were very frequent in many Picard-speaking cities, amongst them also Tournai, an episcopal city which underwent strong French royal influence in this period.[455] In the Flemish-speaking part of Flanders there is a transition from Latin or Picard French to Dutch as the main language used in the city administrations around 1300. So an investigation into resilience of the Picard dyadic strings can be particularly revealing in exactly these cities, and gender inclusivity can therefore also be examined in Ypres in order to test the Kittel-Queller hypothesis. If anything, the Ypres cloth industry defined even more than in Douai the city's social structure. But what is important in this case is that Ypres was not, unlike Douai after the defeat of the Flemish count and the treaty of Athis-sur-Orge in 1305, transferred to royal control. It remained under the firm control of the counts. The city did not, therefore, in the fourteenth century experience a similar 'French' influence to its Walloon-Flemish counterpart, although the counts of Flanders did not hesitate to develop centrally organised institutions that were partly inspired by the example of French royal institutions. Political power in the fourteenth century was, however, very much shared and the three leading cities were very anxious to defend and broaden the scope of their privileges and autonomy; above all, they abhorred political intervention in their own affairs.[456]

First, it must be stated that the legislative material for Ypres is not as good as that for Douai, in part, of course, because the Ypres archives were destroyed in the First World War. The materials start only in the 1280s (considerably later than the Douaisien sources). Nonetheless, they reveal a very similar pattern to the Douai case. Before and shortly after 1300 dyadic references are very obvious in the Ypres privileges and they look very much like the Douaisien *homme/femme* and *bourgeois/bourgeoise* terminology. For example the statutes of the clothiers (*drapiers*) of the late thirteenth century typically use gendered dyads for the most crucial textile occupations: 'it is ordered that all people involved in the manufacture of woollen cloth, men and women,

---

[455] The position of Picard French and its relation with Middle Dutch are described in Lusignan, *Essai d'histoire sociolinguistique*, more in particular 187-233. For Tournai see also the recent edition of the city ordinances in Billen and Boone, *Bans et édits*.
[456] For the general orientation of the political position of the big Flemish cities in late medieval Flanders see Boone, *A la recherche d'une modernité*.

should use the town's seal or else be fined to 20 shilling'.[457] The clothiers' statutes of 1280, written in the same Picard French as those in Douai, even explicitly mention that when a man and a woman are joined in marriage, each is allowed to continue her or his business, even after they have together formed a household, with the exception of those who sell small goods (*menues denrées*), a retailing occupation that could not be combined with being a clothier.[458]

Just as in Douai, particular occupations in Ypres around 1300 seem as a rule to have been gendered from a very early stage. Male fullers, but in particular female occupations in the preparation of wool, were never integrated in the dyadic terminology. Hence the clothiers' statutes from around 1300 mention female combers (*cammigghe, pineresse*), carders (*treckigghe*) and spinners (*fileresse*).[459] The statutes regulating wool preparation in the same period do not take into account even the possibility of male workers. In setting the conditions of putting-out – in an industry thriving on differential product qualities as an essential prerequisite for guaranteeing standard quality – the statutes stipulated that 'no woman' (*nule femme*) could take wool out of the city for treatment.[460] These types of statutes addressing female occupations are used throughout the fourteenth century and changes in the language used from Picard to French or Dutch do not seem to have had any consequences. In the spinning regulation (dated before 1363) wool merchants were not allowed to use a labour force from outside the city to spin wool, because wool, once processed, should not leave the city to avoid the mixing of the expensive English Cotswold and March wool with cheaper raw materials. But citizens, or rather female citizens (*poortigghen*), were allowed to spin it.[461]

The chronology of the disappearing occupational dyadic references in the Ypres cloth industry does, however, also differ from the Douai case. In general the tendency towards male occupational titles happens earlier. It is probably no coincidence that Ypres was one of the first cloth cities to seize with open arms the industrial changes in favour of luxury fabrics. Exclusively masculine occupations regularly appeared as early as 1300, while in Douai such changes were not visible in the regulations until at least half a century later. Ypres statutes from 1300 often even indicate the guild status of master craftsmen, by mentioning, for example, master weavers (*maistres tysserands*), master fullers (*maistres foulons*), master shearers (*maistres tonderes*), and so on. But even occupational titles in the statutes that are not immediately linked to the status of mastership are no longer expressed in a dyadic form; nor are they given a dyadic he/she addition like *homme/femme*. Thus, the early fourteenth-century statutes mention only masculine versions for dyers (*tainteniers, vaerwere*), shearers and cloth finishers (*scerre, drapscerre, lakenreder*), wool cleaners (*wullespoelre*), wool beaters (*batteur de laine*),

---

457 *Il est ordeneit que nus ne soit hardis des ore en avant, ne homme ne femme, qu'ils fachent pieche de draep a liste* (Espinas and Pirenne, *Recueil*, 3, 461-462).
458 *Et sil avenist que doi venissent ensamble par mariage dont li uns fust drappiers et li autres dautre mestier, ke chascuns pouisse faire son mestier* (Espinas and Pirenne, *Recueil*, 3, 453-454).
459 It is remarkable that the charters in Picard French often use the Flemish occupational title of *spinnigghe, treckigghe* etc., rather than the Picard terminology (Espinas and Pirenne, *Recueil*, 3, 461-462.
460 Espinas and Pirenne, *Recueil*, 3, 503-504.
461 Espinas and Pirenne, *Recueil*, 3, 553.

dyers in blue (*ketelcnape, waidiers*), tenterers (*recwaghtere, utslare*) and, of course, the exclusively male guild officials (*stockenaere*, ...), etc. Other, less cloth-related guild activities which appear in the textile statutes of this period also mention exclusively male occupations: coopers (*cupere, commakere*), comb makers (*cammakere*), coppersmiths (*ketelare*), etc.

Even the clothiers (*drapier*) and merchants (*coopman*) tend to be described preferably using only a masculine occupational title.[462] The *homme ne femme* dyad is replaced by the omnipresent Flemish Dutch for 'no one, whoever he is' (*niemen wie hij zij*). The increasing guild influence on cloth production (and on urban policy) had probably been a catalyst for such changes. The hierarchical labour market in a guild economy pops up again and again in the cloth statutes. Workers are identified more and more with their labour status. Already in the clothiers' and weavers' statutes from around 1300 the hierarchies between masters (*maistre, meester*), apprentices (*apprenti, leercnape*), journeymen (*valès, cnape*) and unfree workers (*garchon, garsoen*) are clearly expressed and leave no room for women at all.[463] As such, the dramatic manufacturing changes of the late thirteenth and early fourteenth centuries were not only catalysts for the guild economy and guild control at large, they also provided a platform from which guild masters were able to claim higher levels of social prestige, economic independence and, although in Ypres mostly indirectly, even political power. As a result, labour markets became increasingly formally organised, a process that came at the cost of women's opportunities for independent economic activity.

Instead of the individual worker, the unit of labour became the guild master's workshop, and female work was more and more limited to strictly controlled systems of putting-out for the preparation of wool on the one hand, and work within the household as wife, daughter or (domestic) servant on the other. Already the dyer's charter from around 1300 mentions the household as a defining criterion for the organisation of production (*ketelcnape ki taint a caudiere ne sa femme*).[464] The statutes not only enforced a kind of economic solidarity between guild members, they described the companionate household of a husband and his wife as an economic unit. In the early fourteenth century the terminology of the household became even more apparent. The cloth broker's privilege after 1300 forbade a broker (*corretier*) and those residing with him, including his sons (*filg*), to form partnerships with other brokers or with members of their households (*compaignie avoec corretier ou avoec sa maisnie*). Cloth brokership was certainly a sensitive occupation in this city that depended on cloth exports. A few years before, neither brokers nor their wives, assistants (trained journeymen) or other members of their households (*meisnie*) had been allowed to be active in the money and bullion trade.[465]

The household, however, also had its limits in the eyes of the urban authorities. Partnerships between grown-up children and their parents were looked on with great

---

[462] Espinas and Pirenne, *Recueil*, 3, 507-508 and 511-512.
[463] Espinas and Pirenne, *Recueil*, 3, nrs. 752 to 765.
[464] Espinas and Pirenne, *Recueil*, 3, 478-479.
[465] Espinas and Pirenne, *Recueil*. 3, 486-487.

suspicion. The children of cloth sellers (*lakensniders*) or cloth entrepreneurs (*upsetters*) had to come before the aldermen and representatives of the clothiers once they reached marriageable age (*die te huwene zijn*). There, they received permission to be active in the same line of business as their parents, but on the condition that, once independent, they would not form partnerships with either of their parents and that they would not live under the same roof with them.[466]

Although the general pattern is clear, the process was also nuanced and complex. Independent female labour continued in the fourteenth century also to exist in other than the low-paid and low-status jobs of wool preparation; and even dyadic references and, therefore, the expression of gender inclusivity still concerned some textile occupations even as late as the second half of the fourteenth century. The 1309 charter for the production of stamforts – in this case it is probably no coincidence that it concerns the manufacture of lower quality woollens – still contains the same *homme-femme* dyadic references as the thirteenth-century statutes.[467] But even in the statutes regarding the quality of wool dating from 1363 and the following years dyadic occupational expressions still appear occasionally (*wullebreiker noch wullebreikigghe*).[468] But as a rule such semantic strings had by then all but disappeared in the key guild-controlled manufacturing processes.

For cloth traders and cloth entrepreneurs in Ypres, however, the situation is rather different. At the high end of the economic chain, among clothiers and merchants, women were paradoxically much more evident than in the key stages of the production chain from weaving to cloth finishing. The statutes for the production of the famously expensive *dickedinne* woollens in 1303 state that all citizens of Ypres, men and women (*poorters ende poortigghen*), living in the city's jurisdiction, apart from some occupational categories like brokers, dyers, wool cleaners, combers and spinners (the latter two indicated, not surprisingly, by exclusively feminine occupational titles), greasers and mercers, were allowed to be active as clothiers.[469] Even as late as 1363 the Picard *drapier/drappiere* expression of the thirteenth-century statutes is mirrored in the Flemish Dutch clothiers' charter which states that no cloth entrepreneur, male or female (*drapier of drapierigghe*), or cloth merchant was allowed to enter the site of the cloth press without the clothiers or merchants who owned the pressed woollens being present.[470]

If entrepreneurship seems to have remained gender-inclusive in Ypres throughout the fourteenth century, the cloth trade or other mercantile activities related to the cloth industry were even more open to women. The cloth merchants' charter dated before 1300 and other regulations concerning the wool trade or the trade in the new luxury woollens (*dickedinne*) in the same period leave little doubt that women were active as merchants. All citizens of Ypres, 'whether men or women', were addressed (*bourgeois,*

---

466 Espinas and Pirenne, *Recueil*, 3, 544).
467 Espinas and Pirenne, *Recueil*, 3, 466-467.
468 Espinas and Pirenne, *Recueil*, 3, 633.
469 Espinas and Pirenne, *Recueil*, 3, 518-519.
470 Espinas and Pirenne, *Recueil*, 3, 557.

ne home ne femme; bourgeois ne bourgoise; man of wijf).⁴⁷¹ In 1362 the clothiers' statutes still use the same dyadic reference of 'clothier, male or female' (*drapier of drapierigghe*), but also add an explicit reference to the household economy: regulation also applied to those in the clothier's (man or woman) household who were also involved in the cloth business.⁴⁷² Elsewhere in the same charter or in others, however, the reference to gender inclusivity becomes less explicit as gradually the masculine form of the occupational titles becomes dominant. Foreign merchants are referred to only as *marchans* or *home estrainge*. The cloth sellers' statutes of 1363 and the following years refer to *cleetsnidere*, 'whoever he is' (*niemen wie hij zij*). Cloth selling was, however, a typical retail activity and, therefore, also a guild-based activity. The cloth trade itself and entrepreneurship in cloth production were not guild-based activities; they fell under the jurisdiction and control of the urban authorities and enjoyed the same customary regulation ubiquitous in most Low Countries cities that guaranteed women a certain amount of independence in economic affairs.⁴⁷³ The tenacity of the dyadic semantic strings in trade and entrepreneurship throughout the fourteenth century is not, therefore, surprising. It suggests, however, that it was the guilds (and the guild-regulated economic activities) that were the real catalysts for long-term changes in gender inclusivity, rather than the civic governments themselves.

It is (Becoming) a Man's World

Historians have offered very different interpretations of the role of women on the late medieval labour markets and the labour status they could achieve. On the one hand optimists have stated that women profited from the labour shortages that were caused by massive mortality in the fourteenth century and the inevitable rise of real wages caused by them. As a result women were attributed more agency in the final centuries of the Middle Ages, and recent scholars have pointed at the sixteenth century as a transitional period with declining labour opportunities for women.⁴⁷⁴ On the other hand, other researchers have put forward a continuing decline in labour opportunities, stating that craft guilds in particular had been instrumental in the demise of job opportunities of all sorts. Data for the urbanised Low Countries suggest, however, a much more nuanced pattern. On the one hand, the region was able to escape from cataclysmic population decline, paradoxically probably because of its urbanised character and the strong migration flows that continued to supply labour in sufficient quantities.⁴⁷⁵ The

---

471 Cloth merchants before 1300: *nus bourgois, ne homme ne femme*; wool trade around 1300: *Item ke nus bourgois ne bourgoise ne achachetent laine encontre Englès ne autres gens*; and statutes for the 'dickedinne' woollens in 1303: *onder enighen man of wijf diet te venten stelde* (Espinas and Pirenne, Recueil, 3, 494 and 501).
472 *Noch enich van haren mesnieden die hem gheneren met lakenen te copene* (Espinas and Pirenne, Recueil, 3, 557).
473 Hutton, *Women and Economic Activities*.
474 Recently Pilorget, 'La fin du Moyen Âge', 95-107 for Amiens and her *Des femmes dans la ville*.
475 Empirical evidence for urban migration rates in medieval Flanders concerns mostly the fourteenth and fifteenth centuries (see Thoen, 'Immigration to Bruges', 453-491 and Stabel, *De kleine stad*, 34-50 and a more general assessment of urban stability in the demographic crisis of the late Middle Ages in Stabel, 'Composition et recompositions des réseaux urbains', 29-64).

cities of the Low Countries did not, therefore, experience the same levels of population loss as were identified for other urbanised parts of Europe, from Italy to southern England. The result was that wage evolution presents a more mitigated and, above all, more cyclical pattern whereby labour shortages do not seem to have been as acute as elsewhere in Europe. Thus, women were less needed to fill the gaps in a male labour market.

On the other hand, the economic changes in the Low Countries cities of the thirteenth and fourteenth centuries also caused structural social changes, which would eventually lead to the guild-dominated urban economies of the late Middle Ages and Early Modern Period. Hence the massive export-oriented textile industry of the twelfth and early thirteenth centuries, where relatively free labour markets were controlled by capitalistic merchant-entrepreneurs, changed into a still very much export-oriented industry, but by the end of the thirteenth and early fourteenth centuries more and more geared towards the manufacture of high-quality woollens and to luxury industries. The result was a more central position for the emerging craft guilds, which were able very efficiently to organise systems of quality control and to coordinate training systems for industrial processes based on very expensive raw materials and skill. In other economic sectors similar processes of guild organisation were also taking place.

The guild economy was, however, based not upon individual workers as before, but on family units under the supervision and control of the patriarchal and male head of the household. Only when the male head of the household died could his widow ensure the continuity of the workshop, and, therefore, of the household. As such, women's status became less dependent upon work and independent income, but more on inclusion in a household and on marital status.[476] The effect on labour opportunities for women around 1300 must have been enormous. On the one hand, the process, which had already been apparent before, whereby low-paid and low-status jobs (for example in the preparation of wool) were increasingly feminised became stronger throughout the fourteenth century. On the other hand, women all but disappeared from the guild-organised, key industrial functions in the dominant textile industry (from weaving to cloth finishing). That is to say, they disappeared from the formally and hierarchically organised labour in the guild itself (apprentices, journeymen, masters); they remained, however, active as wives and daughters (and probably also as domestic servants) in the household economy. The low end (wool preparation) and the top end of economic activity were, however, the exception. Single, but also married women were heavily involved in the labour-intensive but badly paid preparatory stages of the industry. As we have seen, most labour input in cloth manufacture occurred in spinning, carding and combing. Women seem to have been engaged in the industrial process during the fourteenth and fifteenth centuries as independent workers, just like the female weavers, shearers and dyers in the twelfth and thirteenth centuries. But entrepreneurship itself and even mercantile activities also seem to have attracted women throughout the

---

476 This does not mean, however, that women's identities were not partly shaped by their economic and occupational status. For England see Beattie, 'The Problem of Women's Work Identities', 1-19 for England and Franceschi, 'Famille et travail', 109-110 and more general remarks in Groppi, *Il lavoro delle donne* for Italian industrial cities.

period. The more egalitarian Flemish (and, by extension, West-European) legal system provided an institutional framework in which women could retain agency, on the condition, of course, that they also owned or had access to capital and financial markets.

The consequences of this very layered labour market were important. Thus, the late medieval period in the Low Countries cities probably did not witness a rise in independent labour opportunities for women. The low-end industrial jobs had already been the realm of women in the period of growth in the twelfth and thirteenth centuries, while their situation did not change drastically as regards (the fewer) entrepreneurial and commercial activities. But women were massively ousted from most key guild occupations before 1300 (except when they were widowed). This stands in stark contrast to, for example, the important role still played by female *socie* in late medieval Florence, who carried out subordinate tasks for the clothiers in weavers' workshops but were also involved in the actual weaving process itself, an activity which women were no longer allowed to undertake in Flemish cities after 1300.[477] Almost 40 per cent of the estimated workforce in Florence were women, a figure which cannot be very far removed from the Flemish gender relations in cloth manufacture, but in Italy women were therefore clearly also allowed to manufacture the fabric, and not just to prepare wool and spin yarn.[478] Late medieval prosopographical analysis has shown that only those guilds where training did not play an important role (retailing guilds such as mercers) retained a lot of women. The only unknown factor is the number of domestic servants. One cannot, however, doubt that the newly established household economy of small commodity producers required more (in this period relatively expensive) female domestic servants than before, as the households themselves contained even cheaper female domestic labour, the wives and daughters of the master. In the past, the greater agency of women on labour markets was directly linked to the emergence of a 'West-European marriage pattern' which, in line with David Herlihy's models of the household economy, was situated chronologically in a period of great mortality in the fourteenth century.[479] Declining population offered opportunities to intensify their labour input. According to this pattern women married relatively late, they moved out of their family networks while setting up their own households, and all these elements combined stimulated them also to engage more actively in labour markets. But in Ypres and Douai, and most likely also in all other cloth cities of the Low Countries, job opportunities for women seem to have declined, women were banished to less rewarding activities outside the guild economy or they were absorbed more in a household economy under patriarchal supervision. The growth of independent job opportunities for single women in the late Middle Ages is therefore not straightforward, and neither is the emergence of the West-European marriage pattern and its chronological link with the demographic cataclysm of fourteenth-century Europe.

---

477 Franceschi, *Oltre il tumulto*, 174-175 and id., 'Famille et travail', 112. For Flanders, Stabel, 'Working Alone?', 27-49.
478 Franceschi, *Oltre il tumulto*, 272.
479 Herlhy, *The Black Death*; De Moor and Van Zanden, 'Girl Power', 1-33.

CHAPTER 9

A Time to Protest

Cloth and Revolt

Medieval Revolts in Flanders

Bruges and Ghent, the most populous cities of medieval Flanders, both have the reputation of also having been uneasy cities under comital rule, since the early twelfth century constantly alert for any breach of their privileges, harbouring ambitions to broaden the scope of their power in the city itself and beyond in their hinterland, always also erupting in internal friction and strife among members of the elite families but, as industrial expansion fired up the impact of craft guilds and new elites emerged, gradually also between more popular factions and the political elites. When, shortly before and after 1300, the so-called 'democratic' revolts destroyed the political monopoly of the traditional 'patriciate' and regional or international conflicts in the fourteenth century such as between, for example, the count of Flanders and the king of France, or the Hundred Years War between France and England, were piled on existing frictions, the troubles only became fiercer and more violent. In the final century of the Middle Ages it was the struggle between the centralising state and the large, politically influential cities that came to the fore. That was also linked to the continuing internal struggle between some groups in society, usually among them the elites themselves, some of whom favoured the policies of the dukes of Burgundy while others were more reluctant to accept state intervention, and among the more popular factions of the middle and lower classes, those were usually organised into the craft guilds.

Traditionally, the historians of the Burgundian Period have certainly long considered Ypres as a kind of backwater. The troubles in Bruges – guild unrest in 1407-1411, a wide-ranging revolt in 1436, the city's leading role in the demands put before the new ruler, Mary of Burgundy, in 1477 after the violent death of her father, and again the struggle with Maximilian of Habsburg in the 1480s and early 1490s, culminating in the capture of the Austrian prince in 1488 – and even more in rebellious Ghent – with, besides many smaller events, the general revolt in the late 1370s and early 1380s, and with the long struggles with Burgundian power in the 1450s and in the 1470s and 1480s – are considered eponymous with the political ambitions and social frictions in the cities of the Low Countries. In fifteenth-century Ypres, however, the urban governments were most of the time still being controlled by the same mercantile and landowning elites that had achieved the communal changes in the twelfth century, and the influence of the craft guilds was more or less limited to lower level institutions in the neighbourhoods or in the corporations themselves, or to a counselling role in one of the advisory boards of the city. Real power remained firmly in the hand of the elites, therefore, and as the city's main industry went into decline it was also less and less challenged internally. Although Ypres was, as a truly industrial city, characterised by higher levels of inequality and of social polarisation even between the wealthy mercantile elites and relatively poor textile workers with, in sharp contrast to Bruges, only a relatively small and less prevalent middle class, the decline of the industry must have affected the social composition in the long run, and the city in the fifteenth century probably became less prone to sharp social polarisation. In Ypres, declining numbers of craftsmen and the greater relative importance of middling groups – social phenomena we see much more pervasively in Bruges and even in Ghent – did not apparently lead to the stronger internal organisation of those middling groups or to greater antagonism towards the city elites, which tended to favour strong central power. Ypres was, nonetheless, with Ghent and Bruges (and the rural district of the *Franc* of Bruges), one of the Members of Flanders, which allowed the county organised participation in comital and ducal policies. As Flanders was still by far the richest territory of the Burgundian Dukes, the large cities to a large extent also held the purse of the Burgundian dukes and later the Habsburg monarchs. Yet Ypres was undoubtedly in this period also a mitigating factor, never in the forefront of dissension. It joined in some of the common urban unrest in the fifteenth century, most notably the friction after the death of Duke Charles the Bold in 1477 and the early opposition to Maximilian of Habsburg. It was, however, never one of the ringleaders. It was the first to capitulate, and its depleted population probably also did not allow it to adopt such a prominent revolutionary role.

A century earlier, however, from the 1280s to the 1380s, the situation was completely different. Ypres was politically and socially one of the most polarised, and also one of the most volatile cities in the County of Flanders. There were major troubles in 1280 during the *Cokerulle* and in the events surrounding 1302, leading to the murder of half of the bench of aldermen in 1303. There were revolts and troubles before and during the short period of 'democratic' city government in the late 1320s and again in 1348, when the count laid siege to the city. This was only a prelude, however, to periods of chronic revolt in 1359-1361, 1367, 1370, 1377, 1379-1380 and finally 1382.[480] Ypres was, with Ghent, the main hotspot for urban resistance to the encroaching power of Count Louis de Male. In the meantime smaller but no less violent conflicts arose about internal political relations and the organisation of labour. Ypres was therefore anything but a tranquil city. Every generation experienced major political conflict and these conflicts were often interspersed with smaller and more localised bouts of unrest, primarily characterised by industrial action.

The reasons for all this turbulence are easy to pinpoint. In chapter 3 we saw how in the first half of the fourteenth century the city was marked by extremely high rates of inequality, with enormous differences of wealth and access to economic opportunity. At the same time, it had also been a very polarised political city. Political power and control of the city's government were jealously guarded by the traditional elites. From the twelfth into the fifteenth centuries the same families of Belle, de Brune, Van Dixmude, Piet de Soile, Paeldinc and a limited number of others continued to fill most influential political positions, and although there had been openings for new mercantile families

---

480 Verbruggen, *Geweld in Vlaanderen*, 40-45.

and also for some members of the so-called *poortersneringhen*, usually capital intensive crafts, the elites were successful in resisting all attempts by the common people and the textile guilds to reach a comprehensive agreement about structural systems of power-sharing. At best, the craftsmen had access to some of the counselling bodies or neighbourhood institutions. In chapter 4, we also saw that the mercantile elites remained key figures in the cloth industry itself, because of their hold on the flows of capital.

It is surprising, nonetheless, that the stronger middle groups in the late medieval period did not gain similar political influence to that they had in Ghent or Bruges. Although scholars have pointed to the rallying force of craftsmen and of the lower classes in social and political friction, generally it is also assumed that the political demands of the guild-organised middle groups were a crucial factor in the frequency and intensity of political conflict in Flanders. One group in particular was all set to open the doors to political power: the Ypres clothiers. After 1280 they had truly become the crucial figures in industrial organisation. Their occupation was intrinsically linked to the accumulation of capital, which they needed to buy the increasingly expensive raw materials for the manufacture of woollens. Their role in the emancipation of the entrepreneurial class in the economic life in the late thirteenth and early fourteenth centuries is generally accepted to have been crucial, although we have seen that their financial dependence upon the elites probably did not stop at that time. Yet the clothiers did not gain systematic access to the centre of political power in the city. They were not able to control the main levers of economic decision-making, the bench of aldermen. Unlike, for example, the dyers, who had almost unlimited access to the formal financial market in the late thirteenth century, they had to rely on their role in the weavers' guild, paradoxically a guild that was very active in social and political friction for political agency throughout the long fourteenth century. Still, the clothiers' position in the weavers' guild was also slightly ambiguous; as entrepreneurs, many clothiers were indeed master weavers and members of the weavers' guild. Because of their social clout and economic hold they probably controlled the guild's daily activities, yet their social identity was also completely different from that of most other guildsmen. Their access to capital and their status in the industrial process set them apart from the usually very poor master weavers and from the journeymen in the weavers' guild. This ambiguity seems also to have defined their political role in the tensions and conflicts that defined the political cycle in fourteenth-century Ypres. At times they seem to have participated in the unrest, at other times they were obviously absent from the unrest and from the violence.

The past decades have seen interest in medieval popular uprisings increase exponentially. Scholars have tackled various issues related to popular discontent in different timeframes, from the communal uprisings of the twelfth century to the 'industrial' conflicts of the thirteenth and the 'political' revolts of the late fourteenth and fifteenth centuries. While the first were traditionally linked to the emancipation of the civic community from its feudal surroundings and the emergence of the urban landowning and mercantile elites, in older studies inevitably called the 'patriciate', the second were associated with the rise of the guilds, culminating in what were once described by Henri

Pirenne as 'medieval democracies' after the events of 1300-1302, and the third are usually described as attempts by the urban communities to resist the encroaching power of the feudal territorial state and defend the autonomy they had so laboriously gained from the early twelfth century onwards.

Scholarship has increasingly targeted the processes that constituted the mechanisms of revolt. In particular, Ghent historians such as Walter Prevenier, Marc Boone, Jan Dumolyn, Raf Verbruggen and Jelle Haemers in Belgium, but also Anglo-American scholars such Sam Cohn, Wayne te Brake and Patrick Lantschner, have identified particular dominant features. All these revolts were, of course, accompanied by violent outbursts and emotional attacks of one urban group against another. The use of violence during revolts was, however, also part of a highly ritualised process. The breakdown of social order needed to be legitimated by the action of revolt itself, both by its modus operandi and by the social performance of its actors.[481] The expression of violence was therefore not random, nor was it unplanned. It served a purpose and this purpose was clearly linked to the fact that the idea of community needed to be performed and staged. It built on those aspects of public culture, social and political organisation and the continual re-enactment of these in urban ritual that so defined urban social life as a whole.[482]

Therefore, the instruments of social and political unrest were often familiar, and as a result even in the case of the collapse of a particular regime the new social and political order had to make use of and consider the processes that constituted that social order. It is striking that the revolutionaries of the fourteenth century were called the 'common people' (*tcommun*), undoubtedly referring to the communal nature of the city, terminology previously reserved for the urban community as a whole. While in earlier periods the notion of commoners primarily was primarily reserved for the mercantile and landholding elites, the so-called 'best' or 'wisest part' of the city (*melior pars, sanior pars*), the term was in this period increasingly used primarily for the urban craftsmen and guilds. Although the notion of 'common good' was central to all city governments as an instrument of legitimation, the communal terminology of 'commoner' therefore moved from elite circles to the lower strata of urban society.[483] This phenomenon has inspired recent scholars working on urban revolts in the Middle Ages to link the outward characteristics of revolt (peaceful or violent, inclusive or antagonistic, bargaining or hegemonic) and the level of success they brought to the prior institutional and social arrangements in place for solving tensions. Urban conflict is defined, therefore, 'within a spectrum of readily available rationalities of political action'.[484]

This reflection on what is in essence urban culture and social identification was often necessary, as revolts were not always solely based upon class, and the ranks of

---

481 Lantschner, *The Logic of Political Conflict*, 15-16.
482 Peter Arnade's book (*Realms of Ritual*) was the first of a multitude of studies dealing with the relationship between urban space, the urban social fabric and political rituals in peacetime and during revolts (for references to this strand of scholarship see Boone and Haemers, 'The Common Good', 93-127).
483 Haemers and Merlevede, '*Le commun se esmeut*', 177-204.
484 Lantschner, *The Logic*, p. 17. See also Dumolyn and Haemers, 'Patterns of Urban Rebellion', 369-393.

both the insurgents and the people in power against whom the insurgents operated had gradually become socially diffused when guilds and other associations had managed to enter the ranks of city governments. Yet class still mattered, as many of the grievances that were ventilated in collective action were triggered often directly by social injustice and inequality. The masses of textile workers provided in almost all cities of medieval Flanders the rank and file for the shock troops of revolt, yet it is the urban middle classes who often reaped the benefits and lasting results would primarily consist of the further institutionalisation of guilds in city governments and reinforcement of the hold of middle groups on urban governance, inside or in close cooperation with the institutions of urban government. This does not mean that class was completely irrelevant. At least rhetorically, the idea of the common good integrates social concerns in the political arena. Such concerns were expressed by many groups in urban society, and even in times of crisis these channels of political communication seem to intensify even more. So-called 'cryers' (*creesers*) shouted out, sometimes very literally, the complaints and demands of popular groups in the public sphere, while more formal arrangement of 'requests' to the urban governments, petitions in which often very specific demands, but also broader concerns about access to political participation, were ventilated provided an outlet for popular frustration and anxieties.[485] Yet none of these mechanisms of participation, of course, matched the influence that urban middle classes could achieve by formal arrangements of political participation and power-sharing.[486] And it was the craft guilds that had become the true vehicles serving the interest of the urban middle class. They could sometimes radicalise, for example in the revolt in the late 1370s and early 1380s in Ghent or during the Ciompi regime in Florence in the same period, but mostly, once the ambitions of their leaders were attained, they just as easily turned into instruments for preserving the status quo.

In such circumstances social order was challenged continually, however, and popular movements tried to respond to the changing economic and cultural frameworks to which urban society had to adapt. This led to very uneven outcomes and sharp differences from one region to another, even from one city to another. In Northwest Europe, where guilds became more firmly entrenched in local power constellations, the struggle for internal dominance usually set mercantile-entrepreneurial elites against the leading strata of the craft guilds. Moreover, the internal conflicts were often linked to the external relations of the city, vis-à-vis their territorial lords, the counts of Flanders. These were not mere bystanders but, on the contrary, they sometimes made very volatile alliances with urban stakeholders in order to preserve their authority.

In recent studies, therefore, class, the dominant feature in the older studies of the 1920s and 1960s, has not been forgotten, but has still been somewhat sidelined as the main cause for insurrection and political turmoil. A refined analysis of discourses points rather to ideas that go beyond class identity itself, but are constructed out of common standards of community-building. In other words, whether it was the urban elites of the twelfth century, the guildsmen in 1280 or 1300, or the political lobbies behind urban

---

485 Haemers, 'Révolte et requête', 27-56.
486 Dumolyn, 'Criers and Shouters', 111-135 and Dumolyn and Haemers, 'A Bad Chicken was Brooding', 45-86.

decision-making in the late fourteenth and fifteenth centuries, they all shared a common language, not to say a common identity. It is the communal idea, the concern for the common good or commonwealth, that defines political action, whether this action is directed towards what are considered to be the private interests of the political elites that did not conform to a sense of 'common good', or towards an external force, the prince, who limits or even eradicates legal and political rights that are considered to be crucial for that common good.

But where does this leave class conflict itself and the actions of the less privileged in political conflict? One of the common threads in the ideas and practices of revolt in late medieval Flanders (or elsewhere for that matter) is that the driving force of turbulence is closely associated with the rise of the burgeoning middle classes. We have already seen how notions of middle class were also paramount in the analysis by Martha Howell of the Ypres letters obligatory in the latter part of the thirteenth century. The fact that one third of the city's population seems to have been involved in these formal debt arrangements and that – at least that is Howell's reasoning – new ambitious entrepreneurial groups such as the clothiers, but also other guild-organised trades, were very active in this field is surely proof of the importance of these middle classes. Howell's conclusions cannot, therefore, be much clearer. The old ideas of class struggle must be rethought in this dynamic field of economic ambition and the social aspirations of ever larger parts of the urban population, also, and perhaps even particularly so, in an industrial city like Ypres.

The idea that an industrial giant is also a place with strong and dynamic middling sorts of people, however, runs counter to the patterns of social inequality. In chapter 3 we saw that inequality rates in Ypres calculated from taxation records in 1325-1326 were extremely high. Ypres was a very unequal city, and this high inequality rate was intrinsically linked to the much smaller impact of urban middle classes of small commodity producers and retailers. This was also true for all real industrial cities in the medieval Low Countries, and the pattern can be found also in, for example, Leiden and, although to a lesser extent, in Ghent. Even in Bruges, a city at the end of the fourteenth century characterised by very low inequality rates, the more industrial districts of the city were substantially more unequal than the more commercial districts.[487] So the Ypres clothiers (together with some of the guilds that catered for the city's food supply and other services) may have constituted, alongside the merchants who did not yet belong to the urban elites, those ambitious *homines novi*, the new men, who tried to grab power around 1300; they were far from constituting a demographically dominant group. Late thirteenth-century Ypres was not late-fourteenth century Bruges, where exactly those middle groups became one of the driving forces of a Smithian process of developing specialist fashion, durable consumer goods and luxuries. And even in Bruges the demographically dominant middle groups never achieved complete control over political power, although they did, of course, influence urban politics. Ypres in this period was a much more polarised city, with large segments of the population living off

---

[487] Stabel, *A Capital of Fashion*, forthcoming and recently for Ghent also Dumolyn, Ryckbosch and Speecke, 'Did inequality produce medieval revolt?', 372-405.

(low) wages in return for industrial work, hardly the self-conscious guild artisans who boosted demand for material goods in the late fourteenth and fifteenth centuries. So does the question not need to be asked again? Was the old idea about class struggle in the social and political conflicts of the 1280s and 1300s so wrong, and should we not rather try to blend the new research on processes of revolt with those older ideas?

Paradoxically, it is one of the leading voices in the new research paradigms, Jelle Haemers, who has recently voiced similar concerns. In a case study on urban revolts in Leuven, one of the capital cities of the Duchy of Brabant, he again demanded attention to be paid to a return of class as a decisive factor to explain medieval revolts.[488] Even in Ypres, the urban oligarchy of the late Middle Ages became more open and to a certain extent also meritocratic, absorbing relatively frictionless newcomers who had achieved commercial success. Thus, the conflicts that arose during the fourteenth century tended to be much more based on class difference and on social demands. Subaltern groups, united in guilds or other associations, tried to carve out their own place among the urban administrations or to develop institutions that allowed political influence to be brought to the decisions that mattered, while the powers that be resisted them. It was a period characterised by a new self-confidence among city dwellers, a new 'lust for liberty', to use Samuel Cohn's expression, and this lust expressed itself all over Europe. Cohn clearly links the greater willingness for revolt to the shattering effects of the Black Death and other crises that struck late medieval society. In Flanders, and in Ypres in particular, these conflicts clearly built on earlier frictions in urban society.[489] While in Italy the clash between the traditional elites and the *popolani* in the thirteenth century had really been predominantly an affair of urban middle classes aspiring to power; in the industrial cities of western Europe the tensions involving lower classes in urban society had already surfaced, most notably in the industrialised cities of Flanders. But in particular during the fourteenth century they returned with much more vigour and their impact was reinforced by two other variables. They were accompanied by similar social difficulties in the countryside (for example in Flanders in the 1320s). And upon the internal social and political frictions in urban society was laid another political layer, the relationship of cities and their territories with the expanding territorial state. The turbulent history of fourteenth-century Ypres cannot be dissociated from all these elements, and always the central role of industrial organisation and social inequality, of the economic cycle and of the relative balance between the stakeholders in the industrial process, in other words of the changing features of class relations, must be considered as essential ingredients, creating exactly in this period an explosive mix.

---

488 Haemers, "Bloed en inkt", 141-164.
489 Cohn, *Lust for Liberty* and id., 'Popular Insurrection and the Black Death', 188-204. See also Mollat and Wolff, *Ongles bleus, Jacques et Ciompi*.

Cokerulle: A True Social Conflict?

This was, of course, certainly the case in the most acute phases when Ypres commoners challenged the political and economic hold the elites had on them. The best studied example for Ypres is, of course, the *cokerulle* of 1280 or, in the eyes of Count Guy of Flanders, the 'very grave events and horrible acts which because of God and good reason could not be left unpunished' (*mout de grief chas et de fais oribles ki selonc Dieu et raison ne doivent demorer sans estre amendei*).[490] What occurred had, however, been much more complex than the simple conflict described by the comital officers as a struggle between the old mercantile elites ('the aldermen and those of their party') and the craftsmen (clothiers, weavers, fullers, shearers and 'a great number of other people who supported them'). It is striking, for example, that not all textile guilds are named: the position of most cloth finishers and of the dyers is not discussed. In particular the position of the dyers is remarkable. They belonged to the *poorterneringhen*, or the citizens' crafts, and because of the capital-intensive nature of their businesses they probably did not entirely sympathise with the other craftsmen. Already before 1280 the dyers had acted almost independently of the merchants at the financial market. The clothiers, on the other hand, had gained some level of agency in the markets for raw materials and woollens, yet, if we look at the Ypres debt contracts, it is likely that they did not emerge completely from the financial hold of the elites as many dyers were able to do. Despite the financial clout some clothiers must have had, even compared with the dyers, their relations with the elites in the final decades of the thirteenth century were still asymmetrical, and they would probably remain so well into the fourteenth century. Moreover, most clothiers were guildsmen anyway, belonging as masters to the weavers' guild.

The events surrounding the *cokerulle* may have triggered the most fundamental shift in the social relations between merchants and clothiers in medieval Ypres, but from a distance and compared to the very violent conflicts of the fourteenth century, the events during the *cokerulle* revolt were not much more than a storm in a teacup. The revolt was not characterised by massive and uncontrolled bloodshed, nor was the repression by the count and the city elites very harsh. In the end a tax was imposed on the textile crafts which the political elites could keep for themselves, in exchange for financially supporting the count in the future. And indeed, in contrast to the predominantly 'Lily' faction in the political elites of Ghent or Bruges, the elites of Ypres would remain loyal to the comital family in the conflict that set the count against the king of France before and after 1300, even leading an Ypres expeditionary force to the battle of Kortrijk in 1302. Still the effects of the revolt would be felt in the internal relations of the Ypres cloth industry in the following centuries. It shook up the relations between merchants, cloth entrepreneurs and guild entrepreneurs.

Everything started in the summer of 1280, when two underlying local conflicts surfaced: industrial relations were becoming tense because of the structural changes in the industry (with declining outputs of cheaper worsteds affecting the volumes

---

490 Espinas and Pirenne, *Recueil*, 3, 679.

being manufactured and creating friction among textile workers) and because competition among the elites for political power had increased (with new wealthy families challenging the entrenched position of the old Ypres elites). But in truth, unrest had been brewing for a decade already in most industrial cities of Flanders, Artois, Hainaut and even Liège. The close political and economic relations between cities in this densely urbanised region can explain why all these revolts seem to have occurred almost simultaneously. The end of medieval growth, when standards of living were gradually being eroded and cities exploded because of push-migration from the overcrowded countryside, was felt by ever larger portions of the urban population, and nowhere were tensions felt as acutely as in industrial cities with their high numbers of semi-proletarianised textile workers. Furthermore, in order to hang on to their export volumes, the merchants and the clothiers, at this stage probably still primarily their 'foremen' (to use Doudelez's eloquent description), there must have been a push to reduce manufacturing costs and implement downward pressure on wage levels. The wage settings of 1280 can probably be interpreted in this context (rather than in the context of trying to smooth relations with workers during a conflict between merchants and clothiers). The result was therefore not appeasement, but rather the intensification of friction. The charter issued by Count Guy in 1281 talks of illicit gatherings without his consent, which the count did not hesitate to describe as 'conspiracies' (*conspirations, toutes aloiances et tout aconpaignement, comment c'on les apiat, ki sunt faites sans congiet de seigneur*), and one of the sanctions he proposed was a ban on gatherings of more than ten people, which he probably associated with the potential danger of generating further unrest.[491]

Social frictions remained very real, and labour conflicts lay also very much at the heart of social unrest. This was already the case long before 1280 and it would remain so also after the *cokerulle*. On 18 June 1281 six craftsmen were sentenced to a fine of £3 for refusing to go to their work stations.[492] In chapters 6 and 7 we saw that textile workers were not allowed to refuse work once they were asked to work by the clothiers. And a couple of days later, on 2 July, another ten craftsmen were sentenced to a fine and banishment from the county for refusing work (*de prohibitione operis*). Similar cases (*de tensamento et prohibitione operis*) had surfaced occasionally in preceding years, but they are mentioned only randomly in the city accounts, so it is impossible to study the frequency of such labour conflicts in any systematic way.[493] The regulatory framework even allows one to note a steady tightening of rules regarding disobedience to the count, the aldermen or even to employers. The cloth statutes of the early 1280s, shortly after the troubles of the Cokerulle, state that all apprentices in the guilds of the weavers, the fullers and the shearers had to come before a commission of two city aldermen with two pledgees who would swear on their behalf that they would not get involved in any 'conspiracy' or revolt against the count. Apprentices who were found out lost

---

[491] Espinas and Pirenne, *Recueil*, 3, 681.
[492] Des Marez and De Sagher, *Les comptes*, 1, 61: *Hanninus Keie, Lambertus Kelelbotere, Willelmus Pillecoc, Boudinus Pillecoc, Claikinus Hemeric, Willelmus Dobbelsergand: 3 lb. quilibet de non eundo ad opus post Pentecostes sicut ei demandatum fuerat.*
[493] Des Marez and De Sagher, *Les comptes*, 1, 2 and 63.

their status and masters who willingly employed such people forfeited the right to ply their trade for a year.[494] In the fourteenth-century regulation, shearers who refused to stand by the orders given to them by the guild officials or did not respect a verdict of the guild were similarly severely fined, and could be brought before the aldermen for justice.[495] Fullers were, in the middle of the fourteenth century, not allowed to employ people, journeymen or others, who had been on strike or had refused work before, even in other cities, nor were clothiers allowed to hire a master fuller who had been involved in a strike, called an 'exit' or *uutganc*, whereby the workers left the city.[496]

In the tense circumstances of 1280 a single spark was enough to cause massive disturbance, and the spark came not from the textile workers themselves, but from factional violence among ambitious wealthy merchant families, who were not yet among the leading families of Ypres. It was the Oudewijn family that fired the revolt. Jan Oudewijn asked his brother Hendrik in late September or early October 1280 to raise a (smallish) group of insurgents in the nearby textile town of Poperinge, and when this group arrived in the Ypres suburb outside the Butter Gate (in the western suburb of the Holy Cross parish, developed partly on the lands of the Order of the Knights Templar), the textile workers of Ypres did not hesitate to join the movement. The rebels entered the city and attacked the houses of some members of the political elites. Two aldermen who had not succeeded in hiding or fleeing were killed in the process. But, all in all, violence remained limited: the discontent was ventilated in plunder and symbolic action. The name *cokerulle* itself points more to a kind of charivari-like demonstration of discontent, rather than to violent conflict.[497] Everything was over in a couple of days, and the local representatives of the counts and the city elites were able quickly to recover from the onslaught.[498] The count restored the peace, and in his decree of 1 April 1281 he ordered there to be peace between the elites on the one hand and the textile workers and entrepreneurs on the other, and also that all internal strife among the elite families themselves be ended (*bone pais soit entre les parties et les linages*). The Oudewijn family was punished only symbolically and the revolt did not prevent another family who had instigated the event, the Van Eeckhoute family, from being among the city officials and aldermen in the next century. Internal elite conflict was appeased after one violent outburst, and the bench of aldermen was opened up to some of these new families in the following decades without jeopardizing the position of the traditional elites. The incident would, nonetheless, have grave social consequences, as the position of the clothier in the manufacturing process was strengthened, but again without really endangering the mercantile elites' hold on the industry. In the long run clothiers would indeed constitute a middle group which, as the industry moved to manufacturing almost exclusively luxury cloth, started to acquire an economic

---

494 *Ke il jamais ne fera kuere, ne conspiration, ne alloianche contre le seigneur de le terre ne encontre la vile dYpre* (Espinas and Pirenne, *Recueil*, 3, 464-465).
495 Espinas and Pirenne, *Recueil*, 3, 600.
496 Espinas and Pirenne, *Recueil*, 3, 572.
497 Dumolyn and Haemers, 'Takehan, Cokerulle', 39-54.
498 For a more detailed description of the events see Doudelez, 'Une revolution communale', 188-294; Hooghe, 'De Cokerulle', 293-348 and Boone, 'Social Conflicts', 147-155.

position more independent of local mercantile capital. More than a breakthrough in political participation, which was never completely achieved in the Ypres institutions of government, it is the economic success of the clothiers that may help to explain their ambiguous attitude in the following conflicts in the city, which were also significantly more radical and more violent.

Revolt and Restoration 1302-1328

The relative low profile of the events in 1280 and their aftermath did not mean, however, that the social tension that had been at the origin of the unrest had completely evaporated. The next great crisis occurred in the wake of 1302 and the Revolt of Bruges against the French occupation of the county. In Ypres, the events of 1280 had created new possibilities for the textile trades, and despite their continuing dependence upon mercantile capital, textile entrepreneurs became more important nonetheless. Some clothiers and the *upsetters*, a typically Ypres phenomenon of entrepreneurship in the final stages of cloth manufacture and a strange blend of cloth entrepreneurs and merchants who managed only the final stages of cloth manufacture, must have accumulated new wealth, and some probably also knocked at the door to become members of the merchant class. These were frictions that were present in nearly all Flemish cities, but in Ypres the tensions were further exacerbated because of the closed nature of political office. New elites could almost not force an entrance into the political elites of the city. It is uncertain whether dire economic circumstances for cloth workers added to the tension, as they undoubtedly did in other cities. All in all, Ypres entrepreneurs were still enjoying some success in the manufacture of semi-worsteds, the stamforts, which remained popular on Mediterranean markets.

Ypres had already played a role in the events leading to the battle of Kortrijk on 11 July 1302. The Ypres militia led by a member of the Belle family had pinned the French garrison down in Kortrijk during the battle. The city elites with their involvement in the wool and cloth trade and their anglophile sympathies were certainly little inclined to favour the *Lily* faction. So it is hardly surprising that they favoured the comital party of the Lion (*liebaert*) – the lily, of course, representing the royal coat of arms, the lion the Flemish coat of arms. After 11 July 1302 and the successes of the guild-led Bruges militia at Kortrijk, however, the pressure to adhere to the movement opening the urban governments to the guilds must have been felt in Ypres as well. Across Flanders and even in Brabant the old elites tried to build new compromises with the guilds and looked at systems of power-sharing.

Probably this had not at all been the Ypres elites' intention. Despite the efforts of 1280, political power was still a monopoly of the traditional elites, and they did not want to give in immediately. Unrest was inevitable, and violence erupted in the night of 29 November 1303. A number of aldermen and councillors were killed in the riot, while the others fled. A charter of Philip of Chieti, one of the younger sons of the count of Flanders and regent of Flanders during the imprisonment of his father, Count Guy, and his two elder brothers in France, mentions that the events had been caused by the misdeeds the ruling elites had committed against the common people (*commun*).[499] Philip, governing a rebellious county against a possible new French invasion and whose position was maintained only with the goodwill of the powerful large cities, was continually forced into a balancing act. The old bench of aldermen in Ypres had been chased away, and it was replaced by a new city government controlled by the commoners and the guilds, in first instance the guilds of weavers (including the clothiers) and fullers. So the count's son and the other cities of Flanders (Ghent, Bruges, Lille and Douai) had little choice other than to sanction the new situation on 16 December. The murderers were pardoned.[500] Thirty members of the old elite were targeted for their earlier misdeeds: they were put on a list of those who had to pay compensation for what had been stolen from the commoners (*biens et revenues que li dis communs a paiés a tort*). Philip also confirmed the new revolutionary bench of aldermen. As the aldermen in Ypres were traditionally appointed by co-optation, henceforth the commoners would be allowed to nominate the aldermen starting at the next legislature the following August.

Still the old elites felt threatened and wanted to regain their old positions as fast as possible. The revolutionary regime did not last long. It had probably also overplayed their hand and the aldermen of Ghent and Bruges probably did not want anarchy to reign further in one of the largest cities of the county in the context of the continuing struggle with France and of still very insecure urban governments in most other cities. Already in April and much more radically in a charter of 4 May 1304, only four months after his initial charter, the regent and the leading cities changed course. Philip of Chieti reinstated the aldermen who had escaped the onslaught of 29 November and nominated seven others to replace those who had been murdered.[501] In the same process the revolutionary administrators were ousted from all functions, and the new bench would therefore still be nominated by the old elites. In other words, nothing would change. But the tone had changed completely. While the first charter accused the old elites of fraud and deceit, now the aldermen's murders were called evil deeds (*vilains*). There was no more talk of pardoning the rioters of 1303: 47 named culprits were to be executed (on the wheel and by hanging), unfair taxes levied by the guilds (*li bonne gens des mestiers*) during the winter months had to be returned, and the aldermen would deal with all complaints about extortion and theft during the months of the revolutionary regime. This was indeed a complete volte face: the old order was restored. Yet the legitimacy of government needed to be guaranteed and the guilds were allowed to continue the election of their own leaders (*capitaines*) from their midst and perhaps they retained a level of political participation in the broader council, which had advisory powers. The guilds' position in urban society was therefore not necessarily weakened. All was set for another showdown.

---

499 Espinas and Pirenne, *Recueil*, 3, 718-721.
500 The charter mentions pardon from the death penalty, from mutilation, from confiscation and from infamy (*de cors, de membres, de biens ne de fame*: ibid., 720).
501 Diegerick, 'Les drapiers yprois', 192-194; Espinas and Pirenne, *Recueil*, 3, 722-730.

And tensions did remain, even immediately after order was restored. A new violent outburst occurred in June 1304. It is not clear what exactly happened next. The sources speak of a riot after a riot on 7 June (*debate ende discorden*). But journeymen weavers – about the position of the master weavers, the *conventers*, we know nothing – and fullers had probably left the city in a so-called exit shortly after the judgment of the regent and the four large cities. It is likely that the commission, appointed by the four other large cities (Ghent, Bruges, Lille and Douai) in May, that had tried to identify the damage caused to the property of the elites in the winter months of 1303-1304 was among the main causes of this discontent. The elites claimed to have suffered enormously and wanted to be reimbursed at the expense of the city and the guilds.[502] The antagonists were now, however, different. This time the tensions were not primarily between the clothiers, with the guilds on the one hand and the merchants on the other, as they had been in 1280 and again in 1303; they cut across the old alliance of cloth entrepreneurs and cloth workers, and set the craftsmen against their direct employers, the clothiers. The new fault line lay therefore in the industry itself, between the cloth entrepreneurs on the one hand and their salaried workers and subordinate entrepreneurs on the other. It was a fault line that would appear again and again during the fourteenth century. In a letter of 21 July 1304, the journeymen weavers (*cnapen wevers*) and the fullers (probably in this case the master fullers) accepted the mediation of Philip of Chieti and the aldermen in a conflict that set them against the clothiers and 'the good people of the city'. The guilty people 'on both sides' were to be brought to justice, and in the meantime the weavers and fullers promised to return peacefully to the city and go to work normally without causing riots or discord in the city. Craftsmen who broke their oath and ran riot nonetheless would be considered enemies 'of the count, his knights, of the good cities and the whole county'.[503] Despite the fact that only the journeymen weavers were bound by this letter, it was signed with the seal of the guild itself (and with that of the fullers' guild). The memory of the violent revolt in 1303 must still have been very vivid, and the aldermen, again completely controlled by the mercantile elites and the regent, promised to judge all by the customs of the city, so order was restored.

Social Friction and Political Dissent 1328-1377

It was a fragile peace that had descended on Ypres during the reign of counts Robert de Béthune and Louis de Nevers. In fact, unlike in other cities of the County of Flanders, nothing much had changed in 1303-1304. The mercantile elites still completely controlled the urban government, and although the guilds were now well entrenched in the social organisation of the city, their access to political power remained merely indirect via the broader councils that advised the bench of aldermen.[504] It was inevitable that new frictions would erupt. As in 1303, they took place within the context of

---

[502] Espinas and Pirenne, *Recueil*, 3, 730-739 contains a long list of complaints about illegal taxes and confiscations, running into tens of thousands of pounds.
[503] Espinas and Pirenne, *Recueil*, 3, 740-742.
[504] Trio, 'Bestuursinstellingen', 335-336.

general revolt in Flanders. The so-called Coastal Revolt is often considered to have been primarily a rural phenomenon, but in fact it was also embedded in urban society. The events had severely undermined the position of the count, Louis de Nevers, and the popular party in Ypres, driven unequivocally this time by the textile guilds, tried to take advantage of this.

This time, however, there is little doubt that internal factors also played their part. In the 1320s exports of the successful Ypres *coverture* (striped half stamforts) to the Mediterranean stalled. If the decline in Ypres says and *enforchiés* in Italy and France in the final decades of the thirteenth century had been compensated for by the expansion of the stamforts, this time there was no remedy. The manufacture of worsteds and semi-worsted, responsible for half of the Ypres cloth industry, almost completely disappeared inside a decade, and the Ypres entrepreneurs had to fall back on the production of fine heavy woollens: they had to trade quantity for quality with, probably, devastating effects on levels of employment. It is no coincidence that from this period the actions of the city government against cloth manufacture in the rural surroundings and in the small towns in the vicinity intensified.[505]

After a failed attempt to take over power in 1324 and a revolt in May 1325, the rebels, under the command of Nicolaes Zannekin himself, conquered the city on 15 June 1325. Again, the old regime was ousted from power.[506] So, after the short-lived experiment in the winter months of 1303-1304, a city government defined by the commoners again took control of Ypres. This time it would last more than three years; until the rebellion was defeated by French and comital troops at the battle of Cassel in August 1328 and the old elites recovered their lost position. At the last stage of the revolt the cities had, however, already withdrawn from the insurrection.[507] So, it must have been somewhat surprising for contemporaries that this time repression was harsh and immediate. And the fierce reaction was not because the elites themselves wanted retribution. By chasing away the count and his representatives, who had acted on behalf of the French King, the rebels had committed lèse-majesté against the royal sovereignty, and the king in a charter of 10 September 1328 insisted on severe sanctions against the aldermen of the city, the council and the community of citizens (*advoués, eschevins, conseil et communauté de la dite ville*). Ypres was to be hit in the heart of its economic identity: 500 weavers and 500 fullers had to leave the city and the County of Flanders, and settle for at least three years in the Kingdom of France beyond the River Somme, while the others involved in the rebellion were to be duly punished in Ypres itself. The guilds could also no longer appoint their own leaders (*homanz, ne autre gouverneur ou capithainnes*). Henceforth this right was given exclusively to the aldermen.

---

[505] Louis de Nevers on 16 February 1325 granted a charter forbidding cloth manufacture within a radius of three Flemish miles (Espinas and Pirenne, *Recueil*, 3, 747-748).
[506] Sabbe, *Vlaanderen in Opstand 1323-1328*, 34-45, Verbruggen, *Geweld in Vlaanderen*, 41-42; and TeBrake, *A Plague of Insurrection*.
[507] A recent assessment in van Bavel, 'Rural Revolts', 250-268.

All men without property were also to be disarmed, so they could no longer threaten the peace.[508]

Some sanctions were already revoked in the following months. At the request of the new aldermen, members of the elite and therefore also closely associated with the success of the Ypres cloth industry, a great number of textile workers were in fact allowed to return to Ypres if they had left the city at all. But many more had to go to France or remain there and did not return.[509] As already discussed in Chapter 1, it is not entirely clear what effects the royal decision had on the cloth industry itself. The forced removal of so many textile workers came at a moment when the industry had already met adverse conditions on its export markets. So the decision probably did not deliver a direct blow to the survival of the industry; it can even have slightly alleviated the levels of structural unemployment: a forced correction of the current imbalance between declined output and employment figures. It is also not clear whether many of the banished workers actually returned. It seems that some remained in France, while others moved to England, which received a lot of immigrant Flemish textile workers around this period.[510] But many more of these artisans probably came from other textile cities as well. So emigration to England was certainly caused not just by the political upheaval, it was the result primarily of the crisis in the industry and the loss of the Mediterranean markets for Flemish worsteds and semi-worsteds. In fact the position of greased cloth manufactured in Flemish cities, most of them coming from the towns on the River Leie, even improved in Italy, Southern France and Spain in the second half of the fourteenth century. So the link between these political circumstances and the decline in cloth output in Ypres is at best indirect.

The severe punishment of Ypres clearly shows, however, that, according to the king, textile workers and most of all weavers and fullers had been the driving force of the political and social unrest. By targeting the workers, the king wanted to get rid of what they saw as an imminent threat to the social order and political peace in the County of Flanders. It is unclear, however, who these textile workers really were. The list of weavers explicitly mentions only one clothier, Michiel de Hert, who was allowed to return in October 1329. Given the conflicts that had earlier set clothiers against weavers and the different interests of the various groups within the weavers' guild, it is likely that most banished artisans must in fact have been journeymen weavers or master weavers who did not necessarily operate as clothiers. Among the fullers, too, there is little indication about the numbers of masters and journeymen who were forced to leave.

The conflicts in Ypres during the following decades were entirely different and less bloody. Even when the guilds recovered some of their privileges in the period when the Ghent leader, Jacob van Artevelde, defined politics in the county and access to political

---

508 Espinas and Pirenne, *Recueil*, 3, 750-753; Diegerick, 'Les drapiers yprois', 285-310. In the end only 422 weavers, 224 fullers and 154 other guildsmen were banished (Verbruggen, *Geweld in Vlaanderen*, 41 citing Vandermaesen, 'Brugse en Ieperse gijzelaars', 124-127).
509 Espinas and Pirenne, *Recueil*, 3, 756-758.
510 For the conditions of Flemish workers in England see Lambert and Pajic 'Immigration and the Common Profit', 633-657.

power was made easier, the conflicts themselves were much less eventful.[511] Still, major conflicts between the city and the count of Flanders, Louis de Male, erupted in 1348, and again there were textile workers among some of the punished ringleaders. The position of the old elites in the urban government, now confirmed by both royal and comital power, was no longer successfully challenged, however. Instead unrest moved from the urban political arena to economic friction between the various stakeholders in the industry itself. In 1339, in the midst of the Artevelde period, the Members of Flanders, the aldermen of Ghent, Bruges and Ypres, intervened in a conflict between the guilds of weavers and fullers. At stake were the contributions to the weavers' guild of fullers who were also active as clothiers. In Ypres most clothiers were, of course, master weavers, and therefore members of the weavers' guild. In fact, older statutes even explicitly forbade fullers from becoming clothiers. Yet apparently this formal incompatibility was not always respected. Some fullers were clearly also active as clothiers, and as such they had to contribute to the costs of the weavers' guild. The Members of Flanders decided that fullers could henceforth no longer be obliged to contribute to the costs of the weavers. Instead, weavers' children could learn the fullers' trade at the same cost as fullers' children and vice versa, by this rule granting much more entrepreneurial flexibility to those with sufficient financial means to be active in the trade which offered the best possible conditions.[512]

From the 1350s, however, the intensity of internal strife increased. In 1353 there was trouble again: a fuller was convicted of conspiracy against the count of Flanders, banished from the county and apprehended in Lille.[513] Whether this warrant outside the borders of the county (at the time governed directly by the French king) was an individual transgression or symptomatic of collective unrest is not known. Real trouble started only in July 1359, when a meeting of textile craftsmen demanded the restoration of the guilds' privileges and the right to nominate their officials themselves – something they had not been allowed to do since the royal decree of 1328. But then the logic of revolt took over. When Count Louis de Male was forced to agree to most of these demands, the rebellion only really took off. The count, at the time present in Ypres, even had to flee the city and, in an orgy of violence, the rebels, identified by contemporary observers as weavers and fullers, took control of the city, imprisoned the aldermen and killed a number of them, all members of the old families. In the absence of the powerless count and with many elite families that had fled the city, they held on to power for two years. Violence in this period continued and the urban space was occupied by the guilds, which claimed authority symbolically with the sound of the belfry bells and the colours of their banners. In the end, even the count's bailiff and members of his retinue were killed by the guildsmen.

As in most revolts of fourteenth-century Ypres, the position of the clothiers is not entirely clear. It is striking, nonetheless, that they do not figure prominently among the

---

511 In this period the guilds coopted some of the aldermen with the exiting aldermen (Trio, 'Bestuursinstellingen', 337-338).
512 Espinas and Pirenne, *Recueil*, 3, 773-774.
513 Espinas and Pirenne, *Recueil*, 3, 776-777.

craftsmen who were punished and that in both the narrative sources and the surviving administrative or juridical documents the insurgents are usually described only as craftsmen, weavers and fullers. There is little mention of clothiers in the events. It is likely, therefore, that the clothiers had only lukewarm sympathies for the ambitions of the revolt and that they probably did not like its violent excesses that mucfh. At moments of extreme tension it was the journeymen and the *conventers* who took the lead in the weavers' guild. In the fullers' guild no systematic distinction was made between masters and journeymen, so probably here masters, many of them men of considerable means, joined the rebellion.

In an indictment against four Ypres rebels in the city of Tournai two years later, in August 1361, we can clearly see how the rebels had used a mix of real violence and ritualised actions to state their claims. The actions had been aimed both at the count himself and at the ruling elites. The indictment claimed that the revolt had been a rebellion against the authority of count Louis de Male, and that the rebels, again identified as craftsmen weavers and fullers, had organised an assembly (*assamblee*) that made extraordinary demands (*requestes miervilleuses*) and that they had therefore belonged to an illegal conspiracy (*conspiration et sans licence*) and that they had wanted to make laws against the count and his cities (*faire constitutions contre lui et ses boines villes*).[514] Very much like in the 1320s, initially the count was forced to agree to some of the demands and the guildsmen were allowed, like their colleagues in Ghent, to appoint their own officials (*que ils feissent vingres, decres et capitaines*), but they persevered in their 'bad opinion and error' and 'cried out' for more and a return to their rights during the revolutionary era of Jacob van Artevelde. After these events they took control of the city, going around the parishes to appoint their officials and leaders *a leurz plaisirs*. In August 1359 things spun out of control as the demands became more political. The weavers and fullers took up arms, they attacked the building used by the official governing bodies, and installed their own leaders there. The count himself was forced to flee the city, whither he had come to appease the insurrection.

The rebels imprisoned 16 aldermen and councillors in the cloth hall and demanded the keys to the belfry (where all the charters of the city were kept) so that they could sound the bells whenever they wanted to (*pour faire sonner quand il volroient les clokes dicelli bieffroit*). They also had new city banners made and confiscated a horn (*cor*) to rally the inhabitants when necessary. Moreover they also wanted to control the city's finances, probably because they suspected wrongdoing by the ruling elite, and to confiscate some of the public moneys. The demands of insurgents in the late medieval Flemish cities often included control of the public finances. In the ensuing chaos again the city's mayor and three aldermen (members of the elite families of Belle, Piet de Soile, van Dixmude and Stassin) lost their lives, a repetition of the events in 1303. When the count sent in a new bailiff, Jehan le Prisenaere, in November, the armed rebels liberated some of his prisoners with sounding bells and flying banners (*a banieres desployés et a clokes sonnans*). They were accused of committing illegal acts during the revolt. The revolutionary atmosphere continued. Even as late as May 1361, after

---

[514] Espinas and Pirenne, *Recueil*, 3, 781-784.

having been in function already for almost two years, the bailiff himself was arrested and thrown off a tower so that he died from his injuries, and again the violence was accompanied by the symbolism of banners and bells.[515] When the count finally sent in an army in August 1361, the craftsmen resisted with force and again killed a number of other members of the elite families and comital representatives.

After all this violence, reaction was, of course, immediate. But given the overall difficulties in the county under count Louis de Male and the fact that in many cities the guilds now fully participated in the urban administrative institutions and in the textile guilds in particular, reaction was also less swift and decisive than in 1303. Ypres had become an outlier in the urban power structures in Flanders with the traditional mercantile elites' exclusive hold on urban institutions, so perhaps Bruges and Ghent, the two other Members of Flanders, were also somewhat hesitant to allow the count to react harshly. When comital forces ended the textile revolt in August 1361, all the old customs were reinstated, and the guilds were again removed from direct access to power. Members of the guild leadership were executed, but as a whole repression was half-hearted and did not reach the levels of 1304 and 1329. In similar circumstances in Bruges and Mechelen repression typically targeted journeymen. It is likely that this also happened in Ypres. They, together probably with the master fullers and *conventers*, had after all been the ringleaders of the revolt in 1359-1361.

But discontent rumbled on nonetheless, and new incidents occurred in 1367, 1370, 1371 and 1377, each time focused on the control of internal guild administration or on working conditions. In September 1377, according to the chronicler Olivier van Dixmude, a prominent member of the city elites, the common people started to cause unrest. The people thought they were being cheated (*begonste tcommun roeren ende dochten dat zy verdult waren*). There were calls to start a strike. But the aldermen reacted promptly. They arrested and executed one of the inciters, a broker called Hannin de Werd, and the craftsmen feared that they would share his fate and returned to work. They did this grudgingly (*bleef altoos in quaeder meeninghe*), so a lot of friction remained.[516]

Generalised and extreme violence as in 1303 and 1359 did not occur on these occasions and swift repression (Olivier van Dixmude calls it *scaerpe wet and groote justicie*) usually prevented full rebellion, although in 1370 a plot existed to attack one of the supervisors of the weavers' guild, Pauwel van Passchendaele, and in 1371 the city's policemen (*scerrewetters*) were ambushed from a shearer's house.[517] Ypres citizens, some identified as fullers, shearers or weavers, were banished from the city nonetheless for inciting rebellion (*faire meute et conspiration*), for sounding church bells to incite rebellion (apparently they could not reach the bells in the city's belfry any more), for threatening civic officers or for speaking insulting words in guild assemblies (*horriblez paroles ... a le place dez tisserans en le presence dez gouverneurs*).[518] But it was

---

515 Nowé, *Les baillis comtaux*, 384.
516 Van Dixmude, *Merkwaerdige gebeurtenissen*, 1.
517 De Sagher, 'Notice sur les archives communales', 43-44 cited in Verbruggen, *Geweld in Vlaanderen*, 178.
518 On each occasion a number of rebels were banished from the city, a number of them weavers or fullers (Espinas and Pirenne, *Recueil*, 3, 788-790).

not only threats to the public order that were punished. In 1377, before the beginning of the Western Schism when the county of Flanders sided with England and chose the pope in Rome against the wishes of the King of France, fuller Paul de Haestigghe was condemned for heresy and referred to the aldermen as the secular court. He was burned in the marketplace.[519] The 1360s and 1370s remained a tense period throughout and, as often happened, the frictions surfaced also in conflicts which had little to do with local power relations. The clear antagonism between the political elites and the guilds' aspiring autonomy and participation was exacerbated every decade by violence and repression. But in no case were the guildsmen able to turn the tide. Industrial Ypres was not only a city of social polarisation between the wealthy and the poor; it was also a politically city polarised between the elites and the craftsmen.

The Last Revolts (Late Fourteenth-Fifteenth Centuries)

The situation changed almost overnight with the great revolt of Ghent in 1379, and this time discontent in Ypres was not apparent only among the usual suspects: the semi-proletarianised weavers and the fullers (with the occasional shearer); it was shared by broader segments of the population, although the ringleaders of revolt were still recruited from among the craftsmen. Strikingly the clothiers seem to have taken on a much more active role this time, reminiscent of the *cokerulle* of 1280, a century earlier. When troops from Ghent approached Ypres in September 1379, the count's garrison and many wealthier citizens realised what was going on and fled the city. The people, according to Olivier van Dixmude, were hungry because of the general dearth of food in the county and angry (*verstorbeirt ende gram*). The craftsmen from the suburbs, again primarily weavers and fullers but among them now also some clothiers, flooded with the Ghent troops through the southerly Comines Gate, linking the industrial suburb of St Michiel to the inner city, into the central market square and seized power, under the command of Jacob van der Berst.[520] But success was only short-lived. Already in August 1380 the combined forces of Ghent and Ypres were defeated by a comital army, and the count retook the city, punishing the rebels who had stayed behind. In May 1382, when the Ghent militia defeated the comital faction in Bruges, the craftsmen regained the initiative, but only for a short period. Already in November 1382 the old elites returned to power, and the city would thereafter remain on the side of Count Louis de Male (and later of his son-in-law Philip the Bold, the duke of Burgundy). This did not mean the end of the troubles, however. When the Ghent forces received reinforcements of English troops, they laid siege to Ypres.[521] The suburbs were abandoned, and when the English left without having conquered Ypres, the industrial suburbs were abandoned for good. The official explanation was that this measure was intended to fight the imminent danger of the concentration of so many textile workers. They were to be relocated to

---

519 Espinas and Pirenne, *Recueil*, 3, 790.
520 For more details about these events see Van Dixmude, *Merkwaerdige gebeurtenissen*, 1-5; Verbruggen, *Geweld in Vlaanderen*, 43-44.
521 Mus, 'Het beleg van Ieper', 20-30.

other towns or they had to move to the inner city. In chapter 3 already we saw that probably other motives also came into play.[522]

The struggles of 1379-1382 proved decisive. The spine of the revolutionary textile workers was broken and their claims to guild autonomy and political participation were abandoned for a long period to come. Fewer craftsmen were now making fewer woollens. If anything, the tendency towards producing ever more luxury woollens continued, so the craftsmen became more specialised, worked with ever more expensive raw materials, and targeted ever more exclusive markets. As a result, massive unemployment of the craftsmen must have become a structural phenomenon, but at the same time the demand for highly skilled labour must have increased, so some successful textile workers probably fared much better. A charter of Philip the Good laments the pitiful condition of the city's textile workers who, because of their unemployment, had become so poor that they could not sustain themselves or their families.[523] Around the same time, probably to appease the restless masses of textile workers, the attempts to limit cloth manufacture in the city's surroundings increased. All textile manufacture was forbidden within a radius of three Flemish miles (about 16km) around the city, of course with the usual caveats that privileged cloth industries could maintain their activity.

The clothiers' position became even more crucial. In 1379-1382, the clothiers had already been more involved in the political unrest than in the other fourteenth-century revolts and troubles. Still, their role in an industry that saw no other way forward than to manufacture ever more expensive woollens had become more crucial. The clothiers were, after all, the guarantors that quality requirements could be implemented across the production chain. So, the clothiers' position, apparently weakened politically after the repression following the revolt of 1379-1382, must have strengthened economically. In the by now rapidly de-industrialising city, their impact had therefore become more important. And perhaps more than the merchants, with their free roaming capital moving their investments from city to countryside and back again, they were dependent on the success of the urban industry itself. They demanded from the city government the execution to the letter of the comital ban on rural textiles. This had become a pressing issue, because gradually some rural centres turned, as Poperinge had done earlier, to the production of greased woollens and not only to the worsteds and semi-worsteds that were no longer produced in great numbers in Ypres. The period witnessed the start of the growth of new semi-rural industrial centres such as Nieuwkerke for fine woollens and Hondschoote for says, a growth that would continue until the late sixteenth century. This time, discontent with the political elites had less to do with participation in urban government structures, therefore; it was directly linked to the lamentable fate of the cloth industry, by now in full decay.

In 1428, the clothiers questioned the actions of the Ypres aldermen as regards the rural industries. They incited the textile workers to strike and not to return to work until the looms and fullers' workshops in the countryside had been destroyed and

---

522 See also Chapter 3.
523 Diegerick, 'Les drapiers', 7-8.

cloth manufacture stopped (*voor de ghewanden ende de commen in de doorpen te nieuten ghedaen waren*). The events were witnessed by the chronicler Olivier van Dixmude – as his name already indicates, a member of the Ypres elites, not a particularly neutral observer – so we know quite well what happened during the unrest.[524] He describes these words as *spitelike*, meaning both pitiful and spiteful. It is clear in this episode that the elites hesitated between two very different goals: on the one hand protecting the industry by imposing protectionist measures, but on the other hand protecting their own interests, which were also located in the countryside. In the course of the unrest they were regularly called traitors by the craftsmen. Unrest had been brewing for a long time. One year earlier, in 1427, there had already been talks between the fullers in Ghent and their Ypres colleagues about mutual support in supporting their demands about wages and working conditions.[525] From that moment the troubles ran their usual course: there was uproar (*rumoer*) and there were strikes. The textile workers were expected to gather in the three central parishes of the city, St Peter, St Nicolas and St James (at that time the industrial suburbs and their parochial organisation no longer existed) and to march to the central market square with their banners flying and shouting their rallying call.[526] The authority of the aldermen was further undermined by the public performance of satirical poems.[527] The plan failed, but before the discovery of the plot, there had been nightly assemblies of the textile workers (*assemble de nuict*).

This does not mean that the authorities did not use similar concepts and terminology in the language of repression. In fact it is often underestimated that the same vocabulary was used by the various social layers and stakeholders in urban society. Hence in the indictment of one of the rebel leaders of 1428, the bailiff of Ypres accuses Olivier van Koyeghem of crimes 'by the common voice of the city' (*par la voix commune dicelle ville*). The authorities also acted on behalf of the 'common good', the idea of a commonwealth stemming already from the communal ideas of the twelfth century.[528] Yet there was a difference between that communality defined by the whole city and the illegal acts of assembling at night done by the 'commoners' (*du commun*). The first is associated with the rule of law as a guarantor of the peace and welfare of the city, the latter by the particular interest of a part of the city that was harmful to those ideas of peace and welfare. The commoners were therefore rhetorically juxtaposed to commonality, by associating them with unrest and commotion, with the murder of 'notable' members, with taking up arms against the commonality and with nightly gatherings and therefore secret acts. The public nature of government, with public decrees, bells and banners, is rhetorically juxtaposed with secrecy and plotting. Rebels may want to appropriate the public acts of government by making use of the bells in the belfry or in church towers or by deploying their banners or the city colours; in the eyes

---

524 Van Dixmude, *Merkwaerdige gebeurtenissen*, 119-122.
525 Boone and Brand, 'Vollersoproeren', 179.
526 Diegerick, *Les drapiers yprois*, 10.
527 Lamin Fabriel was banished from the city. He was accused of composing and spreading a song entitled 'Ypres, you were a sweet garden of delight' (*Ypre, ghi waert een zoet prayel*), about how the city government had failed to preserve the wealth in the city (Haemers and Vrancken, 'Libels in the City', 165-187).
528 Boone and Haemers, 'The Common Good', 93-127.

of the authorities, these are mere outward expressions of what is in essence opposed to the public cause of government.

Among the ringleaders were, as usual, a number of textile workers (weavers), but clothiers are also mentioned this time. It is striking that the convictions were primarily aimed at the craftsmen (*tisserands de laine*) and that among the list of people executed in Ypres itself there were mainly journeymen weavers (*cnaepwevers*).[529] The clothiers, who began the protest, disappeared almost completely from view once the troubles started. It was as if they had not joined the movement, once it took on the form of a real rebellion. While the leaders of the revolt were executed at once, banished or brought to justice even outside the borders of the county, only some clothiers were banished for shorter periods.

Labour Conflict, Political Conflict

The fact that the demands of the rebels in 1428 did not focus primarily on political representation, but on the economic policy of the city government, is telling. In the course of a century and a half of sometimes very bloody revolts, the elites, in collaboration with the prince, had successfully defended their political hold on the city and on the economic levers of power in the city and its surroundings. Ypres would in the course of the fifteenth century often join the efforts of the other Members of Flanders in opposing some of the centralising initiatives of the Burgundian dukes. They would do so, however, in much less radical ways than Bruges or Ghent. Without a real internal guild-led opposition, the elites usually sided with the dukes, and they were inclined to mitigate and appease tensions in the county, rather than sounding the drums of resistance. After a dramatic fourteenth century, Ypres indeed had become a sea of tranquillity. Economic decline had broken the power of the textile guilds, and all energy that remained went into a desperate and doomed strategy of fighting rural competition, implemented only hesitantly by the mercantile elites who also had a vested interest in the countryside.

In the end, the craftsmen organised into guilds had not been able, except for some short interludes which were thereafter succeeded by harsh repression, to break that stalemate. In the process, the new urban middle classes of retailing guilds and industrial entrepreneurs, the clothiers, joined these revolts only very half-heartedly. Instead of leading, the clothiers kept a low profile, in the process weakening the striking force of the guilds because in the end they provided the leading groups in one of the most important guilds (and in many other cities one of the driving forces of dissent), the weavers. In Ypres the elites and the count mostly faced a divided and hesitant opponent. With the levels of social inequality and polarisation in this most industrial of all Flemish cities, the relative underdevelopment of true urban middle classes and the clothiers held an ambiguous position in the urban social fabric. As their role in the industry increased during the fourteenth century, and their relative wealth probably increased as well, their

---

529 Documents published in Diegerick, *Les drapiers yprois*, 19-26.

political demands seem to have been superseded by their anxieties about the industry itself. It was the ambition to influence economic policy that defined their political involvement, rather than a more general ambition to participate in urban government and governance. Hence their active involvement in 1280, when they acquired a new level of independence from mercantile capital, or in 1380 or 1428, when competition from rural cloth producers came high on the political agenda. Moreover their equally ambiguous, even schizophrenic, position in the weavers' guild seems to have undermined the guilds' potential for resistance against the power of the mercantile elite, which could always count on the support of the count and his officers.

This does not mean that all other revolts failed completely. The crucial role of the two main textile guilds of weavers and fullers and of other textile guilds which were organised within a more collective framework of common or bourgeois guilds was never questioned, even in periods of severe repression by the traditional elites and the count/king. Issues of guild leadership were more sensitive, but in the end the guilds clearly profited from relatively high levels of autonomy and they broadened the impact of their political influence in the subaltern urban institutions. The guilds, and of course primarily the guild masters, were and remained important stakeholders in the organisation of the cloth industry. The rank and file in the revolts were often guildsmen, drawn mostly from the poorer strata of the guild (journeymen and master weavers, the so-called *conventers*; the only exception being some master fullers). In this sense the social profile of the rebels mirrored the poorer social background of textile insurgents in fourteenth-century Bruges.[530] But the differences between industrial Ypres and middle-class Bruges were also very important. Indications that the textile workers found many allies among other occupational groups in Ypres are scarce. Textiles and class identity seem to have constituted separate networks of dissent in the city.

After the failed incident in 1428, revolt brewed once again in 1477. As in many other cities in Flanders and Brabant, the death of Duke Charles the Bold fanned chronic discontent with the centralising policies of the Burgundian dukes into open revolt. In Ypres as well, although slower and less forcefully than in Ghent or Bruges, the craft guilds tried to change the political constellation, and for a short while with some success. Yet by 1478 everything was back to normal, and the Ypres political elites would continue their loyalist tradition. A chronicle written by a sympathiser with the traditional elites, Peter de Letuwe, could not hide his disdain for the insurgents. But behind broad categories such as 'the guilds', it is extremely difficult to pinpoint their social identity. Some of the punished craftsmen were, of course – how could it be otherwise in Ypres – linked to cloth manufacture (weavers and fullers), yet beyond the very temporary inclusion of guildsmen in the city's political institutions, no systematic political programme was formulated, other than to put an end to fiscal abuse.[531] The social and economic composition of the population in Ypres had changed dramatically by now, and the textile workers could no longer muster enough levels of coercion to challenge the elites with some chance of success. The candle of revolt died by itself.

---

530 Dumolyn, Ryckbosch and Speecke, 'Did Inequality Produce Medieval Revolt?', 372-405.
531 Haemers, *For the Common Good*, 248-262.

CHAPTER 10

Roads of Capitalism

In his brilliant synthesis of 1997, *Transitions to Capitalism*, Bob DuPlessis, pointed to some of the structural changes in late medieval and early modern society which defined the course of capitalism. Two broad developments were symptomatic of the changing nature of capitalism in the premodern period. On the one hand mercantile capitalism became more dominant, altering the balance with feudalism as a defining criterion in moulding society and social relations between groups. The entanglement of feudalism and capitalism therefore changed in favour of a greater role for mercantile initiative, financial technology, trade flows and less control of military elites using extra-economic power to coerce other economic actors into particular economic relations of dependence. Instead, the increasing role of the state (and in some regions also of large urban centres) compensated for the decline of feudal power. On the other hand, the rise of proto-industrial organisation in the rural economy also became a constitutive element in new types of agrarian capitalism, whereby either landholding or labour markets came under the influence of capitalistic tendencies, in some regions leading to larger estates depending on waged labour, while in others smallholdings dominated, but also requiring the input of industrial labour, very often (but as we have seen for the English cloth industry not always) in the service of urban merchants and entrepreneurs.[532] In these places, the development of capitalism was therefore linked directly to the strong hold of urban merchants and entrepreneurs on a burgeoning rural economy and on the spread of cottage industries.

Rural historians working in a Brennerian paradigm used this framework to distinguish between various regions and to look at regional divergence to trace the differing capitalistic nature of society.[533] In some regions an economy built upon secure property relations and with equitable inheritance customs developed into smallholdings, which gradually, despite (or rather because of) enormously high land productivity, became too small to survive without an external input of income through industrial labour. More fluent property relations and a tendency towards concentration stimulated leaseholding, investment of urban landowners and higher labour productivity. This model has recently been linked to the neo-institutional approach of markets.[534] In late medieval Flanders the former system, consisting of small peasant-owned holdings with industrial labour input, can be found in Interior Flanders, the latter consisting of larger leaseholdings with wage-earning labourers in Coastal Flanders. A recent survey of

---

[532] DuPlessis, *Transitions to Capitalism*.
[533] Brenner, 'The Low Countries', 169-241. For Flanders see Thoen, *Landbouwekonomie* and Soens, *De spade in de dijk*, and the synthesis of their work in Thoen and Soens, 'The Family or the Farm', 195-224.
[534] Van Bavel, *The Invisible Hand*, and for the Low Countries id., *Manors and Markets*.

property relations in the region of Ypres suggests that the countryside in the hinterland of the city was somewhere between these two systems.[535]

In an effort to recalibrate the urbanised medieval Low Countries in this transition – the urban factor is missing from most Brennerian research, urbanisation being considered a dependent variable – Martha Howell more recently reframed the discussion by integrating commercialisation as a primary factor of capitalistic organisation, while looking at the increasing monetisation in society and its social and cultural consequences. She stressed that in an urbanised society like the Low Countries, where commerce took hold precociously, commerce affected all levels of society and changed ideas about 'property, marriage, and exchange', and therefore 'forced alterations in associated social practices'. Although, unlike most Marxist historiography, she is careful to not explicitly address issues about the nature of mercantile capitalism and about inevitable transitions towards true capitalism in the late eighteenth century, in her eyes processes of commercialisation (and therefore of urbanisation) had caused dramatic societal change, nonetheless. In a true Braudelian fashion a world between was cretad, in between a capitalistic market economy, based on neoclassical assumptions of self-correcting and self-regulating market mechanisms, and a more traditional system of exchange. The late Middle Ages and the start of the early modern period are, therefore, for Howell a period of a shift towards loosening traditional social boundaries and social customs about property, exchange and social organisation.[536]

In these changing social landscapes, the Ypres cloth producers had to negotiate their course of action. And, indeed, the cloth industry in Ypres (or in all other large Flemish cities for that matter) does not fit very comfortably into the teleological models of mercantile capitalism, proto-industries and the transition towards the industrial capitalism of the eighteenth and nineteenth centuries. The massive industrial organisation of cloth manufacture, starting probably already in the late eleventh century and increasing its hold on society in the late twelfth and thirteenth centuries, initially created almost a merchant capitalist paradise. The concentration of thousands of semi-proletarianised textile workers, men and women, all of them depending upon wage income and the strong and undisputed hold of the mercantile elites on markets for raw materials and finished commodities, even on society itself through elaborate credit networks and property structures, the social separation between the mercantile elites and the rest of urban society, with only limited chances for social mobility within the industrial system, were all very precocious and unbalanced. In all aspects, industrial Ypres was a very unequal city and the accumulation of wealth and economic initiative, of social prestige and power was extremely unbalanced.

But gradually during the thirteenth century, other forces also came into play, and they were helped by changing political and economic contexts. This was not a straightforward route to an ever more powerful position in society of mercantile capital. The latter part of the thirteenth and the fourteenth centuries witnessed the rise of other

---

535 Soens, Stabel and Vandewalle, 'An Urbanised Countryside?', 35-60.
536 Howell, *Commerce before Capitalism*, 5-13, 32-33 and 299-302, citing amongst others Braudel, *Wheels of Commerce*, 456.

stakeholders, who had remained hidden in the previous period. In this sense, Ypres started to conform more to the pattern of rising middle groups in all other Flemish cities. When Flemish active trade was curtailed during the late thirteenth century and the Mediterranean markets for cheaper fabrics were lost – both developments are usually linked to sudden changes, but both were, as we have seen, also very gradual developments – other stakeholders saw their chance to acquire a new role in society. The guilds that had come of age in Ypres in the middle of the thirteenth century were keen to organise labour relations in occupations defined by access to skill, but most of all the cloth entrepreneurs themselves – in Ypres taking on the very hybrid identity of free-standing entrepreneurs and of guildsmen – who had organised cloth manufacture for the mercantile elites, gained more independence from the merchants. Again, this was a very gradual process, with ups and downs, and never completed to a full disentanglement of industrial entrepreneurs and mercantile capital, but in Ypres society the changes must have been felt and caused a lot of anxiety among the traditional elites.

Instead of dominating mercantile capital, the Ypres industry became a battlefield of social and economic negotiation between different stakeholders, in which some (women, unskilled workers and even the guild journeymen) clearly lost, while others could profit and carve out a new position in urban society. These included the clothiers, a very hybrid group of entrepreneurs, and, through the control of the labour markets, also the guild masters (or at least those in the weavers' guild when masters could also become clothiers, and in the fullers' and dyers' guilds). These struggles within the industry prefigure to a certain extent the direction all cities in late medieval and early modern Flanders would take, with strong middle groups in urban society and very fragmented wealth. In this sense the Ypres pattern fits almost seamlessly into the model proposed by Hugo Soly: guilds or 'guildlike' groups with their own sense of social identity like the Ypres clothiers succeeded in gaining more independence from the overarching influence of mercantile capital when they operated in a field where 'different power groups with divergent or even opposing interest existed'.[537] In Ypres the conditions for such development occurred when mercantile capital changed course in the late thirteenth century (or rather when local mercantile elites were forced to abandon their position of strength in trade and industry). This does not mean, of course, that mercantile capital became completely dissociated from the industry. Ypres cloth manufacturers were, as they had always been, dependent on international outlets and on imports of raw materials, and both were, of course, dominated by (now mostly foreign) merchants. It was the changing economic position of the local elites, taking on the role of credit suppliers and of brokers with international trade, that defined the new position of local stakeholders, and of course these local mercantile elites also succeeded, unlike in the other cities of Flanders, to hang on to a quasi-monopoly of political power. Moreover, the changed bargaining power of the different stakeholders in the industry suited their purposes: it allowed them to spread risk more easily, to avoid the trappings

---

37 Soly, 'Political Economy', 70-71.

of dramatic commercial change that characterised late-medieval Europe and to engage more intensively in other more secure investments.

But even in this new equilibrium the industry did not last. After more than three centuries of skilful adaptation, creative innovation, changing commercial outlets and changing social positions, Ypres merchants, entrepreneurs and textile workers were forced to abandon the industry, some of them fleeing into safer and probably also more profitable investments in regional trade and rural property, while others moved into servicing trades or left the city to work in other textile settlements. The Ypres cloth manufacture had been to a large extent a closed circuit, pooling credit and cheap or skilled labour from inside the city. Even spinsters were recruited in the city itself. This clear separation between the urban and the rural labour markets can be compared to the manufacture of woollen cloth in Florence. In Tuscany, rural proto-industrialisation was no alternative for cloth entrepreneurs in a system of sharecropping that offered little basis for a labour reservoir in the countryside.[538] But in Ypres, the rural hinterland, with its smallholdings producing a lot of surplus labour, was always in the background to the urban cloth industry's developments. It provided a permanent migration reservoir for the city, allowing entrepreneurs to profit from the downward pressure of wage levels. It also provided, however, a permanent alternative for the industrial organisation in the city. In the end, regional rural and small-town competition drained away a lot of the potential for innovation or adaptation to international demand for different types of woollens.

A Rural Epilogue to an Urban Industry?

In the late fifteenth century little remained of what had once probably been the highest concentration of textile labour in medieval Europe. Not much more than a dozen looms were still in operation for supplying export markets with luxury fabrics. Textile workers were still obvious in the streets of Ypres around 1500, but their impact could no longer be compared with that of the hundreds of looms and the dozens of fulleries that were dispersed during the fourteenth century in the four industrial suburbs of the city, and of the thousands of women, most of them living in the inner city, who were involved in the industry as badly paid spinners, carders and combers. Around 1500, the immense cloth hall, built in the thirteenth century at the height of Ypres' success, must have been a pathetic sight, occupied as it was only by a couple of clothiers, lacking the presence of foreign merchants and the hustle and bustle of complex financial deals. The remaining cloth entrepreneurs probably went to the Bruges or Antwerp markets to sell their cloth, like so many other clothiers from Flanders. This direct dependence upon a distant gateway market also created new social thresholds, and stimulated hierarchical networks of clothiers, only some of them having access to enough capital to cater for these external trade links. Like in Menen or Kortrijk, it is these clothiers who brought wool to the city and took out the woollens, monitored often by other clothiers, to their

---

538 Goldthwaite, *The Economy of Renaissance Florence*, 282 citing Brown, 'The economic decline', 101-115.

domestic or international consumers, controlling in this way a wider range of craftsmen dependent upon their commercial role.

Still, textiles remained the bread and butter of the city, its main livelihood in the hearts and minds of the Ypres guildsmen. Plans to resuscitate the industry were made almost continually. The memory of past successes did not fade immediately and, as in Bruges, attempts to attract craftsmen from elsewhere for their skills and expertise and to set up new lines of production abounded. The continuing success of cloth manufacture in some of the neighbouring towns and villages, places like Hondschoote, Armentières and Nieuwkerke, or of the finishing industries in Lille, in Bruges in the fifteenth, or in Antwerp in the sixteenth century, must have reminded the Ypres entrepreneurs and textile workers nonetheless of the almost unstoppable decay of their own old industry, the pride and glory of the city with its huge visual *lieu de mémoire* in the central market square. In such circumstances it is not surprising that people looked to the outside for culprits, and these were almost too easy to identify: the still successful cloth manufacturers in neighbouring villages and towns. In the eyes of the Ypres entrepreneurs, they had undercut the Ypres quality standards for cloth, they had copied Ypres products and had sold inferior qualities on foreign markets using the reputation of the Ypres cloth producers, they were profiting from unfair and dishonest competition and were prepared to sacrifice quality for a reduction in the overall cost of manufacture.

In fact, relations with neighbouring cloth industries had always been a delicate issue in Ypres, even at the height of its industrial expansion in the thirteenth and early fourteenth centuries. And friction with producers elsewhere was always felt, particularly at moments of crisis, when in the final decades of the thirteenth century worsteds could no longer be exported, when in the 1320s Ypres lost its Mediterranean markets for striped halfcloth, or when in the late fourteenth century the output of even luxury woollens started to decline. In the historiography of the medieval cloth industries, relations with the rural surroundings, which may (for example in Flanders, Normandy and England) or may not (in the case of Tuscany) have been involved in cloth manufacture themselves, has always been given a primary role in the development of the urban textile industries. The essence is, of course, that in rural surroundings and in so-called proto-industrial environments, wages did not have to be the sole source of income for households; they were only a supplement for income generated otherwise by agricultural activities. In general, therefore, rural wages tended to be substantially lower, and rural craftsmen were prepared to work for lower pay for their industrial output than their urban counterparts. If the levels of productivity yielded by urban economies of agglomeration did not compensate for these lower wages, production inevitably moved to those places where the highest profits could be made, in this case the countryside.

As a result – and this is particularly true for late medieval Flanders – a kind of organic distribution of industrial manufacture came into being, a process that has recently been described as 'medieval offshoring'.[539] Fabrics using cheaper materials and requiring less sophistication (cheap linens and woollens, so-called *doucken*) were

---

39 Van der Meulen, *Woven into the Urban Fabric*, 209-215.

produced primarily in the countryside. In the smaller towns, middle-tier woollens and cheaper copies of high-quality woollens were produced. On average, wages were lower in smaller towns than in the large cities and the less well-developed regulation and guild organisation allowed for more flexible manufacturing circumstances.[540] Finally the large cities and some of the smaller production centres as well specialised in expensive fabrics, made from the most exclusive (English) wool and using prime quality dyes and finishing processes. These woollens targeted elite clienteles. The market for luxury fabrics was less elastic because elite demand did not change suddenly with changing relative prices. Indeed, elite demand was less influenced by sudden shocks in standards of living, and the potentially higher price of labour in large cities was dwarfed by the cost of the raw materials required for making luxury cloth anyway. As a result, these woollens suffered less from the rising transaction costs in trans-European trade shortly before and after 1300 that had undermined demand for low quality woollens across Europe, explaining the ever-increasing focus on luxury fabrics in the larger cities.

But, of course, even this seemingly logical distribution according to manufacturing costs and productivity does not always sit easily with stubborn historical processes. For the liberal historian Henri Pirenne, the decline of the Flemish urban textiles was caused by nothing else than the self-inflicted policies of the larger production centres themselves.[541] Guilds tightened regulation and secured relatively high wages, undermining the competitiveness of Flemish woollens on foreign markets. To make matters worse, the subsequent rise of cloth industries in the countryside (and in the smaller towns) was held back by aggressive military interventions in the rural production centres. The militias of Ghent and Ypres (and, although less enthusiastically, also of Bruges) started smashing the industrial infrastructure in villages and small towns and from the 1320s they secured from the successive (weaker) counts of Flanders charters limiting cloth manufacture within a three-mile zone (about 18km) to a small number of chartered towns. This explanation has since been nuanced and corrected by North-American scholars such as David Nicholas and John Munro, but is surprisingly tenacious among economic historians.[542] Although in particular in the political turmoil of the late 1330s and 1340s, when urban revolts successfully challenged comital power, the policies of the large cities can indeed be described as aggressive, and Ypres in particular continued to challenge, sometimes with armed expeditions, cloth manufacture in its hinterland, in the end results were relatively limited. Ghent could control rural manufacture in its immediate hinterland, yet failed to curb the expansion of the so-called 'new draperies' in the small towns in its region.[543] Bruges never tried to limit cloth manufacture with any great conviction and started from the second half of the fourteenth century to specialise in finishing raw woollens produced elsewhere, just like Lille and Saint-Omer.[544]

---

540 Stabel, *De kleine stad*. See also Chapter 7.
541 Pirenne, 'Une crise industrielle', 489-521.
542 Nicholas, *Town and Countryside*, passim, Munro, 'Medieval Woollens', 255-259. For a recent Pirennian approach: van Bavel and van Zanden, 'Economy', 385-402.
543 Stabel, *De kleine stad*, 138-141.
544 Sortor, 'Saint-Omer and its Textile Trades', 1475-1499, Clauzel and Calonne, 'Artisanat rural', 531-573, Munro, 'Medieval Woollens', 255-259 and Stabel, *A Capital of Fashion*, forthcoming.

The fourteenth-century expansion of Flemish cloth manufacture took place primarily in smaller chartered towns anyway, and not in the countryside. In that sense, the traditional framing of increasing internal competition for textile markets as a clash between industrial towns and the proto-industrial countryside is not quite accurate. It is much more correct to describe the process of continuous industrial dislocation within fourteenth- and early fifteenth-century Flanders as competition among cities and towns, large and small. The competitors of the cloth industries in Ghent, Douai or Ypres came from within the urban network in Flanders itself. Moreover, the claims of the 'three cities' were not always without cause. Indeed many smaller towns targeted market niches that were considered by the cloth entrepreneurs in the large cities as their own, and some of these smaller towns were very successful, in particular those along the Leie River in the shadow of Kortrijk and Lille. Towns like Wervik, Menen and Comines achieved huge success on Mediterranean markets from the 1350s to the 1450s and their woollens were around 1400 one of the staple products of the large Italian firms, like Francesco di Marco Datini in Prato.

In fact, the true expansion of rural cloth manufacture occurred only much later, in the late fifteenth and early sixteenth centuries, when already well established but usually small production centres like Hondschoote or Nieuwkerke started to target new markets with new products, dry woollens (worsteds and semi-worsteds) in the *sayetterie* of Hondschoote and fine woollens made from domestic and Spanish wool in Nieuwkerke and Armentières. In the process, these initially rural settlements started to urbanise rapidly, losing many of their proto-industrial characteristics. In Flanders, manufacturing export woollens was clearly an urban phenomenon for which regulation and quality control were essential, even when initially industrial development took place in a rural context. But this time, the large cities were no longer able to put up much of a fight anyway. Their cloth output had diminished to insignificant levels. Instead of conducting real military interventions such as they had organised in the 1320s and 1340s, the large cities tried to curb competition in the courts of the Burgundian dukes. But these attempts also failed. In fact, around this time it was no longer the rural and small-town cloth entrepreneurs who copied the fabrics of the big cities, it was entrepreneurs from Bruges, Ghent and Ypres who tried to introduce the woollens made in the countryside into their own industry. The late fifteenth and early sixteenth centuries saw the resurrection in the larger cities and secondary cloth towns of the *draperies légères*, the manufacture of worsteds and semi-worsteds, a line of fabrics that had all but disappeared as an export product around 1300. Although some centres like Hondschoote were much more successful in switching to these new 'old woollens', they were produced in nearly all the remaining cloth industries, from those in the large cities (Bruges) to the small towns (Dendermonde, Bergues) and the countryside, where some of the rural boroughs in Western Flanders saw the production of their *doucken* expand again.

And so it was with the cloth cycle in Ypres as well. In the decades before 1500, the Ypres entrepreneur and politician, Pieter Lansaem, made a fortune. Like hundreds of Ypres clothiers before him, his father had been a small-scale entrepreneur who was mainly active in monitoring a part of the output of luxury cloth. But Pieter chose another business strategy. He became a merchant and was involved in overseas trade. He had family relations with Portuguese traders active in Bruges, and perhaps he himself became involved in cloth trade with Portugal. If such commercial links did exist, they surely no longer involved the traditional luxury woollens of the Ypres industry, in the early 1470s limited to the production of at best a couple of hundred woollens per year, but rather cheaper textiles, woollens that are traditionally associated with small towns and even the countryside. In the final decades of the fifteenth century, Ypres again tried to develop the manufacture of what in a fiscal document of 1474 were called *gheheele doucken ende crempers*, cheaper fabrics made from Spanish, Scottish and domestic wool. And quickly, they were again being produced in their thousands.[545] Probably this range of products had never been abandoned completely, but worsteds and semi-worsted had not been exported abroad since the 1320s, and they were therefore made exclusively for domestic consumers. The census of 1431 does still mention five weavers of *doucken* in one of the four districts of the inner city. But at this time their number is still dwarfed by those of the traditional clothiers, weavers and fullers active in the manufacture of greased cloth made almost exclusively from English wool, and there are only precious few indicators that the manufacture of cheap dry cloth became more important in the following decades. In the late fifteenth and early sixteenth centuries the manufacture of cheaper cloth gained momentum, however. The number of stalls in the cloth hall allocated to clothiers active in the market for cheaper woollens started to increase from fewer than 10 in the 1470s to more than 30 in the late 1490s. Around the same time the Ypres aldermen also increased their efforts to curb the success of nearby villages, primarily, of course, the successful centre of Nieuwkerke.

The late success of cheap woollens in Ypres seems to have been an anomaly, however. As a rule, it was rural production centres that held the trump cards in organising the manufacture of coarse woollens, for which no or only a limited finishing capacity was needed. Moreover, some cities, Bruges in the fifteenth century, Lille and Antwerp in the sixteenth, had started to specialise in finishing industries anyway for raw woollens brought in from elsewhere. But still the short-lived success of Ypres (and of Bruges in the same period) as a manufacturing centre for cheaper textiles is a warning against exaggerating the seemingly obvious and inescapable logic of allocating industrial production in function of only the production cost and labour productivity. Nor was production in the countryside limited to cheaper fabrics. Nieuwkerke started to urbanise from the late fifteenth century onwards and it was able to develop an infrastructure for producing mid-range woollens destined for export via the Antwerp market. And in other parts of Flanders as well, specialist industries surfaced in rural and proto-industrial contexts. In the region between Aalst and Oudenaarde a massive deployment of rural tapestry weaving occurred in the late fifteenth and early sixteenth centuries. This was a region already previously characterised by proto-industrial development, more particularly for linen production. The rural tapestry weavers were supervised mainly by merchants and entrepreneurs in the small town of Oudenaarde. And, similarly, Nieuwkerke clothiers could rely on urban commercial infrastructure and

---

545 Mus, 'Pieter Lansaem', 61-88 and Demey, 'De mislukte aanpassingen', 171-187.

urban investment to develop their cloth industry. So, more elaborate and refined rural industries either tended to be supervised very closely by urban entrepreneurs, or they developed in settlements, such as Hondschoote, Armentières and even Nieuwkerke, which tended to experience a degree of urbanisation. A rural production of fine woollens, the main feature of the cloth industry in fifteenth- and sixteenth-century England, did not really appear in Flanders. The region was just too strongly characterised by dense urbanisation, and wage differences between smaller and larger towns already provided for a degree of entrepreneurial flexibility in any case.

The situation around 1500, when the traditional Flemish, Artesian and Brabantian cloth industries in larger cities such as Ghent, Bruges, Douai, Arras, Brussels, Mechelen, Leuven and, of course, Ypres were already in decline, was, however, nothing new. Internal competition from other production centres had constituted the very nature of cloth manufacture in Flanders from its heyday in the thirteenth century. The introduction of the horizontal loom had probably never completely erased rural cloth manufacture. So, even long before the surge in urbanisation in the latter part of the thirteenth and in the early fourteenth centuries (when small market towns all over Flanders and Brabant acquired their own textile industries, some of them semi-rural towns such as Eeklo and Kaprijke between Ghent and Bruges), smaller textile centres such as Diksmuide, Aardenburg and Dendermonde had competed even on foreign markets with the woollens manufactured in the large cities.[546] Perhaps no other region in Flanders was so marked by this internal competition than the rural surroundings of Ypres.

In the fourteenth century, relations were particularly tense between Ypres on the one hand and cloth manufacturers in Langemark (one of the more ambitious cloth-producing villages in the region) and Poperinge (a small town no more than 10km from the city) on the other. The most fearsome competitor for Ypres woollens had undoubtedly been Poperinge. In fact, already in the thirteenth century Poperinge cloth manufacturers had produced cloth for export purposes and Poperinge became with the large cities of Flanders one of the staple names in Flemish cloth exports. David Nicholas has even suggested that there was symbiosis between Ypres and Poperinge. It was Poperinge workers who had started the *cokerulle* revolt in 1280, and Ypres merchants also exported in the thirteenth century so-called 'Ypres-Poperinge' cloth, probably copies manufactured in Ypres of a type of woollen produced in Poperinge. It was not always the smaller centres that copied from the larger ones. In the same period Bruges clothiers produced, for example, so-called *Ghistelsayen*, worsteds probably copied from an example produced in the small town of Gistel in the vicinity of Bruges.

When, however, in the late thirteenth century, because of rising transaction costs in Mediterranean trade, the exports of worsteds and, after the 1320s, also those of stamforts started to disappear, relations became more tense. Flemish cloth entrepreneurs switched more and more to fine greased woollens – considered by John Munro to be price-makers, rather than price-takers. And export markets started to change. Although this did not happen suddenly, Ypres woollens were during the fourteenth century more and more directed to the eastern, Hanseatic export markets, where Poperinge

---

546 Stabel, *Dwarfs among Giants*, 138-157.

woollens were also marketed. In an industrial environment of declining output figures, competition drove manufacturing centres against each other, and the 'Three Cities', of course, used their political power in Flanders in this period to try to curb the success of the smaller cloth towns and cloth villages. The complaints of the Ypres aldermen about Poperinge were very clear and to the point in this respect. They complained that Poperinge clothiers were used to making light cloth and not greased woollens, and that they had recently switched to also manufacturing fine woollens. In fact, what they described was also exactly what had happened in Ypres itself in this period. The Poperinge clothiers' reply was equally correct: they claimed to have been forced to change to greased woollens because otherwise Poperinge textile workers would not have been able to sustain themselves. The scramble for the market for fine woollens on the Hanseatic market was in full swing, and each cloth-producing centre wanted to increase its own market share. Because Ypres clothiers had lost or were losing their Mediterranean markets, Ypres had to broaden its hold on those Central- and East-European markets, and so did Poperinge clothiers.

The Ypres aldermen also complained about unfair competition in the Leie towns. But it is striking that, despite some lukewarm attempts to challenge cloth manufacturers in Comines or Wervik in the 1340s, little was done in the end to achieve these goals. The Leie towns still targeted Mediterranean markets, markets that had been lost to Ypres clothiers. Moreover, the Leie cloth towns close to Kortrijk were well outside Ypres' reach, and many would gradually be integrated into the zone of influence of Ghent, rather than that of Ypres. Poperinge was different though, and the Ypres aldermen persevered, with a combination of both military coercion and attempts to challenge the rural industries by legal means. But even in the late 1330s and early 1340s, when in the Artevelde era the three cities ruled the county almost unopposed by the count, they were never quite able to achieve success.

This was different as far as the village industries were concerned. Although the village of Langemark had possessed a chartered cloth industry since the 1240s, the interventions of the Ypres militia and the political actions of the Ypres aldermen in the 1340s were much more successful than those against Poperinge. Langemark produced not only the *doucken* that were no longer among the leading products of the Ypres clothiers, but also greased cloth that was dyed in colours according to the wishes of the merchants. Langemark cloth was sold, as were all other woollens manufactured in Flemish chartered cities, at the fairs of Flanders and they were exported to the Hanseatic lands. After a few attacks on the industry by Ypres militiamen in the 1320s (called by the count in 1329 'murders, arson, robberies and destructions perpetrated by those from Ypres'), and again in the 1340s, Louis de Nevers, count of Flanders, was forced in 1342 to retract all the charters that he had himself issued for the Langemark industry and he forbade any further cloth manufacture in the village. Only when the balance of power was restored in 1348 in favour of the count did the new count, Louis de Male, again confirm the cloth privileges of the village, deploring the fact that the

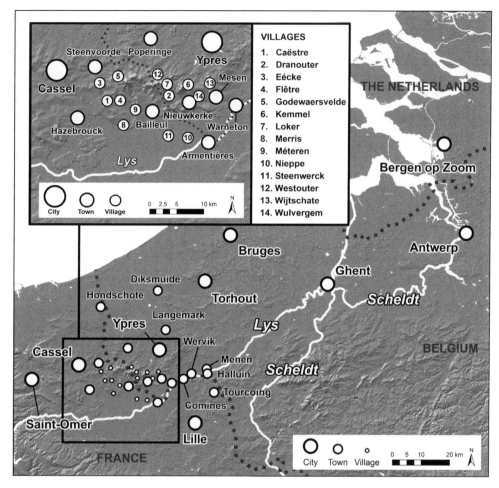

Figure 10.1 Map of the cloth producing towns and villages in the western part of the county of Flanders (© Iason Jongepier, University of Antwerp).

'weavers and those from the cloth industry in Ypres' had destroyed the looms, fullers' troughs and tenterers' fields in Langemark.[547]

Both John Munro and David Nicholas have attributed this lack of result to the limited levels of coercion the smallest of the 'Three Cities' could muster, even in a period when the counterforce of the counts of Flanders had all but disappeared.[548] This may be true, although even the most powerful city in Flanders, Ghent, failed to reduce the success of the cloth industries in the smaller towns of its own hinterland. On the contrary, almost all towns in the river basin of Interior Flanders experienced economic growth in this period. Ghent was more successful with its militia raids in the villages in Interior Flanders, where cloth manufacture all but disappeared in this

---

[547] Espinas and Pirenne, *Recueil*, 3, 9-14.
[548] Munro, *Medieval Woollens*, 255-259 and Nicholas, *Town and Countryside*, 211-215.

period. But why would Ypres be any weaker than Ghent as regards disorganised rural weavers? The city militia of Ypres in the first half of the fourteenth century participated wholeheartedly in most of the conflicts that ravaged the Flemish countryside in that period. And the documents about the actions of Ypres against the villages show that in the 1340s Ypres was effectively pursuing with some success the destruction of the cloth industry in nearby villages. Later, when in the latter part of the fourteenth century under counts Louis de Male and Philip the Bold and during the fifteenth century the Burgundian dukes could once again intervene as a counterforce to the large cities of their hinterlands, this was no longer the case. Ypres was indeed inclined to bow to comital power sooner than the other two larger and wealthier cities, but in the second quarter of the fourteenth century power relations were much more in favour of the cities.

The key to understanding Ypres' limited success in banning rural and small-town cloth manufacture lies probably much more in the ambiguous attitude of the city itself towards those industries. We saw already in the previous chapter that the town administrations, controlled by the mercantile elites, were suspected by the guilds of playing a double game. Outwardly they were seen acting against the competitors of the urban industry in the hinterland of the city by acquiring or (re)imposing the ban on rural cloth manufacture within a range of three comital miles of the city or by directly challenging the small-town industries which allegedly copied the Ypres woollens. Yet, at times of crisis, they were accused by the leaders of the revolt of implementing such policies only reluctantly, or even of not doing this at all. Would it not be likely that this suspicion of the craft guilds and the artisans was indeed founded on reality? As we saw elsewhere in this book, the mercantile elites who controlled the urban government in Ypres had vested interests in the countryside. They possessed a lot of the land in the vicinity of the city, and they had not hesitated to parcel these lands and rent them out to the Ypres craftsmen in the four suburbs, profiting in the process from higher land values. But their possessions went, of course, much further than just the immediate surroundings of the city.

Moreover, it is plausible that they were also involved in the trade in woollens produced in these towns and villages and that they were also involved in credit relations with the clothiers and craftsmen in those villages. Before 1300, borrowers from Langemark were only rarely involved in borrowing money from Ypres merchants (there are only three cases of formal loans among the thousands of chirographs that were kept in the city archives). But the Ypres merchants were also not very much involved in lending to Ypres artisans and clothiers under formal IOUs because, as we stated in chapter 4, they were probably tied up in more informal credit arrangements with them.[549] It is equally striking that armed expeditions of the Ypres militia occurred primarily in those periods when the craftsmen themselves gained direct access to or control of the urban government, from 1325 to 1328 and again in the early 1340s. It is only in those (limited) timeframes that armed action took place against rural and small-town competitors. A new military expedition to Poperinge in 1363 was primarily linked to

---

549 Database Martha Howell, see for full reference chapter 4.

matters of jurisdiction, although rivalry about cloth undoubtedly also played a part in the motivation of the Ypres aldermen.[550] On all other occasions the Ypres government went to comital courts only to gain an advantage over the city's rural competitors, and during the reign of Count Louis de Male the issue at stake was always the suspicion that small-town clothiers copied the woollens of Ypres cloth manufacturers.

The fact that by now in most villages some cloth manufacture took place was no longer challenged after 1349. And only occasionally, when rural weavers were suspected of manufacturing greased cloth, did Ypres try to intervene. But, with the exception of the occasional military statement, for example in 1352, coordinated actions of the city militia were a thing of the past.[551] The rural woollens, usually called *doucken*, were in this period undoubtedly still primarily worsteds intended for domestic markets, rather than export products, so not an immediate threat to the luxury fabrics produced in Ypres. This may explain why the Ypres city administrators relied solely on the count to safeguard their rights and why their privileges were enforced only legally. In the 1430s a legal dispute with Nieuwkerke before the Parliament in Paris confirmed the status quo.[552] The real competition continued as before between Ypres and the chartered secondary towns in its quarter. In a well-documented legal conflict between Ypres and Poperinge in 1373, the Poperinge clothiers relied successfully on the confirmation of their privileges by the count and continued to produce greased woollens that were popular on the Hanseatic markets, the same markets on which the Ypres clothiers were also active, although the entrepreneurs in Poperinge wrongfully claimed that Ypres was still more oriented towards the Mediterranean markets.[553] But everything ended in a stalemate, and everybody continued as before. The distribution of various types of woollens across the industrial landscape also took hold in Ypres and its hinterland. This lack of direct result in the eyes of the Ypres craftsmen must have aggravated tensions in the city itself. As a result, the Ypres aldermen and political elites were suspected by the craftsmen of defending the city's privileges in only a lukewarm fashion, an accusation that would be repeated henceforth in all conflicts that set the elites against the commoners in the late 1370s and early 1380s and again in the failed revolt of 1428.

It is therefore not so much the traditional explanation in historiography, the lack of political and military coercion of the third city of Flanders, Ypres, but rather the strategies of the urban elites of Ypres themselves that may have caused the failure of the city to control the rural and small-town textile manufacturers in its vicinity. The allegedly strong lobby in Ypres favouring craftsmen's interests was clearly not efficient enough to define the political strategies of the mercantile elites in the city.[554] Defending the cloth industry at all costs was just no longer in the interests of the leading bourgeois,

---

550 Nicholas, *Town and Countryside*, 215-216.
551 Nicholas, *Town and Countryside*, 207-208 and Vander Meulen, *Woven into the Urban Fabric*, forthcoming, chapter 4, mentioning the expedition of 55 Yprois in 1352 under the command of count Louis de Male's bastard son.
552 Dauchy et al. (eds), *Les arrêts et jugés*, 1, 576-578.
553 De Pauw, *Ypre jeghen Poperinghe*.
554 The traditional view on the Ypres city administrators was upheld recently in Van der Meulen, *Woven into the Urban Fabric*, 143-174.

and as a result they only paid lip service to such strategies, probably to avoid social unrest in the city.

Furthermore, we have seen that around 1300, when foreign merchants took over their role in the wool and cloth trade and when clothiers gained entrepreneurial independence, the involvement of the mercantile elites certainly did not stop abruptly. They retained a crucial role in the distribution of capital in the industry and in commercial contacts with foreign merchants, but this pivotal role must have diminished during the fourteenth century, when Ypres clothiers started to focus on smaller numbers of ever more expensive woollens. So, the investment portfolios of the elites undoubtedly shifted towards obtaining a greater share of rural income and reducing the importance of urban income. Although direct empirical research into the financial interests of the Ypres elites in the fifteenth century is still lacking for the moment, it is possible that the role of the political elites in the urban economy no longer coincided with the industrial interests of the cloth entrepreneurs and textile craftsman in Ypres. So, in this case, a lot of elements point to a process, linked traditionally by scholars such as Henri Pirenne or Fernand Braudel with a 'treason of the bourgeoisie'.[555]

By the fifteenth century nothing much seems to have changed, except for the fact that the need to restrict competition was felt even more urgently by the craftsmen. The rural industries had always been a bone of contention. In the 1370s and 1420s it was the main reason for their revolts against the political elites. The Ypres industry was moribund by this time. But, similarly, many rural and small-town industries had also got into difficulty. Cloth entrepreneurs in Poperinge and Roeselare, the two most important secondary cloth towns closest to Ypres, also lost most of their export markets for their woollens, and in the latter part of the fifteenth century even the Leie towns and the secondary towns in Interior Flanders, the region controlled by Ghent, saw their output diminish substantially. The fine greased woollens from Flanders were starting to disappear from the Hanseatic markets. The initiative went to new production centres. As we have seen, the most spectacular case was the say production in Hondschoote, which in the early sixteenth century saw it even outgrow Ypres as the third most populated urban settlement in the Dutch-speaking parts of Flanders. But also, the traditional production of fine greased woollens was continued in places such as Armentières near Lille with its famous *oultrefin* woollens and Nieuwkerke (and in some of the older, smaller cloth towns of Interior Flanders, such as Menen, Dendermonde and Kortrijk). Other rural centres of production seem to have focused primarily on worsteds (*doucken*), but by the late fifteenth century here too the traditional greased woollens were exported, despite token protests from the capital city of the region, Ypres. Even cloth manufacturers in villages such as Wulvergem, Eécke, Kemmel and Dranouter used broadlooms to produce woollens that were comparable to those produced in small towns or even in Ypres. In the late fifteenth and early sixteenth centuries the Flemish textile industries acquired a distinctively English-style rural flavour, therefore. But this development seems never to have been challenged with any conviction be the urban cloth industries; no military expeditions in the countryside were organised any longer,

---

555 Pirenne, 'The Stages', 512-513 and Braudel, *Civilisation matérielle*, vol. 2, 574-576.

no legal challenges achieved any kind of result. If anything, the urban industries seem to have adapted, again, as they had done around 1300, after the middle of the fourteenth century and in the early fifteenth century, by specialising and by product innovation. Sometimes these attempts were successful as in the case of the Oudenaarde tapestries, the Kortrijk linens, the Menen fine woollens and the light woollens in Dendermonde and Ronse (*bays*); sometimes these attempts met with disaster.

If the institutional boundaries between town and countryside started to become blurred in the late fifteenth century when places such as Nieuwkerke and Hondschoote attracted central functions that were traditionally associated with urban settlements, the urban status of individual textile workers became ambiguous much sooner. Indeed, many of the rural textile craftsmen acquired the status of out-burghers of Ypres. In the 1560s almost a third of the clothiers in the thriving industry at Nieuwkerke were out-burghers of Ypres, and it is likely that in earlier periods figures had been very similar.[556] Some Nieuwkerke clothiers probably even had urban backgrounds themselves. In a growing cloth centre such as Nieuwkerke in the late fifteenth and early sixteenth centuries several textile workers had certainly emigrated from Ypres, where employment opportunities had radically diminished. So, despite all the bans and legal actions that Ypres organised against the rural textile centres in its hinterland, which continued indeed well into the sixteenth century, a kind of *modus vivendi* was arrived at nonetheless. Around 1500, Ypres' traditional cloth industry was no longer a match for those in Nieuwkerke and Armentières, so the city's elites looked for occasions to profit from this rural expansion instead. Ypres became, together with Antwerp, one of the leading outlets for Nieuwkerke clothiers. Brokers specialising in rural woollens were also active at the Ypres market and the city was also important for bringing flows of raw materials to the rural clothiers. Clothiers from Nieuwkerke or the nearby village of Kemmel were, certainly, at the beginning of the sixteenth century still regularly attending the Ypres fairs to do most of their business.[557] By this time the old balance had shifted completely. After a last upsurge of the city's cheaper woollens, sixteenth-century Ypres would gradually move to its new role of administrative and commercial centre for its hinterland.

Ypres and Florence: Two Sides of the Same Coin?

In the Mediterranean, in North and Central Italy, another model of industrial organisation emerged. Although here, as in Flanders, decentralised manufacture, organised in family units, was omnipresent, the links between mercantile capital and textile manufacture developed differently from in Ypres and most other Flemish textile centres. Instead of a gradual separation of mercantile investment from industrial enterprise across the late thirteenth and during the fourteenth centuries, the opposite occurred in Florence, which in this period became the leading manufacturing centre for woollen

---

[556] Van der Meulen, *Woven into the urban fabric*, 143-174.
[557] Van der Meulen, *Woven into the urban fabric*, 107-142.

fabrics in Italy. There was a steady rapprochement of mercantile capital and industrial manufacture. Before the middle of the thirteenth century the dense urban system in Italy was not particularly geared towards producing fine woollen textiles for export. There were certainly concentrations of cloth manufacture in the cities of, particularly, Northern Italy, in Lombardy and in what would later become the Venetian *terraferma*: Milan, Bergamo, Brescia, Verona and Mantua produced woollens made from domestic and imported wool, and gradually also the large cities in Tuscany, Florence and Pisa, and some smaller towns like Siena, Prato and Pistoia started developing important cloth industries. Eventually, Florence's *Arte della Lana* would, of course, become the leading producer in Italy.[558]

But before 1300, Italian merchants imported most of their quality woollens from Flanders or France, some of which were finished by local cloth finishers and dyers, and its cloth manufactures produced primarily coarse woollens, worsteds and mixed fabrics. When in the late thirteenth and early fourteenth centuries more expensive woollen fabrics were also produced, they were called 'French woollens' (*panni franceschi*).[559] As elsewhere, in English, French and German cities manufacture was organised in small-scale workshops, and households were the economic units that were organised by entrepreneurs into a production chain. The overall structures of urban cloth manufacture in medieval Europe resembled each other, and it was only differences in the scale of the operations that distinguished the massive export industries in Flanders and Artesia or in Chalon in Burgundy from manufacture elsewhere.

In Italian cities the balance between mercantile capital and manufacturing artisans, however, became different. Paradoxically, it resembled a little what was common in Flemish cities before the 1250s. In this sense, fourteenth-century Florence mirrored the earlier social relations in twelfth- and thirteenth-century Ypres, Saint-Omer, Douai and Ghent. After 1300, Italian cloth manufacture changed dramatically in some cities. Instead of medium-quality domestic wool or wool imported from North Africa, Italian merchant companies started to import fine English wool (which they had also already started to market in Flanders), and cloth manufacturers (*lanaiuoli*) started also to produce more expensive fabrics. In the process, Florence conformed to the pattern in many North-European textile cities: a growing focus on luxury textiles and the gradual abandonment of cheaper worsteds and other coarse woollens. This massive import substitution not only drove cheaper Flemish and Brabant woollens from their traditional Italian and Mediterranean markets, as we saw in Chapter 1; in the longer run they carved out new markets all over Europe for the very fine Florentine woollens which could compete with the most expensive Flemish scarlets. It is also around this time that the social organisation of cloth manufacture in Flanders and Italy starts to diverge from the European model.

Whilst in Flanders the drive towards luxury fabrics signified the beginning of the end for direct mercantile involvement in cloth manufacture, in Florence for the same

---

558 Dini, 'L'industria tessile', 13-49.
559 Munro, 'Medieval Woollens', 262-266 and Goldthwaite, *The Economy of Renaissance Florence*, 267-271.

reason mercantile involvement in cloth manufacture seems to have increased.[560] In Ypres, clothiers became the crucial figures in cloth production; in Florence (and Prato), a lot of the cloth production was channelled through the large *botteghe*, owned jointly by merchants and by specialist cloth entrepreneurs, whom the merchants employed or with whom they formed temporary firms. This was, of course, still no factory system. The infrastructure required to manufacture woollens in any medieval urban environment still consisted of dispersed workshops, many of them still owned by small-scale craftsmen. But merchants and their wool shops became much more dominant in financial and industrial relations. Like true Boinebrokes a century earlier (and probably also like the De Brune, Van Scoten and Belle merchant dynasties of Ypres), the fourteenth-century 'shops' of the Strozzi, Acciaiuoli and Datini, and, of course, in the fifteenth century the Medici, organised the handling of wool (wool beaters, cleaners and carders) and the finishing of woollens (tenting, dyeing) themselves. For this purpose, production units were organised directly by central wool shops, sometimes even on the ground floors of urban mansions, while other stages of production were entrusted to semi-proletarianised weavers and fullers or to domestic workers such as spinsters. The hold of mercantile capital on industrial manufacture was therefore almost complete in very similar ways to those in Flanders and Artois a century earlier.

How we must explain this apparent different direction taken in very similar circumstances is still matter for debate. While Ypres merchants chose to abandon direct involvement in cloth manufacture when a drive for luxury made quality control and the regulation of the labour market even more crucial than before and clothiers and guild masters became the crucial operators in the industry, Florentine merchants chose to associate themselves with the actual cloth entrepreneurs, entrusting them with their capital investments and even sometimes themselves organising large workshops. Not all these merchants can be compared to the so-called super-companies like the Bardi or Peruzzi, so the scale of operations was probably comparable to the capital used by the Ypres elites themselves earlier on. The path-dependent tracks that opened in both cases could not be more different, however.

In Flanders, even in Ypres where the mercantile elites could hang on to most of their coercive power during the late Middle Ages, the cloth industry became a battleground for its different stakeholders. Each of these stakeholders (merchants, clothiers, craft guilds, workers) carved out its own field of interest. The supervision of the industry lay in the hands of the public authorities, of the city aldermen (and indirectly, therefore, of the mercantile elites), while the coordination of the industry was in the hands of the clothiers, entrepreneurs with close ties with the artisanal world. So, access to finance remained in the hands of the merchants, entrepreneurship became the realm of the craftsmen, guilds acquired important functions in adjusting labour markets, and workers could in function of desired standards of living offer their labour to the system at whatever level they had access to, defined by skill and gender. Relations between all these levels of activity were negotiated and the outcome was defined by internal

---

560 The organisation of the industry is discussed in Franceschi, *Oltre il tumulto*. The most detailed analysis of the structure of a textile firm remains De Roover, 'A Florentine Firm', 85-118.

power relations or by external demand: what kind of cloth was produced and marketed and what kind of balance of skill (guildsmen and workers), capital (merchants) and monitoring (clothiers) it required. So, we see struggles between the merchants and the clothiers for the distribution of profit and about the balance between manufacture and trade, the first in the fourteenth century, once they had withdrawn from the industry itself, wanting a clear separation, the latter an osmosis so that they gained better access to markets for raw materials and woollens. But there was also competition between the clothiers and the guilds about the levels of skill required in each production stage, within the guilds also between masters and journeymen about labour conditions, wage levels and the input of unskilled labour, and finally between the clothiers and the unskilled workers, so crucial because these undertook the most labour-intensive stages of production and the small-scale clothiers worked with very low profit margins. The aldermen themselves, of course, no neutral actors, had to take care that these different equilibria between all these stakeholders were kept under control and still allowed innovation and adaptation.

In the Florentine *Arte della Lana* many of these relations were no different. The basic structure of production was, after all, the same. So, workshops tended to be dispersed and organised at the level of the family unit. The power relations between the different stakeholders, however, led to a wholly different outcome. As the stakes went up when Florence started to produce the 'French woollens', the role of capital increased and the involvement of the merchants increased with it. While in Ypres it was small-scale clothiers who became the pivotal figures and they gradually became more independent of merchant interference, in Florence the links between the *lanaiuoli* and the merchants became stronger, and in many cases this led to the so-called 'wool shop', a partnership with a common investment in which the merchants delivered most of the capital and the clothiers (if we may use this terminology from the northern industries) mainly their expertise in running the enterprise. As such, like the Flemish clothiers, the Florentine cloth entrepreneurs were primarily managers, but they were in fact managing the merchant's enterprise as paid employees, a situation that must have looked much more like the position of the clothiers in the Flemish industries of Douai or Ypres during the thirteenth century. This does not mean that the organisation of the industry in Florence or Prato differed completely from its Ypres counterpart. As a rule, most wool shops were not very sizable operations, except for a couple of larger ones incorporated into the business strategy of large merchant firms like Datini or Medici. Many managing directors were, like the Flemish clothiers, also of modest origins and had only modest means with which to organise the industry, although some came from the merchant class themselves. And most of all, the operations they controlled were, like those of the Ypres clothiers, based upon the ownership of raw materials and finished commodities, therefore upon a substantial investment in movable capital goods, rather than in fixed capital goods.

But some elements were clearly very different. Certainly, in the first part of the fourteenth century, before the Black Death, the wool shops still organised a lot of the labour input directly, by hiring employees at time-rate wages for the early and late stages of the manufacturing process. To control production stages that were carried out at home or in the workshops of specialist artisans, from weavers to dyers, they used intermediaries or brokers paid on a piece-rate basis.[561] Moreover, the people involved in investing in wool shops also owned a lot of property that was used by craftsmen: weavers' workshops, fulleries or tenting and dyeing infrastructure. We saw earlier that in Ypres the mercantile elites also invested in providing land and manufacturing infrastructure to the craftsmen; there are, however, no indications that the clothiers were very much involved in these practices. For Florentine merchants, a wool shop (or a silk shop for that matter) was a relatively safe investment, a way to spread risk, but at the cost of a relative low return. The merchants probably accepted this disadvantage in order to broaden the scope of their enterprises and reduce the risk of being wholly dependent upon external supply chains. The wool shop became as such an intrinsic part of the commercial venture, and it was, therefore, also intrinsically linked to mercantile capital. The wool shop, however, not only complemented the range of exports of merchant companies, but it also delivered to other merchants or supplied itself from other merchanting activities. The wool shop, in other words, both reinforced the commercial position of the merchant firm and became a part of commercial networks cutting across the boundaries of individual firms. Because of their scope and the fact that a lot of the wool preparation and the cloth finishing was directly organised by the wool shops, the other stages of production were much more dependent upon their mercantile-entrepreneurial activities.

Unlike in Flanders, the all-encompassing cloth guild (the *Arte della Lana*) was dominated by entrepreneurs, not by master craftsmen as in the specialist guilds of weavers, fullers, shearers, cloth finishers and dyers in red and in blue of Ypres. The specialisation in different trades in Ypres and Florence was perhaps similar, their corporative organisation was not. This means that the guild in Florence was primarily occupied with the relations between the wool shops and their workers. The guild did not become a separate stakeholder in the industry defending the interests of very specific groups of craftsmen. In Ypres, despite the relative weak political position of the guilds compared to those in other Flemish cities, the guilds had in fact since the middle of the thirteenth century been self-organisations of homogenous groups of craftsmen. The homogeneity concerned, first and foremost, the nature of the occupation, the position of the group vis-à-vis the whole production chain, and the requirements of the occupation for the career development of guildsmen and their relative position on the labour market. It did not, of course, concern social homogeneity because the guilds in essence included both employers and employees, masters and journeymen. In the end, the most essential interventions of the Flemish textile guilds lay in defining the standard quality of the end-product they delivered (to the clothier as organiser of the production chain or, in the case of the dyers, to the merchant or consumer) and in regulating the labour market in which the guild entrepreneurs, the masters, had to organise their workshops. The craft guilds, of course, also provided a framework in which guildsmen developed their social and cultural identity. Nothing of the kind happened in Florence. The regulating

---

561 Goldthwaite, *The Economy of Renaissance Florence*, 319, see also Franceschi, *Ultro il tumulto*, 183-198 and Dini, 'I lavoratori', 141-171?

function of the *Arte* in this respect resembled much more the regulating activities of the city aldermen in Ypres: defining how entrepreneurs (or firms) had to deal with the systems of outsourcing that were abundant in the industry. As such the function of the *Arte* was not equal to the actions of the Flemish guilds. It was similar rather to what the (merchant-dominated) civic authorities did in Ypres. Florentine clothiers were members of the guild; Ypres clothiers were not, unless they were associated with one of the craft guilds, in most cases the weavers, in their quality of artisan.

A second different feature of the Florentine industry compared to the organisation of manufacture in Ypres was the omnipresence of partnerships at all levels of industrial organisation.[562] This was the case not only at the top of the production chain, the *bottega* or wool shop, which was often a partnership between the merchant who brought in most of the capital and an active managing partner; it was also the case at the bottom. Even proletarianised textile workers who provided only their labour, for example spinsters, are seen in the account books of the wool shops to be acting as partnerships, and the semi-independent weavers, men and women, fullers and cloth finishers operate in 'companies', linking their infrastructure to each other. Franco Franceschi claims that this was done primarily to achieve more income security.[563] Employment in textile industries was always unpredictable and volatile. By combining their effort in a partnership craftsmen and textile workers could spread risk more easily. A temporary fall in employment for one partner could be compensated for by another partner who could hang on to a particular job opportunity. Because the *Arte* was an overarching organisation in which the cloth entrepreneurs themselves were the most influential members, the guild did not intervene so much at the level of individual artisanal workshops, or at the level of individual employment.

In Ypres from the middle of the thirteenth century, this was very different. The focus on monetised relations between the craftsmen and entrepreneurs (and, although less strictly, between merchants and entrepreneurs as well) and the reluctance to allow partnerships or even loose associations for investing in workshops atomised the labour market to a large extent and individualised the artisanal workshops. Thus, spinsters were not allowed to associate amongst themselves, if only to safeguard the quality of the wool owned by the merchant or the cloth entrepreneur. Hence also the strict regulation of associations among guild masters and the prohibition of journeymen from investing in masters' workshops. As such, the lack of partnerships must to a certain extent have weakened the bargaining position of workers. Wage negotiations in the cities of the Low Countries were mostly a private matter between employer and employee, and were ruled by relations of scarcity. This was, however, compensated for by the collective action of the guilds and the Intervention of the public authorities. In periods of social unrest and of pressure on wages (and a threat of rising wages in particular), wages were set at a particular level. As we saw in Chapter 7, wage settings were not very frequent (in the period of the *cokerulle* revolt in 1280, and again after the middle of the fourteenth century when high mortality must have exercised upward pressure on wage levels). In

---

562 Goldthwaite, *The Economy of Renaissance Florence*, 330-332.
563 Franceschi, *Oltre il tumulto*, 47-66.

both cases, it is likely that it was the guilds (and the clothiers) that were demanding to curb wages. As such the guilds acted as defenders of the artisanal workshop and of the guild masters, not of the employees, even the journeymen, the skilled employees. Only occasionally did the concerns of the journeymen seep through, when, for example, wages were set for the journeymen dyers in 1375. So, the old cliché that guilds kept wages artificially high in the Flemish textile guilds must be nuanced. In fact, most of the time they did exactly the opposite. Any association among journeymen or, even worse, financial interest of the journeymen in a master's enterprise, therefore, would have weakened the grip of the guild masters on the labour market. And the same is true for the relations between the clothiers and the unskilled workers in wool preparation and spinning. So, in the end the true winners of the Flemish guild system in the late Middle Ages were, unsurprisingly, the middle class of entrepreneurs, both the clothiers and the guild masters, the same people who in fourteenth-century Florence had to form partnerships to organise protection from the overwhelming dominance of mercantile capital. Surprisingly in Florence it seems to have been the weavers who were the least inclined to arrange partnerships with other weavers. This is a striking parallel with the fact that the weavers in Ypres were also the trade with relatively less institutional hold on their own weavers' guild. The guild was controlled mainly by the clothiers, most of them owning a weaver's workshop, and the master weavers who were not clothiers, the so-called *conventers*, were, like the journeymen, on average only poor craftsmen lacking the resources to play an important role in the guild. Although sources do not allow us to investigate the social relations in Ypres before 1250, it is likely that in the pre-guild period such protection of small artisans in the successive stages of manufacture against overarching mercantile dominance must have been sought in partnerships as well. There would have been little alternative, and the fact that such associations were looked at with great suspicion after the guilds came of age was probably part of the social negotiation process between the old and the new stakeholders.

In the end, the fundamental and structural differences between Ypres (and probably the whole urban cloth industry in Flanders-Artois-Brabant) and Florence were caused primarily by the fact that in Flanders mercantile capitalists became dissociated from the industry (at least directly). All the differences between the Ypres clothiers and the Florentine *lanaiuoli* and between the Ypres guild craftsmen and the Florentine weavers, fullers, dyers and cloth finishers who operated without their own guild, and between the atomised labour force in the wool-preparing stages in Ypres and the occasional partnerships among textile workers, can be explained by the changing investment strategies of the elites, who gradually preferred income from rural holdings and from regional trade networks and, as a result of this process, the greater independence of the clothiers and the guild artisans. They used their corporate organisations and their hold on the labour markets as a protection against the vicissitudes of the market. This process did not happen without friction, as the previous chapters have shown. But the apparent hold of capital on cloth manufacture in Florence was also accompanied by sometimes harsh social conflict. The iconic Ciompi revolt of 1378 in Florence was very much an attempt by the skilled artisans to acquire their own corporate organisations, separated from the central Wool Guild, which was controlled by the cloth entrepreneurs, and it is perhaps not a complete coincidence that among the craftsmen were also Flemish immigrants, who were used to the guild organized structures.[564] In Ypres guilds were, of course, already present, so large-scale conflicts were more about the political influence of the guilds and on the political strategies of the urban authorities to protect and stimulate the industry.

Rise and Fall of a Textile City

At the end of this survey an uneasy feeling remains. In the introduction we stated that the history of medieval Ypres was characterised by two periods, one of rapid industrial expansion, when the city had up to 30,000 inhabitants, most of them in one way or another depending on cloth manufacture, and one of industrial decline, until in the fifteenth century the city was only a shadow of its former self and its population steadily fell below 10,000. In this period the city was doomed to become a regional servicing centre, still capitalising on institutional inertia to hold on to the last remnants of its once great cloth industry and to profit from the central administrative position it had gained in its heyday in the surrounding countryside. Recently, Jim van der Meulen did not hesitate to describe the sensational rise in the late fifteenth century of the cloth industry in Nieuwkerke, 14km south of the city, as 'born amidst the rubble of its crumbling predecessor', meaning, of course, the traditional Ypres industry.[565] Doom and gloom irrevocably befell the desperate and stubbornly short-sighted clothiers of the big city.

The difficult source situation, with detailed regulation starting to appear only after the 1280s, documents primarily the second period, so precious little can be said about the period of expansion. As a result, Ypres has in a lot of the historiography bec9ome a cliché of itself. It became associated with ill-advised industrial and political conservatism, with ill-fated attempts to reverse a situation that was caused primarily by its own weakness, the monopoly of an industry that could no longer compete successfully on international markets. Inevitably, these markets were lost one by one. The strong hold of the craft guilds on the organisation of labour effectively stopped any attempt at fundamentally altering the conditions of manufacture. The natural inclination to turn to those solutions that had worked in the past, but were no longer able to turn the tide, led to a conservative strategy of hitting out almost randomly at any competitor in the vicinity that was able to continue its cloth activities. Ypres was a former industrial juggernaut unable to adapt to changing times.

And yet ... which other industrial city in medieval or early modern Europe had been able to remain, as Ypres did for such a long period, from the 1150s to the 1450s, a leading centre of manufacture? Ypres was, almost uninterruptedly for a period of three centuries, one of the quintessential cloth cities of Europe, its products so successful and coveted by consumers, and not only by the one-percenters of medieval society, the super-wealthy elites of princes and noblemen, but also the socially ambitious

---

564 Stella, *La révolte des Ciompi* and Goldthwaire, *The Economy*, 323.
565 Van der Meulen, *Woven into the Urban Fabric*, 209-216.

urban middle classes. The strong image of decline, so much promoted by historians in the past as a warning against guild organisation and high wages, against the strong institutional hold on labour relations, against tightening control of the urban hinterland, against the refusal of technological change and the unrelenting defence of existing industrial processes and social relations, is therefore also at odds with a more nuanced and certainly more reluctant historical reality. Ypres had been a huge industrial (and commercial) success for a very long period. And even after 1300 when the Mediterranean markets were gradually lost and cloth entrepreneurs were forced to specialise in particular niches, causing output figures to drop and unemployment levels to rise, these adaptations were often very imaginative.

In truth, many Flemish textile cities, large and small, adopted similar strategies. They were equally resilient during the alleged late medieval decline of the industry. Entrepreneurs and guild-organised craftsmen adapted seemingly effortlessly to fundamentally changing trade routes, to new commercial partners, to changing fashion and taste. They took entrepreneurial decisions that not only guaranteed the survival of the industry but also caused a radical shift to another kind of production, in which high-quality output required the intervention of the craft guilds as guarantors of standard quality and of well-oiled labour markets. In the process, guilds are no longer to be considered bastions of conservatism and a liability, as was stressed by most scholars from Henri Pirenne in the early twentieth century to Sheilagh Ogilvie a century later; they were in fact a life insurance for the industry, facilitating product innovation and labour specialisation. In this, the old and big guilds of textile craftsmen in Ghent and Ypres operated in very similar ways to the slicker and smaller guilds organising the fashion and luxury industries in late medieval Bruges. And, just as in middle-class Bruges, also in industrial Ypres the action of the guilds was curbed, moulded and in the end defined by other stakeholders as well, by the city authorities, the mercantile elites and, in the case of the Ypres cloth industry where, unlike in the specialist industries of Bruges, entrepreneurs were operating for the most part outside the guild framework, also by the clothiers.

Viewing the Ypres industry not merely in the light of decay, but in the light of changing and adaptive mercantile or entrepreneurial strategies and through the lens of labour relations has allowed us to bring to the fore some of the essential characteristics of what the organisation of the *grande draperie* did to the social fabric of a medieval city. At the end of our narrative some remaining questions must, however, still be addressed. How inevitable was the development of cloth manufacture in Ypres and, for that matter, in all the other large production centres of the Low Countries, of Flanders and Artesia, of Brabant and Holland? Ypres constituted the prime example of massive industrial organisation in a Northwest-European city. Production had always been decentralised into family units that were linked to each other in a chain of production: there was no viable option yet for concentrating manufacture in larger units and for producing within a framework of economies of scale. In the process, the levers of power were, however, firmly controlled by mercantile elites. Yet the active organisation of industrial manufacture was in the hands of separate cloth entrepreneurs, the clothiers. Hence the fragmentation of economic initiative constituted the core of industrial organisation. This was not an unchanging feature. We have seen that the relative position of the different stakeholders changed over time. The local merchants, in the first phase of the industry the undisputed leaders of the cloth trade and heavily involved also in the manufacturing networks, gradually retreated to a more passive involvement based upon credit relations, brokerage and landownership, up to the point where they lost all interest in the fifteenth century and because of their interests as rentiers even matched to a certain extent with the rural competitors of the urban industry. The clothiers retained their original function of coordinating the production chain but changed from passive actors working with and for mercantile capital to more independent entrepreneurs, who themselves got involved in the trade of wool and woollens. In the fourteenth century they became the pivotal actors around which the industry was organised. The specialist craftsmen, organised in guilds since the latter part of the thirteenth century, were able to define their position in the production chain through collective action, while securing their income as far as possible by carefully monitoring the market for skilled and unskilled labour. Wage earners, both the skilled and unskilled workers inside the guild systems, and the many unskilled workers in the processing of wool, most of them women, were subjected to ever more detailed regulation, an insurance system for the entrepreneurs for attributing liability in case of damage and for securing the continuity of the industry by guaranteeing the availability and flexibility of labour. But, despite these changing positions of the various stakeholders, the structural organisation remained the same.

The starting position before 1300 was different, however. The Ypres mercantile elites, controlled the flows of raw materials and finished textiles, and became involved in complex commercial and financial arrangements in England and at the fairs of Champagne. But they had a stake in the manufacturing system as well by controlling the workforce as landlords and through credit arrangements. But instead of developing these networks further and engaging in manufacture directly, they retreated from active involvement, leaving manufacture completely to the cloth entrepreneurs themselves, while fending off these clothiers from commercial networks with only mixed success. So, no mercantile *botteghe* developed in Ypres after 1280, and manufacture remained a game of linking many individual artisans to each other in a chain of production, a task for which only the clothiers and their artisanal know-how concerning the production process were suited. But because the clothiers did not wield the same financial clout as the merchants and because they could probably not exercise the same levels of extra-economic power either – they were, after all, for the most part kept away from direct political power in the city – at the level of the production chain another kind of equilibrium had also to be reached between the clothiers and the guild-organised masters, entrepreneurs in their own right. These were backed up by the collective power of the craft guilds.

Some of these structural differences were even caused by the technologies involved in organising cloth manufacture. There is no doubt that the social position of fullers, usually entrepreneurs controlling what was for a medieval city a substantial workforce on their own premises, or of dyers, who required substantial capital investment to organise their trade, and weavers and shearers, usually small craftsmen when they could not acquire another economic role as clothiers, differed significantly. Furthermore, many small-scale and badly paid domestic workers, usually women, who undoubtedly constituted the majority of the textile workforce in the city were again wholly different from the guild-organised craftsmen in the main textile trades. Some of these differences were caused by access to capital, by gender, but also by the logistics involved in organising workshops.

In the fourteenth century the Flemish and Artesian cloth industries, weakened by the loss of their markets for cheaper fabrics and forced to specialise in high-quality fabrics, met with increasing competition. This competition came from within, from the 'new draperies', mostly located in the smaller towns of the county, from within the Low Countries (Brabant and Holland), but also from abroad. In the end, the taxation of English wool exports and competition from the mainly rural English cloth industry proved fatal for the traditional urban cloth industries, both the old centres and the small-town 'new draperies', yet for almost two centuries Flemish cloth entrepreneurs were able to adapt to changing market and manufacturing circumstances. They did this, however, without significantly altering the overall organisation of manufacture. Product innovation and small adaptations of technology were absorbed within an existing framework which was only partly guild-organised. Mercantile capital, foreign and domestic, was not directly involved in the main stages of production; cloth entrepreneurs were the driving force implementing product innovation while adapting the chain of production to those changing circumstances; skilled craftsmen, in an industry defined by ever more expensive raw materials, became crucial stakeholders in guaranteeing quality and continuity, yet they did not acquire a similar pivotal role to that of the clothiers, so to define the industry in terms of guild organisation is not correct; finally labour markets were gradually formalised and, through the action of guilds and above all guild masters, who monopolised the reproduction of skill from about the 1250s, they were designed to cater for flexible procedures of hiring and controlling the workforce.

So the system evolved. It did not, however, fundamentally change. In the end changing social positions were forced upon the economic actors, and they seem to have accepted quite willingly a new trade-off between production volumes and quality. Merchants retired into the comfortable and safer position of rentiers, investors and regional traders; clothiers gained economic independence; and guild masters achieved more control over labour markets and guild regulation in order to reinforce their economic position. And those new positions in fourteenth-century Ypres seem to have suited all those actors. The true cost of economic change was paid by skilled and unskilled wage earners who could find employment less easily. For all others the unpredictable and high-investment markets of the massive thirteenth-century woollen manufacture with its costly export crises concerning says before 1300 or striped semi-worsteds in the 1320s were abandoned, and instead the emphasis on luxury cloth made markets more predictable and still allowed cloth entrepreneurs and guild masters to have returns upon their investments. This new equilibrium was not easily achieved. The harsh political and social conflicts that characterised fourteenth-century Ypres are evidence of this. But these conflicts, and the involvement of the textile guilds and, although more haphazardly, the cloth entrepreneurs, not only demonstrate heightened social tension (also within the guilds) but also show that small-scale entrepreneurs inside or outside the guilds still hung on to levels of political ambition and social clout.

The Ypres industry, and by extension also most other urban cloth industries in the Low Countries, was therefore a continuous balancing act between all these various stakeholders. In Ypres, an essentially industrial city with high levels of social inequality, but also in Ghent this led to violent clashes between those stakeholders. Conflicts not only clustered around industrial issues (wage levels, entrepreneurial freedom, etc.), but quickly also crystallised in political demands. But it was not only political conflict that affected social organisation. The cloth industry employed substantially more than half of the urban population, from single women spinning yarn to unskilled male and female workers in the weavers' and fullers' workshops to the skilled craftsmen who were employed often on a weekly basis by the guild masters as journeymen. It is they who finally paid the price of the industry's capacity for flexible product innovation. As Ypres geared towards luxury textiles, total employment figures dropped, the share of unskilled workers declined, and the use of expensive raw materials forced entrepreneurs more carefully to control the outworking systems they made use of. Women were ousted from skilled work as guild regulation tightened. In literature, textile workers are often associated with low wages, insecure employment and social polarisation. As employment in the industry declined, paradoxically the share of skilled workers must have risen; as the population fell, Ypres started to conform more to what would be the essence of the late medieval and early modern Low Countries cities, places with strong urban middle classes built around servicing functions and industries with high added value. It is perhaps this evolution, more than the misery of unemployed textile workers, that helps to explain why in the end Ypres abandoned textile manufacture so easily in the early modern period.

Bibliography

Abraham-Thisse, Simonne, 'Kostel Ypersch, gemeyn Ypersch. Les draps d'Ypres en Europe du Nord et de l'Est (XIIIe-XIVe siècles), in Dewilde et al. (eds), *Ypres and the Medieval Cloth Industry*, 125-145.

———, 'Le commerce des draps de Flandre en Europe du Nord : faut-il encore parler du déclin de la draperie flamande au bas Moyen Âge ?', in Boone and Prevenier (eds), *Drapery Production*, 167-206.

Ammanati, Francesco, 'Francesco di Marco Datini's Wool Workshops', in Nigro, Giampiero (ed.), *Francesco di Marco Datini: the Man the Merchant*, (Firenze: Firenze University Press, 2010), 489-514.

Ammann, Hektor, 'Deutschland und die Tuchindustrie Nordwesteuropas im Mittelalter', *Hansische Geschichtsblätter*, 72 (1954), 1-63.

Arnade, Peter, *Realms of Ritual. Burgundian Ceremony and Civic Life in Late Medieval Ghent*. (Ithaca: Cornell University Press, 1996).

Arnoux, Mathieu, 'Relation salariale et temps du travail dans l'industrie médiévale', *Le Moyen Âge*, 115:3 (2009), 557-581.

Bardoel, Agatha Anna, 'The Urban Uprising at Bruges, 1280-1281.Some New Findings about the Rebels and the Partisans', *Revue belge de philologie et d'histoire*, 72 (1994), 761-791.

Bautier, R.H., 'Les foires de Champagne, *Recueils de la Société Jean Bodin*, 5 (1953), 97-148.

Bautier, Robert-Henri, Jeanine Sornay, Francoise Muret, *Les sources de l'histoire économique et sociale du Moyen Âge. 2: Les états de la Maison de Bourgogne*, (Paris: CNRS, 1984).

Beattie, Cordelia, 'The Problem of Women's Work Identities in Post Black Death England', in James Bothwell, P.J.P. Goldberg and W. Mark Ormrod (eds), *The Problem of Labour in Fourteenth-Century England*, (York: Boydell and Brewer, 2000), 1-19.

Beck, Patrice (eds), *L'innovation technique au Moyen Âge. Actes du VIe Congrès international d'Archéologie Médiévale (1-5 Octobre 1996, Dijon – Mont Beuvray – Chenôve – Le Creusot – Montbard)*, (Caen: Société d'Archéologie Médiévale, 1998).

Bell, Adrian R., Chris Brooks and Tony K. Moore, 'The Credit Relationship between Henry III and Merchants of Douai and Ypres 1247-70', *Economic History Review*, 67 (2014), 123-145.

Benoit, Paul, 'Au four et au moulin: innovation et conjoncture', in Beck (ed.), *L'innovation technique au Moyen Âge*, 293-301.

Bervoets, Leen, *Quicumque in villa per annum unum et per diem unum manserit, liber erit. De genese van het poorterschap in de dertiende-eeuwse steden van de Vlaamse ruimte*, (Ghent: unpublished Phd Ghent University, 2022).

Bigwood, Georges, *Le régime juridique et économique du commerce de l'argent dans la Belgique du Moyen âge*, (Brussels: Hayez, 1920-1921).

Billen, Claire and David Kusman, 'Les affaires, la clienteèle et les scrupules de Jehan Biérenghier, usurier tournaisien († 1305). Crédit et usure à Tournai au XIIIe et au début du XIVe siècle', *Histoire urbaine*, 51 (2018), 41-70.

———— and Marc Boone, 'Pirenne in Brussels before 1930. Guillaume Des Marez and the Relationship Between a Master and his Student', *Revue belge d'histoire contemporaine*, 41 (2011), 459-485.

———— and ————, *Bans et édits pour la ville de Tournai en temps de peste (1349-1351). Les transcriptions retrouvées de Frédéric Hennebert*, (Brussels: Commission royale d'Histoire, 2021).

Blockmans, Wim, 'Transactions at the Fairs of Champagne and Flanders, 1249-1291', in Simonetta Cavaciocchi (ed.), *Fiere e mercati nella integrazione delle economie europee, secc. XIII–XVIII: atti della trentaduesima settimana di studi, 8-12 maggio 2000* (Florence: Le Monnier, 2001).

Blondé, Bruno, Frederik Buylaert, Jan Dumolyn, Jord Hanus and Peter Stabel, 'Living Together in the City: Social Relationships Between Norm and Practice', in Blondé. et al. (eds), *City and Society*, 59-92.

————, Marc Boone and Anne-Laure Van Bruaene (eds), *City and Society in the Low Countries, 1100-1600*, (Cambridge: CUP, 2018).

Bonenfant, Paul, John Bartier and Andrée Van Nieuwenhuysen, *Ordonnances de Philippe le Hardi, de Marguerite de Male et de Jean sans Peur, 1381-1419, t. I (1381-1393)*, (Brussels, 1965).

Boone, Marc and Hanno Brand, 'Vollersoproeren en collectieve actie in Gent en Leiden in de 14de-15de eeuw, in: Tijdschrift voor sociale geschiedenis', 19 (1993), 168-192.Boone, Marc and Jelle Haemers, 'The common good: governance, discipline and political culture', in Blonde et al. (eds), *City and society*, 93-127.

———— and Walter Prevenier (eds), *Drapery Production in the Late Medieval Low Countries: Markets and Strategies for Survival (14th-16th Centuries)*, (Leuven/Apeldoorn: Garant eds, 1993).

————, 'Apologie d'un Banquier Médiéval: Tommaso Portinari et l'Etat Bourguignon', *Le Moyen Âge*, 105: 1 (1999), 31-54.

————, 'Centre et périphéries: les facteurs de croissance économique au Moyen Âge', in *La crescita economica dell'Occidente medievale. Un tema storico non ancora esaurito. Pistoia, 14-17 maggio 2015* (Rome/Pistoia: Viella, 2015), 363-382.

————, 'Destroying and Reconstructing the City. The Inculcation and Arrogation of Princely Power in the Burgundian-Habsburg Netherlands (Foureenth-Sixteenth Centuries)', in Jonas Braekevelt et al. (eds), *City and State in the Medieval Low Countries. Collected Studies by Marc Boone*, (Turnhout: Brepols, 2021), 163-186.

————, 'L'industrie textile à Gand au bas Moyen Âge ou les resurrections successives d'une activité réputée moribonde', in Boone en Prevenier (eds), La draperie ancienne des Pays-Bas, 15-58.

————, 'Nieuwe teksten over de Gentse draperie: wolaanvoer, productiewijze en controlepraktijken (ca. 1456-1468)', *Bulletin de la Commission royale d'Histoire*, 154 (1988), 1-61.

————, 'Social Conflicts in the Cloth Industry of Ypres (Late 13th-Early 14th Century): The Cockerulle Reconsidered', in Marc De Wilde, et al., *Ypres and the Medieval Cloth Industry*, 147-155.

———, *A la recherche d'une modernité civique. La société urbaine des anciens Pays-Bas au bas Moyen Âge* (Brussels: ULB, 2010).
Bossuyt, Stijn, *Rijke stinkerds. Editie en analyse van de middeleeuwse grafinscripties te Ieper (1118-1566)*, (Leuven: unpublished MA, 2000).
Boussemaere, Pieter, 'De Ieperse lakenproductie in de veertiende eeuw opnieuw berekend aan de hand van de lakenloodjes', *Jaarboek voor Middeleeuwse Geschiedenis*, 3 (2000), 131-161.
Bove, Boris, 'Une sombre affaire de teinturerie: organisation corporative et territoires de production à Saint-Denis à la fin du XIVe siècle', *Médiévales: Langue, textes, histoire*, 69 (2015), 105-128.
Braekevelt, Jonas, Frederik Buylaert, Jan Dumolyn, and Jelle Haemers, 'The Politics of Factional Conflict in Late Medieval Flanders', *Historical Research*, 85 (2012), pp. 13-31.
Brand, Hanno and Peter Stabel, 'De ontwikkeling van vollerslonen in enkele laat-middeleeuwse textielcentra in de Nederlanden. Een poging tot reconstructie' in Jean-Marie Duvosquel and Erik Thoen, *Peasants and townsmen in medieval Europe. Studia in honorem Adriaan Verhulst*, (Gent: Snoeck, 1995), 203-222.
Braudel, Fernand, *Civilisation matérielle, économie et capitalisme XVe-XVIIIe siècles*, (Paris: Colin, 1979).
———, *Material Civilization and Capitalism. Vol. 2. The Wheels of Commerce*, (London: Collins, 1982).
Braunstein, Philippe, 'Savoir et savoir-faire: les transferts techniques', in Beck (ed.), *L'innovation technique au Moyen Âge*, 303-311. Cardon, Dominique, 'Des toisons aux étoffes, la deuxième vague d'innovations dans l'industrie lainière médiévale', in Beck (ed.), *L'innovation technique au Moyen Âge*, 35-42.
Brenner, Robert P., 'The Low Countries in the Transition to Capitalism', *Journal of Agrarian Change*, 1 (2001), 169-241.
Brown, Judith C., 'The Economic Decline of Tuscany: the Role of the Rural Economy', in *Florence and Milan. Comparisons and Relations*, (Florence: La Nuova Italia, 1989).
Brulez, Wilfrid, 'De handelsbalans der Nederlanden in het midden van de 16de eeuw', *Bijdragen voor de Geschiedenis der Nederlanden*, 21 (1967), 278-310.
Cardon, Dominique, *La draperie au Moyen Âge: essor d'une grande industrie européenne* (Paris: PUF, 1999).
Carlier, Myriam and Peter Stabel, 'Questions de moralité dans les villes de la Flandre au bas Moyen Âge', in Cauchies. and Bousmar, *Faire bans*, pp. 241-262.
Carolus-Barré, Louis, 'Les XVII villes, une hanse vouée au grand commerce de la draperie', *Académie des inscriptions et belles-lettres*, 109: 1 (1965), 20-30.
Carus-Wilson, 'Technical Innovation and the Emergence of the Grande Industrie', in S. Marotti (ed.), *Produttività e tecnologie nei secoli XII-XVIII*, (Florence: Le Monnier, 1981), 359-360.
Carus-Wilson, E.M., 'An industrial Revolution of the Thirteenth Century', *Economic History Review*, 11 (1941), 39-60.
Cauchies, Jean-Marie and Eric Bousmar (eds), *Faire bans, edictz et status. Légiférer dans la ville médiévale*, (Brussels: Presses de l'Université Saint-Louis, 2001),
Chorley, Patrick, 'The Cloth Exports of Flanders and Northern France During the Thirteenth Century: A Luxury Trade?', *Economic History Review*, 40 (1987), 349-379.

———, 'The Ypres Cloth Industry, 1200-1350: the Pattern of Change in Output and Demand', in Dewilde et al. (eds), *Ypres and the Medieval Cloth Industry*, 111-124.

Cipolla, Carlo M., *Clocks and Culture, 1300-1700* (New York, 1967).

Clark, Peter and Denis Menjot (eds), *Subaltern City? Alternative and Peripheral Urban Spaces in the Pre-Modern Period (13th-18th centuries)*, (Turnhout: Brepols, 2019).

Clauzel, Denis and S. Calonne, 'Artisanat rural et marché urbain: la draperie à Lille et dans ses campagnes à la fin du Moyen Âge et au XVIe siècle', *Revue du Nord*, 72 (1990), 531-573.

Cohn Jr, Samuel K., *Lust for Liberty: The Politics of Social Revolt in Medieval Europe, 1200-1425*, (Cambridge, Mass.: Harvard University Press, 2006).

———., Samuel K., *Popular Protest in Late Medieval Europe: Italy, France, and Flanders* (Cambridge: Cambridge University Press, 2004).

Coornaert, Emile, 'Draperies rurales, draperies urbaines. L'évolution de l'industrie flamande au Moyen Âge et au XVIe siècle, *Revue Belge de Philologie et d'Histoire*, 28 (1950), 60-96.

———, *Un centre industriel d'autrefois. La draperie-sayetterie d'Hondschoote. XIVe-XVIIIe siècle*, (Paris: PUF, 1930).

Coppejans-Desmedt, Hilda, 'Handel en handelaars op de Vlaamse jaarmarkten in de tweede helft van de XIIIde eeuw', *Albym Carlos Wyffels* (Brussel: Algemeen Rijksarchief, 1987), 69-88.

Dauchy, Serge (eds), *Les arrets et jugés du Parlement de Paris sur appels flamands conservés dans les registres du Parlement*, 3 vols (Brussels: Ministère de la justice, 1966-2002).

Dauphant, Léonard, *Le royaume des Quatre rivières. L'espace politique français (1380-1515)*, (Paris: Seyssel, 2012).

De Hemptinne, Thérèse and Martha Howell, 'The "Lettres de Foire" of Ypres (Second Half of 13th Century): Windows into the Commercial Culture of a Late Medieval Industrial Giant', in *Les documents du commerce et des marchands entre Moyen Âge et époque moderne (XIIe-XVIIe siècle)*, (Rome: Collection de l'École française de Rome, 2018), 133-152.

De La Roncière, Charles, *Prix et salaires á Florence au XIVe siècle. 1280-1380*, (Rome: Ecole française de Rome, 1982).

De Moor, Tine and Jan Luiten van Zanden, 'Girl Power: the European Marriage Pattern and Labour Markets in the North Sea Region in the Late Medieval and Early Modern Period', *Economic History Review*, 63:1 (2010), 1-33.

De Munck, Bert, *Guilds, Labour and the Urban Body Politic. Fabricating Community in the Southern Netherlands, 1300-1800*, (London: Routledge, 2019).

De Pauw, Napoleon, *Ypre jeghen Poperinghe angaende den verbonden. Gedingstukken der XIVe eeuw nopens het laken*, (Brussels: Koninklijke Vlaamse Academie voor Taal en Letterkunde, 1899).

De Pelsmaeker, Prosper, 'Le courtage à Ypres aux XIIIe et XIVe siècles', *Bulletin de la Commission royale d'histoire*, 74 (1905), 439-484.

———, *Coutumes des pays et comté de Flandre: quartier d'Ypres, VI, Régistres aux sentences des échevins d'Ypres*, (Brussels: Royal Academy, 1914).

———, *Registres aux sentences des échevins d'Ypres. Coutumes des pays et comté de Flandre. Quartier d'Ypres*, (Brussels: Goemaere, 1914).

de Pleijt, Alexandra M. and Jan Luiten van Zanden, 'Two Worlds of Female Labour: Gender Wage Inequality in Western Europe, 1300-1800', *The Economic History Review*, 74: 3 (2021), 611-638.

De Poerck, Guy, *La draperie médiévale en Flandre et en Artois: Technique et terminologie*, (Bruges: De Tempel, 1951).

De Roover, Raymond, 'A Florentine Firm of Cloth Manufacturers: Management and Organization of a Sixteenth-Century Business', in Julius Kirchner (ed.), *Business, Banking, and Economic Thought in Late Medieval and Early Modern Europe*, (Chicago: Chicago University Press, 1974), 85-118.

De Sagher, H.-E., J.-H. De Sagher, Hans Van Werveke and Carlos Wyffels (eds), *Recueil des documents relatifs à l'histoire de l'industrie drapière en Flandre. Deuxième parie. Le sud-Ouest de la Flandre depuis l'époque bourguignonne*, (Brussels: Commission royale d'Histoire, 1951-1965).

De Smet, J., 'Les keures inédites du plus ancien livre de keures d'Ypres', *Bulletin de la Commission Royale d'Histoire*, 94 (1930), 389-481.

De Valériola, Sébastien, 'Le corpus des chirographes yprois, témoin essentiel d'un réseau de crédit du XIIIe siècle', *Bulletin de la Commission royale d'histoire*, 185 (2019), 5-74.

De Witte, Hubert, 'Craft in the Town of Brugge: Archaeological Evidence', in *Lübecker Kolloquium zur Stadtarchäologie im Hanseraum, V: Das Handwerk*. Ed. Gläser, Manfred, (Lübeck: Schmidt-Römhild, 2006), 115-122.

Delumeau, Jean, *L'alun de Rome, XVe-XIXe siècles*, (Paris: SEVPEN, 1962).

Demey, Jules, 'De mislukte aanpassingen van de nieuwe draperie, de saainijverheid en de lichte draperie te Ieper', *Tijdschrift voor Geschiedenis*, 63 (1950), 222-235 en Mus, *Prisma*, 171.

———, 'De Vlaamse ondernemer in de middeleeuwse nijverheid: de Ieperse drapiers en "upsetters" op het einde der XIIIe en in de XIVe eeuw', *Bijdragen voor de Geschiedenis der Nederlanden*, 4 (1949-1950), 1-15 en Mus, *Prisma*, 143-156).

———, 'Proeve tot raming van de bevolking en weefgetouwen te Ieper van de XIIIe tot de XVIIe eeuw', *Revue Belge de Philologie et d'Histoire*, 28 (1950), 1031-1048 en Mus, *Prisma*, 157-170.

Derville, Alain, 'Les draperies flamandes et artésiennes vers 1250-1350 (Quelques considérations critiques et problématiques)', *Revue du Nord*, 54: 215 (1972), 353-370.

———, *Histoire de Saint-Omer*, (Lille: Presses universitaires de Lille, 1981).

———, *Saint-Omer. Des origines ou débuts du 14e siècle*, (Lille: Presses universitaires de Lille, 1995).

Des Marez, Guillaume and E. De Sagher, *Comptes de la ville d'Ypres de 1267 à 1329*, (Brussels: Commission royale d'Histoire, 1902-1913).

———, *Etude sur la propriété foncière dans les villes du Moyen Âge et spécialement en Flandre*, (Brussels: Engelcke, 1898).

———, *La lettre de foire à Ypres au XIIIe siècle. Contribution à l'étude des papiers de crédit*, (Brussels: Académie royale des Sciences, 60:6, 1900-1901).

Dewilde, Marc and Stephan van Bellingen, 'Excavating a Suburb of Medieval Ypres (Belgium): Evidence for the Cloth Industry?', in Dewilde et al., *Ypres and the Medieval Cloth Industry*, 57-72.

———, Anton Ervynck and Alexis Wielemans (eds), *Ypres and the Medieval Cloth Industry in Flanders. Archaeological and Historical Contributions*, (Brussels: Institute for the Archaeological Heritage, 1998).

Diegerick, Isidore, 'Les drapiers yprois et la conspiration manquée. Épisode de l'histoire d'Ypres (1428-1429)', *Annales de la Société d'Émulation de Bruges*, 14 (1855-1856), 285-310.

Dini, Bruno, 'I lavoratori dell'Arte della Lana a Firenze nel XIV e XV secolo', in id., *Manifattura, commercio e banca*, (Fiesole: Nardini, 2001), 141-171.

———, 'L'industria tessile italianan nel tardo Medioevo', in id., *Saggi su una economia-mono: Firenze e l'Italia fra Mediterraneo ed Europa (secc. XIII-XVI)*, (Pisa: Pacini, 1995), 13-49.

Doehaerd, Renée, *Les relations commerciales entre Gênes, la Belgique et l'Outremont aux XIIIe et XIVe siècles*, (Brussels: Palais des Académies, 1941).

Doudelez, Georges, 'La révolution communale de 1280 à Ypres', *Revue des Questions historiques*, (1938), nr. 2, 58-78, nr. 3-4, 3-25 and (1939), nr. 1 21-70 and Mus, *Prisma*, 188-294.

Dumolyn, Jan and Bart Lambert, 'A Chemical Compound in a Capitalist Commodity Chain: The Production, Distribution and Industrial Use of Alum in the Mediterranean and the Textile Centers of the Low Countries (Thirteenth-Sixteenth Centuries)', *Journal of Early Modern History*, 22 (2018) 238-258.

——— and Jelle Haemers, 'Patterns of Urban Rebellion in Medieval Flanders', *Journal of Medieval History*, 31 (2005), 369-393.

——— and ———, 'Reclaiming the Common Sphere of the City: The Revival of the Bruges Commune in the Late Thirteenth Century', in Jean-Philippe Genet (ed.), *La Légitimité implicite*, 1, (Paris: Publications de l'École française de Rome, 2015), 161-188.

——— and ———, 'Takehan, Cokerulle, and Mutemaque: Naming Collective Action in the Later Medieval Low Countries', in Justine Firnhaber-Baker and Dirk Schoenars (eds), *The Routledge History Handbook of Medieval Revolt*, (London: Routledge, 2017), 39-54.

——— and ———, 'A Bad Chicken Was Brooding. Subversive Speech in Late Medieval Flanders', *Past and Present*, 214 (2012), 45-86.

———, 'Criers and Shouters. The Discourse on Radical Urban Rebels in Late Medieval Flanders', *Journal of Social History*, 42:1 (2008), 111-135.

———, '*Le povre peuple estoit moult oprimé*: Elite Discourses on "the People" in the Burgundian Netherlands (Fourteenth to Fifteenth Centuries)', *French History*, 23 (2009), 171-92.

———, Georges Declercq and Jelle Haemers, 'Social Groups, Political Power and Institutions I, c. 1100–c. 1300', in Andrew Brown and Jan Dumolyn (eds), *Medieval Bruges c. 850-1550*, (Cambridge: Cambridge University Press, 2018), 124-151.

———, Wouter Ryckbosch & Mathijs Speecke, 'Did Inequality Produce Medieval Revolt? The Material Position and Political Agency of Textile Workers During the Flemish Revolt of 1379-1385', *Social History*, 46:4 (2021), 372-405.

DuPlessis, Robert S. and Martha C. Howell, 'Reconsidering the Early Modern Urban Economy: the Case of Leiden and Lille', *Past and Present*, 94 (1982), 49-84.

———, *Lille and the Dutch Revolt: urban stability in an era of revolution 1500-1582*, (Cambridge: Cambridge University Press, 1991).

———, *Transitions to Capitalism in Early Modern Europe* (Cambridge: Cambridge University Press, 1997).

Endrei Walter, Changements dans la productivité lainière au Moyen Âge, *Annales. Economies, sociétés, civilisations*. 26: 6 (1971), pp. 1291-1299.

Endrei, Walter, 'Manufacturing a Piece of Woollen Cloth in Medieval Flanders: How Many Work Hours', in Erik Aerts and John Munro (eds), *Textiles of the Low Countries in European Economic History*, (Leuven: Peeters, 1990), 14-23.

———, 'The Productivity of Weaving in Late Medieval Flanders', in Negley B. Harte, and K. G. Ponting (eds), *Cloth and Clothing in Medieval Europe*, (London: Heinemann Educational Books, 1983) 108-119.

Epstein, Stephan R. and Maarten Prak (eds), *Guilds, Innovation and the European Economy 1400-1800.* (London: Routledge, 2008).

———, 'Craft Guilds in the Premodern Economy: a Discussion', *Economic History Review* 61:1 (2008), 155-174.

———, 'Craft Guilds, Apprenticeship, and Technological Change in Preindustrial Europe', *Journal of Economic History* 58 (1998), 684-713.

Espinas, Georges and Henri Pirenne (eds), *Recueil des documents relatifs à l'histoire de l'industrie drapière*, 4 vol. (Brussels: Commission royale d'Histoire, 1904-1920).

———, *La draperie dans la Flandre française au Moyen Âge*, (Paris: Picard, 1923).

———, *La vie urbaine de Douai au Moyen Âge*, 4 vols (Paris: Picard, 1913).

———, *Les origines du capitalisme I: Sire Jehan Boinebroke patricien et drapier douaisien*, (Lille: Raoust, 1933).

Farmer, Sharon, *The Silk Industries of Medieval Paris. Artisanal Migration, Technological Innovation, and Gendered Experience*, (Philadelphia: University of Pennsylvania Press, 2017).

Fecheyr Selma, 'Het stadspatriciaat te Ieper in de 13e eeuw', *Jaarboek van het XXXVIe Congres van de Federatie van de kringen voor Geschiedenis en Oudheidkunde van België*, 2 (1956), 197-204 and Mus, *Prisma*, 295-303.

Franceschi, Franco and Ilaria Taddei, *Les villes d'Italie du milieu du XIIe s. au milieu du XIVe siècle : économies, sociétés, pouvoirs, cultures*, (Rosny-sous-Bois: Bréal, 2004).

———, 'Famille et travail dans les villes italiennes du XIIIe au XVe siècle', in Myriam Carlier and Tim Soens (eds), *The Household in Late Medieval Cities, Italy and Northwestern Europe Compared*, (Leuven: Garant, 2001), 105-120.

———, 'Les enfants au travail dans l'industrie textile florentine des XIVe et XVe siècles', *Médiévales*, 30 (1996), 69-82.

———, 'The Economy: Work and Wealth', in John M. Najemy (ed.), *Italy in the Age of the Renaissance, 1300-1550*, (Oxford: Oxford University Press, 2004), 124-144 and 277-280.

———, *Oltre il tumulto. I lavoratori fiorentini dell'Arte della Lana fra Tre e Quattrocento*, (Firenze: Olschki, 1993).

Francesci, Franco, 'Woollen Luxury Cloth in Late Medieval Italy', in Bart Lambert and Katherine Anne Wilson (eds), *Europe's Rich Fabric: The Consumption, Commercialisation, and Production of Luxury Textiles in Italy, the Low Countries and Neighbouring Territories (Fourteenth-Sixteenth Centuries)*, (Farnham: Ashgate, 2016), 181-204.

Geens, Sam, *A Golden Age for Labour? Living Standards and Income Inequality in the Southern Low Countries and the Republic of Florence Before and After the Black Death (1275-1550)*, (Antwerp: University of Antwerp, forthcoming).

Gilliodts-Van Severen, Louis, *Coutumes des pays et comté de Flandre: quartier d'Ypres, II, Sources et développement de la coutume d'Ypres*, (Brussels: Royal Academy, 1908);.

Goldthwaite, Richard A., *The Economy of Renaissance Florence*, (Baltimore: The Johns Hopkins University Press, 2009).

Greve, Anke, *Hansische Kaufleute, Hosteliers und Herbergen im Brügge des 14. und 15. Jahrhunderts*, (Frankfurt: Peter Lang, 2012).

Groppi, A., *Il lavoro delle donne*, (Rome/Bari: Laterza, 1996).

Gustafsson, Bo, 'The Rise and Economic Behaviour of Medieval Craft Guilds', in id. (ed.), *Power and economic institutions. Reinterpretations in economic history* (Aldershot, 1991), 69-106.

Haemers, Jelle and Dries Merlevede, '*Le commun se esmeut*. Een onderzoek naar het politieke optreden van "het gemeen" in het kader van de Gentse opstand (1379-1385)', *Belgisch tijdschrift voor filologie en geschiedenis*, 88 (2010), 177-204.

——— and Valerie Vrancken, 'Libels in the City. Bill-Casting in Fifteenth-Century Flanders and Brabant', *Medieval Low Countries*, 4 (2017), 165-187.

———, 'Bloed en inkt. Een nieuwe blik op opstand en geweld te Leuven, 1360-1383', *Stadsgeschiedenis*, 7 (2012), 141-164.

———, 'Filthy and Indecent Words. Insults, Defamation and Urban Politics in Flanders and Brabant, 1400-1600', in Jan Dumolyn et al. (eds), *The Voices of the People in Late Medieval Europe. Communication and Popular Politics*, (Turnhout, Brepols, 2014), 247-267.

———, 'Révolte et requête. Les gens de métiers et les conflits sociaux dans les villes de Flandre (XIIIe-XVe siècle)', *Revue historique*, 318 (2016), 27-56.

———, 'The Identity of the Urban "Commoners" in 13th Century Flanders', *Imago Temporis: Medium Aevum*, 10 (2016), 191-213.

———, *For the Common Good. State Power and Urban Revolts in the Reign of Mary of Burgundy (1477-1482)*, (Turnhout: Brepols, 2009).

Haquette, Bertrand, 'Des lices et des joncs: rivière et draperies de la vallée de la Lys à la fin du Moyen Âge', *Revue du Nord*, 79 (1997), 859-882.

Haverkamp, Alfred, (eds.), *Information, Kommunikation und Selbstdarstellung in mittelalterlichen Gemeinden*, (München: Oldenbourg, 1998)Herlihy, David, *The Black Death and the Transformation of the West*, (Cambridge, Mass.: Harvard University Press, 1985).

Hillewaert Bieke en Van Besien Elisabeth, *Jaarverslag 2005: Raakvlak, Intergemeentelijke Dienst Archeologie Brugge & Ommeland*, (Bruges: 2005).

Hofenk-De Graaff, Judith H., 'The Chemistry of Red Dyestuffs in Medieval and Early Modern Europe', in Negley B. Harte and K.G. Ponting, *Cloth and Clothing in Medieval Europe: Essays in Memory of Professor E.M. Carus-Wilson. .*, Pasold Studies in Textile History, 2, (London: Heinemann Educational Books, 1983), 71-79.

Holbach, Rudolf, *Frühformen von Verlag und Grossbetrieb in der gewerblichen Produktion*, (Stuttgart: Steiner, 1994).

Hooghe, Filip, 'De Cokerulle (1280-1285). Een conflict tussen Ieper en zijn hinterland over de lakennijverheid', *Handelingen Genootschap 'Société d'Emulation' Brugge*, 143 (2006), 393-448.

Howell, *Commerce before Capitalism in Europe 1300-1600*, (Cambridge: Cambridge University Press, 2010).

Howell, Martha C., 'Achieving the Guild Effect without Guilds: Crafts and Craftsmen in Late Medieval Douai', in Pascale Lambrechts and Jean-Pierre Sosson (eds), *Les métiers au Moyen Âge* (Louvain-la-Neuve: Institut d'Etudes médiévales, 1994), 109-128.

———, 'Credit Networks and Political Actors in Thirteenth-century Ypres', *Past and Present*, 242 (2019), 3-36.

———, 'Un réseau de crédit à Ypres au XIIIe siècle. Les reconnaissances de dettes de 1249-1291', *Histoire urbaine*, 51 (2018), 19-40.

———, 'Weathering Crisis, Managing Change: the Emergence of a New Socioeconomic Order in Douai at the End of the Middle Ages', in Boone and Prevenier (eds), *La draperie*, 85-88.

———, *The Marriage Exchange: Property, Social Place, and Gender in Cities of the Low Countries, 1300-1550* (Chicago: University of Chicago Press, 1998).

———, *Women, Production and Patriarchy in late medieval cities*, (Chicago: University of Chicago Press, 1986),

Hunt, Edwin S., *The Medieval Super-Companies: a Study of the Peruzzi Company of Florence*, (Cambridge: Cambridge university Press, 1994).

Hutton, Shennan, *Women and Economic Activities in Late Medieval Ghent*, (London, Palgrave, 2011).

Kaptein, K., *De Hollandse textielnijverheid 1350-1600: conjunctuur en continuïteit*, (Hilversum, Verloren, 1998).

Kittel, Ellen and Kurt Queller, 'Whether Man or Woman… Gender Inclusivity in the Town Ordinances of Medieval Douai', *Journal of Medieval and Early Modern Studies*, 30 (2000), 63-100.

Kusman, David, *Usuriers publics et banquiers du Prince. Le rôle économique des financiers piémontais dans les villes du duché de Brabant (XIIIe-XIVe siècle)*, (Turnhout, Brepols, 2012).

Lambert, Bart and Milan Pajic 'Immigration and the Common Profit: Native Cloth Workers, Flemish Exiles, and Royal Policy in Fourteenth-Century London', *Journal of British Studies*, 55: 4 (2016), 633-657.

Landes, David S., *Revolution in Time: Clocks and the Making of the Modern World*, (Cambridge MA: Harvard University Press, 1983).

Langhals, Heinz, 'Die Farben des Mittelalters aus der Sicht des Naturwissenschaftlers', in *Farbe im Mittelalter: Materialität – Medialität – Semantik*. Ed. Bennewitz, Ingrid and Schindler, Andrea, (Berlin: Akademie Verlag, 2011), 1017-1024.

Lantschner, Patrick, *The Logic of Political Conflict in Medieval Cities: Italy and the Southern Low Countries, 1370-1440*, (Oxford and New York: Oxford University Press, 2015).

Laurent, Henri, *Un grand commerce d'exportation au Moyen Âge: la draperie des Pays Bas en France et dans les pays mediterranéens, XIIe-XVe siècle*, (Paris: Droz, 1935).

Le Goff, Jacques, 'Temps de l'église et du marchand', *Annales ESC*, 15 (1960), 417-433.

Lecuppre-Desjardin, Elodie and Anne-Laure van Bruaene (eds), *De Bono Communi. The Discourse and Practice of the Common Good in the European City, 13th-16th Centuries*, (Turnhout, Brepols, 2010).

Lee, John S., *The Medieval Clothier*, (London: Boydell & Brewer, 2018).

Leroux, Laure, *Les cloches et société médiévale. Les sonneries de Tournai au Moyen Âge*, (Tournai: Art et histoire, 2011).

Lesnikov, Michail P., *Die Handelsbücher des hansischen Kaufmanns Veckinchusen*. (Berlin: Akademie Verlag, 1973).
Liagre, Léone, 'Le commerce de l'alun en Flandre', *Le Moyen Âge*, 61 (1955), 177-206.
Lis, Catharina and Hugo Soly, *Worthy Efforts: Attitudes to Work and Workers in Pre-Industrial Europe*, (Leiden: Brill, 2012).
—— and Soly, Hugo. 'Subcontracting in Guild-Based Export Trades, Thirteenth-Eighteenth Centuries'. In Stephan R. Epstein and and Maarten Prak (eds.), *Guilds, Innovation, and the European Economy, 1400-1800*. (Cambridge: University Press, 2008), 81-113.
Lloyd, T.H., *The English Wool Trade in the Middle Ages*, (Cambridge: Cambridge University Press, 1977).
Lusignan, Serge, *Essai d'histoire sociolinguistique. Le français picard au Moyen Âge*, (Paris: Garnier, 2012).
Maire Vigueur, Jean-Claude, *Cavaliers et citoyens. Guerre, conflits, et société dans l'Italie communale XIIe-XIIIe siècles*, (Paris: Editions de la EHESS, 2003).
Melis, Federigo, 'La diffusione nel Mediterraneo occidentale dei panni di Wervicq e delle altre città della Lys attorno al 1400', in *Studi in onore di Amintore Fanfani*, vol. 3, (Milan: Giuffre, 1962), 219-243.
——, *Aspetti della vita economica medievale (Studi nell'archivio Datini di Prato)*, (Firenze: Olschki, 1962).
Merlevede, J., *De Ieperse stadsfinanciën (1280-1330): bijdrage tot de studie van een Vlaamse stad*, (Brussels: VUB Centrum voor sociale structuren, 1980).
Mertens, Wenceslaus, 'Changes in the Production and Export of Mechelen Cloth (1330-1530)', in Erik Aerts and John Munro (eds), *Textiles of the Low Countries in European Economic History*, (Leuven: Peeters, 1990), 114-123.
Milgrom, Paul R., Douglass C. North and Barry R. Weingast, 'The Role of Institutions in the Revival of Trade: the Law Merchant, Private Judges and the Champagne Fairs', *Economics and Politics*, Vol. 2 (1990), 1-23.
Moerman, Marieke M., Diepgaande analyse van twee Ieperse kaarten: het stadsplan van Thévelin-Destrée (1564) ende gravure over het beleg van Ieper van Guillaume du Tielt (1610). (Ghent: unpublished Master's thesis Ghent University, 2010).
Mokyr, Joel, *The Gifts of Athena: Historical Origins of the Knowledge Economy*, (Princeton: Princeton University Press, 2002).
Molà, Luca, *The Silk Industry The Silk Industry of Renaissance Venice*, (Baltimore: Johns Hopkins University Press, 2000).
Mollat, Michel, Philippe Wolff, *Ongles bleus, Jacques et Ciompi: les révolutions populaires en Europe aux XIVe et XVe siècles*, (Paris: Calmann-Lévy, 1970).
Monnas, Lisa, 'Some Medieval Colour Terms for Textiles', *Medieval Clothing and Textiles*, 10 (2014), 25-57.
Moore, E.W., *The Fairs of Medieval England: an Introductory Study*, (Toronto: Pontifical Institute of Mediaeval Studies, 1985).
Moreels, Renilde, *Een web van verhaaldraden. Een onderzoek van lokale Ieperse stadskronieken over de middeleeuwse historiek, verwantschap en uitgave*, (Leuven: unpublished MA, 2000).

Muldrew, Craig, '"Th'ancient Distaff" and "Whirling Spindle": Measuring the Contribution of Spinning to Household Earnings and the National Economy in England, 1550-1770', *The Economic History Review*, 65:2 (2012), 498-526.

Munro, John H., 'Builders' Wages in Southern England and the Southern Low Countries, 1346-1500', in Simonetta Cavaciocchi (ed.), *L'Edilizia prima della rivoluzione industrial*, (Florence: Le Monnier, 2005), 1013-1076.

———, 'Industrial Protectionism in Medieval Flanders: Urban or National?', in H.A. Miskimin, David Herlihy en A.L. Udovitch (eds), *The Medieval City*, (London/New Haven: Yale University Press, 1977), 229-268.

———, 'Industrial Transformations in the North-West European Textile Trades, *c.* 1290-*c.* 1340: Economic Progress or Economic Crisis?', in Bruce M. S. Campbell (ed.), *Before the Black Death: Studies in the 'Crisis' of the Early Fourteenth Century* (Manchester: Manchester University Press, 1991), 110-148.

———, 'Medieval Woollens: Textiles, Textile Technology, and Industrial Organisation, *c.* 800-1500', in David Jenkins (ed.), *The Cambridge History of Western Textiles* (Cambridge: Cambridge university Press, 2003), 181-227.

———, 'Medieval Woollens: The Western European Woollen Industries and their Struggles for International Markets, *c.* 1000-1500', in David Jenkins (ed.), *The Cambridge History of Western Textiles* (Cambridge: Cambridge university Press, 2003), 228-324.

———, 'The Medieval Scarlet and the Economics of Sartorial Splendour', in *Cloth and Clothing in Medieval Europe: Essays in Memory of Professor E.M. Carus-Wilson*. Ed. Harte, N.B. & Ponting, K.G., Pasold Studies in Textile History, 2 (London: Heinemann Educational Books, 1983), 13-70.

———, 'The "New Institutional Economics" and the Changing Fortunes of Fairs in Medieval and Early Modern Europe: the Textile Trades, Warfare, and Transaction Costs', *Vierteljahrschrift für Sozial- und Wirtschaftsgeschichte*, 88 (2001), 1-47.

———, 'The Origins of the English "New Draperies": the Resurrection of an Old Flemish Industry, 1270-1570', in Nigley Harte en D. Coleman (eds), *The New Draperies*, (Oxford/New York: Pasold Studies, 1997), 35-127.

———, 'The Symbiosis of Towns and Textiles: Urban Institutions and the Changing Fortunes of Cloth Manufacturing in the Low Countries and England, 1270-1570', *Journal of Early Modern History*, 3 (1999), 1-74.

———, 'Urban Regulation and Monopolistic Competition in the Textile Industries of the Late Medieval Low Countries', in Erik Aerts and John H. Munro (eds), *Textiles of the Low Countries in European Economic History*, (Leuven: Peeters, 1990), 41-52.

———, 'Wage-Stickiness, Monetary Changes, and Real Incomes in Late-Medieval England and the Low Countries, 1300-1500: Did Money Matter?', *Research in Economic History*, 21 (2003), 185-297.

Munro, Jonh H., 'Wool-Price Schedules and the Qqualities of English Wools in the Later Middle Ages, *c.* 1270-1499', *Textile History*, 9 (1978), 118-169.

Murray, James M., *Bruges, Cradle of Capitalism, 1280-1390*. (Cambridge: Cambridge University Press, 2005).

Mus, Octaaf and Paul Trio, *De geschiedenis van de middeleeuwse grootstad Ieper: van Karolingische villa tot de destructie in 1914,* (Ieper: Stad Ieper, 2010).

——, 'De localisatie van de Ieperse 12de-eeuwse vesting', *Handelingen van het Genootschap voor Geschiedenis te Brugge,* 136 (1999), 33-101.

——, 'De verhouding van de waard tot de drapier in de Kortrijkse draperie op het einde van de 15e eeuw', *Handelingen van het Genootschap voor Geschiedenis te Brugge,* 98 (1961), 156-218.

——, 'Het aandeel van de Ieperlingen in de Engelse wolexport 1280-1330', in *Economische Geschiedenis van België. Behandeling van de bronnen en* problematiek, (Brussel, 1972, 233-259, and Mus, *Prisma,* 322-355.

——, 'Het beleg van Ieper in 1383. De vernietiging van de buitenwijken en de gevolgen voor de binnenstad en de bewoners ervan', in *Verwoesting en wederopbouw van steden van de middeleeuwen tot heden,* (Brussel: Gemeentekrediet, 1999), 21-50.

——, 'Pieter Lansaem, promotor van de nieuwe draperie te Ieper in de tweede helft van de 15de eeuw', *Handelingen van het Genootschap voor Geschiedenis te Brugge,* 130 (1993), 67-72.

——, *Inventaris van het archief van de Commissie van Openbare Onderstand Ieper: Oud regime zonder oorkonden,* (Ypres: Gemeentebestuur Ieper, 1972).

——, *Prisma van de Ieperse Geschiedenis,* (Ieper: Gemeentebestuur Ieper, 1972).

Nicholas, David, 'Commercial Credit and Central Place Function in Thirteenth-Century Ypres', in Lawrin Armstrong, Ivana Elbl and Martin M. Elbl (eds), *Money, Markets and Trade in Late Medieval Europe: Essays in Honour of John H. A. Munro,* (Leiden: Brill, 2007), 310-348.

——, *Medieval Flanders,* (London: Longman, 1992).

——, *The Domestic Life of a Medieval City. Women, Children and the Family in Fourteenth-Century Ghent,* (Lincoln: University of Nebraska Press, 1985).

——, *Town and Countryside: Social, Economic, and Political Tensions in Fourteenth-Century Flanders,* (Bruges: De Tempel, 1971).

Nightingale, Pamela, *A Medieval Mercantile Community. The Grocers' Company and the Politics and Trade of London, 1000-1485,* (New Haven: Yale Un iversity Press, 1995).

Nowé, Henri, *Les baillis comtaux de Flandre. Des origines à la fin du XIVe siècle,* (Brussels: Lamertin, 1929).

Ogilvie, Sheilagh C. and Markus Cerman, 'Proto-Industrialization, Economic Development and Social Change in Early Modern Europe', in id. (eds), *European Proto-Industrialization: An Introductory Handbook,* (Cambridge: Cambridge University Press, 1996), 227-267.

——, *The European Guilds: An Economic Analysis,* (Princeton, NJ: Princeton University Press, 2019).

Ogilvie, Sheilagh, 'Whatever is Right? Economic Institutions in Pre-Industrial Europe', *Economic History Review,* 60:4 (2007) pp. 649-684.

Oldland, John, 'The Clothiers' Century, 1450-1550', *Rural History,* 29 (2018) 29, 1-22.

——, *The English Woollen Industry, c. 1200-c. 1560,* (London: Routledge, 2019).

Papin, Kristof 'Gids voor het Fonds Merghelynck', *Westhoek-Info,* 9 (1993-1994), 133-145.

Pilorget, Julie, 'La fin du Moyen Âge, un moment charnière pour l'histoire des femmes? Les embarras de la périodisation', *Questes,* 33 (2016), 95-107.

———, *Des femmes dans la ville: Amiens (1380-1520)*, (Paris, unpublished PhD Paris IV-Sorbonne, 2018).

Pirenne, Henri, 'Draps d'Ypres à Novgorod au commencement du XIIe siècle, *Revue belge de Philologie et d'Histoire*, 9 (1930), 563-566 and Mus, *Prisma*, 356-358.

———, 'Les dénombrements de la population d'Ypres au 15e siècle (1412-1506)', *Vierteljahrschrift für Sozial und Wirtschaftsgeschichte*, 1 (1903), 1-32 and Mus, *Prisma*, 359-390.

———, 'The Stages in the Social History of Capitalism', *American Historical Review*, 9 (1914), 494-515.

———, 'Une crise industrielle au XVIe siècle: la draperie urbaine et la "nouvelle draperie" en Flandre', *Bulletin de l'Académie royale de Belgique, Classe des Lettres*, 5 (1905), 489-521.

———, *Les anciennes démocraties des Pays-Bas* (Paris: Flammarion, 1910).

———, *Les villes et les institutions urbaines*, (Paris-Bruxelles: Alcan, 1939).

Posthumus, N.W., *De geschiedenis van de Leidsche lakenindustrie. 1. De middeleeuwen (veertiende tot zestiende eeuw)*, (The Hague: Rijksgeschiedkundige Publicatiën, 1908).

Preneel, Aenold, 'Ieperse stadskwartieren en -wijken tijdens het Ancien Regime', *Westhoek. Tijdschrift voor geschiedenis en familiekunde in de Vlaamse en Franse Westhoek*, 30:1 (2014) 51.

Prevenier, Walter, 'Bevolkingscijfers en professionele structuren der bevolking van Gent en Brugge in de XIVe eeuw', in *Album Charles Verlinden*, (Wetteren: Universa, 1975),

———, 'Conscience et perception de la condition sociale chez les gens du commun dans les anciens Pays-Bas des XIIIe et XIVe siècles', in Pierre Boglioni, Robert Delort and Claude Gauvard (eds), *Le Petit Peuple dans l'Occident médiéval. Terminologies, perceptions, réalités. Actes du Congrès international tenu à l'Université de Montréal, 18-23 octobre 1999* (Paris: Editions de la Sorbonne, 2002), 175-195.

Puttevils, Jeroen, *Merchants and Trading in the Sixteenth Century: the Golden Age of Antwerp*, (London: Pickering and Chatto, 2015), pp. 28-29.

Roch, Jean-Louis, 'De la nature du drapier médiéval. L'exemple rouennais', *Revue Historique*, 302 (2000), 3-31.

———, 'Innovations et résistances dans la draperie : exemples normands', *Médiévales*, 39 (2000), 46-56.

———, *Un autre monde du travail. La draperie en Normandie au Moyen Âge*, (Mont-Saint-Aignan: Presses universitaires de Rouen et du Havre, 2013).

Sabbe, Jacques, *Vlaanderen in Opstand 1323-1328: Nikolaas Zannekin, Zeger Janszone en Willem de Deken*, (Brugge: Van de Wiele, 1993).

Scholliers, Etienne, 'Werktijden en arbeidsomstandigheden in de pre-industriële periode', in: id. and Peter Scholliers (eds), *Werktijd en werktijdverkorting. Durée de travail et diminution du temps de travail*, (Brussels: VUB, 1983) 11-13.

———, *Loonarbeid en Honger. De Levensstandaard in de XVe en XVIe eeuw te Antwerpen*, (Antwerp: De Sikkel, 1960).

Schulz, Knut, 'Denn sie lieben die Freiheit so sehr...' Kommunale Aufstände und Entstehung des europäischen Bürgertums im Hochmittelalter (Darmstadt: Wissenschaftliche Buchgesellschaft, 1992).

Simons, Walter, *Bedelordekloosters in het graafschap Vlaanderen: chronologie en topografie van de bedelordenverspreiding vóór 1350*, (Bruges: Cobbaut, 1987).

———, *Cities of Ladies: Beguine Communities in the Medieval Low Countries, 1200-1565*, (Philadelphia: University of Pennsylvania Press, 2003).

Sjoberg, Gideon, *The Preindustrial City: Past and Present*, (New York: Simon and Schuster, 1960).

Smail, Daniel Lord, *Legal Plunder. Households and Debt Collection in Late Medieval Europe*, (Cambidge MA: Harvard University Press, 2016).

Smithuis, Justine, 'Popular Movements and Elite Leadership: Exploring a Late Medieval Conundrum in Cities of the Low Countries and Germany', in Justine Firnhaber-Baker and Dirk Schoenaers (eds), *The Routledge History Handbook of Medieval Revolt* (Abingdon and New York: Routledge, 2017), 220-235.

Soens, Tim, *De spade in de dijk? Waterbeheer en rurale samenleving in de Vlaamse kustvlakte (1280-1580)*, (Ghent: Academia Press, 2009).

———, Stabel, Peter, and Van de Walle, Tineke, 'An Urbanised Countryside? A Regional Perspective on Rural Textile Production in the Flemish West-Quarter', in Remi van Schaïk (ed.), *Economies, Public Finances, and the Impact of Institutional Changes in Interregional Perspective: The Low Countries and Neighbouring German Territories (14th-17th Centuries)*, (Turnhout: Brepols, 2015), 35-60.

Soly, Hugo, 'The Political Economy of European Craft Guilds: Power Relations and Economic Strategies of Merchants and Master Artisans in the Medieval and Early Modern Textile Indistries', *International Review of Social History*, 53 (2008), 45-71.

Sortor, M., 'Saint-Omer and its Textile Trades in the Late Middle Ages: a Contribution to the Proto-Industrialization Debate', *American Historical Review*, 98/5 (1993), 1475-1499.

Sosson, Jean-Pierre, *Les travaux publics de la ville de Bruges XIVe-XVe siècles* (Brussels: Crédit communal de Belgique, 1977).

Stabel, Peter '*Dmeeste, oirboirlixste ende proffitelixste let ende neringhe*. Een kwantitatieve benadering van de lakenproductie in het laatmiddeleeuwse en vroegmoderne Vlaanderen', *Handelingen van de Maatschappij voor Geschiedenis en Oudheidkunde te Gent*, 51 (1997), 113-153.

———, 'Ambachten en textielondernemers in kleine Vlaamse steden tijdens de overgang van Middeleeuwen naar Nieuwe Tijd', in Catharina Lis and Hugo Soly (eds), *Werelden van verschil. Ambachtsgilden in de Lage Landen*, (Brussels: VUB Press, 1997), 79-98.

———, 'Composition et recompositions des réseaux urbains des Pays-Bas au bas Moyen Âge' in Eisabeth Crouzet-Pavan and Elodie Lecuppre-Desjardin (eds), *Villes de Flandre et d'Italie : relectures d'une comparaison traditionnelle* (Turnhout, 2007), 29-64).

———, 'Entre commerce international et économie locale. Le monde financier de Wouter Ameide (Bruges fin XVe-début XVIe siècle)', in Marc Boone and Walter Prevenier (eds), *Finances publiques et finances privées au bas Moyen Âge*, (Leuven: Garant, 1996), 75-100.

———, 'Guilds in Late Medieval Flanders: Myths and Realities of Guild Life in an Export-Oriented Environment', *Journal of Medieval History*, 30 (2004), 187-212.

———, 'Labour Time, Guild Time? Working Hours in the Cloth Industry of Medieval Flanders and Artois (Thirteenth-Fourteenth Centuries)', *The Low Countries Journal of Social and Economic History*, 11 (2014), 27-54.

———, 'Les draperies urbaines en Flandre au XIIIe-XVIe siècles', in Giovanni L. Fontana and Gérard Gayot (eds), *Wool: Products and Markets (13th-20th Century)*, (Padua: CLEUP, 2004), 355-380.

———, 'The Move to Quality Cloth. Luxury Textiles, Labour Markets and Middle Class Identity in a Medieval Textile City. Mechelen in the Late Thirteenth and Early Fourteenth Centuries', in Bart Lambert and Katherine Anne Wilson (eds), *Europe's Rich Fabric: the Consumption, Commercialisation, and Production of Luxury Textiles in Italy, the Low Countries and Neighbouring Territories (Fourteenth-Sixteenth Centuries)*, (Farnham: Ashgate-Routledge, 2016), 159-180.

———, 'Urban Markets, Rural Industries and the Organization of Labour in Late Medieval Flanders: the Constraints of Guild Regulations and the Requirements of Export Oriented Production', in Bruno Blondé, Eric Vanhaute and Michelle Galand, *Labour and Labour Markets between Town and Countryside (Middle Ages - 19th Century*, (Turnhout: Brepols, 2001), 140-157.

———, 'Working Alone? Single Women and Economic Activity in the Cities of the County of Flanders (Early 13th-Early 15th Century)', in Julie De Groot, et al. (eds), *Single Life and the City 1200-1900.* (London: Palgrave McMillan, 2015), pp. 27-49.

———, *A Capital of Fashion. Guilds and Economic Change in Late Medieval Bruges*, (Oxford: Oxford University Press, forthcoming).

———, *De kleine stad in Vlaanderen: Bevolkingsdynamiek en economische functies van de kleine en secundaire stedelijke centra in het Gentse kwartier (14de–16de eeuw)*, (Brussels: Koninklije Academie voor Wetenschappen, 1995).

———, *Dwarfs among Giants. The Flemish Urban Network in the Late Middle Ages*, (Leuven-Apeldoorn: Garant eds, 1997).

Stabel, Peter', Entre commerce international et économie locale. Le monde financier de Wouter Ameide (Bruges fin XVe-début XVIe siècle)', in Marc Boone and Walter Prevenier (eds), *Finances publiques et finances privées au bas Moyen Âge. Public and Private Finances in the late Middle Ages*, (Leuven/Apeldoorn: Garant eds, 1996), 75-99.

Stella, Alessandro, *La révolte des Ciompi. Les hommes, les lieux, le travail*, (Paris: EHESS, 1993).

Stieda, Wilhelm, *Hildebrand Veckinhusen. Broefwechsel eines deutschen Kaufmanns im 15. Jahrhundert.* (Lepizig: Verlag S. Hirzel, 1921).

Sutton, Anne F., 'The Merchant Adventurers of England: their Origins and the Mercers' Company of London', *Historical Research*, 75 (2002) 25-46.

Taft, Robert F., *The Liturgy of the Hours in East and West. The Origins of the Divine Office and Its Meaning for Today*, (Collegeville, Minnesota: Liturgical Press, 1986).

TeBrake, William H., *A Plague of Insurrection: Popular Politics and Peasant Revolt in Flanders, 1323-1328*, (Philadelphia: University of Pennsylvania Press, 1993).

Thijs, Alfons K.L, 'Les textiles au marché anversois au XVIe siècle', in Erik Aerts and John H. Munro (eds), *Textiles of the Low Countries in European economic history*, (Leuven: Peeters, 1990), 81-84.

Thijs, Alfons K.L., *Van "werkwinkel" tot "fabriek". De textielnijverheid te Antwerpen (einde 15de-begin 19de eeuw)* (Brussels: Gemeentekrediet van België, 1987).

Thoen, Erik and Eric Vanhaute, 'Pirenne and Economic and Social Theory: Influences, Methods and Reception', *Belgisch Tijdschrift voor Nieuwste Geschiedenis*, 41:3-4 (2011), 323-353.

―――― and Tim Soens, 'The Family or the Farm: a Sophie's Choice? The Late Medieval Crisis in the Former County of Flanders', *The Medieval Countryside*, 13 (2015), 195-224.

――――, 'Immigration to Bruges during the Late Middle Ages' in S. Cavaciocchi (ed.), *Le migrazione in Europa (secc. XIII-XVIII)* 25. Settimana di Studio. Istituto Internazionale di Storia Economica F. Datini (Firenze, 1994), 453-491.

――――, 'Technique agricole: cultures nouvelles et économie rurale en Flandre au bas Moyen Âge', in *Plantes et cultures nouvelles en Europe occidentale au Moyen Âge et à l'époque moderne*. (Flaran 12, 1992), 51-67.

――――, *Landbouwekonomie en bevolking in Vlaanderen gedurende de late Middeleeuwen en het begin van de Moderne Tijden. Testregio: de kasselrijen en van Oudenaarde en Aalst (eind 13de – eerste helft 16de eeuw)*, (Leuven: Belgisch centrum voor landelijke geschiedenis, 1988).

Thompson, E.P., 'Time, Work-Discipline, and Industrial Capitalism', *Past and Present*, 38 (1967) 56-97.

Trio, Paul, 'Bestuursinstellingen van de stad Ieper (12deeeuw-1500)', in Walter Prevenier and Bea Augustyn (eds), *De gewestelijke en lokale overheidsinstellingen in Vlaanderen tot 1795*, (Brussel: Algemeen Rijksarchief, 1997), 44-63.

Van Bavel, 'Rural Revolts and Structural Change in the Low Countries, Thirteenth-Early Fourteenth Centuries', in Richard Goddard et al. (eds), *Survival and Discord in Medieval Society: Essays in Honour of Christopher Dyer*, (Turnhout: Brepols, 2010), 250-268.

van Bavel, Bas and Jan Luiten van Zanden, 'Economy', in Peter Clark (ed.), *The Oxford Handbook of Cities in World History*, (Oxford: Oxford University Press, 2013), pp. 385-402.

――――, *Manors and Markets: Economy and Society in the Low Countries AD 500-1600* (Oxford: Oxford University Press, 2010).

――――, *The Invisible Hand? How Market Economies Have Emerged and Declined since AD 500* (Oxford: Oxford University Press, 2016).

Van Bellingen, Stephan and Marc Dewilde, 'De verdwenen Sint-Michielswijk te Ieper (prov. West-Vlaanderen Interimverslag 1994)', *Archeologie in Vlaanderen*, 4 (1994), 149-167.

Van der Meulen, Jim, *Woven into the Urban Fabric. Cloth Manufacture and Economic Development in the Flemish West-Quarter (1300-1600)*, (Turnhout: Brepols, 2022).

Van der Wee, Herman, 'Prices and Wages as Development Variables: A Comparison between England and the Southern Netherlands, 1400-1700', *Acta Historiae Neerlandicae*, 10 (1978), 58-78.

――――, 'Industrial Dynamics and the Process of Urbanization and De-Urbanization in the Low Countries from the Late Middle Ages to the Eighteenth Century. A Synthesis', in id., *The Rise and Decline of Urban Industries in Italy and in the Low Countries (Late Middle Ages - Early Modern Times)*, (Leuven: Leuven University Press, 1988), 321-336.

Van Dixmude, Olivier, *Merkwaerdige gebeurtenissen vooral in Vlaanderen en Brabant en ook in de aengrenzende landstreken van 1377 tot 1443*, ed. by Jean-Jacques Lambin (Ypres: Lambin, 1835).

Van Houtte, Jean A., 'Makelaars en waarden te Brugge van de 13e tot de 16e eeuw', *Bijdragen voor de Geschiedenis der Nederlanden*, 5 (1950), 1-30 and 177-197.

Van Laere, Raf, 'Loden penningen en aanverwante objecten opgegraven in de Verdronken Weide te Ieper (14de eeuw)', *Revue belge de numismatique et de sigillographie*, 163 (2017), 269-364.

———, 'Loden textielzegels opgegraven in de Verdronken Weide te Ieper (13de-14de eeuw). Een aanzet tot materiaalstudie', *Revue belge de numismatique et de sigillographie*, 162 (2016), 257-322.

van Nederveen Meerkerk, Elise, 'Market Wage or Discrimination? The Remuneration of Male and Female Wool Spinners in the Seventeenth-Century Dutch Republic', *The Economic History Review*, 53:1 (2010), 165-186.

Van Uytven, Raymond, 'De korte rokken van de jaren dertig: mode en conjunctuur in de veertiende eeuw', in Willem Frijhoff et al. (eds), *Bewogen en bewegen. Liber amicorum prof. Dr H.F.J.M. van den Eerenbeemt*, (Tilburg, 1986), 219-231.

———, 'La draperie brabançonne et malinoise du XIIe au XVIIe siècle : grandeur éphémère et décadence', in M. Spallanzani (ed.), *Produzione, commercio e consumo dei panni di lane (nei secoli XII-XVIII)*, (Florence: La Monnier, 1976), 85-97.

———, 'Technique, productivité et production au Moyen Âge. Le cas de la draperie urbaine aux Pays-Bas', in S. Marotti (ed.), *Produttività e tecnologie nei secoli XII-XVIII*, (Florence: Le Monnier, 1981), 283-293.

———, *Production and Consumption in the Low Countries, 13th-16th Centuries*, (Aldershot: Variorum reprints, 2001).

Van Werveke, Hans, 'Das Wesen der flandrischen Hansen', *Hansische Geschichtsblätter*, 76 (1958), 7-20.

———, 'De koopman-ondernemer en de ondernemer in de Vlaamsche lakennijverheid van de middeleeuwen', *Medelingen van de koninklijke Vlaamse academie voor wetenschappen, letteren, en schone kunsten van Belgie, Klasse der letteren*, 8 (1946) 1-26.

———, *De medezeggenschap van de knapen (gezellen) in de middeleeuwse ambachten*, (Antwerp: Koninklijke Vlaamsche Academie voor Wetenschappen, Letteren en Schoone Kunsten van België, 1943).

———, 'De omvang van de Ieperse lakenproduktie in de veertiende eeuw', (Antwerp: Koninklijke Vlaamse Academie van België, 1947) and Mus, *Prisma*, 496-520.

———, 'Die Stellung des hansischen Kaufmanns dem Flandrischen Tuchproduzenten gegenüber', in *Beiträge zur Wirtschafts- und Stadtgeschichte: Festschrift für Hektor Ammann*, (Wiesbaden: F. Steiner, 1965), 296-304.

———, 'Hansa in Vlaanderen en aangrenzende gebieden', in: id., *Miscellanea Mediaevalia. Verspreide opstellen over economische en sociale geschiedenis*, (Gent: Story-Scientia, 1968), 60-87.

———, 'Industrial Growth in the Middle Ages. The Cloth Industry in Flanders', *Economic History Review*, 6 (1954), 237-245.

———, *De Middeleeuwse hongersnood*, (Brussels: Royal Academy, 1967).

———, *Jacob van Artevelde*, (The Hague: Kruseman, 1982).

van Zanden, Jan Luiten, 'The "Revolt of the Early Modernists" and the "First Modern Economy": An Assessment', *The Economic History Review*, 55:4 (2002), 619-641.

Vandenbussche, P., 'De huizen van de Ieperse Grote Markt in de 15e eeuw. Een topografische studie', in: id., *De Ieperse markt Een historisch fenomeen. Drie bijdragen gebundeld ter gelegenheid van de tentoonstelling in de lokalen van de Kredietbank te Ieper van 18.1.1985 tot 1.2.1985* (Ieper: Kredietbank, 1985), 29-48.

Vandenpeereboom, Alphonse, *Ypriana. Notices, études, notes et documents sur Ypres*, (Bruges : De Zutter, 1880 ff.)

Vandermaesen, Maurice, 'Brugse en Ieperse gijzelaars voor koning en graaf, 1328-1329. Een administratief dossier', *Handelingen van het Genootschap voor Geschiedenis te Brugge*, 130 (1993), 124-127.

Vannieuwenhuyze, Bram, 'Reading History Maps: the Siege of Ypres Mapped by Guillaume du Tielt', *Quaerendo* 45 (2015) 292-321.

Verbist, Botho, *Traditie of innovatie? Wouter Ameyde, een makelaar in het laatmiddeleeuwse Brugge*, (Antwerp: unpublished PhD University of Antwerp, 2014).

Verbruggen, Raf, *Geweld in Vlaanderen: macht en onderdrukking in de Vlaamse steden tijdens de veertiende eeuw*, (Brugge: Van de Wiele, 2005).

Verhille, Bernard, 'La guède en Picardie (XIIe au XVe siècle)', *Société des antiquaires de Picardie*, 675 (2005), 393-399.

Verhulst, Adriaan, 'La laine indigène dans les anciens Pays-Bas entre le XIIe et le XVIIe siècle. Mise en oeuvre industrielle, production et commerce', in *La lana come materia prima. Atti della Prima Settimana di Studio 18-24 aprile 1969*, (Florence: Le Monnier, 1974), 11-42.

———, *The Rise of Cities in North-West Europe*, (Cambridge: Cambridge University Press, 1999).

Verlinden, Charles, (eds), *Documenten voor de geschiedenis van prijzen en lonen in Vlaanderen en Brabant*, (Bruges: De Tempel, 1959-1974).

Vermaut, Jos, 'Structural Transformation in a Textile Centre: Bruges from the Sixteenth to the Nineteenth Century', in Herman Van der Wee (ed.), *The Rise and Decline of Urban Industries*, 187-203.

Wickham, Chris, *Sleepwalking into a New World: The Emergence of Italian City Communes in the Twelfth Century*, (Princeton: Princeton University Press, 2015).

Wyffels, Carlos, 'De Vlaamse Hanzen opnieuw belicht', *Academiae Analecta*, 53 (1991), 3-17.

———, 'De Vlaamse handel voor het Engels-Vlaams konflikt van 1270-1274', *Bijdragen voor de Geschiedenis der Nederlanden*, 17 (1963), 205-213.

———, 'De Vlaamse Hanze van Londen op het einde van de 13de eeuw', Handelingen van het Genootschap voor Geschiedenis te Brugge, 97 (1960), 7-30.

———, *Analyse de reconnaissances de dettes passées devant les échevins d'Ypres (1249-1291) éditées selon le manuscrit de Guillaume Des Marez*, (Brussels: Commission royale d'Histoire, 1991).

———, *De oorsprong der ambachten in Vlaanderen en Brabant*, (Brussels: Royal Flemish Academy, 1951).

Glossary of textile terms (in the Ypres sources)

D. = Middle Dutch / Fr. = (Picard) French / It. = Italian
For more details about the technical terminology of cloth manufacture in Dutch and French, see also De Poerck, *La draperie médiévale*, vol. 2 and 3 and Cardon, *La draperie*.

Alum mordant imported from Italy or Asia Minor used to fix colours
***Averecht* (D.)** more felted side of a woollen after wet shearing (see also recht)
***Batteur de laine* (Fr.)** wool beater
Biffes (*pijffelaer*, D.) type of light cloth, in Ypres associated with the striped *enforchiés*
***Blauververs* (D.)** see dyers in blue
Blue cloth cloth woven from blue yarn dyed in the fibre or yarn
***Boom* (D.)** winch at a tenterer's frame or warp/cloth beam (see warping)
Brazilwood imported red dyestuff from the Sappanwood tree (in India), used to achieve dark and deep reds (for example for blood red or *sanguine*)
Broker (*ostelier*, Fr.; *hostelier*, D.) usually local intermediary in business transactions between foreign merchants and local merchants and/or entrepreneurs, providing mostly also space for storage and accommodation (hence also the name of hosteller)
Burling removing knots or lumps from the woven fabric
***Caerden* (D.)** see carding or teasel
Carding after beating the wool, carders use small wooden planks laden with nail to loosen and straighten the wool fibre before spinning, see also combing
***Cleet snider* (D.)** cloth retailer
***Clocke* (D.)** Clocke des ouvriers (Fr.), worker's bell

Cloth beam beam at the weavers' side of a broadloom used for the woven raw woollen
***Cnaepe* (D.)** journeyman
***Cnecht* (D.)** servant
***Com* (D.)** see fuller's trough
Combing after beating the wool, combers use two combs with long teeth to loosen and straighten the longer wool fibre before spinning, see also carding
Comb maker (*cammaeker*, D.) producer of the textile combs
***Conventer* (D.)** person who agrees on taking on a particular assignment (work). In the Ypres industry mostly used for a master weaver taking on a weaving assignment for a clothier, so for an independent weaver who was not active as a clothier
***Courretier* (Fr.)** see broker
***Coverture* (It.)** Ypres stamforts exported to the Mediterranean
***Crap* (D.)** see madder
***Cru* (Fr.)** see raw woollen
***Derdelinghe* (D.)** heavy cloth made with a specifi type of comb in a 2/1 weave
***Dickedinne* (D.)** thick and heavy cloth among the top products in Ypres
Distaff or rock (see also rock spinning) tool to hold unspun fibers for the spinning process with a spindle
***Doucken* (D.)** coarse, mostly dry woollens which did not fit the traditional sizes of the Ypres heavy woollens
***Draperie ointe* (Fr.)** see greased cloth

Draperie sèche (Fr.) see light cloth

Draperie légère (Fr.) see light cloth

Drapier *drapenier*, fem. *drapierigghe*, *drappiere* (D. or Fr.), clothier

Draps de sorte (Fr.) unspecified term for a type of cloth around 1300

Drapscerre (D.) shearer

Dueten (D.) a less refined version of the expensive *dickedinne*

Dyeing dyers were divided between dyers in blue and dyers in red. Woollens wer dyed in the fabric at the end of the manufacturing process or in the wool or yarn

Dyers in blue dyers using woad to dye wool fibre, yarn of woollens

Dyers in red dyers using a mordant to fix the colour in the fabric (madder, grain, weld, etc.)

Enforchié / Afforchi (Fr.) striped Ypres woollen from around 1300, considered by De Poerck as light woollens, but by Patrick Chorley because of their price range and quality as a type of woollen belonging to the heavy cloth

Estainfort (Fr.) see stamfort

Eswardeurs (Fr.) see guild controllers

Faisceur de draes (Fr.) clothier

Foulon (Fr.) fuller

Fuelge (D.) see alum

Fuller's Earth is a mixture of floridin with hydrous aluminium silicates or kaolinite which, mixed with water and sometimes urine, is used to scour, degrease and cleanse the raw woollen

Fuller's trough usually dug in the ground and reinforced with a wooden casement where fullers could 'walk' on the woven cloth to stimulate the fulling process

Fulling (or walking) the manufacturing involving the cleansing of woollen cloth to eliminate grease and impurities, to make it thicker

Fulling mill water- or animal-powered mill with a system of wooden hammers. The process was considered in most Flemish textile industries as harmful for the quality of fine woollens and banned from the manufacturing process. Fulling mills are, however, attested in medieval Ypres

Gaersoen (D.) (young) unskilled male worker

Garenboem (D.) see warp beam

Ghesmoutte Draperie (D.) see greased cloth

Grain expensive red dye imported from the Mediterranean and made from the dried bodies of the females of an insect (*kermes vermilio*). The dyestuff was used particularly for the bright scarlets, the high end of the Ypres woollens

Greased Cloth expensive and heavy woollen woven from greased and usually short-stapled wool

Grein (D.) see grain

Guild controllers officials appointed by the craft guild or the city authorities who controlled the quality and due process of raw materials and the manufactured goods

Kermes see grain

Kersey very popular coarse woollen, originally produced in England (and taking its name from the village of Kersey in Suffolk)

Ketelcnape (D.) dyer in blue

Laboureur fem. *labouresse* (Fr.), unskilled workers

Lakenboeters (D.) artisans taking care of final stages of cloth finishing

Lakenreders (D.) cloth finishers

Lakensnider (D.) cloth retailer

Leercnape (D.) apprentice

Lice (Fr.) tenterer's frame

Light Cloth woollen woven with ungreased wool

Liste (D. and Fr.) hem or edge of a piece of cloth to protect the woollen from unravelling. In the weaving process the edges of different types of woollen were given their own distinctive identity (for example by using a particular colour, for example *roliste*, with a distinctive red edge) to guarantee the woollen's quality

Madder or *rubia tinctorum* domestic plant used to dye red. The plant was grown in Coastal Flanders and Zeeland

***Marchand drapier* (Fr.)** ambiguous term used for clothiers who also were active as merchants or for merchants dealing in cloth

***Meygron* (D.)** 'May green'

***Moreit* (D.)** dark brown-purple colour

***Nieuwe Ghaernine* (D.)** Ypres woollen form around 1300 considered by De Poerck as belonging to the heavy cloth, but considered by Chorley to be dry cloth

***Noppen* (D.)** see burling

***Onghesmoutte draperie* (D.)** see light cloth

***Ostelier* (Fr./D.)** see broker

***Ourdissage* (Fr.)** see warping

***Peckers* (D.)** type of Ypres woollen from around 1300 belonging to the category of the *derdelinghe*

***Pijfelaer* (D.)** see biffe

***Plache* (D.)** open square (in Ypres a part of the central market square) used for hiring labour

Plain woollen heavy cloth woven in a 1/1 weave

***Raem* (D.)** tenterer's frame

***Raeu* (D.)** see raw woollen

Raw woollen woollen at the end of the weaving process, so not fulled or finished

***Rec* (D.)** tenterer's frame

***Recht* (D.)** less felted side of a woollen after wet shearing (see also averecht)

***Recwachters* (D.)** see tenterers

Reed (or comb) long comb at a horizontal loom, separating and guiding the warp yarns and allowing to tighten the weft yarns in the weave

Reeling (or spooling) winding yarn on a cylinder or spool before the weaving process

***Riet* (D.)** see reed

Rock spinning see distaff

***Roodververs* (D.)** see dyers in red

***Ros* (D./Fr.)** see reed

***Sadblau* (D.)** clear blue, one of the key colours used by Ypres dyers

***Sanguine* (Fr.)** 'blood red', dyed mainly with madder and brazilwood

Say light and ungreased woollen

***Scaerlaken* (D.)** see scarlet

Scarlet both used for the colour (dyed with grain) and for the top quality woollens manufactured in Flanders

***Scerre* (D.)** shearer

***Scherdisch* (D.)** downward-sloping working table of shearers, see shearing

***Schering* (D.)** see warping

***Schietspoel* (D.)** see shuttle

Shearing delicate process in which the napping of woollens is clipped and the surface of the fabric is smoothened with large blades or scissors. Is is a crucial part of the finishing process of woollens

Shuttle holder carrying the weft yarn. It is passed back and forth through the alternating warp yarns on a loom to producte the desired weave

Spinning process making use of either a distaff and spindle or a wheel to spin the weft and warp yarn from loosened and straightened fibre

***Spoeler* (D.)** reeler

Stamfort from *stamine forte* (strong warp yarn), type of woollen, mostly striped, and with a warp spun from carded wool. One of the top export products of Ypres to the Mediterranean just before and after 1300

***Standvoord* (D.)** see stamfort

Striped Cloth type of woollen woven with dyed wool yarn. By alternating the weave, the weavers managed to add a (coloured) striped pattern to the fabric, lengthwise or breadthwise. Striped cloth was particularly in high demand before and after 1300

***Taintenier* (Fr.)** dyer

***Tainteniers a le caudiere* (Fr.)** dyers in blue

Teasel instrument consisting of a collection of thistles/teasels used for cleaning and teasing the fabric during the fulling and tentering stages of cloth manufacture

Tellier (**Picard Fr.**) weaver

Tentering manufacturing process in which after fulling the wet fabrics are stretched on a frame and in which the cloth is dried and cleaned

Tonderes (**Fr.**) shearer

Tysserand tisserand (Fr.), weaver

Ungreased Cloth usually cheaper cloth made from yarn which still has its natural lanolin

Upmaecken (**D.**) see fulling

Upsetter (**D.**) cloth entrepreneur invoved in organizing the final stages of cloth manufacture, but lacking the encompassing role of the clothier

Utslares (**D.**) see tenterers

Uutdragers (**D.**) deliverers of raw materials or half-finished goods in the production process, also used for second-hand cloth dealers or ragpickers

Vaerwere (**D.**) dyer

Valès (**Fr.**) journeyman

Vermeil (**Fr.**) bright red

Vinders (**D.**) see guild controllers

Virgati (**It.**) see striped cloth

Vulre (**D.**) fuller

Waidiers (**Fr.**) dyers in blue

Warping (*oudissage*, **Fr.**; *schering*, **D.**) before the weaving process warp yarn is winded, measured, and fixed uniformly to a warp beam

Weld or *Reseda luteola* yellow dye widely used in medieval cloth industries. The plant was grown in Interior Flanders

Wercwijf (**D.**) unskilled female worker

White cloth undyed woollens, woven with undyed yarn

Woad *isatis tinctoria*, biannual plant used for dyeing in blue

Wool beating process in which the wool is beaten with sticks to loosen it and separate the fibres to allow the combing or carding process

Worsted name taken from the village of Worstead (Norfolk) and given to a model type of cheaper, lighter and coarser cloth than the traditional heavy cloth, woven from ungreased and long-fibre wool

Wullebreiker fem. *Wullebreikigghe* (D.), wool beater

Wulledragers (**D.**) wool carrier, sometimes bringing the wool to carders, combers ot spinsters

Wullespoelre (**D.**) wool cleaner

Ypersch-Popersch (**D.**) light Ypres cloth, probably made after a model from the nearby town of Poperinge.